'*An entire generation pumping gas, waiting tables, slaves in white collars. Advertising has us chasing cars and clothes, working jobs we hate so we can buy shit we don't need. We are the middle children of history. No purpose, no place. We have no great war, no great depression. Our great war is a spiritual war; our great depression is our lives. We've all been raised on television to believe that one day we'll all be millionaires and movie gods and rock stars. But we won't. We're slowly learning that fact. And we're very, very pissed off.*'

Chuck Palahniuk, *The Fight Club*

ACKNOWLEDGEMENTS

My thanks for their love, support and faith go to:

My editor, Brenda, designer, Lizzy, and my agent, Andrew.

My colleagues, Ian, John, Laura and Jane at Straight Forward Productions for their energy and support on the 'Vodou' film project.

My spiritual mother and father, brothers, sisters and the friends I have met and worked with in shamanism and Vodou: Mambo Kati, Bon Houngan Yabofe, the members of the Millennium Kanzo, Ekun (to whom I am also grateful for his insights into Tibetan Buddhism and Cuban Santeria), Palo and Vodou Priest Lance, 'Jamie from South America', 'Moon Shaman' Tim, Vera Waters, Simon Buxton of The Sacred Trust, and Howard Charing – all of them good friends and good healers.

My friends Les Prince and Ken Gray (for the fun-time we spend together on the rare occasions we get to meet), John Doyle; Mick, Hilary and Mikita; as well as the clients, students, spirits, and colleagues who have shared their stories and their journeys with me. False names have been given and some details changed in order to preserve anonymity, but they all exist, and you know who you are.

There are modern shamans all around us, who weave worlds with their poetry and entertain us to a musical healing of the spirit, as shamans have done throughout time. So I would also like to thank the following musicians, whose music provided a background for me in writing this book: Counting Crows, James, the Smashing Pumpkins, Nick Cave, Crowded House, Manic Street Preachers, Sparklehorse, Elvis

Costello, Leonard Cohen, Leftfield, Travis, Moby, David Gray, Patti Smith and Julian Cope.

My thanks also to Guido Casale, one of the best teachers I ever had, who taught me to question *everything*, to stand up for what *I* believed and never to accept authority just because it had appointed itself an authority. And to Elizabeth Kübler-Ross, whose brilliance and compassion have opened a million doors for a million souls in need.

This book, as ever, is dedicated to my best friends, my daughters, Amelia and Jodie, in thanks for everything they are and do, and the constant lessons they teach me about life.

Acclaim for *Spirit in the City*

'Ross has done for shamanism what Deepak Chopra has done for complementary health'
Nick Wood, author of *Voices From the Earth* and Editor of *Sacred Hoop* magazine

'A pioneering work that communicates the wisdom of shamanism . . . Eloquent and expressive, inspiring and profound, this is a vitally important presentation of an immense wisdom'
Simon Buxton, Founder and Director of The Sacred Trust and UK Faculty for the Foundation for Shamanic Studies

'Ross Heaven's warm style reflects his compassion and understanding of the plight of the citified man or woman seeking for the spiritual. This is a friendly book, a conversational book, a book which, with simple exercises, shows how any of us can take the journey of the shaman'
David V Barrett, author of *The New Believers*

'Ross Heaven has the mind of a scientist and the heart of a healer, writing with both clarity and compassion. In *Spirit in the City* he eloquently fuses science and spirituality, psychology and shamanism, to provide a visionary perspective of our urban reality. This book offers a way out of the mess and stress of modern life that is both intelligent and practical . . . reading it will bring you to your senses and wake you up to the power of positive change that lies within us all!'
Amoda, author of *Moving into Ecstasy*

Also by Ross Heaven

THE JOURNEY TO YOU

and published by Bantam Books

SPIRIT IN THE CITY

THE SEARCH FOR THE SACRED
IN EVERYDAY LIFE

ROSS HEAVEN

BANTAM BOOKS

x

LONDON · NEW YORK · TORONTO · SYDNEY · AUCKLAND

SPIRIT IN THE CITY
A BANTAM BOOK : 0 553 81324 2

First publication in Great Britain

PRINTING HISTORY
Bantam edition published 2002

1 3 5 7 9 10 8 6 4 2

Copyright © Ross Heaven 2002

The right of Ross Heaven to be identified as the author of this work has been
asserted in accordance with sections 77 and 78
of the Copyright Designs and Patents Act 1988.

I am grateful to Duen Hsi Yen at Noogenesis, to Earth Transitions, and to
Mambo Racine Sans Bout, for permission to quote from their research and
materials. I have tried to ensure that their, and all other, references and sources
are clearly quoted in this book. If any have slipped through the net, please let me
know and I will do all that I can to put things right.

Please note: a number of real case studies and experiences are quoted in this
book. In order to protect the identity of individuals concerned, names have been
changed in all cases and, in some, incidental details and locations have also been
altered. These changes do not affect the substance of these case studies and all
events referred to essentially happened as described.

Furthermore, the exercises in this book have been tested in many workshops and
other real-life applications. No harm has arisen to any participant as a result.
However, any application of the recommendations set forth in the following
pages is at the reader's sole risk. The author and publishers disclaim any liability
arising directly or indirectly from the use of this book.

Set in 10.5/13pt Sabon by
Phoenix Typesetting, Ilkley, West Yorkshire.

Bantam Books are published by Transworld Publishers,
61–63 Uxbridge Road, London W5 5SA,
a division of The Random House Group Ltd,
in Australia by Random House Australia (Pty) Ltd,
20 Alfred Street, Milsons Point, Sydney, NSW 2061, Australia,
in New Zealand by Random House New Zealand Ltd,
18 Poland Road, Glenfield, Auckland 10, New Zealand
and in South Africa by Random House (Pty) Ltd,
Endulini, 5a Jubilee Road, Parktown 2193, South Africa.

Printed and bound in Great Britain by
Cox & Wyman Ltd, Reading, Berkshire.

CONTENTS

BEAUTIFUL MUTANTS

There is so much exquisite beauty in the world that one mind, one human body cannot contain it. It hurts to feel so much, which is why, perhaps, we teach ourselves to feel so little.

I sank into a soft bed of insect song, a backbeat to the *icaros*, the sacred songs of the ayahuasca shaman whose cadence directed the balance of energy in this wooden church, deep in the full moon night of the jungle.

Ayahuasca, the visionary vine of souls, brings waking dreams and sensual things; puts two and two together in the vast underground caves of the mind; draws down the wisdom of the universe for those of us who drink it in the sacred night. It had been brown and thick and sickly-bitter at first taste, but with the passing of the nausea which followed, the deep painful beauty had descended.

The room was dark and completely at peace, all of us drifting in a private universe of ecstasy, an awareness of how the world we shared was *truly* shared: with the insects who chant the sacred song of the cosmos to hold the world in check and call down the night. With the jaguars and spider monkeys moving in the jungle, stirring up the undergrowth so the trees can breathe and grow for us. With this small group of frail humans dwarfed by the immensity of night and the distant specks of light that shine there, each of them a human soul hanging in a web of magic, evolving into stars. And, around these blessed pioneering souls, perhaps other worlds like ours where a similar ceremony is now taking place and other magic coming into being.

The shaman sang of the worlds he had visited, of Ether and Orion, and the sanctity of desert places, inner spaces, silent vast galaxies hidden in our cells.

And suddenly, gently, I was there, in that landscape of vines and snakes and DNA and curling spirits who dance like smoke. I knew the secrets of the clouds and oceans. I swam like dolphins swim in whale songs, their deep-sea echoes floating on the sailor's vast horizon. I heard the gentle laughter in our unborn children's voices. And I danced for them with torches for the orphans and unwanted.

Across the pink and mauve of our primitive sky, the clouds were the dreams of the Infinite. They were the same clouds that had looked down since prehistory, skittering like birds across the moon.

The moon is made of water, sang the shaman, and the thoughts and souls of every man and woman who has ever lived still live there. And life on Earth? An experiment, a cosmic joke, an accident with purpose . . . a beautiful mutation. Only the paradox makes sense – and, like children's games, unbound by rules, a game, a beautiful game.

Why else should it be that we began our existence as single-celled proto-creatures flowing peacefully with the tides, that we chose complexity, became fish to swim the oceans and explore the deeper places, then reptiles able to leave the seas for land, then apes, then men – if not in play? If not to explore and experience new sensations of being?

If we looked back far enough, to the first second of life itself, we were all the same energy and matter. We shared the same cosmic genetics as the jungle trees, the air of the night, the songs of the shaman, the insects and the creatures of the forest, all of whom are mutating too into new life-forms and expressions of life. There is no real difference between us.

We are the Beautiful Mutants of the universe, precious cosmic children rolling and falling in the soft down of new sensations. And because we know that, we are the future.

We have choice: to evolve *consciously* and to explore at will. To *choose* our future To be *free*. We have the power to create anything we want of ourselves and of the world around us.

What we have made so far is not the end, it is the beginning. We are the Beautiful Mutants – and the universe is well pleased with us.

Amazon Rainforest Lodge, November 2000

PREFACE

by Bon Mambo Racine Sans Bout Sa Te La Daginen

We live in a steadily collapsing world. Space and distance have collapsed to the point where travel from anywhere to anywhere is merely a matter of the cost of the ticket. We are surrounded by goods from all over the world, in such abundance that any supermarket in the United States offers foods from every part of the globe. A walk down the main street of Boston's shopping district leads from Vietnamese restaurants at one end to Italian and German leather goods merchants at the other – a walk of perhaps 200 yards.

Time, likewise, has collapsed. The musical forms of many different eras, sold on compact disc, are to be had for the buying in department stores. Waltz and blues and Gregorian chant, swing and Renaissance classical, are all appreciated during the current era. Likewise the literature and arts of the ages. A university student can expect to read from *Beowulf* to Browning, from Kant to Koontz. Museums display the mummies of Egypt across the hall from the most modern abstract sculptures.

Most importantly, our communities have collapsed. Unlike the 'natural' human social structure, where a person knows perhaps fifteen to twenty people with whom they pass their lives, humans are now grasping for relationships that endure. At the same time that we are given more and more 'choices', as we are provided with electric light and antibiotics, we are thrown more and more on ourselves and our own resources to cope with the collapsing world.

In both developed and underdeveloped countries, normal and peaceful ways of life are disrupted by the collapse of the world. In the United States, families move every few years, and divorce between moves, it seems. Even halfway around the world in traditional Angola, life expectancy is a mere thirty-eight years due to civil war, famine as the agricultural cycle is disrupted by war, and epidemic disease. Communities which used to include four or five generations now have atrophied into parent–child or husband–wife pairings, as if no relationship involving more than two people can endure any longer.

Above all, we are faced with the uneasy certitude that the physical world itself is collapsing, losing its ability to sustain our lives. Holes in the ozone, changes in the Gulf Stream, global warming, the mass destruction of the rainforests; all are catastrophic changes in the biosphere which supports our existence.

In response to this collapsing world, we now search for the sturdiest, most experiential spiritual traditions. It seems that people who watch the most television, who spend the most time on the Internet (the ultimate time-and-space collapser) are the people who need the most tangible experience of the divine spirit. It is not enough to be carefully instructed in spiritual matters by clean priests in beautiful buildings. Today's spiritual seeker wants to be transported by the visions of the sweat lodge, overwhelmed by the hallucinatory power of the ayahuasca vine, possessed by Vodou gods!

And why not? Direct experience of the divine is our birthright, our heritage, it is born into us. We have the ability to dream prophetic dreams, see visions, undergo possession, heal through spiritual means. We are the 'Beautiful Mutants' as Ross puts it, and we have no parallel on this planet.

So now, as indigenous populations are urbanized, urban populations turn to indigenous traditions for spiritual growth. The cities are nerve centres of information – Buddhist monks from Tibet lecture one week, Vodou priestesses another, shamanic practitioners a week later. We are free to choose what is helpful from each and every tradition which presents itself.

Of course these traditions also change as they are urbanized. Rural Haitian peristyles (Vodou churches) are brightly painted, obvious structures, and the membership of these congregations often follows family lines. In Boston and New York and Miami, Vodou services are conducted in basements, not secretively, but not openly either, and membership is drawn from the surrounding area, since the biological family is fragmented through emigration.

When I met Ross Heaven, I was preparing to conduct only the second initiation ceremony I had ever done. I was delighted to discover the sincerity of those who joined the Millennium Kanzo, as we came to call it. Participants came from the UK and the USA as well as Haiti, they were black and white and Hispanic.

Ross impressed me above all with his fearlessness and his good humour. He is a man committed to living fully, without regret and without excuses. His personal appearance shows self-esteem, his manner combines the brashness of an adult man with the fun-loving spirit of a happy child.

During the two-week long kanzo ceremony which consecrates initiates in Haitian Vodou, there is a point where the initiates are removed from the surrounding community. They are guarded by men armed with machetes to prevent them from running away! They are then given a series of ceremonial baths, which cut off the initiates from the world of the living. The mournful songs sung at this time refer repeatedly to the death of the initiates, to the loss of their personal identity. Ross approached the waters of dissolution wearing a T-shirt bearing the words:

Absolutely
Positively
Definitely

NO FEAR

(Not even a little bit)

17

When I saw that, I knew I had someone special in my charge, and I did everything in my power to ensure correct and authentic ceremonies. I was rewarded with a loyal initiate son who brings me happiness, challenges my imagination, and communicates the Vodou tradition faithfully to others. His sacred name, *Bon Houngan Reve We Chemen Ginen*, means *Good Houngan Who Dreams and Sees the Road of Gine* (Gine being the land of the ancestors, where we all come from, the root and source of our existence).

Ross's spiritual patron, the *loa mét tét* or 'owner of the head', is Ogoun Badagris. All Ogouns are loa of power, in all its myriad aspects. Ogoun Badagris is the negotiator, the mediator, the one who obtains and uses power by establishing balance, so much needed in our collapsing world.

Vodou, shamanism, other root traditions, provide the healing balance to the artifice of modern life. We become spiritually and emotionally healthy in the measure to which we are able to reclaim our true selves.

Ross Heaven's work has been to bring this balance to others, through his writing and through his life. I wish him continued success, and look forward to learning and to enjoying this mysterious, ecstatic voyage with him.

Bon Mambo Racine Sans Bout Sa Te La Daginen
(Kathy S. Grey, MSc.)
Haiti, 2001

INTRODUCTION

*Throughout life, we get clues that remind us of
the direction we are supposed to be headed in. If
you do not pay attention, then you make lousy
choices and end up with a miserable life. If you
stay focused, then you learn your lessons
and have a full and good life . . .*

Elizabeth Kübler-Ross, *The Wheel of Life*[1]

This book could have been called 'Spirit in the *System*', I
suppose, since it is really the Western way of life which is
under examination here and, more particularly, the faceless,
nameless system we have put in place to govern our lives. We
slip into this 'system' each day as we board the commuter
train, become anonymous consumers of the world around us,
the 'advertised life', and no longer 'ourselves' any more (or
who we think we are), in the crowds on the street. Finally we
arrive at our work, where we shuffle our papers or dig our
ditches in jobs which bolster and reinforce 'the system' itself.
Then we return home, to TV dinners and a TV diet which tells
us who we are, how we feel, and where we 'should' be going.
We are so used to this routine that we hardly even question it
any more, even if we find the lifestyle itself intrinsically unsat-
isfying, even damaging to our health and well-being. After all,
how can we escape, for the system is everywhere?

There is a saying in Keltic shamanism, that 'nature is the
visible face of spirit', and if that is the case, then it seems to
me that the city is the visible face of the system. It is where
most of us live, work and spend our lives, and in the rush,

19

crush and pressure of the city, it is also where the system most reveals itself, and where we find it easiest to forget who we are – and *what* we are: simply human; creatures of joy who delight in new experiences and have come here to this Earthly life to *play*. In my ayahuasca vision, which I have called Beautiful Mutants, I saw very clearly that we are here to enjoy life, not to suffer; we have simply forgotten that. The system we put in place was designed to serve us, to help us to explore the adventure and the beauty of this exquisite world, but we have somehow allowed it to take over so that we have become its servants.

All things are alive and all things have a spirit, say the shamans. I have journeyed to the spirit of the system and seen it as a tyrant; humourless, unforgiving, relentless and vast. It has the ability to drain our sense of fun, and even take our humanity away from us, turning us all into robots simply following its rules.

Let me give you an example: traffic wardens!

I moved to a new flat in Hastings in April 2001, which has a residents' parking zone in front of it. I applied for a parking permit on the first available day and, while I waited for it to come through, I put a note on the windscreen of my car to tell the wardens that I *was* a resident and had applied for a permit. I even gave them my address so they could check this if they wished. That didn't stop them giving me a ticket every single day for a week until my permit finally arrived. On the day when it did arrive, I walked downstairs to put it in my car window, only to find another ticket, and on this one, the warden had hand-written a note: 'Your permit does not start till May 1'. I looked at the permit in my hand. He was right – but what was the point?

He *knew* I was a resident all along; he had my address; he obviously knew that I had been granted a parking permit for the area, and yet he still had to follow the rules of the system and issue me with £120 of parking tickets, even when I had a permit.

This is a small example but it illustrates a point. The *system* was designed to protect residents and enable them to park outside their own homes, but it had become more important in its own right than the exercise of common sense, human relations or consideration for another person. How often do we hear similar stories of 'red tape' and 'bureaucracy' from faceless officials who are the first-line agents of the system?

In this book, then, I am using the word 'city', by and large, to stand as a metaphor for the urban myth of modern living, that bigger is better, that more is greater, that faster is automatically fitter for purpose, and that the system is there to be followed.

At the same time, when I talk about 'traditional' communities, I do not necessarily mean pre-industrial societies where some form of mythological rural idyll is being played out. Many of these societies have problems of their own which we would find unbearable. And yet (or, perhaps, *because* of these problems), they have found a way to *be* in their lives which keeps them connected to the sacred moment – the ever-present Now – which we have simply forgotten.

Rather, the difference is one of intent, of how we choose to view the world – whether we decide that the commuter trek and meeting the hire purchase payments are more important to our lives, or whether a reconnection with our true selves as joyous children of the universe, and with more holistic, sacred, living would ultimately bring us greater happiness than a life of consumption to appease the admen and keep the system going. It is this sense of connection, the community of mutual care, and the appreciation of the spiritual world around us, which is key in the 'traditional' societies I am describing, even today, even if they exist alongside a technological world or are a community in their own right in the very heart of the city.

'Traditional' is a way of mind rather than a place or time. The exercises in this book will, I hope, help you to discover that way of seeing the world around you.

The difference between these two cultures – the 'collapsed' world of the 21st century and the spiritual world of traditional peoples – was described by the dancer, artist and student of Vodou, Maya Deren, in her work *At Land*,[2] when she remarked that: 'The universe was once conceived as a vast preserve, landscaped for heroes, plotted to provide them with appropriate adventures. The rules were known and respected, the adversaries honourable, the oracles articulate.' This is the essence of a 'traditional' society, based on real community and caring. But today 'the rules are ambiguous, the adversary is concealed in aliases, the oracles broadcast a babble of contradictions. One struggles to preserve, in the midst of such relentless metamorphosis, a constancy of personal identity.'

I believe that we are all born perfect, our minds junk-free and unfettered, our potential as vast as the oceans from which all life came. I watch my children grow and I see this energy and potential in them; the way they relate to the world with purity and trust; their natural compassion; their warm and unpretentious love which asks nothing in return; their sense of fair play, of equality and community. They are just being themselves, just being alive, *naturally* alive, and in that being, knowing and instinctively trusting that all will be well. And all *is* well.

I can barely remember how that must feel. I am an adult and I have lived too long for that. I have too many memories of people showing me 'for my own good' that this view of the world was somehow wrong, naïve, 'un-civil-ized' . . . 'childish'. We are even taught in the West that asking for help in order to understand the world, or ourselves, is somehow wrong. We are told to keep our problems to ourselves and to suffer quietly and stoically, struggling on in spite of our questions. Our Christian religion tells us that life was designed as an unpleasant interlude on the way to a better world which we must earn the right to; even the First Noble Truth of Buddhism is that 'life is suffering'.

Seeking help, however, and trying to understand our world and the part we play in it, is *not* wrong. It is an act of liberation from this mindset of suffering and a realization that we all have an absolute right to the enjoyment of our lives in this world, *right now*.

My friend, Nick Williams, quotes research in his book, *The Work We Were Born To Do*,[3] which shows that, by the age of about 10, we will all have shared the experience of being praised for our beliefs and behaviour in the world maybe a few dozen times, and told we were 'wrong' or criticized for our actions *several thousand* times. But, after all, who says we are 'wrong'? Only the system – and the system is really in no position to say so, for it is there as a tool to serve us; *we* are *its* masters!

There is a definite division between the child's view of the world as a place of excitement and fascination, and the less enticing world of adults. How do we go from this innocent acceptance, this innate knowledge of how to blend and flow with the world, to *be part of life* – to the chaos and competition, anger and alienation that we see every day on the streets of our cities?

All that we are and all we can become on Earth is still unwritten when we enter this world and this potential remains always intact; things don't *have* to change just because we grow up. We can still, legitimately, see the world with all the freedom and potential of our children, if that is what we choose. Who says we cannot? We remain free to create a world where angels or devils walk beside us, into a future we have yet to make. The choice is always ours. The moon hangs over the same Earth and the same clouds fleck the sky. Only we are different.

And what has changed for us, exactly? This is a question which has involved me deeply over recent years. How have we managed to get from childlike acceptance and joy at life, to become the casualties of the city that we read about each day? And, more to the point, why? Why on Earth did we ever agree to this?

This book grew out of answering those questions for myself. In my view, what we lose above all else as we grow – from children to adults, and from tribal to city dwellers – is our connection to the sacred, to the community, to the spirit which is all around us, and to what it truly means to be alive beneath blue skies and rainbows and nights full of stars. And without these, we can lose our way completely.

Spirit in the City is my attempt to find a solution to the central issue which faces us all in this 21st century world: how can we reconnect with the sacred, with a simpler, more traditional lifestyle, while still in the flux and crush of modern living? How can we become more like our children, more honourable, loving, forgiving and accepting? How can we save ourselves from the future we read about each day, of global warming and climatic chaos, inner city decay, starvation for thousands, rage and hatred on the streets, violence in the classroom, a city choked with fumes and cars?

Along the way, I have looked for answers to a number of other important questions which have concerned me and which will ultimately concern us all. Questions like:

- How do we *really* live our lives in the modern world, behind the gloss and the glamour of expense account lunches and designer labels? What dreams are we living by – and are they enough to sustain us? If not, what do we really want?
- What do traditional societies have that we do not which accounts for their more spiritual orientation to, and greater happiness within, the world? Is it, perhaps, that they expect less of life? Or do they actually expect *more* – and manage to find it too – although it is a different 'more' from the one we are habituated to? How can we learn from them and apply some of these same principles to our own lives, even in the narcotic whirl of the city?
- How can we use traditional spiritual practices to strengthen and protect ourselves from the impact of the city, to heal ourselves, and to envision and live a better life? And, in doing so, how can we use these powers to start a chain reaction of love and compassion which will literally, physically, change the world and create a healthier planet for ourselves and our children?

As you read through this book, these questions will remain as a backdrop to the subject matter which will take us, chapter by chapter, through a reconsideration of the modern world as we have been taught to view it, into the shaman's world where everything is primarily composed of energy and the entire world is open to redefinition and change, and finally into real-life examples of how others are integrating the shamanic message into their own lives in the city, in work, in the family, and in their own self-healing – and how you can too if you wish.

I will be truly delighted if you challenge my views throughout. I will be equally delighted if you remain open to challenging your own. Because, when it comes right down to it, how many of the views that we carry with us in this world are actually *our own* – and how many have we just accepted without question as they have been given to us? If I am honest, many of my own views, until I began to truly question them, were based on received wisdom rather than personally discovered truth, and they were often contradictory at that. Ask me what I think about war, for example, and I will tell you to make love instead, but tell me another Hitler is about to invade and I will be there fighting to keep him out.

The truth is that we live smack bang in the middle of a paradox called Life. Nothing is black or white. If you can accept that, really feel it, really sense the truth of that, you have already heard the most important message in this book.

The modern world is dualistic and likes its reality as 'either-ors', because that is the way the system talks – in binary code. The truth, however, is more ambiguous.

Let me give you an example. I recently heard about a research company which conducted a poll of some hundreds of people and asked them if it was OK to smoke while they were praying. A horrified majority said 'No! Of course not.'

The same company then asked another several hundred people if it was OK to pray while they were smoking, to which the same majority replied 'Yes! Of course.'

The action of smoking and praying is exactly the same in either case; it is only the *intention* that changes. So what, then, really, is the truth in this complex, collapsing world? Does 'the truth', as it is given to us daily, even really exist? Or is the answer merely 'our intention'? You will find your own truth, but the lesson is the same for us all: Be absolutely crystal clear on what you accept as a 'personal' belief because the paradox of living underpins it all.

Another example: in the Western world, we are proud to live in a democracy and we have fought wars to ward off the 'dark powers' of communism and Fascism. We believe in our freedoms and our rights and we are passionate about our individual liberty. But what exactly is 'democracy'? As I sit here writing, the UK has just taken part in an election which the incumbent party won with the votes of 25 per cent of the electorate. Democracy in action.

Yet, what this also means is that 75 per cent of people did not vote for the party which now runs the country for us, dictating the dream, and controlling the system we will live by for the next four years.

To compound the conundrum, voting returns show that almost 50 per cent of people did not vote *at all*. Now, if we truly lived in a democracy, of course, that is a pretty clear signal that the country is really not interested in politics or politicians *of any party*! What we really want is something more, something better, a different, more holistic way of life where the system is not the issue.

The system talks in doublespeak, the city is a monochrome paradox of bright lights and misery, and beneath it all, the world we think we know is illusory. The shamans and the mystics have been long aware of this, and so, in answering the questions I have posed above, I have been guided by the teachings of such shamans from ancient times to the modern day, from cultures as diverse as the Sioux and the Saami, and in settings as different from one another as rural Africa, the rainforests of Peru, the Vodou night of Haiti, and the hidden worlds of central London.

There is an enduring wisdom and a powerful model for living available to us in the teachings of these spiritual guides, which is just as relevant today as it ever was.

As well as shamanism, this book includes some of the wisdom and practices of Vodou. Trace any Vodou tradition back to its roots and you will arrive at shamanism. The practices are almost identical, and the way of communicating with, and relating to, the gods also very similar – which is perhaps not so surprising, since all of human life stems originally from Africa, the spiritual home of Vodou and, more fundamentally even than this, all human beings sprang from the same genetic source.

The Oxford Ancestors research project by Oxford University recently used DNA genetic fingerprinting to examine evolution over the last 150,000 years. It concluded that 99 per cent of all Europeans can trace their maternal ancestry back to just seven women, whom the researchers call the Seven Daughters of Eve. They began their lives in Africa.

Closer to home, in Europe, frozen in ice in a glacier on the border of Italy and Austria, the remains of a Bronze Age man, dating back some 5,000 years, were discovered at the end of the 1990s. The body taken from the ice had curious, unidentifiable tattoos on its legs, a practice that is known to be connected with some European shamanic lineages, and he carried crystals and herbs in a pouch strung round his waist. Some people feel that this ancient man was, indeed, a shaman – and statistical evidence has shown that, genetically, every person in Europe could well be related to this one distant ancestor. So, not only may we in Europe all stem from one source, but that source may have been a shaman.

Somewhere in your ancestry, *you* were African and lived naturally, shamanically, and in harmony with the practices of Vodou, practices which were carried throughout Europe, in the body of your 5,000-year-old nomadic shaman ancestor. In that sense, the information and exercises in this book are simply a coming home for you.

The tragedy of Vodou – thanks largely to the tabloids and to Hollywood – is that it has been so dreadfully misrepresented and misunderstood. This is our loss more than the religion's, since there is much we can learn from it and much of value it can introduce into our lives. It can reintroduce us to our ancestral past as well as giving us an honourable framework for modern living and a better design for the future.

The problem for Hollywood, and even for serious anthropologists, is that the real essence of Vodou, the secret teachings at the heart of the religion, are only available to initiates and take place in the *djevo*, the inner sanctum of the Vodou temple, and away from the cameras and notebooks. Those unwilling to become initiated are left standing on the outside trying to catch a glimpse of what is happening within – and failing. What you then read about or see on your TV screen is the reporter's attempt to make sense of the unexplained and the hidden, and clichés are often the only way of doing so. Those who are initiated are sworn to secrecy about what actually happens in the *djevo*.

I became initiated as a priest of Vodou (a *houngan*) in the year 2000 in order to fully understand the religion, and what you will read in this book is the closest I can get, without betraying my oath of secrecy, to the real truth about Vodou. I have included exercises and teachings from shamanism and from Vodou and have looked at the parallels between them. At the heart of both spiritual traditions is a fundamental belief in a very real, very different universe – one where pure, nameless energy, is the one single truth of the cosmos, and it is only the definitions we apply to this which give it shape and form. And that, ultimately, is the point: *we can choose to create any world we wish* – the one we currently live in or one which better serves us.

In this book, then, we begin with a look at the underlying beliefs and philosophy of our Western culture (Chapter 1) and then examine how this translates into the physical world we have built around ourselves, which is the expression of these beliefs (Chapter 2), before moving on, in subsequent chapters, to contrast this with the shaman's view of the world as composed of energy instead of 'a hard world of physical objects', as Castaneda's don Juan once put it.[4] Since this energy can be used purposefully and directed by us to create any world we choose, I have included discussion and exercises which enable us to better understand these forces, relate to them, and employ them in our daily lives to protect and heal ourselves from the onslaught of the city. In the final chapter, we look at how the shaman's view of the world can give us not only a better philosophical framework for living, but how some people are using this approach in the world of business, medicine and other disciplines. For shamanism is a *practical* approach to the world, not an empty spirituality, and it is open to all of us. Taking the work of these pioneers as an example, we can *all* learn to be shamans in our cities.

But why would anyone *want* to be a shaman? What is the point? As Mayan shaman Martin Prechtel remarks in his book, *Secrets of the Talking Jaguar*: 'I don't know why people in modern life want to be shamans . . . we just go around capturing monsters, re-sweetening the Earth, and making people's memories taste good again'.[5]

I know why. I believe that we all know at some very deep level within us that there is indeed more to life than the world we have created in 3D physical 'reality' and that we all long for reconnection with this sweeter, more spiritual world, which we sometimes catch a glimpse of, just at the periphery of our vision, out of the corner of our eye.

And, in fact, Martin knows the answer too, if truth be told. He goes on: 'In modern culture where people are no longer initiated, the spirit goes unfed. To be seen, the uninitiated create insane things, some destructive to life, to feel visible and powerful. These creations are touted as the real world. They are actually forms of untutored grief signalling a longing for the true reality of village togetherness.'

We want this reconnection; we want to feel at one with the universe and whole in ourselves, and the '3D physical reality' of life in the system simply cannot give us that.

We have got ourselves into a bit of a mess at the start of the 21st century – like children making castles in the sand who are so intent on their next great creation, they do not realize that the tide has come in behind them and washed the first of their castles away. But here's the thing: the modern world is not the end, it is just the *beginning*. Once we know the problems, and the dangers, we can find a new part of the beach to play on, and a safer foundation to build upon. Our new consciousness, our new awareness, has given us options on the future so we can more fully understand the world around us and find a better outcome.

We truly are the Beautiful Mutants of the universe and, as we become more and more conscious of our role in life and in the cosmos itself, we have greater choice to *consciously* evolve at will. Our thoughts, our decisions, our ambitions, our actions all change the nature of reality itself and can create a new path for us to walk.

It is exactly as Maya Deren depicted it:

> *The laws of the macrocosm and of the microcosm are alike. Travel in the interior is as a voyage in outer space: we must, in each case, burst past the circumference of our surface – our here-space and/or now-time – and cut loose from the anchorage of an absolute, fixed centre, to enter worlds where the relationship of the parts is the sole gravity. This is a ballet [and] the dancers are constellations which orbit and revolve in the night sky.*[6]

So now, as we walk through our rainy city streets at night, we can choose to see the litter in the gutter or the moon and the stars reflected there.

Shamanism and Vodou give us this power of choice, as well as the tools to reconnect with the sacred nature of life and of the city, so we can find the meaning which is inherent in the universe and available to us all, and start to dream this better world.

I really hope you will work with these tools to find this new sense of reality, for as Einstein once famously said: 'The problems that exist in the world today cannot be solved by the level of thinking that created them'.

To make a better world, we desperately need visionaries who can see beyond the darkness of the night sky in order to reach for the moon, especially as it hangs over our cities.

SOME NOTES ON THE SHAMANIC JOURNEY

The key approach of all shamans, ancient and modern, is the shamanic journey, a special state of trance consciousness which enables communion with the spirit energy of the universe. Its parallel in Vodou is the possession trance where the spirits enter our lives directly and carry out their healing actions through us.

There is absolutely no danger in this at all and, in fact, the possession trance is well known in many traditional and modern societies – and even to the mediums and psychics of our own Western spiritualist churches and the ecstatic celebrants of our Southern Baptist and Pentecostal churches, as well as our scientists who have been studying altered states of consciousness since at least the 1960s.

Spirit possession is also a well-documented phenomenon and a fundamental aspect of many religious practices, including the Shinto and Dojo religions of Japan (hardly a backward nation in terms of science and technology), and a central part of the trance journey of shamans throughout the world.

'It is just a relationship between the spirit and the body,' said Western spiritist, Druid and author, Emma Restall Orr.[7] 'Ultimately everybody is possessed by spirits . . . in Jungian terms you would talk about different facets of behaviour and personality. So, as in therapy, it is purely a matter of working out which spirits you want to work with.'

Even so, recognizing the reticence on the part of most of us in the West to hand over total control of our bodies, I have tended to steer away in this book, from exercises in full possession, though there is some guidance on how to call the spirits in this way. But I *have* included many gentle shamanic journeys; I will introduce the technique now so you will be able to use it throughout this book.

The shaman's world (like that of Vodou, and of most religions) has two dimensions – the material or physical and the immaterial or spiritual – and in most societies the spiritual world is further split into three main levels: the upper, middle and lower worlds. All three are linked.

- The upper world is a place of philosophers and archetypes where spirit helpers tend to appear in human form.
- The lower world is a place of more 'Earthy' energies, where essentials and primary beings live, often taking the form of animals – what we have come to call 'power animals' since they provide the shaman with energy or power in his or her out-of-body journeys.
- The middle world is the energetic parallel of our own and is the shadow or the mirror of human life. It is the place of the ancestors and of all sentient beings who have once lived – or continue to live – on Earth. It is the *essence* of ourselves, of humanity and of all living things that we find in the middle world.

All three realms are connected – in many cultures by the World Tree, which grows from the Earth and reaches up to span the sky. The shaman may climb this tree to reach the upper world; descend via its root system to the lower world; while its trunk remains his primary co-ordinate for middle world journeys, the place he will return to.

To take any journey, find a quiet time where you won't be disturbed for 20 minutes or so, and, if you wish to, you may adopt a position often used by shamans because of its effectiveness in stimulating the trance consciousness needed for journeying.

Lie down on your back, right arm at your side, left arm bent with your forearm resting just above your eyes, as if shielding them from a strong light from behind you. Your legs remain straight, feet allowed to fall naturally to the side. You may wish to use a scarf to cover your eyes. This is known as the

Jivaro posture and is particularly good for lower world journeys, though it will work for you whatever your destination.

Take a few moments to relax and breathe deeply and calmly to 'centre' yourself.

The shamanic journey is usually taken to the sound of drumming or rattling, a sound which helps to shift the consciousness into a trance state. Nowadays, drumming and rattling tapes can be bought from many new age stores and ordered from the web (also see the back of this book), and it is very beneficial, if not essential, to purchase one of these. They are usually not expensive.

When you start your drumming tape, you will find it begins with a slow, introductory beat. This is the time for you to express your intention, your purpose for this journey – whether it is simply to explore the spirit worlds, to find a wise teacher there, or to work with a healer who can help you with an illness or a problem.

Be very clear about your intention. It is this which acts as your map *and* your destination.

Visualize your starting point for the journey. This may be the World Tree, standing tall before you in a beautiful meadow or, better yet, a real place in ordinary reality that you know or have visited. For a lower world journey, somewhere that takes you deep into the Earth is ideal – a cave, a well, or the burrow of an animal, perhaps. For an upper world journey, you may choose to climb a ladder, a vine or a tree, or to ascend into the sky in the arms of a powerful wind.

The introductory beat on your drum tape will be followed by a faster one which will help you to enter shamanic consciousness. You may find yourself in a cave or a tunnel at this point, if you are journeying to the lower world. Your senses will be keener – you can see in the dark, hear through the silence, speak without words, fly like an eagle, swim like a dolphin. In this world you are a being without limits. Follow the tunnel out into the light and into the new world. Remember your intention and follow your goal – and your heart – once you are there.

Your journeying tape will end with a slower beat, usually two rounds of seven single beats, followed by more rapid drumming or rattling. This is your call-back signal. At this point, thank any spirit helpers you are interacting with, and retrace your steps through the tunnel, to the landmark in ordinary reality that you journeyed from. You are now back to physical reality and everyday consciousness.

Remain quiet and still for a few moments, then write down your experiences, or perhaps draw them, or act them out. The journeying log that you create in this way will become an *aide-mémoire* and a map for you to use in coming journeys, and you will notice that patterns and motifs begin to emerge. Your personal journey of discovery has begun.

KEY POINTS: TAKING THE SHAMANIC JOURNEY

- Find a time and place where you can be undisturbed for 20 minutes or so.
- Dim the lights or cover your eyes so you are not distracted by the light, then lie down on your back, legs outstretched, and make yourself comfortable.
- Keep your right arm at your side, fingers straight, and the whole arm relaxed. Bend your left arm and place it over your forehead so that it shields your eyes. This is the special trance position known as the Jivaro posture.
- You will be journeying, as the shamans do, to your spirit teachers – the intelligent energy of the universe – to seek answers to your *specific* questions. So it is crucial to express your intention and to keep this focus and hold your question in mind as you journey.
- Most shamanic journeys are taken to the sound of drumming, which encourages a specific mental state of trance. Drumming tapes can be purchased or you can drum for yourself or ask a friend to help you with this.
- As soon as the drum sound begins, see yourself entering a place which will take you down into the Earth, such

as a cave or a well, and, via the tunnel that you will find there, into the otherworld of wise teachers and spirit beings who can help you with your question.

- Remember to stay focused on your intention throughout and, if you lose your bearings at any time on the journey, come back to your purpose and focus again on the sound of the drums.
- When you hear the call-back signal of the drum, or when you are ready, come back to normal awareness and record your thoughts and feelings.

Much more detail on this technique is offered in my book, *The Journey To You*,[8] but these, in a nutshell, are the steps by which shamans for centuries have entered the otherworld and continue to do so. It is really a very simple technique, much simpler than it sounds.

Perhaps you would like to journey now so that you have the experience of using this approach and can then do so at any time you wish in the following chapters to check out for yourself the validity of the information you read there, according to the insights offered by your own spirit teachers. Let's try a simple journey to get the hang of things.

EXERCISE: JOURNEY TO THE EVENTS OF THE DAY

Cast your mind back to a significant event or incident of the day – a meeting with someone, for example, where you were unable to say what you needed to for whatever reason – or something else which is not life or death, but which seems important to you.

This is the event we will journey to. As well as allowing you to practise the journeying technique, it also means you can check the information you receive from your spirits, if you wish, by going back to the person you were too rushed to speak with today, in order to finish your conversation or to change the outcome of today's events, *in the spirit world*.

According to the shamans, we each have a spiritual double, a soul or an energy self which is connected with, but exists independently from, the physical body. This soul-self is quite aware and very capable of out-of-body movements or 'flight' using the journeying technique.

By allowing your body double to journey away from your physical body, it is still *you* who is interacting with the outside world, but in an energy-place outside of time and space, so you can visit other places and times (like earlier today) and bring back useful and practical information on the events of the day.

Crucially, you can then test this information by seeing what happens between you and the person your soul-self visited next time you meet *in the everyday world* of physical reality, by observing their behaviour to see if it has changed in any way, or by simply asking them, 'Is this what you meant?' or, 'Is this what you were about to say?', based on the information you receive during your journey. In this way, you will be able to see if journeying is a useful technique for you.

Find some quiet time and prepare yourself for your journey. Lie down in the position I have described, and have in mind a clear question (let's say, for example: *'I'd like to know how that conversation with John would have turned out if I hadn't had to run for the train'*). Now phrase your question as an intention. For example: *'I am making this journey to the shamanic otherworld to continue my conversation with John and to find an appropriate resolution to it.'*

If you have a drumming tape, start it now and begin to orientate yourself. See yourself standing before a place – preferably one you know from real life – which is an entrance into the Earth. It could be the burrow of an animal, a well, or even a drain; whatever feels right for you.

Enter this place and find yourself in a dark and peaceful tunnel, which goes down further into the Earth.

It is very relaxing here and you feel safe and secure.

Eventually, you will see an opening in the tunnel which leads you into another land, the otherworld of the shaman. Here you will be met by a wise and loving being, whom you may recognize or feel that you know in some way. This is your spirit helper, who may appear as a human being or, sometimes, as an animal, or even as a symbol or a sensation. It is not important that you 'see' them; you might hear or simply 'sense' their presence instead.

Develop a relationship with them. Bear in mind that they have access to a great deal of information about your life – and John's – and have a wisdom which they have accumulated over lifetimes. You may ask them any questions you wish.

Ask them now to take you to John – the spiritual 'essence' of John – which exists in the otherworld as the energetic double of the physical person you know by the same name.

When you meet with 'John', continue the conversation you began today and see how it develops. Treat this interaction quite naturally, just as you would an actual conversation with John were he here in the flesh. Make a mental note of his responses so you can ask the 'other' John about them later if you wish.

When you are ready or when the drum calls you back, retrace your steps and, thanking your spirit guide, return to ordinary consciousness.

How you test the information you have received is up to you. You might just call John and ask him, for example, or say nothing but put the information and recommendations from your spirit guide into practice next time you meet and see how your relationship with John then changes. Whatever you decide to do, I urge you to test it so you can be certain you have a method that works for you. Do bear in mind that journeying, like all things, can take some practice, so don't give up on it just yet if you find you are not 100 per cent accurate. By the same token, you may be surprised at how accurate you are.

If you found that exercise easy, then the ones which follow will also present no challenge for you. If you found it difficult to relax in order to enter journeying consciousness, there are a number of things you can do to help yourself.

- Take an aromatherapy bath before you attempt your journey. Neroli, orange, rose, bergamot, clary sage and frankincense are all excellent relaxants. Sage is particularly appropriate as the North American shamans believe that the spiritual essence of burning sage will carry our prayers and intentions to the spirit world. (**Special note:** please do check thoroughly the specified uses for, and cautions against, using any and all aromatherapy oils and especially do not use clary sage if you are pregnant as it may 'call' to your baby and induce contractions).

- Practise four-way breathing, a yogic technique for stilling the mind. Breathe in through the nose for a count of four, hold the breath for four, then breathe out through the mouth for a count of four and, again, hold for four. Keep this up for a minute or two, until you are in tune with the cycles of your breathing, focusing all the time on the breath and, in particular, on the pause between outbreath and inbreath, which creates the space for your connection with the Infinite.

- Lie down on your back and, closing your eyes, visualize a glowing ball of blue healing light floating just at the back of your head. Now bring this light down into your body, allowing it to pause at the top of your head, your brow, your throat, your heart, your solar plexus, groin, between your knees and at the soles of your feet. Allow yourself to relax your face, neck, shoulders, arms, stomach and legs as this healing light travels throughout your body. Where it pauses on its journey, notice as all the pooled stress from those areas is absorbed into the light and taken away from you, while new energy is added to your body. When it reaches the bottom of your feet, breathe out with a sigh, pushing away from you the light that is taking all your stresses with it as it drifts off into the universe to be harmlessly released.

Using these techniques (or any others which seem appropriate to you) will enable you to relax sufficiently to let go of the self-reflective 'inner dialogue' – the tiny voice in your mind which wants you to focus on the events of the day – in order to free your mind for more spiritual pursuits. All the spirits require in order to enter our lives is an open doorway they may step through; inner silence provides this.

Now return to the exercise above and try again.

As a last resort, when people tell me they are unable to fully enter the shamanic state of consciousness or to really get much from a journey, my advice is simple: Make it up!

This is not as ludicrous as it sounds. Often our minds fall prey to too much rational thought, which gets in the way of experience and intuition. We suffer what psychologists call 'analysis paralysis' where too much thought leads to an inability to act on anything. Instead of becoming the victim of negative thoughts ('I can't do this', 'I'm a failure', or whatever), simply ask yourself, 'Well, maybe I can't do this, *but if I could*, what *would* I experience?' The result of this is to free your mind from expectations and fear of failure and to give yourself permission to succeed. Even if you get only so far in a journey, you can use this technique, by completing the journey as a story perhaps, picking up from where your experience ended and writing the rest down on paper *as if* it had actually taken place. You will still be using your creative, intuitive mind in this action, and giving yourself access to the domain of shamanic potential.

There are many precedents in shamanic tradition for such 'trickery'. North Americans talk of Coyote, for example, the great trickster spirit, who teaches by the paradox of his stories. Often he intends one action and ends up with a totally unexpected outcome, and you may find this too when you begin to write and slip into a state of light creative meditation, only to find that the ending you had mentally 'prepared' for your story turns out to be totally different on the page.

In Haiti, Coyote becomes Ti Malice, the comical, nasty piece of work who is used as a foil to Bouki, the nice guy who is usually shown the error of his ways by his adversary who may, for example, sweet-talk him into surrendering some precious possession, or even rob him, but who always has a valuable lesson for his trusting friend. Such story-telling always contains the seed of cosmic information inherent in shamanic trickery – perhaps that we have to surrender something of ourselves in order to see what is real and get to the truth of any situation. So be pro-active: 'trick' yourself into a successful journey.

We will be taking many journeys in this book so there will be plenty of opportunity for you to practise the technique. As with all things, you will get better at it with time, so please do not worry that you 'cannot do it' – believe me, *everybody* – but *everybody* – can journey. It is the most natural thing in the world. Indeed, it is your heritage as a spiritual being.

1

'ONLY A GAME': THE STATE WE'RE IN

We all live in our own world. But if you look
up at the starry sky, you'll see that all the
different worlds up there combine to form
constellations, solar systems, galaxies

Paulo Coehlo, *Veronika Decides to Die*[1]

'Our day-to-day life is bombarded with fortuities or, to be more precise, with the accidental meetings of people and events we call coincidences,' writes Milan Kundera in *The Unbearable Lightness of Being*. 'Co-incidence means that two events unexpectedly happen at the same time, they meet . . .

'Guided by his sense of beauty, an individual transforms a fortuitous occurrence into a motif which then assumes a permanent place in the composition of the individual's life . . . Without realizing it, the individual composes his life according to the laws of beauty . . .'[2]

If I had not visited that small jungle church and been transformed by the visions which the ayahuasca brought, I might never have written this book, or written it in the way I have. As a consequence of that, you would not now be holding it. It would not be available to change your life. If it does so, perhaps it will be the result of chance, or of coincidence, or perhaps your choice (and mine) was really guided and we were meant to find each other somehow. For now we are linked together through these words – you, me, the group of us in that distant jungle, and the shaman who sang of us all: we are all part of a new mutual dream and all of us are certain to meet again some time, if only in our thoughts.

The only way we will ever know how this came to be, and if it was meant to be, is to choose a perspective and live by it. For, what, really, is 'the truth'? What is the nature of this life we have and this world we are a part of? It is no easy matter, that is for sure.

Priscilla Cogan, in her wonderful novel, *Winona's Web*,[3] tells a traditional folktale about the nature of truth, which I have updated a little to make it more relevant to the modern world. It is a story about a wealthy investment banker who lives in the most luxurious apartment in the most exclusive part of Knightsbridge, London, and drives the latest top-of-the-range Ferrari. His beautiful wife is intelligent, witty, charming, and totally devoted to him, and his daughters adore him too. In short, he has everything a man could ever want or need to be happy, and then some.

But, of course, he isn't.

Instead, he is restless and seems somehow lost. No-one can understand it because this is the man who has everything. But he knows what the problem is and, one day, he confesses. 'I need to find a meaning to my life; I need to find Truth,' he says.

Always supportive of her husband, his wife gives her blessing, and so he sets off on his search for meaning.

For years he wanders the mountains and the forests, the cities, the seas and the wilderness places of the Earth, but he can find so sign of elusive Truth. Then, one day, just as he is about to give up and return home, at the top of a high mountain peak, he comes upon a deep, dark cave and, entering, finds a wrinkled crone dressed in rags and tatters. Her hair is knotted with grease, her skin dirty and aged, her gaping mouth empty of teeth and her old, misshapen body rancid.

And yet, she speaks with such poetry and deep wisdom that the man immediately recognizes her as Truth. And so he stays with her for a year and a day, learning from her the secrets of the cosmos and the intricacies of life and nature. All she knew, all there was to know, is made clear to him.

As the end of his apprenticeship to Truth draws near, the man begins to realize how much he misses his family and his life of fame and glamour in the city. And so, packing up his few belongings, he makes his way to the entrance to the cave which has been his home and his university of life for so long. Pausing, he looks back. 'Truth,' he says, 'you have been kindness itself to me. You have welcomed me in and shown me all that there is. In the city I am wealthy and I have power. It saddens me to see you living in this way. So tell me, is there anything I can do for you in return?'

Truth thinks for a moment and then answers: 'Money does not interest me, my son, but there is one thing you can do for me – when you tell people that you have discovered Truth, please tell them I am young and beautiful.'

Now, what exactly does that mean? That Truth is a liar, that there is no Truth – or, perhaps the opposite, that wherever you find Truth, it will always be young and beautiful no matter how it appears?

The story is a paradox, like a Zen koan, a question without ultimate meaning, which asks you to describe the sound of one hand clapping or the look of your face before you were born. Actually, there is no objective answer. Whatever you say is a reflection of you, not of ultimate reality. And, again paradoxically, that *is* the answer. As Coehlo's words at the beginning of this chapter suggest, we are all the sole occupants of our own world and our own version of the truth, though sometimes we come together as a collective and decide as a group to see the world in a certain way because it makes life easier to do so. The outcome is 'consensus reality'. We then appoint officials to maintain the consensus for us and so social 'systems' arise – the legal system, the education system, the political system – each with its own hierarchy and system of authority which ensure that we toe the line.

Of course, there is no real collective reality. We just act as if there is. The problem is that we seem to have forgotten that and put in place very rigid and inflexible social systems which, literally, have the right of life and death over us if those in authority don't like the way that you or I or anyone else is thinking and behaving in the world. The way we have decided to view the world and the collective reality arising from it *do* matter, not only at the most symbolic and seemingly esoteric of levels but at the level, sometimes, of our own personal, physical survival. And it goes even deeper than that.

Some say, for example, that we occupy physical space, that our lives are material, that possessions and solid objects are all that there truly is; that only matter matters. This is the way of modern Western societies. Others (most traditional, pre-industrial societies among them) believe that we live in a spiritual universe of energetic potential which can manifest as new realities that we can shape and share and use in our evolutionary growth.

Whichever of these viewpoints we adopt will have profound effects for us as individuals, for humanity as a species, and for the world as a whole.

If we are spiritual beings, if all of life is sentient – the rocks, the trees, the stars, as well as we human beings – and all of us connected, as the shamans believe, then, by necessity, we must approach the world in a different way since all things in life become our closest relations. We cannot continue to exploit the planet for material gain; we must adopt a new way of being in order to preserve our world and protect ourselves and our relations.

But if 'matter' is really all that matters, and we have true dominion over the material and physical world, then we are in control, we can do as we wish with the planet, and we can continue to put in place the social systems and structures which reinforce the primacy of our authority in this world.

Each worldview will lead us to a different world.

I want to share with you this true story which, perhaps, illustrates the difference between these two perspectives. It is the story of my father's death and the events that immediately followed it.

I was 22 the winter my father died. I was away at university and had not seen my parents for six months. It was one of the coldest winters on record that century. Snow had been falling for weeks and the ice was thick on the windows even inside the tiny, damp, basement apartment I lived in at that time. I was trying to find a coin for the electricity meter to warm the place up when I heard a knock on the front door.

Someone answered it, another of the students in the house. There was some muffled conversation in the hall above me, then silence. I was still scrabbling through coat pockets for coins when they knocked on my door.

'I'm afraid I have some bad news for you,' said the policeman standing there. I had seen enough TV movies to know what that meant: a death in the family.

My family was a large one – what historians of the 20th century will call an 'extended family' – and some of my relatives were elderly and unwell. Others liked to believe they were as it added a little drama to their lives, so they had convinced themselves years ago that they were destined for an early grave. Some of them were 90 years old.

At the mention of the words 'bad news' my mind, on automatic, went into search mode through this list of relatives to find the one whose name I was about to hear.

My father wasn't even on the list – whatever else he was, he had always been very much alive. So it was really strange to hear the policeman's next words. 'Your father died this morning.' They were a challenge to my own belief system, my assumption that my father would go on for ever. In that instant, I realized how little I knew him as a man, how much of a mythological figure he had become instead, and how I, in turn, had become a myth to match him.

My father was the living archetype of 'The Father' – very much like your own, perhaps: somewhat distant, uncommunicative, involved in secret things – the work he never spoke of, feelings I assumed he did not have – a figure to be feared or pitied, and grudgingly admired for the secret wisdom he must surely have but that he guarded so well. I had never really known him (as the Father–Son archetype requires); instead, I became the rival son, the prodigal who had not yet returned, as we played out the script between us.

Had he not died, we would eventually have made up our

45

differences, realized a love and respect for one another and, when he passed away peacefully a few years later, I would have come to see him as human, fallible, a man both blessed and cursed in his inability to tell me that he cared. I would regret his having died so soon and missed him, quietly, as befits one man of another. He would have come to see me as a strong and independent young man, able to make his own way in the world, and he would have been proud.

This is the way the Father–Son archetype is supposed to go, at least. But our script had played itself out too soon.

It was a struggle to get home that day. I had no car, the trains weren't running. But at last I made it the 150 or so miles to my parents' house.

Walking into the house that day was strange. Although there were only a few people in the room, it seemed packed with souls. The air was thick: it was like moving through some viscous material that clung to me as I walked, and there was a darkness and an intense energy, like the still silence that comes before thunder, when everything seems to congeal around you and compress the body before the thunderclap that brings relief from the build-up of atmospheric pressure. My immediate thought was that something was wrong, something hadn't been done here.

It is vital in many traditional cultures that the dead are honoured in a particular way, that arrangements are made according to their wishes and that the sacred is upheld and respected at this special moment of passage between the worlds. But in this room there was a pervading sense of things left unfinished, not followed through, a room of spirits trying to make their wishes known to people focused only on their personal grief.

What was it that was not being honoured? I looked around the room for clues, sensing the importance of finding out what needed to be done.

At that moment, I looked up and there, at the window facing me, was a robin. It sat on the windowsill, looking straight in towards me, and then, quite deliberately, began pecking at the glass. This continued for minutes before it flew away, only to reappear at another window and begin again its urgent signal for attention or admittance.

Before long, the bird had completed a full turn of the house, pecking at every window. It was the height of winter, freezing outside, and none of the windows were open so I do not know how it was that suddenly this bird was in the house.

It made directly for my father's antique gramophone, one of his most prized possessions in life – and with none of the panic that most birds have when they manage to fly by mistake into the alien environment of a house. It ignored everything else around it and landed on the funnel of the gramophone, where it perched, looking straight ahead at the people who stood facing it on the other side of the room. As it landed, the needle dropped onto the record. Normally, the mechanism would have to be wound for it to play. Now it just played, some old jazz throwaway song from a more innocent age. 'I'm the sheikh of Araby and your love belongs to me.'

The needle caught in the groove of the record and the words 'Araby', 'Araby', 'Araby' played over and over. Someone eventually walked over to the robin and picked it up. Again, no sense of panic. It allowed itself to be held, trusting that it would not be harmed, and was quietly returned to the outside. The sense of congealed energy I had felt in the room lifted as the bird was released. But it was only two days later, at a family conference, that I realized the full significance of this visitation.

After he was discharged from service at the end of the last world war, my father had become an officer for the Palestine police force. Stationed as a young man in Jerusalem, he had the time of his life for four or five years and had often said later that, when he died, he wanted his ashes to be sprinkled on the River Jordan. Although it was a comment made lightly, my family was determined to honour that request, and, as the eldest son, it became my duty to make his last wish a reality. That last request was the thing still undone that I had sensed when I first entered the house that day.

And so it was, a few months later, that I did, indeed, find

myself in 'Arabia', kneeling on the banks of the Jordan, saying my final goodbyes to my father as the last visible remnants of what he had been sank beneath the waters.

As I sprinkled his ashes on the waters, something caught my eye on the distant bank. It was there for just a second and it did not register at first what it was, then I realized: it was a robin.

I do not know whether robins are found in the Middle East, but it seems unlikely and anyway, that is not really the point. Because even if they are, I think it is more than coincidence that a robin should appear at just that very instant. The archetypes collapsed and we became again just father and son.

This is the reality of the spirit world – a world where all things have significance and even the appearance of a robin can be profoundly healing if we choose to open our eyes to the wider meanings inherent in such an event.

But the story of my father's death does not end at this point, as pretty as that might be. Two days after my experience at the River Jordan, I was back in Jerusalem and passing a cinema just outside the Old City where they were showing the film *Christiane F.* It was hot outside and I had nothing better to do, so I went in.

There were two of us – me and a young woman, aged maybe 20, sitting some distance away, both of us waiting for the film to start. It never did. Finally the cinema manager came over to speak to me. I, of course, didn't understand a word.

And then she was there next to me. 'He said they won't show the film today because there are just us two and it's not worth it,' she said. Somewhat disappointed, we agreed on coffee instead and ended up spending the day and then the night together.

Her name was Deborah and she had, she said, come to Jerusalem to die.

Originally from Texas, she was now studying languages at the Hebrew University. Her home life was a tragedy of richness. The daughter of an oil millionaire, she had always had every material thing that she could wish or ask for. None of it meant much.

The one thing she never had was her father. For him, it was always business, never love or time or investment in her. He had denied her the one thing money could never buy her – himself. For twenty years she had, she said, been the loneliest girl on the planet, living her life as if trapped in a lift between floors; a lift of glass where she was always on show, with no-one to talk or turn to. Hers was a world of parties and politicians, pretty rich boys and yes-men. She no longer wanted to live in a world like that.

In her world, there was no escape, no spirit. Trapped like a bird in a golden cage full of material possessions, she flitted from one joyless party to another. In her future lay the prospect of inheriting her father's money and being married for her cash. The social rules she lived by were prescribed by her family and she would always be measuring her own existence by their values.

There are no relative degrees of pain to a young mind; every one is absolute because no-one truly has a reference point external to themselves. The psychological pain of distance and abandonment is just as great as the physical pain of abuse for the person who is suffering. Whatever happened to Deborah I cannot say. I knew her only for those 24 hours. Whether she is now a millionaire trophy wife in Texas or whether she got her wish to die, I hope all is well for her. We were, in some ways, very close.

By making their intentions clear to me, the spirits had shown themselves to be a real, subtle and deeper force in the world, a force which shows us that life itself is rich, that animals, birds and other life-forms can communicate with us, that there is more to live for than money and status and following the rules of the game, something that Deborah – who 'had everything' – had never had. Even in the context of personal tragedy, the death of a father, the spiritual world-view is able to sustain us with nourishment for the soul, bringing with it a richness that the daughter of this millionaire would never know in her world of duality and separateness. This is the real difference between the two perspectives we may hold of the world: one brings comfort, the other can bring pain.

AND SO, WHAT IS 'THE TRUTH'?

If it is indeed the material world we have been conditioned to accept from birth, then how come this solution – once we have found it – can bring such pain with it? And why are there so many anomalies in our lives and our experience?

I suspect that despite our cerebral and socialized construction of social reality, we all know at a visceral level that we have been trained by our society and by the roles we play within it to view the world in a particular way, to accept that it operates as we are told it does, by certain criteria, and that others know best how we should live. But in reality, we *know* that this is not so.

We pay lip service to the importance of individuality, free thinking and free speech but we are all encouraged to sacrifice our own sense of purpose; to give up the individual quest for a full and fulfilling life in order to remain a part of the consensus dream. The result of such socialization is a tendency to end up with a nondescript and often contradictory view of the world, bolstered by the automatic, textbook delivery of the well-learned lines we have been taught. Such compliance, all too often, leads to a complete denial of ourselves to the extent that our personal opinions do not even enter the equation.

The way the world is presented to us and the contradictions in the system around us is an interesting study in its own right, and one which has kept sociologists occupied for decades. Here are just a few examples of the way society really works:

HOW THE MEDIA CREATE 'REALITY'

In the *Observer* newspaper of Sunday, 11 June, 2000, reporter Peter Preston picks up on the role of the media in helping to create and sustain the social dream which defines our reality and our 'truth' for us. He quotes research conducted by the *Columbia Journalism Review*, which polled 300 American media professionals to ask why stories they think should be covered in their newspaper are often not reported at all.

Their top three answers were:

1. Because they might be damaging to the interests of their own news organization – a case of journalism protecting its own to the detriment of the truth. As Preston himself remarks: 'You can tell the truth, the whole truth and nothing but the truth: but not in your own backyard.'

2. Because writing a certain story might expose the reporter 'to ridicule by other journalists' – 'in short', says Preston, 'don't break away from the pack. Conform: shape up, go with the gang': on no account break with the consensus view. Forty-three per cent of journalists thought the risk of ridicule too great to take a chance on reporting the facts if they contrasted too much with the mainstream accepted view.

3. Top answer, for 62 per cent of journalists, however, was that stories do not get reported because they are 'too complex'. Even if they are of national or global importance, these stories will never see the light of day because they – like life itself – are complicated, interwoven with the strands of multiple realities, and cannot be glibly summed up in easy sentences.

There are many conclusions we can draw from this research, but the overriding one is that the media do not see themselves as there to tell 'the truth' or report the facts if they might damage a vested or partisan interest, make them a laughing stock for taking an anti-consensus stance, or if the facts are too difficult to report. So they churn out the same simplistic half-truths aimed at the lowest common denominator, and never once do they dare to challenge our belief systems with evidence of new facts and information. And our media, of course, are the people we have come to rely on to explain the world to us.

Our Western 'truth' is a consensus dream. It is the world we have decided to create for ourselves, which no doubt once served a very real purpose in helping us to evolve this far. However, I question whether the half-truths and soap box dramas we have become habituated to really serve a useful purpose for any of us any more. This is *our* world, every single one of us. We all have a right to be here and we all see the world through unique, individual, eyes. If we choose consensus with like-minded souls, that is one thing, but to be brought up in one mindset as if there is no other option is another thing entirely – and who does it actually serve?

Furthermore, there is very often a sense of contradiction about this 'one social truth' which the media present to us. Think of the 'movie star anorexia' stories which get splashed all over the front pages, for example, only to be followed by a glowing report of some new miracle diet. This can only mean, of course, that *the truth* is *no truth at all* since, if it were, it would, by definition, be immutable and absolute.

This concept of never quite defining 'the truth', is actually a rather sophisticated and intelligent strategy since, by never quite defining what is 'right' or what is 'a game', we always run the risk of being judged 'wrong' after the event or of not seeing the joke when this suits the social dream of the system itself.

WHOSE LAW IS IT ANYWAY?

This same strategy is also bound up in the dictate that 'ignorance of the law is no excuse' – which, in my opinion, is one of the most ludicrous and arrogant pronouncements ever made. How can you avoid taking a particular action if you do not know it is 'wrong' to do so? Surely the onus is on the legal system to explain its rules and regulations to us if it expects them to be obeyed?

Besides which, of course, the law itself is so convoluted and open to interpretation that our own judges don't seem to understand it, hence the many cases lost in court which are subsequently won on appeal before a different judge when almost exactly the same evidence is presented or, in the worst cases, posthumous pardons are issued when someone is executed in error for a crime they did not commit.

And, on top of all that, the laws themselves are often idiotic. There is a state in America where it is statutorily possible to be prosecuted for painting a sparrow in order to pass it off as a parakeet. I wonder what Earthly purpose that serves. And yet, the law is, by definition, always right.

Oprah Winfrey tells how she was once involved in a lengthy court case against a group representative of US cattle farmers after she had made an innocent remark about BSE on her television programme. She sat there day after day in court, she said, listening to rival lawyers describe her as the archetype of an evil villain or as a saint who was merely voicing the legitimate concerns of the people. Oprah didn't recognize herself in either description; she was just a woman expressing a personal view.

What she realized from this, she said, was that the legal system was a court of fantasy, whose *sole purpose* is to distort the facts in order to present a fabricated person to a jury of people forced to hear these fairy stories which they must then accept as 'truth' and make judgements upon as if they were real, material, and mattered.

'I realized,' said Oprah, 'that the spiritual lesson is not to squander your energy defending against the lie but to retain your energy and find your own stillpoint.' It was, she said, that regrouping of her personal energy which saved her. 'In that moment,' she said, 'I won the case.'

IN SICKNESS AND IN HELL

In February 2000, the UK TV documentary programme, *Panorama*, studied another of our great social institutions, the healthcare system, and revealed that our doctors and our hospitals – the very institutions which exist to protect our most vulnerable people – are not always to be trusted either.

According to the *Panorama* research, doctors at a number

of leading UK hospitals had been removing the organs of children who had died in their care so they could experiment on them at leisure, long after the death of these children. At Alder Hey hospital, *Panorama* reported, doctors had amassed an estimated collection of 2,500 children's hearts. In some cases parental consent was never requested. The grieving parents had no knowledge that their children's bodies had been cut up in this way.

The medical profession was not even apologetic. 'We have to learn how to do these operations at leisure,' said one doctor, 'to go over it again – almost in practice.' Only a game.

A later inquiry, chaired by Professor Ian Kennedy, which called for more than seventy different changes in current medical ethics, concluded that, historically, the healthcare system has been 'characterised by a type of professional arrogance – an arrogance born of indifference', which is a pretty damning indictment of our medical profession's capacity for true patient care.[4]

The doctors concerned had absolutely no recognition of the dignity of these children, no acknowledgement of the sanctity of their souls, no understanding of the distress to their parents. There was even evidence that parental consent forms for the removal of their children's tissues had actually been forged by some medical professionals. 'I felt sick,' said one mother, 'when I realized I had only buried half of my child.'

THE NATURE OF WORK

While all this was happening, I watched two personal friends of mine suffer and almost lose themselves in the dark wash of their working lives. One of them, Daniel, just left work one day. No-one ever spoke of his leaving; it was as if the social ranks at work had closed and nobody spoke of what might be troubling him. So we knew it wasn't good, wasn't just a cold or a backache. Rumours started by colleagues suggested depression, a breakdown, mental fatigue. But it was more than that. Daniel's will had simply collapsed. He saw the futility in what he was doing and suddenly just couldn't go on.

When Daniel came back, his eyes were wild and hollow. He sat, smiling the false smile of the outwardly compliant, but when no-one was looking, he rocked back and forth in his chair, his spirit gone. He was somewhere else, far, far away. The 'funny' thing was, no-one cared. Work went on as usual: as long as there was a body to fill a desk, who could smile politely at clients, it really didn't seem to matter.

And then there was Suzie. Suzie was overworked, highly stressed and lived life on the edge of a vast fall into chaos. Her boss always seemed to be giving her more than she could cope with, so she was flustered, pressured and vague. I watched her tension mount until I knew that one day soon, a serious illness had to result.

One day it came – although, interestingly, not to her. Her husband, a businessman who frequently travelled the world, took it all in his stride, and had always seemed totally confident, calm and in control of his life, suddenly had a massive heart attack on a transatlantic flight. He recovered but had to work at home for six months, and travel was out of the question. Suzie had to work part-time to help him at home and, eventually, she left her job completely.

Such stories are not uncommon in shamanic circles. On a spiritual level, where two people are connected through love, it may often be the case that one partner is deeply willing to accept the pain of another and, through that, to precipitate a life-changing event which is ultimately beneficial for them both. If it hadn't been for Suzie's husband, I am convinced that the heart attack or other illness would have been hers. The universe stepped in to save Suzie.

During this, I realized an essential truth: we are all Daniel and Suzie, all pretending our lives away. The system wants it that way. Until one day, driven by the need for more, the demands of our bosses to give more of ourselves (bosses who are under exactly the same pressure themselves), or an undefined fear of failure, we either see the pretence and collapse in our desire to be free of it all, or we may die as a result of our need to sing the same song of chaos and be a real player in the social game.

The name of this game is 'duality'. We have allowed a society to emerge which is based on division; where we are either 'power-full' or 'power-less'; right or wrong; men or women, black or white, rather than simple human beings in a universe of beauty.

This focus on an 'in-group/out-group', an 'I and That' mentality, is a fundamental reason for the problems inherent in our systems. It is the power of a media baron to present 'the facts' selectively in order to protect his own investment, and the powerlessness of the person wrongly depicted to gain access to those same media in order to defend herself. It is the power of office which enables a politician to deliberately avoid paying massive taxes, while at the same time supporting initiatives by the Inland Revenue to 'ferociously pursue' the rest of us office-less citizens for a few pennies and pounds. It is the power of 'doctor' over 'patient' which puts professional distance between the simple meeting of two people, and the doctor's sworn duty and legal right to do all in her power to preserve life – even if it means keeping the bodies of our children on ice for decades until she can get round to her experiments. It is the power of the Church to play out its Holy Wars and Inquisitions over simple people whose only crime was to choose a different god.

One key word lies at the heart of these problems, and that is *separation*. By seeing ourselves as alone, individually or institutionally, and separate from one another, we allow the system and its roles, rules and regulations to take control of our senses. We define ourselves in terms of what we are not – not black, not female, not Catholic, not 'good enough' – and so we maintain this illusion of duality. And so much is lost. Compassion, humanity and empathy for others is just part of it. But imagine how wonderful and powerful we could be as *people*, as a race, if we were able to see ourselves as we truly are, not separate but united, all in this together, as one human race and connected to a positive dream. Beautiful Mutants, evolving together into a single, *conscious*, future.

To realize this new dream for ourselves as human beings, all we really need to do is understand that the systems we have put in place to represent us are *our* systems. We put *them* there, not the other way around, and we have the right and the power to change them if we wish. The way forward is not by empowering these systems any more, by voting for parties, or writing to *The Times*, or changing the school syllabus, but by changing *ourselves*, empowering ourselves with belief and faith in our own abilities, trusting the universe we are a part of rather than the empty and contradictory promises of the systems that surround us. So we can evolve consciously through this bottleneck we are caught in.

By embracing the spiritual instead of the material we will find one way back from the brink of our own disaster; one way for us to reconnect with all that we have let go, and to find a new sense of balance with a new faith and vision for the future.

EXERCISE: WELCOME TO YOUR WORLD

Shamans say there is not one world, but millions of worlds we all individually occupy. Your world may be nothing like mine since it will be determined – created – by you according to the image you have of it.

Furthermore, the spiritual and the physical, the sacred and mundane, exist alongside each other in this room where you sit right now. These other dimensions are not separated from us by time or space, but only by awareness. We can enter the spirit world now and learn from it, simply by altering our perceptions. We do this by changing our consciousness so that we allow these new possibilities to enter our frames of reference.

Relax now and close your eyes. If you wish, use the Jivaro posture I described earlier, or simply sit quietly in meditation. Breathe out slowly and back in a few times in order to quieten your body and slow it down. Notice any tension in your body and let it go.

Allow an image to emerge in your mind's eye of the life you are living now. This will be the first image which comes to mind, even if it seems to bear no obvious resemblance to 'you' and is not what you expected to see at all.

You might, for example, see your life represented in the form of an animal or a structure or a shape of some kind; it might be a sound or a smell or a sensation. These are all fine; work with the image you get.

Walk around the image in your mind and see it from all sides and angles. Where is this image of yourself, what is its context, who is it with? What is it doing? How does it look or seem to you? Don't try to analyse it, just let it flow for the moment. Talk to the image being: is it happy being what it is? How would it like to change? How does it see its future?

Continue your observations and dialogue until you are ready and then, when you have the feedback you need, *step into* the image being so that you become it.

See the world through its eyes now and look back at yourself and any others who might also be here with you. How do things look and feel from this perspective? What is it like to be you? And how do you look through the eyes of this being?

Now step out of the image and ask it two specific questions:

1. *What is the essence of my life as I am living it now? Does this make me happy and fulfilled?*
2. *What is sacred to me? What would give my life true meaning and purpose?*

Explore and experiment further with these questions and try to get a sense of what it would mean and how it might be possible for you to live in a more sacred manner. Then, when you are ready, come back to yourself, breathe out slowly and open your eyes again.

What insights do you now have into the nature of your life and your place within it?

THE CITY AND THE SPIRIT

Most of us live in cities, or what are ironically called urban 'communities', which are, in many ways, the grandest expression of the modern world we have created, and physical representations of our worldview since, ultimately, every physical thing begins first with an idea of what may be possible. We cannot build it until we think it. In this sense, our greatest cities are no less than the system's celebration of itself.

Today's cities represent our most fundamental humanity and our aspirations for the whole race, and almost all of us are tied to this modern world, whether we like it or not. Though many of us would like to, few of us will ever really escape to a downshifted world of 'rural tranquillity' away from the society which continues to impinge upon us more and more in our contemporary lives. If we did, we would discover that the myth bears little resemblance to the reality. There is little peace and sanctity in the real countryside of daily slog, foot and mouth disease and economic decline, since the system lives there too in the form of quotas and bank balances and foreign competition.

How can we live in this mechanized, urban environment and still create a life which is spiritually meaningful for us – a life *without* the games? How can we find the sacred in the city, reconnect to a deeper sense of living and find absolution for ourselves and then peace in a world beset by problems?

- *Emotionally*, we are distanced from one another, isolated, lonely and, through our lack of connection and community, unconcerned

59

about the welfare of others and they of us. I have lived in city apartment blocks where I have never even spoken to my neighbours; worked in offices where human beings were functionaries who might as well have been robots, all of us uniformed in suits and ties, shackled to desks and processing paperwork like automata without once expressing any other aspect of our human selves. The advertising industry (where I used to work) is full of people like this, who do not believe in the products they promote any more than the clients they serve. Far from being 'creative', it is a mechanical process where the product is king, the corporation rules and the people who work there rarely ever meet as human beings. Perhaps your life is different, your work is the most important thing in the world to you, and you can go home to a street full of friends. But sadly, I doubt it.

- *Physically*, our worldview, our dream of life, is leading to the creation of a world where pollution, the extraction and destruction of natural resources, protectionism which leads to aggression and war, inner city decay and inequality, and a host of other problems, are creating a global as well as a local crisis. Mental and physical illness, stress, trauma and general dissatisfaction with life are all on the increase.*

- *Spiritually*, we feel abandoned. There is no magic left in our lives. We are born, we work, we do our duty and we die, rarely finding a true purpose or a point to our lives.

- *Mentally*, many of us see only a dark future and, since energy flows where our attention leads it, the incredible power of our minds, ironically, will create the very future we envision. We are destined for a dark world unless we can reconnect with our spirits and touch the sacred once again. In the late 1990s the media were full of reports of road rage, plane rage and a new phenomenon, work rage, as we strike out against those closest to us to relieve the dreadful build-up of pressure within us. Our

---

* On Christmas Day 1999, the British National Health Service could offer only one single free bed in its emergency wards to all of the millions of people in the UK, an indication not only of a health service in crisis, but of the incredible need for healing we are experiencing in our cities.

culture offers little in the way of the positive and controlled release of this pressure through ceremony and celebration or rites of passage, for example, which are the backbone of many other cultures still, for we have been socialized into the Western way of blame, aggression and exploitation which somehow validates the violence of our actions.

In contrast to this rather depressing scenario, the Dagara medicine man, Malidoma Patrice Some of Burkina Faso, is a walker between worlds, as a diviner and initiate into the traditional secrets and ancestral wisdom of his West African people, and a Western academic, with three master's degrees and PhDs from the Sorbonne and Brandeis University, Massachusetts. He is superbly qualified to talk of the ancient role of the sacred in uniting people and places and providing purpose in life – and to reflect on the impact of its loss in the West.

'When the focus of everyday living displaces ritual in a given society, social decay begins to work from the inside out . . . Where machines speak in place of the gods, people are hard put to listen, even more hard put to vibrate with the realm of nature.'

For Some, the outcome of such a culture can be only one thing: 'To be in a machinelike culture is to have one's soul constantly at risk of being sucked out . . . there are many cases in which people live separated from their souls in this culture. There are many cases of people actually ending their lives because there was no home to go to nor any kind of ritual to receive.'[5]

Rich or poor, it really makes no difference. For Deborah, in Jerusalem or Texas, there was nothing to look forward to but an empty life of spiritual decay in a 22-carat diamond-encrusted prison; her money would not save her, and her millionaire father could not protect her from her own sense of loss of the sacred and of her self.

At the other end of the scale, we have only to walk the streets of London or New York after dark – if we dare step outside into our own cities after dark – to see the evidence of loss and decay in the homeless, the street gangs, the winos and drug addicts, all of them trying to find meaning in street culture rituals and designer badges – a Coke versus Pepsi of the soul which does not provide the sustenance they need – or to lose themselves in the otherworlds of narcotics and alcohol in an attempt to escape the desolation and despair they feel in this one.

In counterpoint, Some talks of his own African village and the sense of true community and belonging experienced by the people there. This community feeling is created, he says, by characteristics within the social structure which have been consciously evolved by the people and which are deliberately maintained through their communication and interaction with the spirit world. It is an interesting, if sobering, exercise to compare these characteristics with those of our Western societies and the more materially orientated social systems we have created.

• **Every member of the group is valued and, in turn, sees a value in the group.** In the West, quite the reverse is true. We are encouraged to develop a pioneer spirit of fierce individualism – it is how the West was won and it is there in the American Constitution. We must think for ourselves and stand on our own two feet, while our economic system steers towards *laissez-faire* and our political systems towards non-intervention. We are even denied the community of a direct connection with spirit, our religious structures imposing a route to god only through the intermediary of a priest and the rote recitation of hymns and prayers once a week for a few hours in the day. Though we may pray alone, it is true, the god to whom we speak is a Western caricature rather than a spiritual entity we know personally as a friend and, more often than not, we scientifically minded Westerners do not seriously expect our prayers to be answered and would die of fright if they were, or at least visit a doctor to check that we weren't 'hearing voices', should the spirits ever talk back to us.

• **There is a deep sense of trust, based on the natural assumption that everyone is innately good and intends good to their brothers/sisters and neighbours.** In the West, we are born with 'original sin' and the culture of blame remains with us throughout life.

We have only to watch the news to see how this culture of blame seeps through. While we protect our individual rights to the point of violence, we still feel as if we should somehow also be protected and looked after like children, and when this does not happen to our satisfaction, like children we lash out at others who must be blamed for their failings towards us.

Our prison system is a case in point. Recidivism amongst offenders is high, primarily, in my view, because we do not truly treat the cause. We are unwilling to look at the unhappy circumstances in a person's history which caused them to 'offend' and to offer support and help to that person to over-come these problems so that they do not need to take the same action again. Instead, we seek redress by punishing them visibly as a 'warning to others'. But this does not solve the problem, just as building new roads does not solve the problem of conges-tion, it simply creates room for more cars. A happy, fulfilled person does not need to offend (however we define that term). Perhaps if we focused our attention on creating more happiness, instead of more creative punishments, we would also solve the problem of prison overcrowding for minor offences.*

---

* As an example of a 'blame-orientated' culture in operation, on Christmas morning 1999, tons of oil from a sunken tanker washed ashore on the French mainland. The authorities were aware days in advance that this would happen and where the oil would arrive. But they did nothing to prevent it. Instead, they busied themselves taking photographs of the shoreline before the oil arrived there so they could take further pictures later to prove the extent of the damage and thereby strengthen their case during the litigation they already had planned. In a culture where all things are understood to be alive and connected and the environment is an essential part of human life, such behaviour would be unthinkable. Every effort would be made to save the land or, if this was impossible, to mourn its loss and to make amends. In a culture which embraces a psychology of blame, the reverse is true; the land is there for our taking, exploitation and disposal, and we care only for money and litigation when it is 'taken from us' by natural or man-made disaster. The differ-ence between the two is simply a change of mind and a change of heart.

• **People are open with one another and share their problems.** Personal problems become those of the community and all people are involved in their resolution. The load is shared. Men and women, adults and children, old and young are equal, each with defined and agreeable roles, and the importance of the contribution of each is valued in its own right.

In our society, we have a diametrically opposite view. How often have you heard a parent sternly warn their child not to tell tales, that big boys don't cry, to keep it to themselves? We do not encourage trust or the sharing of true emotion.

Our offices and businesses are set up with secretiveness in mind in order to 'maintain competitive advantage' and ensure that, in the ways of office politics, the knowledge that is power remains the province of a select few.

In *The Journey To You* I quoted Liz Tomboline, a psychiatric nurse now turned Western shamanic healer, who reflected that we have little to offer each other any more in the way of social support and a network of care. The architecture of our cities and our lifestyles within them are simply not designed for it. 'It's hard enough to get a decent babysitter for goodness sakes.'[6]

• **Caring and sharing.** Among the Dagara everything is shared. If you have a good crop one year, you share it with your neighbours so that next year, should your crop fail, you will be looked after too. This is more than an exercise in instrumental back-scratching. It is the reflection of a deep-seated ideology of community. 'To have while others don't is an expression of your making up a society of your own,' says Some – a society of one.

I am still moved by an image of the African famine from the broadcast of the Live Aid concert in the mid-1980s, of a starving mother, unable to find food for her baby, who had opened her veins and was feeding her child with her own blood, sharing the very essence of herself with her child as the only thing she had left to give.

Here in the West, we have just survived another Christmas,

which many of us recognize as little more than a commercial mockery of a sacred festival. Just days ago, I witnessed two men arguing in a toy shop over the latest fad toy. There was only one left and, presumably in order to demonstrate their love for their child, which they felt able to show only in material terms, these grown men were prepared to come to blows over a plastic substitute for genuine affection.

In the final twist of cynicism that is a typical Western Christmas, the sales began the next day, and two days after that the same toy was back in stock at less than half price.

Is it really the best we can now aspire to, to fight over toys for our children which will be discarded in favour of the new fashion within days, while half a world away, caring for a child means giving up your own life if necessary so that that child might live?

• **Respect for the Elders.** In shamanic communities, where spirit permeates the whole of life, young children are often cared for by the elderly, the community recognizing the deep connection between these two groups and their greater proximity to the spirit world. Children and babies have recently been born from spirit and are considered to have expert, current knowledge of the state of affairs in this otherworld, which is of deep interest to the Elders as they will soon return to this land. The Elders, meanwhile, 'hold the wisdom that keeps the community together' and are valued in their own right for the deep knowledge and experience they have accumulated over many years of life.

In the West we have, since at least the 1950s, created a culture of youth where worldly and spiritual wisdom have taken second place to the exuberance but relative inexperience of our teenagers and young adults. Our motivation, as usual, has been fast access to hard cash and unformed values which can more easily be focused on fashion and consumerism rather than any deep reflection on life. Taste can be controlled and fashions changed faster than values, and our youth 'market' has money that the corporations want.

Even now, adverts tell us that we need 'younger-looking skin' and the songs which accompany them inform us of our 'duty' to 'keep young and beautiful – if we want to be loved'.

- **Respect for nature.** For traditional communities, if there is any distinction at all between the self and the environment, it is one based in deep respect for nature as a source of nourishment and healing.

Such a concept is not unknown to us in the West. James Lovelock's Gaia model (which we will look at in Chapter Seven) has effectively demonstrated that nature operates as a total system, where all parts have a role to play and where humanity itself is an essential aspect of this vast, interconnected structure.

This does not stop us from destroying her – and ourselves in the process – by burning down our rainforests with increasing ferocity, leading to global warming; or plundering the Earth for its natural resources and siphoning off the oil which is her lifeblood; or polluting the atmosphere with chemicals and gases from our consumer goods and cars.

Our problem in the West is not one of ignorance, but of arrogance. Sometimes it is blind arrogance, when we simply do not know what we are doing. This is perhaps the arrogance which gripped the early missionaries who went to Africa to zealously preach the word of 'the one god' (ours, naturally) and left untold damage in their wake. As Desmond Tutu said: 'when the missionaries first came to Africa, they had the Bible and we had the land. They said "let us pray". We closed our eyes. When we opened them, the tables had been turned: we had the Bible and they had the land.'

It is a story repeated on many continents. The Lakota medicine woman, Winona Pathfinder, in Priscilla Cogan's novel, *Winona's Web*, also relates how 'the black robes came to my people and told them the stories of Jesus. We said they were fine stories, now let us tell you our stories . . . but they were rude people, these black robes. They wanted us to hear only their stories. They told us to throw our stories away, to tell only their stories. They said their stories were the true stories.

And then the Elders knew how foolish these black robes were, for no one story could tell it all, and all stories are true'.

Sometimes, however, it is a deliberate arrogance which drives us. Sometimes we know exactly what we are doing and the consequences of our actions, but we continue all the same. When I was a young child, a teacher told us a story which took the form of a fictional exchange between man and god where this human arrogance was made plain. The dialogue went something like this:

God: Why does man always try to take over from the gods, to do what it is our job to do?

Man: Because I am your equal. Why must everything be your way?

God: But I am the creator of all life.

Man: I can create life in test tubes, with cloning, genetic engineering and genetic modification.

God: I control the seasons.

Man: With just a sprinkling of silver chloride crystals on the clouds, I can create rain; I can emulate the fiery heat of the sun in my nuclear reactors; I can change the weather by melting the ice caps.

God: I have the power to strike you down in punishment.

Man: The power of my nuclear reprisals can kill millions.

God: But I can also raise the dead and give you back your life.

Man: [Silence]

Jim Haskins, in his book, *Voodoo and Hoodoo*, makes this same point rather well.

> *Unlike the more advanced technological man, the primitive man sees himself as an integral part of the universe. There is no such thing as alienation in primitive cultures, no word in their language to describe a sense of separation or differentiation from surrounding forces.*
>
> *We modern, 'civilised' individuals regard ourselves as*

separate from, and above, these forces for, in large measure, we can control them.[7]

And yet, like most things, having done so, we tire quickly of our conquest and the very act ceases to have meaning for us.

We tend not to see the things we control, just as we tend not to see the people we control. We are increasingly separate from our parents as well as our children, from our neighbours as well as our co-workers. And more and more we see ourselves [as] discrete entities placed on Earth for some unknown reason to live a life for which it is impossible to find meaning, and finally to die, allowing for no continuance of our personality. (ibid.)

• **The importance of the ancestors.** 'The ancestors are not dead,' says Some, 'they live on in the spirits in the community.'

A little while before I left for Jerusalem for the funeral ritual of my father, I consulted with a spiritist to see how the trip would go and whether it was right for me to conduct this service. Having never before met me, he described perfectly my father's physical features and spoke of a 'hot desert place and the importance of a river that ran through it'. He went on to describe a number of people I would meet during the trip, including 'a young woman who is tired of life but has not yet given up on living'. For him there was no question of the continuation of the human spirit after death, and he was able to offer considerable and accurate predictions on the future based on his consultation with these spirits.

Immediately prior to my meeting with this man, I had attended a service at his church where a visiting medium conducted the ceremony. She was a specialist in what is known as transfiguration, the ability to take on the physical appearance of the spirit speaking through her.

I watched with the rest of the audience as this diminutive, blond-haired lady became, less than five feet in front of us and with no fancy lighting, the physical being of a dark-haired giant of a man complete with beard. A few seats behind me there was a gasp of recognition and a dialogue began between the spirit now occupying her body and an audience member, where messages of fact, evidence rather than opinion, were exchanged, names named, dates cited, personal memories shared.

I have no doubt that the ancestors are here among us. But even if it were not so, if spirit did not exist, we in the West, who pride ourselves so much on analysis and rational thought, have accumulated libraries of wisdom and research which are the voices of our ancestors in different form. We have only to consult them, to learn from our history, in order to predict the future. But how many of us bother? Our leaders would rather reinvent the wheel, sometimes with disastrous consequences, than examine the past and act upon its wisdom.

There is a true story from Haiti which illustrates how big business, and vested economic and political interests, can have an intensely detrimental effect on an entire people as a consequence of its actions – even when it does not mean to – simply because it does not stop and listen to its own ancestral voices in this way.

A few decades ago, Haiti was a land of pigs – some domesticated, and others wild, roaming free in the natural rainforests. Haiti is a Third World country, but local farmers were able to eke out a living from the pigs, which provided them with food. Occasionally they would rear the pigs – called Creole pigs – and sell them at market to buy other produce.

Then something dreadful happened. There was an outbreak of swine fever in the Caribbean and the US authorities became alarmed. American farmers lobbied the government, big business interests got involved and eventually US officials arrived in force in Haiti and began the massive wholesale slaughter of the Creole pig population, reasoning that Haiti was the 'gateway' into the US from the Caribbean and so if all the pigs there were killed, it would stop the spread of the disease that otherwise could destroy their own pig population.

Every pig on Haiti was wiped out.

Because they had not learned the lessons of the past,

however, what the US authorities could never have predicted was the knock-on effect of this action.

First, the rainforest started to die since fertilizer from the wild pigs had helped to bind the soil. Without this, and exposed to strong sunlight and high winds on the mountainous slopes, it began to dry out and then slip down the steep hills in landslides which took the forest with them.

A lot of this soil and dead plant matter landed in the sea – which killed off the local fishing stock. There were no fish.

Farmers and fishermen, who had once just about survived as a result of the 'pig economy', were now in abject poverty and could not feed their families. The pigs were dead, the fish were dead, people were starving. And so the mortality rate began to increase as the children died – as did the crime rate as people began to steal and kill in order to survive at all. Many people died as a result of this simple action of the pigs being killed. It is a story which demonstrates how all things are connected and how we must be careful in our stewardship of the Earth. Everything is part of Gaia, one huge and interconnected system – which is what the ancients have always told us, if only we had ears to hear them.

But it demonstrates something else too – how our Western arrogance and blind assumptions can almost destroy an entire economy for no benefit whatsoever.

For the irony of this story is that swine fever did still enter the US – because the government and its advisers had got it wrong. Haiti was not the 'gateway' to the States as they had first thought; the disease came in from elsewhere. Even more ironically, it turns out that the Creole pig was the *only* type of pig which was naturally resistant to swine fever – and the US had just killed them all, without even doing tests first (which might have helped, of course, to find an antidote). A whole species was wiped out in Haiti, leading to death and crime and violence and, in a sense, *because* of this, swine fever went on to spread throughout the US.

So now, after doing all in its power to destroy the pigs, the US is having to repopulate Haiti with the selfsame pigs. It has cost the US people in taxes twice: once to kill off the Creole pigs, and then to put the same pigs back again.

Of course, it is the same story told in Britain today. The last outbreak of foot and mouth disease in the UK was in the mid-1960s, yet we have done little to prepare in the intervening forty years for a recurrence, including refusing to introduce a simple vaccination programme, which many other European countries have done. And rather than work with our cattle and sheep to help them overcome what to them is little more than a mild flu, we have decided instead to shoot them in the fields, simply because the alternative does not fit our plans and we live a dream of 'dominion over nature' rather than a partnership with her.

Our desire to be 'separate' from nature so that we can 'control' her means that we must always remain oblivious to the possible effects of our intervention in the natural process. We believe we can control the world – indeed, that we *have* to control the world – and it is always with a sense of renewed surprise that we learn once again the impossibility of doing so and the insignificance of the human race in the face of nature's own powerful vast resources.

For Some, the time to act, in order to stop this madness, to reclaim the sacred and, through this, to deal with the problems of modern living, is NOW. 'Spirit is our channel through which every gap in life can be filled. But the spirit realm will not take care of these gaps without our conscious participation,' he warns.

He is not alone in his view. As the impact of the modern world makes itself felt, tensions build and people are taking action of their own to avoid the pressure-cooker explosion that must otherwise follow – like leaving the cities and

EXERCISE: WHAT IS THE CITY?

Relax and close your eyes, and breathe slowly, exactly as in the last exercise. Now, allow an image to emerge in your mind's eye of the city or town you live in.

Walk around the image so you see it from all sides. What is this image? Where is it? Is it happy being what it is? What does the city-image want? What is its purpose? And how does this meet your own sacred purpose? Are you on the same team?

See the world through its eyes now in order to get a perspective on yourself as you are seen by this city-entity. How does it feel about you?

Are there any opportunities for negotiation, compromise or mutual benefit for the two of you, where you can both get what you need from life? If so, explore these further and decide on a course of action that you can both commit to. If the city is prepared to allow you certain concessions so you can live your sacred purpose, what will you give the city in exchange?

When you are both ready and have made your agreements, come back to yourself and then back to normal reality. What insights do you now have into the nature of the city and your place within it?

Images are *real* things – they could not exist if they were not – and what they have to tell us about themselves, and about *ourselves*, is extremely valuable information.

searching for new meaning in places where they can reconnect with nature, as we will see in the next chapter.

THE NATURE OF TRUTH

And so then, what *is* the 'truth'? Put simply, it is whatever we want to believe – that we are destined, like Deborah, for a life of trivia and unhappiness, or that we are surrounded by richness and blessings, by spirits who care for us and, though invisible to our eyes, nonetheless work with and support us every day; that life is soulless or divinely sacred.

Whatever we decide will make its impact on us since we cannot have a dream of life without also creating life in its image. We are what we see and dream.

Traditional ways of dreaming a life of purpose and meaning and of working to create a more fulfilling and powerful world seem in many ways extremely desirable to us in the West who are locked into our own narrow worldview – and we do not have to sacrifice all we have achieved and learned and gained in the last few hundred years in order to embrace these traditional ideologies. All we actually need do is re-empower ourselves so that a new reality can flow from our vision; a reality of connection in place of separation. There are practical techniques from cultures and traditions so ancient that they are often beyond dates and chronology, which still remain strong allies for our future. All we need do is respect them and use them in our own lives by honouring what others have also learned about this world that we share.

For there is one fundamental and simple truth in life: every one of us has the power to change the world through our own dreaming. We have only to will it so. These techniques will help, and then it is down to us. All of us.

The key is to live your own truth, always, and to look with grace and with patience for the answers. In the beautiful words of Rainer Maria Rilke, to 'try to love the questions themselves like locked rooms and like books that are written in a very foreign tongue'.

*Do not now seek the answers, which cannot be given you
because you would not be able to live them.
And the point is, to live everything. Live the questions now.
Perhaps you will then gradually, without noticing it,
live along some distant day into the answer.*[8]

The way to truth may be a slow one for it is a life's journey. But, like any journey, it begins with a single step, with awareness of your surroundings and with allowing the questions to come about the things you see around you.

EXERCISE: SEEING THE TRUTH FOR OURSELVES

We learn much about what we consider true, not through direct experience, but through intermediaries who interpret our reality for us. This can be very helpful to us on occasion since life is complicated and time is short. We cannot examine and experience everything; sometimes we have to trust others. But often what we get from them is not 'truth' but opinion. We need to develop an attitude of questioning instead of blind acceptance, so we do not take things at face value, but only on their merit, on how they gel with *our* sense of truth.

Pick a newspaper story – any story you like from any paper you like – and read it through *with conscious awareness*. Try to maintain a non-judgmental attitude about the story itself so that you can approach the exercise neutrally, and hold a question in mind throughout, such as 'How does this writer approach issues of gender equality?' or 'What does this writer think about race?' You will find that a worldview begins to appear for you out of the words on the page. This is the 'hidden news', the words between the lines which describe our society's perspective on cultural issues. This is not a conscious conspiracy on the part of the writer; it is simply the way we have been socialized to project meaning onto the world.

Count the number of affirmative statements and negative comments in the story, get a flavour of the style of the piece, its humour or depth. These are all 'clues' by the writer to how we should read and absorb the information she or he is presenting us with. Most of us do not *study* the news, we scan it, and so we absorb not just the news content but the values within it as well. By reading through a story with deliberate awareness, you can get a flavour of these subtle messages and, perhaps, begin to see how these influences start to accumulate in our lives, if so much 'hidden' information is contained in one simple story.

Here is an excerpt from the *Sun* newspaper of 30 March 2000, describing the arrival in the UK of asylum-seekers from war-torn countries such as Kosovo. The facts of the matter are that many people are now homeless and countryless as a result of this conflict and have come to the UK, which, like other countries in Europe, has a legal duty to care for them and to find them a place of safety. In 1999, just over 71,000 people applied for asylum here.

This is how the *Sun* carried the story:

> Refugees **cost taxpayers** more than £300 million last year – that's £13 for each family in Britain [which, of course, isn't actually true, since some individuals and families are, by their circumstances, exempt from tax and social security payments]. The cash went on benefit **handouts**, housing and support services for the **thousands** of asylum seekers who **flooded** into the country.

> Last night Tory MPs said the **shocking** new figures **proved** that Government policy on refugees was in **total chaos** . . .

> A Sun **probe** recently revealed that some refugees were really **cheats** intent on **milking** our **generous** benefits system. Others, **many** of whom had been **sneaked** into Britain by **organized asylum gangs**, were earning a **small fortune** from **begging** . . .

> Bernard Jenkin, shadow minister for London, claimed **bogus refugees** were **costing** the capital £177 million a year. He said: 'Labour has made London a **soft touch** for the **organized asylum rackets** who are **flooding** Britain with **bogus** asylum seekers'.

If you had to explain to a visitor from abroad what our worldview is in the West, based on what you have just read, if this was all the information at your disposal, what would you tell him about us? That we are a caring nation? That we, as a democracy, believe in the sanctity of human life, the freedom of all people to avoid persecution and retain their individual liberty? That we are a Christian people, perhaps?

Remember, these are the images and information you have grown up with since birth. How much of it is really you?

Here is another, somewhat related but very different exercise about truth:

In one of Castaneda's books,[9] the shaman don Juan made the interesting observation that among our friends we will find the poles of ourselves. In other words, if you have two friends, one will be very extreme in one direction about a particular issue, while the other will be equally extreme in the opposite direction, and you will be somewhere in the middle. To put this another way: we choose friends who mirror our moods and also reflect the extremes of our worldview back to us, just as the media do.

Is this true for you? If so, what insights into your true self do your friends provide for you?

2

UNDER PRESSURE: THE PEOPLE OF THE CITY

The breezes at dawn have secrets to tell you –
don't go back to sleep.
Rumi[1]

Ayahuasca, the hallucinogenic vine used in healing ceremonies by Peruvian shamans, is considered to have an identity and spirit of its own. It is a real, sentient, spiritual being which lives in the plant itself.

The actual mixture drunk by those who participate in the ceremonies consists of ayahuasca, which suppresses that part of our brains which normally prohibits visions, and chacruna, which produces the visions themselves. Often, pure tobacco from the jungles, along with extract of datura, are included in the mixture. Both of these have a purgative effect, and it is these two which cause the vomiting and sometimes the diarrhoea which is part of the ayahuasca experience, so that the body may empty itself and make room for the spirit to enter.

The spirit of the plant is drawn from the vine through the sacred songs of the shaman, which are known as *icaros*. The *ayahuascero* don Augustin Rivas Vasquez refers to these *icaros* as 'magical tunes without words'.[2] On top of these are added the *mariris*, the words themselves, which chart the course for the visions and call to the spirit of the universe around us. Both the *icaros* and *mariris* are 'discovered' by the shaman, or given to him by spirit, during his special diets and isolation in the jungles for periods of some months to many years, as he studies and works with the sacred healing plants of the rainforest. He may hear the special cadence of one part of a bird's call to a mate, the protective roar of a jaguar, the way the wind blows through the trees in one particular part of the forest, the lullaby whisper of running water or the tumbling energy of a waterfall, and he will put all these seconds of sound together into one powerful song that speaks of love and protection and, during the ceremony, will guide the participant to that holy place of love and warmth and comfort to meet with the spirits there.

Deep in the jungles of Peru in the ghostly moonlit blackness of a full-moon Amazon, I drank the ayahuasca mixture that was offered to me by the shaman Javier, a man who has spent twenty years learning the special healing magic of ayahuasca and many other of the jungle's 'doctors' – the special healing plants of the rainforest which our own scientists are only now beginning to discover and to marvel at. Every three seconds an entire rainforest species is wiped out by human 'exploration' and 'development' of this region; the world badly needs people like Javier who have taken the considerable time to preserve the healing knowledge that lives in the mysterious leaves of this place.

The ayahuasca was thick and bitter, tasting of chocolate and fungus and raw meat. It took willpower to drink the full cup offered to me, but in four or five breathless gulps it was gone and Javier began to sing and blow tobacco into the night air to protect the sanctity of this midnight space from curious or malevolent spirits that might also be drawn here.

Sparks of light began spitting from the shadow-trees around us: fireflies or falling stars, spirits or visions, I couldn't tell any more. My brain began to disassemble the world around me and my eyes to show me things we normally never see. Perhaps these sparks of light are always there, just below the surface of our senses. Maybe they are what holds the world together.

I closed my eyes and stepped on to a mountain top, looking out over the vast desert of the prehistoric world, the world before human life began. Centuries passed in seconds as creatures emerged, grew, evolved, changed, died, mutated, each new life becoming different and new-formed, blending with its surroundings and adapting together with the world around it, which was changing too. This was evolution – not 'fitness for purpose', 'survival of the fittest', 'dog eat dog', but a beautiful symphony of life supporting life and playing like the rising and falling of the shaman's song.

Then the desert itself was changed and became a vast city at night, the lights of the buildings sparkling like fireflies, each house a sacred space for the families that lived and laughed and played there, not individual lives but connected, like the lights of the houses which blurred into one another, lifetimes taking place in the cells of each family member.

We were playing at life! We were here to experience, to explore, to embrace the sensation of living, to play like children with the brand new toy of existence. Evolution was no dark matter and the outcome was not the point. We were just here to experience the moment and to play beneath the stars at being human for this short lifetime before we returned to the vast silences of space beyond our world and became, once again, sparks of light in the perfect sky. We have created a world of potential, a society built of dreams, not fear and chaos. And what we have made is just the start, all there to be changed and shaped again if that is what we choose.

But we have simply forgotten that. Somehow, along our evolutionary path, we have lost the point of our presence. Life wasn't meant for suffering, life was meant to be fun, that is why we came here in the first place. All we have to do is remember – and then change the dream of our world.

I found myself laughing at the very simplicity of it all – and at the irony of a species which had chosen to enter the beautiful kindergarten of our planet, surrounded by toys and riches, and then forgotten that it was all there for us, all of us, to just enjoy.

I looked up at the sky and the moon laughed back at me. I had the feeling that the universe was pleased with its children, that She loved us all and that, despite appearances, everything, every little thing, would turn out fine . . .

In your silent moments, perhaps you see this too? We are, after all, linked together, you and I, and you have seen through my eyes too.

Human evolution is a paradox. Never before in history has it been easier to communicate with another human being, to listen to them and to understand their perspective. And never has it been so hard; never have there been so many lonely, isolated, separated people in the world. Everybody's talking, but nobody's saying very much and, more importantly, nobody's listening anymore.

With the Internet, web, cable, satellite, digital and mobile communications, the Western world entered the post-global society some time ago. Now we're trying to make sense of what we've created. Today, between getting up and going to bed, you are likely to have been exposed to around 1,500 different advertising messages. How much of it do you consciously remember? What about unconsciously?

Potentially millions of images, bits and bytes of information, hit us every day. As consumers, we live our lives in 'info-slices', fast-response, drive-thru information, but we rarely know the full story. We receive the world in pieces, never seeing beyond the headlines into the total thesis.

We tune in to snatches of the Israeli/Palestinian conflict live on TV, zap into *The Weakest Link*, back to the Jeffrey Archer libel trial, the Bush withdrawal from the Kyoto environmental protection treaty, and finish off the evening with *Have I Got News For You*. There is a feeling of desensitization about the whole thing. The Gulf War may have been about real lives – and deaths – yet it is also just one more TV spectacular in a ratings war with the soap operas.

The simplest thing in the world would be to *remember* that the world really isn't this way, to step back from the mirage and see it all anew, and our place in it, from the wider perspective of play and becoming in a universe which means us no harm.

We can sometimes do this when we take a break from ourselves, go away to a new country, or take a holiday from work. Then we relax and sink into the peace and the excitement of new places and new perspectives. But in our everyday world, in the demands of our jobs and the break-neck speed of city living, the job of remembering – re-membering – ourselves can be harder.

'Stress has become the great epidemic of the modern age,' said Polly Ghazi and Judy Jones in their book, *Downshifting*.[3] According to their figures, 90 million working days are lost every year in the UK due to stress-related problems. More recently, Bryan Appleyard, writing in the *Sunday Times Magazine* in June 2000, tells us that one in four of us in the UK are 'clocking up more than 50 [working] hours a week. Half of our fathers spend less than five minutes a day in direct contact with their children . . . Medical research, incidentally, suggests that working for more than 60 hours a week for over three years permanently damages your health . . . Are we mad? No, just trapped.'*

The way we work at the moment, and the lives we lead in the city and the system we have created, all have very real consequences for our health and our well-being. In a survey quoted in the *Daily Telegraph* on 23 September 1999, more than half the people who responded said they were 'frequently' stressed at work; more than a quarter said their sex life was suffering as a consequence, and a third said their health was also affected. 'Mindless corporate loyalty', writes management guru, Tom Peters, in this article, 'was always a rotten idea'.

---

*In addition to increasing working hours, recent research in the city of London has shown that our failing transport infrastructure now means that an average of 70 minutes extra each week must be spent on commuting to work; time which could otherwise be spent on rest and recovery *from* work. People want more than this from their lives. According to the Henley Centre, a third of us in the UK are planning to devote less time to work and more time to 'a better way of life'. Whatever we might think this is, we know it isn't work: 62 per cent of us want to cut our working hours, 42 per cent want to retire early, 42 per cent would like to work part-time, 25 per cent of us would take a pay cut if it meant less stress and more free time, and 28 per cent would prefer more time off to more money (quoted in *Downshifting* by Ghazi and Jones.

Many people agree and are turning their backs on the social dream which sees work as centrally important in our lives (roughly a third of our waking lives will be spent there), and loyalty to our bosses as paramount. Rather than continuing to sell their souls, they are jumping ship and getting out.

'This desire to flee rather than fight was underlined by a third believing that their organization could not change the way it worked,' said the *Telegraph* article. Consequently, many were planning to change jobs. But where does this escapism lead? 'OK. So you got a new job, a new company and a new level of responsibility and within a year the novelty, challenge and excitement begin to pale.'

There is no solution to be found by running round the job wheel like a rat in a cage and entrenching ourselves further in the Western career model and the social dream of a modern world of work and productivity and more and more consumerism paid for in business lunch ulcers and executive level heart attacks.

Just look at these 1999 statistics:

- 49 per cent of people think morale in their organization is low.
- 55 per cent face frequent stress at work.
- 30 per cent think their health is suffering through work.
- 28 per cent think their sex life is affected.
- 50 per cent have too little time to develop relationships outside of work.
- 19 per cent of men and 24 per cent of women drink to ease work pressures.
- 7 per cent of men and 15 per cent of women are in therapy or counselling.
- 31 per cent of workers do not trust their employer.
- 40 per cent believe their company doesn't respect its own staff.
- 36 per cent of people in large organizations and 25 per cent in small organizations do not trust their employer.
- 54 per cent of people in large organizations and 38 per cent in smaller ones report problems in recruiting new people.
- Top work-related issues which affect our personal lives: lack of

balance between work and life, too much to do, stress and lack of support, insecurity, lack of recognition and reward.

- 48 per cent of women and 49 per cent of men do not think things will get any better in the next five years.
- 33 per cent of men and 28 per cent of women have no-one to talk to about these pressures.[4]

You don't need to see figures like these to understand the impact of all of this. A recent letter in *Metro*, a free newspaper distributed in London, says it all: 'Without doubt, this is the most aggressive place I have ever lived. There is not a moment's peace as someone is always trying to do you down, nick your space or cause a row. Perhaps there are too many people here, perhaps they are all disillusioned . . .'

As Woody Allen once put it: 'I don't want to achieve immortality through my work. I want to achieve it through not dying.' There is a search going on for meaning, for something real to believe in, for a viable way out.

So what's stopping us?

Herbert Marcuse in his *Essay On Liberation*[5] described the modern individual as a flattened personality within a social system which perpetuates this. We may all be quite aware of our lack of fulfilment with what we have and what we have created but, because we are inside the system and a part of it, we are quite unable to see an alternative. It is all we have ever known and it is reinforced by the social dream of consumption. Escape becomes increasingly impossible as the bigger house means a bigger mortgage, the children have to go to the right school, we have to be seen in the right places wearing this season's fashions, drive the right car to get there, and still find the money for a two-week holiday at this year's 'in' resort. At the end of it we find ourselves working a 50-hour week just so we can pretend we are 'free'.

Despite the loss of his individuality, Marcuse's 'one-dimensional man' often has so much invested in the system, both literally and metaphorically, that he must believe himself at least partly satisfied and content with it – anyway, to the extent that he is obviously not prepared to rebel against it. Even though his estrangement from himself and his psychological suffering continues, he has little option but to adapt to it and bear his pain in silent discontent. What other choice is there?

The driving force behind our acceptance of this quiet pain is, for Marcuse, the refusal of the system to allow most of us to take responsibility for our own actions. Instead, the state, by our design, now takes responsibility for us, dampening our fire and individuality so we are never truly able to 'grow up, to mature, to perform efficiently and normally in and for society, which compels the vast majority of the population to "earn" their living in stupid, inhuman, and unnecessary jobs'.

The first step towards reclaiming our minds would be 'a break with the familiar, the routine ways of seeing, hearing, feeling, understanding things . . . [a] radical change in consciousness'.

Marcuse could be describing a traditional, shamanic perspective here, one which enables us to look at the world afresh and change our orientation towards it. We are some way from such liberation at a social level, even though our awareness *has* evolved to the extent that we now at least recognize our pain on a conscious, individual level, as we begin to register the increasing stress, depression and boredom inherent in our city living – 'the madness of everyday life', as John Zerzan put it in *The Mass Psychology of Misery* [6] – which is 'recognition, on the visceral level at least, that things could be different'.

According to Zerzan, mental health experts now believe that the majority of us suffer some form of psychopathological symptoms, while the rest of us go through life acting out a 'pathology of normalcy' as we submit ourselves each day to the requirements of a 'qualitatively unhealthy society'.

These mental 'disorders' – which Zerzan sees as really just the natural outcome of going along with things as they are given to us by society – are treated almost exclusively with drugs which do reduce our awareness of our personal anguish but go no way to addressing the cause. Tranquillizers are now the world's most widely prescribed drugs, and anti-depressants have achieved a record number of sales. While both are addictive and have various unpleasant side-effects, they remain popular principally because of their ability to offer temporary respite from a reality which continues to propagate the cause of our dis-ease.

Castaneda, in *The Active Side of Infinity*,[7] offers anecdotal evidence of the detrimental effects of such dis-ease in the story he relates of his friend, 'Roy Goldpiss', a businessman who set himself the ambition of becoming the richest man in the world. He soon gave up on that after realizing he could never compete with people like the leader of an Islamic sect who was paid each year his own weight in gold and would fatten himself to gigantic proportions just prior to his weigh-in.

So then Roy decided to make himself the richest man in America – then California – then the Los Angeles suburb where he lived – failing each time as he discovered someone richer than himself whom he could never match up to. 'Roy's frustration knew no limits. His drive to accomplish was so intense that it finally impaired his health. One day he died from an aneurysm in his brain.'

There are two parts to this story which are particularly sad. The first is the death of Castaneda's friend through his misguided and impossible dream of becoming the richest man on Earth, which signifies more than anything our drive to 'be the best' in terms defined by the system, always to look forwards and suffer the impossibility of personal contentment with what is. Roy felt that he could only 'accomplish' for himself on someone else's terms – the model of success held up by the Western dream, where achievement is valued only in financial clout and not personal contribution to the world. Eventually, Roy was killed by a dream.

The other aspect to this story which saddens me is the man who was paid his weight in gold. What a tragic life and true slavery to the system to allow your personal worth to be measured in this way, to become literally a walking caricature of the system you serve, spending half the year fattening yourself like a sacrificial offering and the other half trying to lose the weight you gained in order to be yourself again – not to mention the implications for your health.

The sense of frustration and failure in stories like this is paralleled to some degree in the experience of everyone who has had to subdue their individuality to the system, whether it is dressing in the drab grey of the business uniform, ensuring that you have the right haircut and accessories, or simply turning up at the office at the prescribed time despite some emergency or personal problem at home.

This may seem a small imposition, but its effects are vast. According to Zerzan, we are in the midst of a continuing modern crisis. Eighty per cent of Americans admit to having at least considered killing themselves, while 'teenage suicide has risen enormously in the past three decades, and the number of teens locked up in mental wards has soared since 1970'. Serious obesity among children has also increased, while eating disorders such as bulimia and anorexia are now quite common in all areas of society, as we try to become the dream image of someone else. The incidence of panic and anxiety attacks has also risen, to the extent that they are fast overtaking depression as the most common psychological malady in our urban centres, while 'isolation and a sense of meaninglessness continue to make even absurd cults and TV evangelism seem attractive to many'.

And it is not just the 'one-dimensional man' who is the subject of this malaise; the very machinery of society is itself at risk from the same crisis. In November 1989, the entire US Navy was forced to suspend its worldwide operations for 48 hours as a consequence of accidents and incidents over the preceding three weeks which had resulted in deaths and injury. The safety review which followed identified problems with absenteeism, drug abuse, and numerous other problems which were affecting the Navy's ability to perform even its most basic role with any semblance of effectiveness.[8]

Our schools, too, and the children they serve, are not

immune to the problem. As well as the high-profile acts of aggression now centred on our schools – in the USA on 1 March 2000, a *six-year-old* took a gun into school and shot a fellow pupil dead – there is also a growing problem of illiteracy as a rising number of American people of all ages simply refuse to take part in reading and writing classes. In answering the question as to why this should be, Zerzan suggests that 'literacy, like schooling, is increasingly seen to be valued merely for its contribution to the workplace. The refusal of literacy is but another sign of a deep turn-off from the system, part of the spreading disaffection.' To support his argument, he points to survey results which show that work now ranks second to last on a 10-point scale in terms of its importance in the life of American people.

We want, and we deserve, more than society is able, or prepared, to offer us. The problem is – we forget. We were born free and we remain spiritually free throughout our lives, but we become so conditioned to the drudgery that we forget our own power to create an alternative.

Richard Bandler and John Grinder are a couple of heroes of mine. Together they founded Neuro-Linguistic Programming, or NLP, a radical form of psychology which has some very immediate and dramatic curative effects and is, in fact, not so far away from shamanic practices in its approach (indeed, the shamanic approach is now being used in this evolving model of human psychology).

They quote some revealing research about the human condition in their brilliant little book, *Frogs into Princes*.[9]

You have no doubt heard of the work of behavioural psychologist B. F. Skinner, who worked with *operant conditioning*, getting rats to run mazes for the reward of food at the other end of the maze, as signalled by the ringing of a bell or some other stimulus. Pretty soon Skinner's rats were able to find their way round the maze like expert navigators and would do so just to the ring of the bell – even when they found no food at all at the end of it. They had been conditioned by a secondary stimulus (the bell, or whatever) to anticipate a reward and so they set off anyway, their little legs carrying them like sprinters round the maze in the hope and anticipation of some food at the end.

According to Bandler and Grinder, one day someone asked the question, 'What *is* the real difference between a rat and a human being?' And so they built a new maze, at human scale, to find out, and had humans run their maze for the reward of five-dollar bills.

The results showed tiny variations in performance – the humans were a little quicker to learn and got there a little faster, that was about it – but the really interesting statistics turned up when the researchers removed the reward and had both groups run the maze just in response to the secondary stimulus: the *expectation* of reward. In the words of Bandler and Grinder: 'They removed the five dollar bills and the cheese and after a certain number of trials the rats stopped running the maze. However, the humans never stopped! They are still there! They break into the labs at night!'

We just forget. We get caught up in the game, we enjoy our new experiences and our play so much that we don't remember the point of the game. But we need to, because the game we're playing now is beginning to kill us.

'SELF-HELP' VERSUS SOCIAL CHANGE

As the desire for escape grows stronger and society begins to lose its children and its converts, what it offers for their sickness – or perhaps in its own support – is psychology, and there has indeed been a flood of new therapies since the 1960s. At the root of every one is an ideology which places the *individual* at the heart of the problem. The implication is that the sufferer and not the social system (which is, after all, the one common denominator in all stress-related and many physical illnesses) must change to accommodate the social dream, and not the other way around.

'*Self*-help' books continue to sell in their millions, advising us to use affirmations, visualization and positive thoughts in order to address *our* problems, while counsellors and 'Agony Aunts' do their best to reassure us that we are OK, we are not 'abnormal', we are still within the fold. But maybe what we need to hear is that we are *not* normal, we are unique, special *individuals*, not just a drone in a soulless society – and that it is *still* OK.

The self-help books and the work of therapists and counsellors is, of course, highly valuable insofar as they help us to heal. No-one would deny that. But they can only treat the symptoms, not the cause of the problem, so it is often true that the dis-ease will return when the therapy ends or the power of the affirmation begins to fade. Then, once again, it is *we* who must adapt to the system, rather than the social structure adapting to our needs – even though it is we who have created this structure so that *it* may take care of *us*. Perhaps the boat needs rocking.

The self-help outlook forces culpability back on the individual who cannot 'fit in' and so

> *legitimates alienation, loneliness, despair, and anxiety . . . It privatises distress, and suggests that only non-social responses are attainable . . . In the name of mental health, we are getting mental disease.*
>
> *Psychiatry appropriates disabling pain and frustration, redefines them as illnesses and, in some cases, is able to suppress the symptoms. Meanwhile, a morbid world continues its estranging technological rationality that excludes any continuously spontaneous, affective life: the person is subjected to a discipline designed, at the expense of the sensuous, to make him or her an instrument of production.*[10]

And it is not just the 'patients' who are suffering. The psychotherapist, Dr Arnold Mindell, has pointed out that this approach can be equally debilitating for the therapist. Mindell has explored a number of shamanic communities and in *The*

Shaman's Body writes of a healing session he underwent with two witch doctors in Mombasa, Kenya.[11]

'Their openness healed a problem I had been unaware of, a disease I did not know I had,' he says.

> *Deep inside of me was a longing, making me half ill. I had forgotten that I had wished the world I lived in would give me this sense of belonging . . .*
>
> *The psychological community I had grown up in looked down upon therapists interested in group experience and so, in my weakness, I had felt guilty about occasionally inviting group participation in my work with individuals. Now I realised how important this participation was . . .*
>
> *. . . No-one can lead a meaningless life for long or tolerate cities with no purpose.*

This 'science' of psychiatry, which focuses on the individual and forces patients and not systems to accept responsibility for their illness, is a fleeting truth, as volatile and short-lived as social opinion. The sexual 'disorders' which so fascinated Freud are a good example. In the nineteenth century, masturbation was regarded as a mental disease and 'treated' with a variety of methods falling just short of torture, by a repressive society so hung up over its own sexuality that middle-class women would even cover the legs of their sofas and pianos, while at the same time turning a blind eye to their husbands' midnight visits to the local brothel. Now, of course, we can all buy *Joy of Sex* type videos which show us how to masturbate 'properly'.

It has long been recognized, as well, that there is an obvious class component to mental illness – what is 'eccentric' and harmless for the rich is a damaging psychiatric disorder for the rest of us. The logic seems to be that the rich are not a part of the working world anyway and so not needed to uphold the social system, merely to stand as tokens of where hard work might one day get us, while the rest of us are required, as healthy cogs, to keep the wheels of industry turning. The cogs are necessary and cannot be allowed to become 'faulty'.

Mindell points out that

> *from the present viewpoint, it would seem that therapy was developed to support the worldview of the middle classes. It is available to those who have the money, time, and security for introspection. It takes you to the door of other worlds, senses and explains what is on the other side, and closes the door again.*
>
> *The more adventurous methods sniff at the door to the other world or cross over for short periods of time but recommend consensus white reality as a measure of what is good. Look at dreams, feel and understand the body, and find the missing feeling in relationships, and the world ought to be in order again. Except that it is not. Something big is missing. There is no jazz, no colour, nothing interesting happening in the community.*

Shamanic healers, by dramatic contrast, see the door, kick it down, and enter, laughing, into the mystery with their clients, dancing into a colourful and exciting world of spirits and soul and ritual. What they find behind that door will be as unique and challenging as the person who accompanies them, since every person is an individual with their own story, their own needs, their own reality, and every battle for the soul is, consequently, a life and death struggle for the divine right to be.

Amazonian vegetalistas (shamans who work with the spiritual and physical essences of healing plants and herbs) spend years, often decades in training, so that they know the spirit of every plant they use in their cures, and have entered the non-ordinary world many hundreds of times for their patients. Yet every time they do so, there will be a sense of trepidation since the spirits are real and the negotiation with them on behalf of the client may not go so well this time; the shaman could get into trouble, the battle may be fought and lost. No shaman would ever be so bold as a Western medical doctor or psychiatrist in treating any case as 'simply routine' and just prescribing the 'tried and trusted' drugs or following the 'usual approach', even though they are often more highly trained, in their way, than our own physicians, and know more 'routine' methods than our doctors.

The question for us in the West, then, is: how do we break out of our definitions and the colourless world we occupy if it is no longer meaningful or satisfying to us? How, like the shamans, can we find the unique in every moment when we are bound by systems and rules and 'normal procedures'? What escape routes are there when all we know is all we have been taught? What is there outside of the world we know, and how can we find it and finally be free?

The answer is in Marcuse's observation that freedom requires 'a break with the familiar, the routine ways of seeing, hearing, feeling, understanding things . . . [a] radical change in consciousness'.

Another of my heroes is Frank Farrelly. Frank is a radical psychotherapist, the author of *Provocative Therapy*,[12] and something of a genius. He has no time at all for a psychiatric system which works on the basis of economics and treatment 'regimes' and routines. Instead, he sees his job as healing those who need his help – and that's it. The way he goes about it is precisely by offering his patients a break with the routine they have got themselves into and a change of consciousness and perspective outside of the 'normal' doctor–patient rules.

Bandler and Grinder talk of his work with catatonic patients, for example.[13] Catatonics are a psychiatrist's nightmare. They sit immobile, staring into space, nothing going in, nothing coming out, for years at a time. Perhaps they have just given up on the world outside, or are bored or disappointed with it, and their withdrawal is a legitimate way of avoiding the pain of daily life.

They are great for psychiatric *institutions*, though, since they require minimum upkeep, are low cost, non-disruptive, and earn the institution lots of money in fees and grants. The institution sees a pay cheque – but that isn't Frank's way.

He sees a person who needs help and, like the shaman who will voyage to the otherworld of the client in order to find and return her lost soul parts, Frank does the same, entering into the world of the catatonic in order to bring her back to ours. When *that* is done, the therapy and everything else can legitimately begin.

Bandler and Grinder quote a couple of examples of Frank's genius.

In the first of these Frank finds himself up against a woman who has been catatonic for maybe four years. He's not fazed at all. According to Bandler and Grinder: 'He sits down and warns her fairly: "I'm going to get you".' He then reaches over to her and rips one of the hairs from her leg, just above the ankle. No response. So he repeats the exercise, this time ripping out a hair from her mid-calf. No response. So then he moves up towards her knee and pulls out another hair – at which point his patient starts and screams 'Get your hands off me!' Catatonic to fully conscious in seconds – *now* the healing can begin.

'Most people would not consider that *professional*,' say Bandler and Grinder – perhaps because it deals with the individual herself and has no time for the needs of the system – 'But the interesting thing about some things that are not professional is that they *work*. Frank says he's never had to go above the knee.'

The other example of Frank's work that I really like was with a young woman in a mental hospital who believed herself to be the lover of Jesus. When she said this to the staff, of course, their response was a fairly typical 'Of course you're not. This is a mental hospital and you are deluded. Accept what we tell you about your reality and we will make you "better".'

Not Frank though. He trained the patient's social worker to give her quite a different response – one which supported the patient's own worldview and entered into it, to an extreme level, in fact. Again according to Bandler and Grinder: the social worker entered the patient's room and 'the

93

patient went "Well, I'm Jesus's lover", and the social worker looked back and said wryly "I know, he talks about you". Forty-five minutes later the patient is going "Look, I don't want to hear any more of this Jesus stuff!"'

What we can never know, of course, is whether the woman in question really *was* the lover of Jesus. In her reality, totally valid to her (and perhaps to us had it been explained to us or if we had experienced it too), she was. But that is another question. The point of the example is to illustrate how direct, intuitive, *human* interaction can often work where healing 'methodologies' and 'systems' fail.

The 'trickery' of all shamanic healing is to enter the client's world totally, in a non-judgmental, completely accepting way, and then to effect a healing by moving the client away from this towards a new belief system which is more empowering and fulfilling for them. When people have their personal worldview, their unique view of the world, supported in this way they are much more open to change. They can then return to a position of greater personal empowerment with the ability to make more choices which better serve them as human beings and as souls who have elected to be born here to experience the world.

What Frank Farrelly is doing is not only brilliant, it is entirely shamanic. What our therapists and 'self-help' experts have been trained to do, by contrast, is often quite the opposite. They have been taught to work with the system and to forget natural, intuitive, human interaction with another person. As Bandler and Grinder remark, they have been trained in 'a belief system that said "Limit your behaviour. Don't join your client's world; insist that they come to yours" [but] it's much harder for somebody who's crazy to come to a professional model of the world than it is for a professional communicator to go to theirs. At least it's less apt to happen.'

I cannot leave this discussion without one more example of this approach in action, this time from Bandler and Grinder's own experience with catatonics, though the influence of Frank Farrelly can definitely be seen in it!

Bandler and Grinder are in Napa State Mental Hospital in California, being shown around the place by some of the institution's psychiatrists when they come upon a group of residents in one of the day rooms. At this point, the psychiatrists begin to whisper, so Bandler and Grinder begin whispering too. 'Then, finally, we looked at each other and said "Why are we whispering?" And one of the psychiatrists turned to us and whispered "Oh, there's a catatonic in the room. We don't want to disturb him".' *We don't want to disturb him!* The very point of work with catatonics *is* to disturb them, to bring them back from the silent wilderness they have entered into! As Bandler remarks, 'I don't know about your mental hospitals, but in California we've got some real whackos in ours – and we have a lot of patients too.'

'We went into that same ward at Napa,' said Bandler, 'and I walked over and stomped on the catatonic's foot as hard as I could and got an immediate response. He came right out of catatonia, jumped up and said "Don't do that!"'

At that point, with a receptive and responsive patient, capable of interaction with the world, true *therapy* instead of simple patient *maintenance* could begin.

A similar story is told by Elizabeth Kubler-Ross in *The Wheel of Life*,[14] where she records phenomenal success in 'curing' and reintegrating many 'hopeless' cases of schizophrenia in her care at Manhattan State Hospital – so many, in fact, that she is eventually called before her superiors to explain her 'technique'. 'I do whatever feels right after I get to know a patient,' she explained. 'You can't drug them into a torpor and hope they get better. You have to treat them like people.'

'Sometimes the longest journey we make is the sixteen inches from our heads to our heart,' says the Mexican shamanic curandera Elena Avila,[15] which exactly sums up the difference in the above example between a Western-trained professional who has been taught the pre-eminent importance of *analysis* and from this perspective did not even want to disturb his catatonic patient – and the more direct, shamanic approach which actually *cured* the client with one stomp of the foot.

I was fortunate enough to work with and drum for Elena at one of her soul retrieval workshops run by The Sacred Trust. She is a wonderful, poetic, deeply caring and very natural healer. But she tells a story very similar to Bandler's of a direct, perhaps from our Western viewpoint even brutal, intervention she once made in the healing of a client, Donna, who had suffered severe trauma as a child and difficulties with her somewhat aggressive adoptive mother.

One of the things this woman would do, when Donna was just a baby, was force-feed. If Donna was sick, her mother would throw the food back at her and continue to make her eat. This must have been terrifying for a small child and had led to problems of severe power loss for Donna who had been unable to fend off her mother during these attacks.

'I was concerned at how matter-of-factly Donna told this story, without any feelings at all,' said Elena.

Following a gut instinct that she needed to connect with this memory emotionally, I stood up, got some baby food out of the kitchen, and began forcibly shoving it into her mouth. Although she looked terrified, she passively accepted this behaviour, only saying 'Stop, stop' in a voice that was weak and shaky. I encouraged her to hit the palms of my hands and to say these words louder and more forcefully . . . through this, she was finally able to connect with and experience the rage and sadness she had felt as a small child, and to become more forceful and protective of herself. I reminded her that people will push you around and abuse you if you aren't in touch with your own sense of self-worth.

Of course, not all of us are Frank Farrelly, Richard Bandler, John Grinder or Elena Avila, so how can we begin to get beyond the system into the direct experience of healing ourselves and claiming back our own power and sense of self-worth, and jettisoning the – sometimes less than effective – courses of action that the system has laid out for us?

The first step is to redefine the system, the cities we occupy, and to get back to basics in how we view the world, with none of the prescriptive overlay, none of the cultural gloss that society has handed to us as the only natural order.

Changing the world means changing our own minds first and foremost. And the good news is that this *does* seem to be happening.

The World Values Survey (quoted in *Downshifting*),[16] investigated thirty-nine countries and 70 per cent of the global population, to identify what was most important to people in the world today, and found a 'steady trend towards post-materialism', a change in perspective summarized as a move from a social identity as 'global consumers' to one where we are 'world citizens', with the values of each as follows:

Global consumer	World citizen
Me	We
More	Enough
Materialism	Holism
Quantity	Quality
Greed	Need
Short-term	Longer-term
Rights	Responsibilities

The differences between the two could almost be summed up as those between a modern Western culture and a traditional, shamanic one.

IS SOCIETY 'EVIL'?

A few years ago I attended a training course led by a shaman from Tuva, on the Siberian border, where the word 'shaman' originated. As part of her teachings, she asked our group of thirty to divide into pairs. One of us then took a shamanic journey to answer the question, 'What is "*bad*"?' while our partner journeyed for an answer to the question, 'What is "*evil*"?'

When we returned from the journey, we reconvened in the larger group and discussed what we had seen and learned.

Throughout the group, those who had journeyed to discover what was 'bad' were shown images of decay, of things out of balance and out of place. The person to the left of me had seen a sewer full of human excrement and then the same waste filling a cathedral, with the understanding that while the former may be an unpleasant image, a sewer is nonetheless the right place for sewage; a cathedral is not. The sewer is not 'bad', because it is true to its purpose, while the second image is, since it represents something dysfunctional, out of place, and disconnected from the natural order.

Those of us who journeyed to understand 'evil' had also been shown images of things abandoned and removed from their true context. Prisoners of war executed *en masse* simply because of their race; slaves forced to work in inhuman conditions; burning cars in streets full of rioting. The difference with these images was that there was an energy about the disconnection they represented. Here were things which had been *deliberately removed* from the natural flow of the universe and intentionally made to be separate for a purpose which was not natural and right.

The conclusion of the group was that we may interpret something as 'bad' for us as human beings – such as a drought when we need water – but it can still reflect the greater, natural cosmic cycle; just as a drought will follow rain and rain will follow drought in the bigger natural order of the weather cycle. Its 'badness' in the moment, and for us, does not make it 'evil', *per se*.

What does make a thing 'evil' is *the human intention behind it to undo the natural order, a decision taken by a conscious being fully aware of the consequences of this behaviour and acting without heart, irrespective of the outcome for all other living things.*

The shaman who led this journey listened quietly while we explained what we had seen and then nodded to herself. It was the same information she had heard from every other group who had taken this journey, from Siberia to San Francisco. What we consider 'bad' from our human perspective is, in the cosmic order of the gods, simply life playing itself out across the pattern of the whole universe. While we may suffer the effects of a drought, there are plants of the desert and other life-forms which flourish in such conditions; it is merely our human self-importance which allows us to judge something as 'wrong' or 'bad' because it does not fit in with *our* plans and expectations, our comfort and convenience. 'Evil', meanwhile, is a human matter. The creation of an atom bomb which makes a desert of a country and orphans an entire race has no higher purpose attached to it.

Using these same criteria as we look around at the urban landscape and the world we have created for the 21st century, at the lost and alienated souls who occupy its landscape, we might find it interesting to ask if this world we find ourselves a part of best fits the category of 'bad' or 'evil'.

For me, an urban dream which does not truly serve us at a real emotional, physical, mental or spiritual level is best defined as 'bad', purely because it does not really work for us or provide real sustenance and nourishment for the soul. But to carry on enduring it and to further entrench ourselves within it in the name of progress is, at best, totally nonsensical, and it is at this point that we enter the territory of 'evil' since we are then deliberately maintaining this lack of harmony and balance by our own human devices. And, worse than that, we are perpetuating it by teaching our children to accept it as their reality too and bequeathing them a word full of problems.

For some people, the answer to this question of 'bad' or 'evil' is quite clear, and their desire to escape the city has seen them turn their backs on it to plough uncertain futures in rural retreats, lifestyle changes, and the shifts to a simpler form of existence that Ghazi and Jones describe in their book,

Downshifting. It has been estimated that 5 per cent of the American population will have turned away from the machine culture to embrace a less fraught and complex lifestyle by the early 2000s, they say, and possibly the same number or more in the UK.[17]

But for many of us, tied to the city by mortgages, careers, the schooling of our children or the negative equity in our urban homes, this is not an option in our generation (nor is it a real solution since the mortgages and the need to pay the bills simply go with us to the countryside. The city is merely the visible face of the system, while the system itself is every-where). But even if it were possible for us all to escape the city in such a way, we would simply transplant the city structure into the new one we would create when we all reconvened in our new rural sanctuary. We cannot all escape the city or we merely make a new one somewhere else.

What we truly need is to find a way to survive the demands of the modern world, and a new approach to living. That takes a change of mind, not a change of location. We need to see again the sacred that exists around us and to give ourselves back the power of connection with the deeper forces of life. And for that we need to return to simpler values and more traditional ways of being in the world.

The answer is not in more or less materialism, but in using our inherently powerful selves to create and connect with greater spirit.

All of this has been foretold in the legends and predictions of more traditional peoples. The creation myth of the Navajo Indians warns that monsters will come to devour the Earth when the gods are no longer alive to protect us, while Nordic legends talk of Ragnorok, the death of the gods which heralds the end of all human life. The Maya have a sophisticated calendar which predicts the end of one cycle of human exist-ence in 2012 as mankind turns its back on the old ways. Even Christianity has the notion of the Antichrist, which might be envisaged as a state of mind rather than a physical entity, a state of mind which entails the decline of sacred living where the spirits are forgotten. In all cases, however, there is a seed of hope, for if we can reclaim the sacred and tap into the energy of the universe, then we can reclaim the Earth. And every one of us has the power to do so.

THE DREAM OF A NEW WORLD

People are incredibly powerful. When allowed to reconnect with their deeper selves, it has been proven time and time again that quite ordinary people are able to heal themselves and others, demonstrate advanced feats of telepathy and clairvoyance, and even control the actions of their bodies right down to the firing of a single cell.

I say 'allowed to' because in the Western world we are very often *not* empowered to make use of these natural abilities. From the earliest age in our homes and our schools we are discouraged from dreaming, from imaginative and creative play, and from less analytical pursuits. We are told to sit up straight, to arrive on time, to pay attention to our teachers, to address them, not as equals, but as 'Sir' and 'Miss'. As well as a formal curriculum in schools, there is what sociologists call a 'hidden curriculum', which teaches us all of these social rules of time-keeping, respect for authority, sitting quietly so as to cause no disruption to routine, and the use of the rational mind. It is the intuitive, insightful and spiritual parts of us which suffer as we learn that we must abandon these aspects of our whole being if we are to 'get on' in the 'real' world.

Yet it is these very attributes which give us our most powerful and expansive capabilities. In *The Journey To You* I quoted many studies which demonstrate the innate powers we are born with for personal development, for growth and for healing. They include the ability to cure ourselves of cancer, as Carl Simonton's work has shown. Patients using his techniques of active visualization, employing exactly the intuitive side of their brains which we are conditioned to let go of from

101

childhood, have been shown to have twice the chance of recovery than others using standard medical approaches relying only on rational, scientific solutions.[18]

More recently, these results have been confirmed by Professor Leslie Walker of the University of Hull in Britain who reports, according to Reuters news coverage, that 'cancer patients can think themselves to a stronger immune system using relaxation and guided imagery techniques'.[19]

Walker and colleagues tested eighty women with breast cancer in a study funded by the Cancer Research Campaign and presented to the annual meeting of the British Psychological Society. All women received normal medical treatment for breast cancer, but half were also trained in relaxation and imagery techniques where they powerfully visualized the body's own defences taking on and destroying the cancer cells, in a way similar to Simonton's patients.

In subsequent tests, the women who had practised visualization had a higher number of immune cells. Their *mental* imagery had actually – scientifically and unequivocally – influenced the ability of their *bodies* to change the outcome of their disease.

'Our results show that relaxation and guided imagery can bring about measurable changes in the body's own immunological defences,' said Walker. This is true 'even in patients with large tumours receiving immunosuppressive treatment'. Despite the effects of chemotherapy, surgery and radiotherapy, all of which depress the immune system, the use of creative imagery – the powers of our own body and will – can boost our natural defences.

In Peru recently, I had the opportunity to witness at first hand this incredible power of the mind, harnessed to shamanic healing work, as I watched the ayahuasca shaman Javier work on the healing of a brave young woman, who was suffering from a brain tumour.

Gina had developed her tumour years ago and the condition had got progressively worse, to the point where she had been told that she could now expect to live only for the next twelve months. She had undergone various operations over the years. The combination of these operations, the drugs, the chemotherapy, and the work of the tumour itself, had left her in a wheelchair. Much of her hair had been lost, her legs were swollen, and her skin was in poor condition.

Gina joined us in her wheelchair on the first night of the ayahuasca ceremonies as we all sat in circle to receive the sacred liquid. Javier, the officiating shaman, took the ayahuasca too and, in his vision, *saw* that Gina could be healed and *would* walk again. As a result of this vision, he decided to remain with our group for the week and to work with Gina on her healing, even though his original intention had been to leave the Amazon outpost where we were stationed immediately after the ceremony.

He worked untiringly for Gina, going deep into the forest to find special healing plants from which he made balms and lotions for her skin and hair. He journeyed to negotiate with her illness, taking further drinks of the 'doctor' plant ayahuasca to understand the nature of her illness and how it could be removed, and then sucked the spirit of the sickness from her body, spitting it away so it could no longer harm her.

After just four days of this intensive treatment, Gina's hair was visibly growing back and the swelling in her legs had almost gone. Even more remarkable, Gina was walking. Before this treatment, she was confined to her wheelchair apart from sporadic episodes where she was able to walk with the aid of a cane, but even that was a struggle and caused her a great deal of pain. Now she was smiling and laughing, and moving around the jungle compound without her cane and with relative ease. There was fluidity and grace to her movements.

What had happened as a result of these four days? Undoubtedly, the healing plants the shaman had used had worked to stimulate hair growth and reduce the swelling in her legs. But, more than that, Gina had been given hope by the shaman's vision and his dedication to healing her. Her own vast natural resources, stimulated by the love and attention of this shaman and his efforts on her behalf, had mobilized themselves and been focused in a new direction – the direction of her healing instead of the further decline of her health which, before, had been the only direction open to her. As a result of the shaman's efforts for her, and the intervention of the spirits on her behalf, *Gina had begun to heal herself.*

This sounds quite remarkable, but it is not so unusual. Our Western medical authorities are in a position of power over us simple non-medically trained people who present to them as patients. We are in their hands and if, as in Gina's case, we have been led to believe that a certain outcome – continuing decline – is inevitable for us, that is what our minds come to accept and that is the strategy for our future that our bodies respond to.

The Western shaman and soul retrieval expert, Sandra Ingerman, tells a beautiful story to further illustrate this point. It is the story of an elderly gentleman who wears a hearing aid who has gone to his doctor for a prescription to deal with a cold. While he is there, the doctor decides to run a few other routine tests before sending his patient home with the requisite prescription.

A few days later, however, he calls his patient back to his office – and it is not good news. He has the test results back and, it seems, the elderly gentleman has, at best, three months to live.

As he is told all of this, the patient nods sagely and then, sombrely, leaves the office.

Ten years later the same patient returns to his doctor for another prescription. His doctor looks at him in amazement as he appears in his office. 'You should have been dead nearly ten years ago,' he says, to his somewhat bemused client.

Through subsequent investigation it transpires that the patient, when he first presented to his doctor, had experienced some problems with his hearing aid that day and he had not heard the bad news his doctor had told him. He had simply not understood the 'instruction' to go home and die, so his body had carried on regardless!

Stories like this illustrate the power that we all carry within us, as well as the power that others have over us if we give them the authority to determine our life or death. Exactly the same power of *faith, belief* and *hope* was mobilized by Javier in curing his patient that the doctor in our Western example could inadvertently have stimulated in his patient to precipitate his death.

It is not just with cancer that such effects have been noticed. Other research, for example, by Elmer and Alyce Green, show that people are able to withstand the pain of burning and electric shocks simply because they believe they can. Moreover, not only can they withstand this punishment, but their bodies do not register it in the form of injury.[20]

One researcher, Ian Pearce, has pointed to the incredible power of the mind which, once unlocked, can perform all kinds of miracles: in his estimate, 75 per cent of all the illnesses he has treated have been fundamentally psychological in nature. Even patients with an inherited disposition to some illnesses, such as diabetes, do not actually become ill until their life conditions provoke the onset by creating in them a feeling of depression which lowers their energies and their resistance to disease. His most effective method of treatment is simply to convince people that they *do* have the power to cure themselves, thereby giving them access to the vast arsenal of psychic weapons already available to them in their own defence.[21]

If there is one single experiment which demonstrates clearly the power of the mind and of intention – the will to change the outcome of events or to create a new reality – it is the one carried out in Toronto by an eight-member group led by Iris Owen.

This group, comprised of ordinary people, including an accountant, an engineer, a scientist and a number of housewives, none of whom claimed to have paranormal abilities of any kind, decided to *create* a 'ghost' – and did.

Between them, they invented an entire life history for a completely fictional character they named Philip who, they decided, had lived in the times of Cromwell and loved a gypsy girl who was burnt at the stake as a witch. Philip, in his despair, killed himself.

As the group bonded and they grew stronger in their intention over the months of the experiment, something remarkable began to happen: Philip took on a personality and an independence of will. He would begin to call the group and communicate with them unbidden, to lift objects and make them move (he once made a table climb a flight of stairs while television cameras captured the event on film, and was even able to appear before a studio audience and in a documentary film made about him) – all of it without any intervention by the group.

Fantasy had become reality: the Toronto group had created a 'ghost'.

What was central to their ability to do so, says Iris Owen in *Conjuring Up Philip*,[22] was the atmosphere of 'motivation and expectancy' surrounding the group. 'Positive and expectant thought were absolutely necessary to keep the phenomenon "alive" [and] there was a definite correlation between the affirmation of the group mind as to the desirability of a specific question being put to Philip and the loudness of the [table] raps [which followed as his answer].'

'We may, of course, prefer to believe that the being who called himself Philip was an alien entity with nothing better to do,' says Colin Wilson, who reports on this experiment in his *Directory of Possibilities*, 'but a less far-fetched hypothesis is that the unconscious mind of the group had finally obliged them and created a "ghost".'[23]

There is quite a precedent of belief in traditional thought that it is entirely possible for the human will to create sentient thought forms such as this. In *The Secret Oral Teachings in Tibetan Buddhist Sects*, Alexandra David-Neel and Lama Yongden talk of the Tibetan master's ability to conjure up independent entities known as *tulpas* in just such a way. Indeed, 'if the concentration of thought and will is powerful enough – perhaps a joint effort by many people – a human *tulpa* can be more than a phantasm. It can come into being by normal birth, as a stable form with personality. It is then called *tulku* or "phantom body". A *tulku* child is not, or need be, distinguishable from others by inspection alone'.[24]

'Inasmuch as the mind creates the world of appearances, it can create any particular object desired,' says Evans-Wentz in *The Tibetan Book of the Great Liberation*. 'The process consists of giving palpable being to a visualization in very much the same manner as an architect gives concrete expression in three dimensions to his abstract concepts after first having given them expression in the two dimensions of his blueprint . . . A master of yoga can dissolve a *tulpa* as readily as he can create it; and his own illusory human body can likewise dissolve and thus outwit death.'[25]

The shamans of Ecuador have a similar belief, which they express poetically in the words 'the world is as you dream it' – anything is possible – while the medicine men of Africa make no distinction at all between what is 'real' and what is 'imaginary', since when something can be imagined it automatically carries the seed of its own existence. To these shamans, the Philip experiment would not be in the least surprising. Shamans have done things far more incredible than this and for more practical reasons. To them, Philip would be merely parlour trickery for human amusement.

'Many indigenous cultures practice shapeshifting,' says John Perkins, who has spent many years with the Shuar people of the rainforests and witnessed such events at first hand. 'Native American hunters take on the spirit of their prey to ensure a successful hunt; Asian medicine men "ingest" a sickness to heal the one afflicted; Amazon warriors become jaguars to soundlessly travel the jungle.

'Those who shapeshift understand that all of life is energy and that, by focusing your intent, you can change energetic patterns, rendering a new form.'[26]

EXERCISE: SHAPESHIFTING – FINDING A
PLACE OF TEACHING IN THE CITY

In this journey we will explore the city in our energetic form, in order to find a place of meaning which can teach us something about ourselves and our power.

Adopt the Jivaro posture for journeying, which I described in the Introduction, and phrase your intention to *travel in the middle world in order to learn about shapeshifting and to find a place of learning in the city*.

Now close your eyes and relax and, if you have one, start your drumming tape.

You will find yourself in a landscape with a sturdy, tall tree – possibly an oak tree – in front of you. As you stand before this tree, allow your essence, your energetic self, to drift away, directed by your will, merging and blending with the elements. As you feel yourself now becoming a part of all things, focus your intention on shifting your form to become another creature which gives you mobility and power, and can direct you to the location you will soon look for – perhaps an eagle or a cat, both of which have heightened vision.

Travel in the form of that creature through the streets of the city, using their intuitive senses and their powers of smell, hearing and vision, until you find a place which catches your attention and which you understand to have information for you. This need not be a major city landmark, it could be a bench in a park that you have noticed but never visited before. Stop at this point and get a sense of where you are and the directions you would take to find that place in ordinary reality, then return to your starting point at the world tree, and come back to normal awareness.

The next day, take the time to travel the city in ordinary consciousness and find the bench or other landmark that you were drawn to in your journey. Again, relax and, in quiet meditation, ask that place what information it has for you. Make a note of what you are told and see if you can put this teaching into practice in your life.

Reality is a political decision; it serves our social system to have its members think and behave in a certain way. But when this way no longer serves us as individuals, it is time for us to change ourselves and to create a new reality which is more empowering. And the beauty is that, since all things are connected through the same energy which pervades the entire universe, when we change ourselves for the better individually, the whole world changes with us and becomes a better place. Our strong intention to change, the exercise of our will to do so, is all that is required. If you believe in miracles, you will see them everywhere.

I am often struck, in the workshops I run, by the powers which ordinary people do have when they allow themselves to believe that something is possible and within their capabilities, and when they are able to let go of the conditioned reality they have been brought up with in order to let their own natural powers shine.

A few years ago, I ran a workshop where one participant, Chloe, was pregnant. Although it was not scheduled within the workshop programme, I suggested that it would be a nice gesture if we journeyed for Chloe as a group to determine the intention and soul purpose of her incarnating child.

Many traditional societies, from Australia to Tibet, believe that a child comes into this world with an intention for the future and that the events of its life are played out against this purpose. Typical of such societies are the Sora of India, who believe the incarnating soul will bring with it characteristics of a particular ancestor who has been in waiting for a suitable soul to come forward so that it may return to the world as part of the new life energy.

In such communities, the shaman may journey with the expectant mother to speak to the child and to learn of its intended future. From this, the child's purpose will be known and it may even be named in accordance with this soul-purpose. Eskimo cultures, for example, believe that the name given to a child has its own soul and that all people who share this name, whether ancestors or contemporaries, share a common purpose.

In societies where arranged marriages are the norm, mates may even be found for each other on the basis of the complementary purposes of their two souls, so that they may support each other in life and assist each other to achieve their souls' ambition. Such was the case with Malidoma Patrice Some, the Dagara medicine man I referred to earlier, who was named after his soul's purpose and whose name translates as 'One who makes friends with the stranger or enemy'. And, indeed, Some, who comes from an African village which suffered severe religious persecution at the hands of the Jesuits, went on to become an ambassador for his native religion, befriending the Western world, which had been the oppressor of his people, by helping its members to see the beauty of genuine spiritual connection, as an academic spreading the message of traditional values to an initially sceptical audience.

By the same token, in the Cuban Vodou tradition of Santeria, a mother-to-be may visit a Santero priest or *babalao* for divination to discover which of the gods will watch over her child in life and ensure that its purpose is fulfilled. Armed with this information, the expectant mother may pray to that spirit for a safe delivery and begin the initiatory education of the newborn child so he or she will benefit from the protection of this spiritual guardian throughout life.

In our workshop journey, the intention was to discover the purpose of Chloe's unborn child so that the mother could then better understand her child and support the intention of the newborn.

I arranged the workshop participants in a posture known as the 'spirit canoe', which originates with the Salish shamans of America, and enables a whole group of people to journey together, often to retrieve an animal spirit for a patient in order to facilitate their healing. Participants are arranged in an oval, as if seated in a boat, and ride the waves of intention into the otherworld.

Chloe sat at the front and I stood at the back, drumming for the group as they entered the trance journey. Each group member was to take their own journey to meet with the child and to see its future as it unfolded according to its own plan, but to do so as a group to add focus and energy to the journey itself.

Our voyage into the otherworld lasted 20 minutes and, as is characteristic of such journeys, as I stood at the back I watched as a white light began gradually to spread throughout the group, linking each member with the others as their energy fields merged and blended. When this happens, it is a signal that all individuals have received information from the child and that it is consistent for them all. At this point, I called the spirit boat back by sounding the return beat on the drum.

I then asked all participants, one by one, to talk of their vision while I recorded their insights for the mother. As we went around the group, the same images began quickly to emerge; all participants had seen a child who was wise and powerful, who walked between opposites to unite people and to help them grow; a leader who achieved results quietly, not by force but by the power of love and the strength to harmonize. Every single person stated that the child was a boy with dark hair.

It is too early to say, of course, that all the information received from participants will be proven accurate, but a few months later I was pleased to receive a letter from Chloe announcing the arrival of her child, a son, whom she had named Joshua. 'He feels just like I imagined and I'm sure you would all feel you know him too,' she wrote. 'He's very serene and gentle and loves his sleep. He IS dark haired and I am hoping it will stay that way.

'I have felt very connected with him right from the start and I am sure that it is due in part to the spirit boat journey that we did together. It seemed to make a connection on a different level for us. It seems that many of the things that we came up with are essentially true for him and for me, which is very validating.'

111

This emergence of the group mind, the ability to partake of and share in communal wisdom from other worlds, is the hallmark of shamanic gatherings where a heightened sense of true reality at a deep, deep level becomes possible, and people are given freedom and support to exercise their natural abilities to connect with something greater than themselves – the community of human spirit and the energetic realm of universal power.

And, indeed, there is growing scientific evidence to support the shaman's observations about the power of the human individual and the collective, and our innate ability to communicate with each other through the transpersonal space which connects us. Biomedical engineer, Itzhak Bentov, for example, in *Stalking the Wild Pendulum*, writes of the electrostatic field which surrounds the human body and which can be detected by scientific instruments.[27] 'This field couples us well to the isoelectric field of the planet, which means that the motions of our bodies are transmitted far and wide around the planet . . . we may even say that in deep meditation [much akin to the shamanic state of trance consciousness] the human being and the planet system start resonating and transferring energy . . . the signal from the movement of our bodies will travel around the world in about one-seventh of a second via the electrostatic field in which we are embedded. Such a long wavelength knows no obstacles and its strength does not alternate much over large distances. Naturally, it will go through just about anything: metal, concrete, water, and the fields making up our bodies. *It is the ideal medium for conveying a telepathic signal*.' [my italics]

Our realities are not fixed, as the societal dream tells us; there are deeper possibilities for the human soul, and the world, indeed, is open to other dreams. There may be millions of ways for us to enter these dimensions of possibility – through meditation and yoga, by fasting or by sensory deprivation, for example – but the approaches of shamanism and its spiritual brother, Vodou, have stood the test of time and are certainly as effective as any.

Both approaches are far from out of place in the modern urban landscape; in fact, they may offer a route to the salvation of us all if we are to create a better world for the future.

EVERYTHING IS ALIVE – THE SPIRITUAL GIFTS OF SHAMANISM AND VODOU

At first sight, shamanism and Vodou – which Hollywood has introduced into the popular imagination as 'voodoo' – seem to have little in common. The former seems to be based upon peaceful co-existence with nature and with the elements, while the latter, insofar as it is known to us through B movies and sensationalist tabloid stories, has a reputation as a secretive, violent practice concerned with the blood sacrifice of animals and sometimes people, 'black magic', wild sex orgies and the creation of undead zombies.

In fact, the two disciplines are more similar than they seem and are linked fundamentally by the belief that we humans are merely part of an animate and interconnected universe of sentient energies where everything around us is alive. We share our existence with the spirits of our ancestors and with archetypal gods and beings with whom we can interact, and whose powers we can call upon in highly practical matters. Shamanism has its spirit realms of the upper, lower and middle worlds, each populated by somewhat different beings – the upper world of the gods, the middle world of the ancestors and the lower world of power animals and Earth energies – while Vodou has its own pantheon of gods, known as the *lwa* or *loa*, each with its own personality and areas of expertise.

At the root of each is the belief that we are not alone, that we are not separate and isolated in the universe, but an intrinsic part of a vast order with its own logic, laws and shape, and that all things, stripped of their material form, are pure energy at their most basic level. This energy can be respectfully controlled, channelled and co-operated with in

113

order to produce the 'miracle' interventions of spirits which are well known to the practitioners of both approaches.

Such root agreements between the two prompted Maya Deren, who wrote one of the first detailed and reasoned studies of Vodou, to comment in *Divine Horsemen* that 'it is doubtful whether any other two peoples, of different racial and continental origins [as the Afro-Caribbean Vodouissant and the Ameri-Indian shaman] could have discovered such astonishing co-incidence of religious beliefs, not only in basic pattern but in ritualistic and even accessory detail.'[28]

She goes on to list some of these commonalities:

- A belief in an original divine creator and a first human couple.
- A pantheon of divinities concerned with the elements and natural forces.
- The worship of the ancestors, the spirits of those who have gone before us.
- A belief in the spiritual powers of the four cardinal directions (North, East, South and West), and of crossroads and trees.
- The ability to commune directly with spirit via possession and trance states, and a belief that these forces can be controlled by human specialists who, in both cultures, act as spiritual-religious and social leaders and as healers for their people.

Both traditions use power objects and fetishes, especially the rattle and the drum, as a focus for these energies, and ritual and ceremony as an expression of, and route to, connection with them. For both peoples, this connection is direct, practical, pro-active and physical rather than passive and contemplative as it is in our Western religious traditions. It involves respect for these primal energetic forces and the acknowledgement that they are not just there to be *used* but must be met as *equals* in the reciprocal exchange of energy through feeding them with sacrifice and honouring them with ceremony and ritual. Finally, both traditions are polytheistic, believing in many spirits who walk among us every day, rather than a distant and judgmental god who does not concern himself with the affairs of humanity.

'Ignoring the different emotional colourings of the two systems of ritual, the differing tensions in the attitudes of the body in the dancing, and all those nuances in which ethos is manifest, one could confound them entirely,' says Deren.

What will ultimately concern us in this book is precisely this similarity between the two and, more especially, the approach that they offer us for communication with these energies of the universe so that we may work with this power honourably to create a better dream for ourselves and our world.

If you are one of the several million people in our Western cities who do not even *feel* themselves part of a community, who see the city, the world of work, the social system itself, as too limiting, too devoid of passion and spirituality and sense of purpose, then the more spiritual approach of shamanism or Vodou may well hold a seed of hope for you. And, as modern science has shown us, this is not just an empty spirituality but carries profound and practical potential within it for us to shapeshift ourselves, our world, and to create new possibilities and new futures for a more fulfilling and healing existence.

But let us start at the beginning, with a brief overview of each tradition, shamanism and Vodou, before we consider them as a single force for positive change.

3

A DIFFERENT REALITY:
THE SHAMAN AND THE HOUNGAN
– SPECIALISTS IN SPIRIT

*We have lost the ability to even imagine a culture
that lives by the belief that human consciousness can
participate in the natural world and that the natural
world responds to the will of human consciousness.
This is the consciousness of the shaman and, I might
add, the ordinary consciousness of the shaman, for
even in a non-trance state of mind, the shaman saw
and understood a different reality than we do today.*

– Tom Cowan, *Fire in the Head: Shamanism and the Celtic Spirit*[1]

Somewhere, at some distant point in history, there must have
been a moment when people realized, perhaps not even at a
conscious level, that the material world they occupied was,
nonetheless, essentially an energetic one of spirit and that
human nature was fundamentally spiritual. At that point,
shamanism was born as early men and women evolved techniques for communicating with their gods and elementals in
order to divine the future for the practical purposes of finding
food and camps, ensuring the success of the hunt, and healing
the sick of their tribe.

We have no idea where or when this realization took place,
although there is considerable archaeological evidence from
as long ago as 30–40,000 years to suggest that Cro-Magnon
man was deeply involved in the spirit world. The shamans of
the Stone Age sketched cave paintings of deer and bison,
believing that these paintings, and the *intention* behind them

to influence the movements of the animals depicted, would indeed make them available to the hunters of the tribe. 'Nor would it be wise to dismiss such rituals as an expression of ignorance and superstition,' advises Colin Wilson: 'dozens of examples could be cited, from students of modern primitives, to indicate that they often do work.'[2]

One of the examples he offers is the ritual of the calling of the porpoises, which was described by Sir Arthur Grimble in *Pattern of Islands*.[3] The porpoise-caller entered the trance which is typical of the shamanic state of consciousness in order to summon the animals to the Kuma village he served, hours later staggering from his hut to announce to the tribe 'They come, they come!'

'The villagers all rushed into the water and stood breast high; the porpoises began to swim in to the shore in an orderly manner, slowly, as if in a trance, and beached themselves. The villagers dragged them ashore and slaughtered and ate them.'

The fact that rituals like these have survived for 40,000 years, and that they still produce effective results, is evidence of the long-standing and proven ability of people to work harmoniously with the forces of nature to engender success in their enterprises.

Many different societies, separated geographically and culturally, must have realized the potential of this at the same time and quite independently, since there is little evidence of nomadism or trade between the people of Hungary, Polynesia, New Zealand and Crete, for example, although there is plenty of evidence of a shared worldview, including artefacts depicting almost identical shamanic trance postures for healing and divination, as Dr Felicitas Goodman has expertly demonstrated in her book, *Where the Spirits Ride the Wind*.[4]

In order to make sense of this and to identify the points of commonality between these cultures, anthropologists have developed what is known as the 'shamanic archetype' to paint a picture of this spiritual belief system.

In this archetype, the shaman in all societies is always a person of power who is able to move smoothly between this world and the next, to bring back gifts of wisdom and healing in order to serve his or her community, and to ensure harmony with nature and other life-forms so that the mutual good is assured.

Most typically, in order to do so, the shaman uses a trance state which may be induced by the ingestion of sacred herbs and potions, such as the hallucinogenic peyote cactus of Mexico, the San Pedro cactus used in Peru, the fly agaric mushroom of Siberia, or the ayahuasca drink of the Amazon region, which is also known as the vine of souls.

For the shaman, this is not about 'taking drugs'. Rather, she understands that each plant has a spirit, which is able to enter her body and her consciousness when the plant is ingested in a sacred manner. Such plants are referred to as 'teacher plants' because of the special wisdom they can impart. Few shamans use drugs recreationally and many would be horrified by the dangers inherent in this, largely Western, practice (though they would also recognize it as evidence of a deep yearning for reconnection with a more meaningful, spiritual, world).

More commonly than using psychotropic substances, the shaman will attain this state of trance through the use of special diet, isolation from her people, such as when she takes part in the solitary pursuit of the vision quest, which is a way of moving beyond the prescriptions of social rules and entering an inner world where our own personal truth and vision can be found – and especially through the use of drumming and dance to achieve a state of ecstatic purity where her ego is shattered and there are no barriers left between her and the gods.

Once this state is obtained, the shaman is able to exercise control over her own spirit so that it leaves her material body and journeys to meet the gods of the otherworld. At the same time, she has perfect control of her physical body and remains safe and aware in our world, a capability which led Mircea Eliade to describe the shaman as 'a walker between worlds'.[5]

The shaman is guided on her journey by tutelary spirits and other helpers which she meets in these worlds of non-ordinary reality. They will show her what is wrong with a person, for example, and teach her how to cure their ills, sometimes working through her directly in order to do so, as part of a spiritual possession of her body.

These spirits are regarded as partners to the shaman and must be thanked for their help and rewarded, often by sacrifices, although the nature of this sacrifice will vary. While the medicine men of North America may offer tobacco, a plant regarded as sacred to the spirits, the shamans of Tuva and of Africa, the houngans of Haiti, and the santeros of Cuba may all offer animals as a blood sacrifice to their helping spirits.

Common among shamans, too, is the experience of the initiatory crisis which precedes the entry into shamanism, where the candidate is called by spirit and, often failing to understand the summons or resisting the call, falls into a physical or mental illness which may herald a near-death experience until she is clear that she is chosen by the gods to do their work on Earth. At this point she will recover fully and emerge from her crisis stronger and more powerful, with the gods on her side.

The trauma of initiation may be sudden and unequivocal, such as a life-threatening illness for which there is no medical cure, but which mysteriously vanishes once the shaman accepts the call of the spirits, or being struck by lightning – symbolic perhaps of this spiritual 'enlightenment' – and surviving the surge of cosmic energy through the body. Always there is a magical element to the cure. Tom Cowan tells how, in the Celtic shamanic tradition a person may fall into a deep sleep reminiscent of a coma, having been lulled into sleeping by the music of the faeries or the singing of magical birds. She then 'awakens' into the otherworld of the faery kingdom and can escape only with the co-operation of her captors or the heroic intervention of another shaman.[6]

In a similar vein, the Lakota holy man, Black Elk, spoke of falling into a coma which lasted for twelve days, to be saved only by the magical actions of a powerful shaman who was able to heal him and to bring him back when all else failed. When he returned, everything had changed and he '*was not like a boy. He was more like an old man*', with a new depth of wisdom and strength of purpose. His healing career began at that point.[7]

This type of trauma may also precede the initiation of the Vodou priest or mambo. Karen Brown, in *Mama Lola*,[8] tells the story of Maggie, a young girl from a Vodou family, who became seriously ill with tuberculosis or perhaps pneumonia; the emergency room physician was unable to tell and wanted to keep her in for more tests. Having begged to go home, however, she was finally allowed to do so on the promise that she return to the hospital the next day.

That night, as Maggie lay in bed, a shadow fell across her pillow and, as she looked up, she saw a lady standing before her.

> *I wasn't scared of that lady and I was saying, 'Who are you? Who are you?' And then she said, 'You know who I am' . . . And then she put up [her] veil and I could see it was her with the two mark. Erzuli Danto [a female deity in the pantheon of Vodou loa] with the two mark on her cheek. Whooooo! Yeah! And then I start to get scared. She told me 'Don't get scared, I'm your mother'. Then she told me to turn my back around, she was going to heal me; I wasn't going to be sick no more . . .*

'After the visit from Ezili Danto, Maggie was no longer ill,' says Karen Brown. 'The rest of the summer passed without incident and, in the fall, Maggie and the other children started to school.'

Sometimes the initiation crisis is more spiritual or psychological in nature, such as that described by the Eskimo shaman who told Knud Rasmussen that he would fall into passions of uncontrollable weeping and melancholy for no reason that he could fathom and then emerge into a state of overwhelming ecstasy. 'I could see and hear in a totally

120

different way,' he said. All things seemed to emanate a bright white light which 'also shone out from me, imperceptible to human beings but visible to all spirits of Earth and sky and sea, and these now came to me to become my helping spirits'.[9]

In January 2000, I made a trip to Haiti to study Vodou and become initiated there as a priest. *En route*, I made a stop-over in Miami where I also met with members of the Santeria Vodou fraternity. During the course of the entire journey, I was able to speak with many people about their own in-itiation and what called them to follow this spiritual path. The similarities with the examples above were evident. Such was the case with Jacques, now a 38-year-old santero (priest of Santeria), who told me of an accident in his earlier life which had set him on the path to spirituality.

'I was cycling home from college one day, along a route I had taken every day for the last several years. I knew every twist and turn in the road. It was a fine day, perfect visibility and no cars on the road at all when, for no reason that I know of, the bike simply fell from under me and I hit the road. At that precise moment, out of nowhere, a car appeared and was right on top of me in seconds. It had no time to swerve and I had no chance to move.

'I was out of it for weeks. First they thought I wouldn't wake up at all. The pain was excruciating. I couldn't move and fell into a kind of depression. Since I was immobile, the world began to take on a strange, unreal quality. My sleeping and waking patterns all changed and I spent many nights awake while everyone else slept.

'One night as I lay there, I thought I heard a voice in the room and looked up and saw a figure in the room. My powers of seeing the spirits were not well developed at that time and I could not make out who it was. Now, I know exactly who it was.

'He told me that if I wanted to get better, there were certain things I must do, including honouring the gods with the proper observances.

'I agreed to his demands and, within a week, was back on

121

my feet. I began my initiation into the religion almost immediately.'

Surviving the trauma which accompanies the call of the spirit is, in some ways, like taking a homoeopathic remedy – having ingested a small quantity of whatever it is that is causing the illness, the natural resources of the body are strengthened and can work with the dis-ease to find a point of equilibrium once again. The shaman, having met the spirits, is in the same way strengthened by them and can move in the landscape of these forces without now being overpowered by them, just as a person who has recovered from a virus is now immune to it and no longer at risk. Moreover, he has learned from his experience and can use this knowledge to work more effectively on behalf of other sufferers and of his community in general.

THE EVERYDAY POWERS OF THE SHAMAN

As fully initiated shamans, these people of power often developed other magical abilities such as a deep knowledge of herbal and plant medicine, far in advance of our accomplishments in the West with aromatherapy, homoeopathy and herbal medicine. The shaman's approach to healing with plant medicine is an integrated one and includes all of these specialized disciplines, which we have come to see as quite separate.

The shaman intuitively knows which plants to pick for his patient and when to pick them, since the potency of all plants varies with the season, the time of day and the phase of the moon, as well as how to blend them to best effect, and how to use them – as a compress, a lotion or a tonic, for example.

How does the shaman know these things when we in the modern world are only beginning to understand the intricate nature of these cures? Simple: she asks the plant itself, allowing her spirit to engage with the spirit essence or energetic form of the plant.

My Peruvian friend, James Chaytor, wrote a book on the

healing plants of the Andes, called *Plantas en la Cultura Andina*.[10] In it he describes the healing properties and preparations of hundreds of plants, but it was only when he began to journey to the spirit of each plant that he *really* began to understand its nature, its personality and its total capabilities. In many cases, he found that the plants themselves could be used in ways that science had no knowledge of. Jasmine, for example, he describes as 'like a young maiden dressed in flowing white robes', whereas Rosemary is a more mature woman who has learned about the arts of healing. As well as their specifically 'aromatherapeutic' or 'homoeopathic' uses, therefore, both of these plants may be used more generally for healing the sorts of 'female' problems found in youth (Jasmine), such as uncertainty about the future and lack of power of those of middle age (Rosemary), such as the struggles with identity and achievement which often arise at this stage of life. It is not the chemical properties of the plant which are most important in this sense, but its *spiritual nature* and personality.

In the West, Bach Flower Remedies and aromatherapy are very popular treatments, although, interestingly, recent research by German scientists suggests that the use of essential oils has no direct effect on the brain. What they did find, however, was that aromatherapy oils *do* work if people *believe* they will work. If they thought a particular oil was stimulating, for example, people *did* get faster in tests of reaction times. To the Western scientist, this would simply suggest the placebo effect of such oils. The shaman would view it quite differently, arguing that the spirit of the plant cannot be measured and quantified in a laboratory and it is the effect of the plant spirits on the mind and emotions that counts. Whatever the arguments, one way or another essential oils extracted from such plants *do* work, according to the research, but only if we *believe* in them.

Flowers and flower essences such as these are used extensively in Peruvian healing. For problems of *susto*, or soul loss, for example (what we in the West might call trauma or depression), the client will often be wrapped in a blanket filled with flowers and allowed to sleep in the sun, surrounded by the beautiful smells of these flowers and the softness of their petals. The spirit of the flowers will then take away the trauma so that the soul may return. 'We believe that, whenever people relive negative emotions and events, they should be surrounded by beauty and wonderful aromas,' says Mexican shaman, Elena Avila. 'Lovely smells are comforting and take away the pain.'

Does all of this intuitive knowledge of plants sound farfetched and unscientific to you? Then let's look at some of the more scientific evidence which supports the shaman's claims.

Peter Tompkins and Christopher Bird in *The Secret Life of Plants*, cite many cases where plants are able to respond to human requests, emotions, even our thoughts, and to grow sick or healthy precisely according to the amount and quality of attention paid to them, suggesting some form of sentience and individual personality – or spirit – within the plant itself.[11]

In one experiment to test just this, research chemist Marcel Vogel wired two plants to a recording machine and began to cut one of them. What he found was that the second plant responded to the pain of its neighbour – *but only when Vogel himself thought consciously about what the plant must be suffering*. In other words, it was Vogel, his emotions and his conscious intention to cut the first plant, which provided the link between the two. The plants were communicating with each other, through a human intermediary.

In another experiment, Vogel enlisted the help of a friend, Vivian Wiley, who was asked to pick two leaves from a saxifrage plant growing in her garden and leave both without water to see how long they could survive. One of these she kept on her bedside table and each day, as she awoke, would look at it and will it to continue to live; the second she placed in her sitting room and ignored.

A month later, Vogel went to her house to photograph the two leaves. 'He could hardly believe what he saw,' reported Bird and Tompkins. 'The leaf to which his friend had paid no attention was flaccid, turning brown and beginning to decay. The leaf on which she had focused daily attention was radiantly vital and green, just as if it had been freshly picked from the garden. Some power appeared to be defying natural law, keeping the leaf in a healthy state.' Having repeated the experiment himself and achieved similar results, Vogel concluded that this 'power' was 'psychic energy'.

It is this same psychic energy which the shaman uses to effect his cures through consultation with the spirit essences of his plants, and the same energy which he is able to use in many other ways to ensure health and balance within his community. For the shaman is a master of energetic transformation. The psychic surgeons of the Philippines, the extraction doctors of the Jivaro tribe, and bare-hand healers of the Hawaiian Kahunas all use a similar approach to work with the energy fields of the body to remove illness, which they see as spiritual intrusions, and to inject new vitality into their patients in a way similar to that now practised by reiki healers who are able to channel universal energy into the body of their client. In the West we are enamoured by the new fad of feng shui, which is really just the manipulation of energy once again, this time in buildings rather than the human body, but it is the same technique known to the shamans of thousands of years ago for creating more healthy living environments through working with the energy flowing through them.

In the West, we have built our society on a division of labour, on specialisms and expertise and so we have, in many ways, lost sight of the simplicity of the shaman's direct approach. For the shaman, *all* is energy (a concept we will look at in great detail in Chapter 4), and while we may lose ourselves in the nuances of a particular technique and get caught up in the detail, she is aware of a much bigger picture and makes no such separation between these approaches. She is a master of energy in *all* its forms.

Shamanism today remains true to these essential experiences of the tradition, while being flexible and adaptive enough to be effective with the new tools and context of a modern Western society. And interest in it continues to grow.

A quick web trawl using a search engine such as AltaVista reveals just a shade under 42,000 pages dedicated to 'Shamanism' and within these you will find everything from Celtic to Korean shamanism as listed specialities. There are also many popular workshops on shamanism in our major cities worldwide and established training centres such as the Eagle's Wing Centre for Contemporary Shamanism in London, the Four Winds Society and the Dream Change Coalition in America, and the Scandinavian Center for Shamanic Studies in Europe.

Why this recent upsurge in interest? A BBC television programme, *The Soul of Britain*, aired in April 2000, provides some answers. While attendances at mainstream, mainly Christian, churches continue to decline, the number of people on a spiritual quest for meaning in their lives continues to rise. These people want *proof, evidence* of the spirits, and *real* communion with god, not hot air and dogma. (Thirty-three per cent of people polled by the BBC believe that 'there is a way to god outside organized religion'.) Shamanism (and Vodou) provide that new way, offering direct encounters with the ancestors and the ambassadors of god. For a nation seeking *evidence* this is powerful proof.

One man can be credited with this upsurge of interest: Dr Michael Harner, founder of the Foundation for Shamanic Studies in America who, after spending years among the shamans, notably the Jivaro of the Amazon, returned to the West to develop a form which he termed 'core shamanism', a distillation of the essential teachings of these powerful healing traditions into an approach which is most suited to our own environment.

The Jivaro often use the sacred teacher plant, ayahuasca,

whose hallucinogenic and even telepathic effects provide a method of entry into the shamanic state of consciousness and facilitate journeys to the spirits. Harner found, however, that the use of the drum, at a steady 220 beats per minute, will produce a hypnotic effect and trancelike state just as suitable for journeying, enabling those who would rather not work with a psychotropic substance such as ayahuasca to benefit from the experience of shamanism. Making the most of modern technology, drumming tapes are now available to make this even easier.

The core shamanic form teaches journeying as a method of consultation with the spirits, extraction medicine and soul retrieval for healing, and divinatory methods for sensing the future. We will look at these methods later in this book. For now it is enough to understand that what links them all and makes them effective is the fact that underlying all things is a commonality of shared energy of which we are all a part. The universe reveals itself in many ways to us and will provide answers once we have mastered the language of energy, a subject we will look at in the next chapter.

VODOU – THE GODS THAT WALK AMONG US

We know as little of the *spiritual origins* of Vodou as we do of shamanism. What we can do is chart its development as a *religion* in the modern world and work with its teachings, which are just as relevant today, in the heart of the city, as they were thousands of years ago in the heart of Africa.

Just a few hundred years ago in Africa, we can imagine a nation of people co-existing peacefully with nature and meeting with their gods, as they had done for thousands of years, in the same basic way as the shamans of Europe and Siberia, practising the same techniques of healing and divination which still survive today, and honouring the land and the spirits through the power of ritual.

We have a somewhat romanticized view of this world from

our modern, pressurized, perspective; the reality was that tribal life was no bed of roses. Life was harsh, food and drinking water scarce, and tribal conflict common. It was for precisely these reasons that a close connection with the spirits and an understanding and co-operation with nature was essential. Survival depended on an awareness of the spirits of nature and a partnership with the gods to ensure a ready supply of game and to cure the illnesses of the tribe which would otherwise, almost certainly, result in death. It was in solving such practical daily concerns that these African shamans became experts in spirit and in healing.

Then came the slave traders.

Thousands of slaves were transported. Among them, the people of Yoruba, Dahomey, Loango, Ashanti and Mandigo, the Senegalese, Bambara, Arada, Congo, Mondongo, Mine, Ibo, Mahi, Fon, Fula, and many other tribes. All took with them their own traditions, gods, rituals and ceremony. Even on the journey of the slave ships to the Caribbean islands, these different traditions began to be exchanged, commonalities noticed, information shared and agreements reached on the nature of the gods. For, despite the differences, the similarities were clear in the practice of ancestor worship, the ecstatic trance achieved through dancing and sacred song, and the possession of the worshippers by the gods themselves.

Once the slaves were landed, it was politically expedient to separate tribal members in order to weaken the bonds between them and guard against any tendency to rebellion and insurrection. In doing so, the slave owners inadvertently encouraged still further the mixing of ideas and beliefs to create the basis of the new religion of Vodou. This blending can be seen even in the language of the religion, for 'Vodou' is the Fon word for an 'invisible force' or 'deep mystery', while 'loa', the gods who are worshipped, is the Congo word for 'spirit': two different languages and belief systems integrated at the very heart of Vodou.

The evolution of the religion was further enriched and complicated by its absorption of many of the trappings and much of the iconography and symbolism of Catholicism, the predominant religion of the slave owners. Many slaves were forcibly baptized into the Catholic religion, as either a pious and possibly well-meant gesture of 'compassion' for the 'poor Negro', an attempt to educate and enlighten the 'primitive heathens' in their midst or, more likely, as a result of white fear. For the rulers had witnessed the passion of the religious gatherings of their slaves, the wild drumming, the sexually suggestive physicality of the free dance and movement, the intensity of their belief, and the possession of their bodies by the god-energy of the spirits – and they were terrified of this force-fulness and power spilling over into fully-fledged revolt. Their solution was to attempt to replace this 'brutal and earthy' religion with another, altogether more 'civilized' and sedate.

Their methods of doing so often belied any idea that their intentions were honourable and godly. 'As a group, the French were the harshest,' comments Jim Haskins.[12] Slaves in Haiti, for example, were often 'herded into a church with whips and ordered to kneel, whereupon they were baptised en masse. Then they were herded back to work, now officially converts to Christianity.'

The slaves, however, immediately recognized the gods of Catholicism and Christianity as their own. For 'the Catholic church had a pantheon of its own,' says Haskins, and one very similar to that of the Fon people of Dahomey and Yoruba in particular. 'Its Virgin and its saints were under-standable to Africans whose religious structure and traditions included lesser but important deities who were, like the saints, honoured with festivals and rituals and prayed to for help in day-to-day living . . . The Catholic church was also highly ritualistic; its Holy Communion, holy days, and its services could correspond in the African's mind to his own rituals, its rosary beads to his talismans.'

And we must not forget that Christianity has its own extreme, even (symbolically, at least) cannibalistic, rituals of sacrifice in the sacrament where the body and blood of Christ is ingested by his followers. For traditional communities where sacrifice was practised as a form of energetic exchange with the gods, the 'ingestion' of such a powerful loa as Christ, the son of God himself, must have seemed a highly passionate and powerful ritual.

Whether the slaves truly adopted these Western saints and beliefs or merely used them as a mask for the continued practice of their native religion is still hotly disputed by some priests. Vodou today is generally seen as a syncretic mixture of various religious forms, although some people deny this, believing instead that the slaves merely created the impression that they were praying to a 'white saint', while actually in contact with their own gods. They were using the saints as camouflage for their prayers, which was quite possible because of the similarity between them.

Thus, say Jason Black and Christopher Hyatt in *Urban Voodoo*, Chango, lord of thunder, fire, storms and war, 'this most masculine and macho of spirits, has been rather hilariously masked as the ethereal and feminine St Barbara. This occurred simply because of the presence of Chango's symbols in her picture, just as St Patrick became the mask for Dambalah [the snake god] in Haiti for no other reason than that there were snakes in the picture.' Someone praying to St Barbara in a white man's church, according to these writers, is in reality in dialogue with their own god Chango and using the representation of St Barbara merely as a visual reference to remind him of the attributes of the loa.[13]

For others, the situation is quite different and there are some houngans and santeros who will not initiate a person into their tradition at all unless they have first undergone Catholic baptism. Alfred Metraux, in his 1959 book, *Voodoo*, quotes a Marbial peasant who is clear that 'to serve the loa you have to be a Catholic'.[14]

Whatever the truth, it is a fact that the Vodou religion does continue to evolve, to change, and to absorb new cultural elements in order to accommodate the needs of its followers in the new urban environment of the city. Author Karen Brown even mentions a new and emerging form of the spirit

Gede, traditionally a highly masculine, ribald and powerful loa who exudes manliness in his appearances at ceremonies where he takes over the body of one of the worshippers present. In this new form, however, he appeared during the possession of the American mambo, Alourdes, as Gedelia, a *goddess* – with exactly the same attributes as her masculine counterpart.[15] 'She came in like a powerful burst of energy, sexiness and humour. Unfortunately, she did not stay long enough for me to get to know her well, and I have not seen her since. Not long ago, however, I saw Gedelia's name written across the front of a bus in Haiti. Thus, I suspect Alourdes is not alone in recognizing the need for her,' says Brown, reflecting on the fact that in modern American cities there is a harshness to life for women and, in particular, for female Haitian immigrants to the city, just as there is a different, but nonetheless potent, harshness to life in their poverty-stricken homeland.

Such a need is pronounced in the western cities of America, where Alourdes lives, as thousands of displaced and lonely Haitian women, separated from their home culture, and often struggling against poverty as single mothers, strive to make ends meet and to send a little money back to their relatives in Haiti. The power and energy of a female Gede as a model for their lives and a source of practical support is very welcome to such people.

Finally, this 'masking', this double life of the slaves in Haiti, had to end, and it did so in 1791, with the only successful slave revolt in history, as the oppressed and cruelly treated Haitians rebelled against their 'masters' in an uprising led by a Vodou priest named Boukman.

Since then, Vodou has continued to grow openly as well as to evolve. Roman Catholicism may be the *official* religion of Haiti, but Vodou is considered the country's *national* religion, and the majority of Haitians believe in and practise at least some aspects of Vodou. There are around 100 million followers and practitioners of the Santeria form in the States alone, while a further 60 million, according to the Library of

Congress, continue to practise other Vodou forms, such as the Brazilian Candomble, Jamaican Obeayisne, and the Trinidadian Shango cult. If all of these various denominations could be counted *en masse*, 'Vodou' would rank as one of the most powerful religions in the world today – and for one simple reason: it allows its followers to connect with the sacred in their daily lives, which is something all human beings badly need.

THE HOUNGAN AND THE JOURNEY TO PRIESTHOOD

In Vodou, the priest who controls the interactions with the gods and makes their presence available to his congregation is known as the houngan (where male) or the mambo (where female). In this, their role is that of the shaman.

Because Vodou is a *religion*, however, with its own traditions, requirements, format and hierarchy of priesthood, just as in our Western churches, rather than a purely spiritual approach like shamanism, the houngan and mambo must operate within a somewhat more rigid structure and follow guidelines and procedures established and passed down by religious leaders over the years. This is much the same, once again, as our own priests, who must follow the protocols and procedures of their own church. In this sense, the houngan is both a traditional spiritual adviser, interpreter and partner to spirit, healer and diviner, like the shaman, and a more formal church authority and religious leader like our own in the West.

All houngans first begin as *Vodouissants*, uninitiated people who attend ceremonies and may receive counsel and healing from a houngan or mambo. As they prepare for initiation and begin a more serious involvement in the religion, they are then referred to as *hounsi bossale, hounsi* in the Fon language meaning 'bride of the spirit' (although the term actually refers to both men and women), and *bossale* meaning 'wild' or 'untamed'. They are therefore still raw disciples to the spirits.

The first grade of initiation is *hounsi kanzo* which, according to my spiritual mother, Mambo Racine, might be likened to a confirmed member of a Christian denomination. Following further ceremony and ritual challenges, the second grade of *sur point* is achieved, which puts the candidate 'on the point' of patronage by a particular loa. It is then that the candidate is officially recognized as houngan or mambo, at a level similar to that of a Christian minister. The final and highest grade of initiation is *asogwe*, on a par with that of a Western bishop. The asogwe may initiate other individuals at all grades, just as a bishop may consecrate other priests, and is the final authority on ritual procedure, deferring only to a loa who may manifest during the ceremonies through possession of a person present.

Mambo Racine describes the development of her own initiatory houngan, Luc Gedeon, which shows how one may progress to the extraordinary position of priesthood from quite ordinary, and even contradictory, beginnings when the spirit calls. The story is interesting since it parallels very closely many of the stages of shamanic development, including the call of the spirits and the initiation crisis which precedes a shamanic career.[16]

Luc Gedeon was born on 19 April 1930 and had a fairly normal childhood. At the age of 12, however, while in church, he suddenly lost consciousness and was possessed by a loa.

'This inappropriate and unseemly episode caused his respected and reputable family enormous concern,' says Mambo Racine, and Luc was encouraged to become an acolyte in order to refuse the influence of the loa.

But Luc gradually found that the pull of the loa was irresistible. 'The more he fought against it, the more he became tired and overwrought. In 1972 he suffered a crisis, and spent 22 days sleeping under the bushes on the Champs de Mars in the middle of downtown Port-au-Prince. This was the final blow to his family. When Luc Gedeon returned to his home, he was permitted to serve the loa.'

Luc was initiated as houngan asogwe in 1975 and, from

then on, was never again bothered by mental or nervous problems.

Spiritism, it seems, also had deep ancestral roots for Luc Gedeon, which is often the case with those who are destined to become shamans. In many societies, shamanic vocation is hereditary and learned from one's parents and grandparents who are also healers and diviners.

In Luc's case, his great grandmother, Tante Bobo, exhibited spiritual characteristics. According to family legends, she had been abducted by the spirits of the water while washing at the river one day and taken to the otherworld, where she remained for seven Earth years (though, in ordinary reality, her journey may have passed in instants), where she was initiated into the secrets of the spirits and the mysteries of the universe. In this and other elements, her story is very similar to those told by Tom Cowan in his book on Celtic shamanism,[17] where the initiate is taken by the spirits, often in a setting just such as this, while in the heart of nature, and kept in their immaterial realm for a period of seven years – which illustrates, once again, the universality of the spiritual experience.

EXERCISE: MEETING NATURE SPIRITS IN THE CITY

Just as Tante Bobo discovered, the spirits of nature are everywhere around us. Seeing them is not a matter of location or timing; the route to the spirit world is, rather, through *attention*, through choosing to see these entities.

There are elements of nature in every city – trees, rivers, parks, commons, botanical gardens, sometimes even hills – but often they are dwarfed by the surrounding man-made structures and so we pass them by and miss out on the opportunity to connect with the nature which is all around us.

Shamans believe that all individual aspects of nature are representative of the whole, so that *a* river stands for *all* rivers, a single *tree* represents all *trees*, and that each

134

of these life-forms has its own spirit which can reveal for us the combined wisdom of the species.

Find a part of nature in the city that you would like to connect with. For the purpose of this exercise, let's say this is a quiet place on the River Thames in London, or the Seine as it runs through Paris, and then lie down there in the journeying position you are now familiar with.

Let your mind relax and let go of any tension in your body. Allow your spirit to guide you back to the world tree, which is the starting point in the otherworld for all of our journeys.

As you stand before this tree, become aware of an entrance into the Earth, like a cave or a hollow near the roots of this tree, and enter into the ground at this point. You will emerge into a tunnel, which takes you further down into the restful solitude of the Earth. Follow this until you find a source of light, which becomes your doorway into the lower world of the shaman, and step through it into this new world.

Look around you and notice the features of this landscape and then search specifically for the energetic parallel of the landmark you have chosen to work with. If it is a river, follow it back to its source and, at this point, ask that the spirit of the water reveal herself to you.

Know that this spirit is not just the essence of *this* river, but of *all* rivers, as they travel through all the lands of the world and through all times in history. Imagine the changes this spirit has seen and the mysteries which time has revealed to her.

Ask her any questions you may wish in order to better understand our world, its origins, its destiny, the purpose of life on Earth, and the part which we, as human beings, play here. Ask any questions about your own life, your future, your past and the reason for certain events.

When you have finished, thank this spirit for her help

and say your goodbyes. Now retrace your steps and come back to ordinary consciousness.

Look afresh at the natural place you have chosen to work with. Stare deep into the waters of the river, look along its length, let yourself become one with the play of light on its surface, and get a feel for the vast library of knowledge which is carried in its depths. Know that you can come back to this place at any time to seek further information now that there is a connection between you; and, indeed, that you have this connection now with all water, which carries the spirit in equal measure.

One of the ways of divination in Vodou is to fill a crystal bowl with water and then, placing a candle beside it and dimming the lights in the room, to stare into the water until a sense of peaceful meditation is reached and a dialogue can begin with the spirits of the water. Now that you know this spirit, this technique is open to you always when you need guidance on the course of your life.

Once he is on familiar terms with his spirits through the process and commitment of initiation, the houngan can interact with them and seek their counsel, much as the shaman, in order to bring information from the past, the future or the present back from the intangible world to the realm of ordinary reality. The difference between the two, more than anything else, is one of technique – the shaman will journey *out* from his body into the ethereal world where he will meet with his tutelary spirits and voyage together with them on adventures of discovery, or sit in council with them and hear the answers to his questions. The houngan, by contrast, controls the flow of energy and oversees the possession of himself or another so that information may be brought *in* to the material world through the appearance of spiritual forces in our own world.

The reality of the spirits in vodou

In *The Journey To You* I posed the question, 'how do we know that the spiritual entities we are in contact with during the shamanic journey are real beings, independent of ourselves, and not just the agents of our own imagination?' In Vodou, the answer is that some of these entities have a history of their own, as ancestors who were once human in their own right and whose histories can be traced.

One of Luc Gedeon's most loyal loa was a spirit known as Arapice La Croix, an entity who began life as a human being called Antoine Jean-Pierre, born on 2 November 1900 in the slum district of Croix Belair.

According to Mambo Racine,[18] Antoine had an unremarkable childhood and little formal education. As an adult, he had courage and disliked injustice. 'Ironically, this proved to be the downfall of his human existence. One day, in a fit of outrage at the arrogant behaviour of some local *gwo neg*, some big shot, he slapped his tormentor across the face. Predictably, the powerful *gwo neg* arranged his murder, which of course went unavenged. Antoine Jean-Pierre was buried by his family at the age of twenty-five . . .

'But that was not the end of his story. After he spent the prescribed one year and one day beneath the abysmal waters that separate the souls of the dead from the world of the living . . . he passed again into the world of humans, invisible but intimately concerned with their affairs.' During his time away in the land of the dead, he had also been renamed by the loa and now had the sacred name, Arapice La Croix.

'It is a basic tenet of the Vodou faith that the living and the dead work together to help each other,' Mambo Racine continues, so Arapice's first task as a spiritual guardian of the living was to protect a Haitian man serving as a soldier in the Vietnam war. 'Arapice carried him safely through battles, ambushes and booby-traps, until the soldier was honourably discharged.'

The spirit Arapice went on to help others before becoming

lonely and disenchanted with his world. He took refuge from the world as a tree spirit until, one day, he saw another loa at work, assisting Luc Gedeon with the healing of a sick person. Arapice began to help this spirit to heal people, and Luc soon realized that another loa was assisting his cures, though he did not know who this spirit was. And so, one day, Luc's helping spirit took possession of him and made him build a bonfire. He then withdrew from Luc so that Arapice could work with him directly.

Arapice decided on a dramatic gesture to demonstrate his power. Still in possession of Luc's body, he sat down in the middle of the huge bonfire. The flames licked around the mortal body of Luc Gedeon, and searing heat swept across his human flesh. Yet, 'Not a hair of Luc's head or a thread of his garments [were] singed,' says Mambo Racine. 'Members of Luc's society wept, first with fear for Luc's safety and then with awe at Arapice's undeniable power. [Then] Arapice quietly entered his *bagi*, the special chamber consecrated to him in Luc's peristyle. There he remains, faithfully serving the needs of the society and of those who come seeking help.'

As well as his mastery of, or partnership with, the spirits in this way, the houngan or mambo is an authority on divination, the technique by which the future is known, of healing by herbal medicines, and of the transformation and redirection of energetic forces through the use of spells and charms.

DIVINATION

In Santeria style Vodou, divination is normally carried out using cowrie shells, twenty-one in total, filed flat at the bottom. Five of these are discarded, according to inspiration and magical practice, and only sixteen used for the actual divination since Odudwa, the mythical progenitor of the Yoruba people, to whom Santeria can be traced, was said to have had sixteen sons, each of whom spoke an essential truth.

The natural 'mouths' of the shells (the sides with serrated

openings) are considered the mouths of the gods and, when these sixteen are thrown, those with their natural openings facing upwards are said to speak of what the gods have in store for the querist.

'Often the advice on what one must do is practical and pragmatic,' says Ewetuga Atare, a friend of mine who is an American priest of Santeria. 'A person might be told to see a doctor, or to call her sister up, or prepare a great meal and invite her brother in order to reconcile familial differences. Or a person may simply be told not to listen to gossip. Many priests do not take any journey or embark on any new project without asking the advice of the spirits in this way.'

Ewetuga has a story which illustrates the practical nature of this divinatory method and also the mysterious way in which the gods sometimes work, which demonstrates why it is so important, sometimes, to just follow their advice without questioning it too much to see how it works out in logical terms.

A man once came for divination in order to seek protection and greater personal safety, and was told to walk to a nearby cliff and throw seven coconuts into the water below, bound together with rope. The man thought this strange since it did not seem to connect in any obvious way with his current predicament, but he knew better than to question the gods, so he did as they asked.

A week later, he passed the same spot where he had thrown this bundle into the sea, when he was set upon by robbers who took a few possessions from him and then threw him from the clifftop into the crashing waters below.

As soon as he surfaced, the man saw the bundle of coconuts which he had thrown into the sea the week before. He was able to pull them towards him with the rope and then use them to keep himself afloat while he swam to the shore. He emerged from the water unharmed, reported his attackers to the police and recovered his possessions.

He had come to the diviner seeking personal protection – and that was exactly what the spirits gave him!

The method of divination in Santeria is complex and wide-ranging. You can, however, get a feel for the approach by using similar techniques which put us in touch with our deeply intuitive selves. One such technique, described by Luke Rhinehart in his books, *The Dice Man* and *The Search for the Dice Man*, is to use dice in order to make our decisions for us, so that we introduce an element of 'chance' into our lives instead of relying on the 'rational' decision-making, which Rhinehart would see as merely a form of social programming. As Rhinehart's character, Luke, says in one of his books: 'The purpose of society is to train human beings to take themselves and their roles seriously. Our purpose is to free human beings from the training of society. It is necessary to resign from the human race – with a forged signature, of course.'[19]

Despite the comical style, there is a sound psychological principle behind the idea of 'dice living'. As another character puts it: 'All humans in complex and contradictory societies are filled with many inconsistent attitudes and desires. The normal self fights these contradictions and is miserable. The wise man embraces them and flows.'

To use the technique that Rhinehart describes, simply focus on a particular event in your life or a question you have, and then write down on a piece of paper six possible outcomes, corresponding to the numbers, 1–6, of the die. The basis of this 'divinatory' system is that all things are connected one to another and your *intention* provides the tangible link between these forces: the unseen world of energy and the seen – the number showing on the die as it lands face up when thrown.

Phrase your question so that it allows for *possibility* rather than a precise answer limited to 'yes' or 'no' (for example, '*What is the outcome of my going into business for myself?*' rather than '*Should I go into business for myself?*'), since the essence of this system is to help you focus your own intuitive powers instead of answering categorically for you.

The number on the die will then correspond to the answer you have written down. The shamans believe that since all things are connected, you already know the likely outcome of any situation and the answer to your question, if you only access this pool of universal knowledge through the power of your intuition.

This technique can be used as a guide to the future as well as a means of overcoming our habitual dependence on analytical thinking as it offers a more intuitive guide to the solution of life problems and choices.

SACRIFICE

Divination can, in itself, be a kind of healing for, if the words of the shaman or *babalowa* empower us to avoid a potentially damaging situation or to make amends for our part in a mutually hurtful situation, then the good is served for all.

But there is another form of healing common in Vodou where physical sacrifice is often required. This will seem more disturbing to our modern sensibilities which have been trained from birth to accept a pre-packaged lifestyle where life and death is never an issue, even at the dinner table, and we are reluctant to engage with a religion which we see as primitive, brutal, and barbaric enough to make sacrifices to its gods.

That, to my mind, is primarily because we are shielded from the reality of everyday sacrifice and of life and death in our own culture. We do not have to take personal responsibility for our own decisions and to witness the true nature of living any more, or the interplay of life and death, the full circle of existence, which all the time surrounds us. We visit the supermarket and buy 'beef', or 'pork' or 'burgers' – cellophane at the top, polystyrene at the bottom and chewy in the middle. Our language belies the truth on our plates, for these meals we eat were once living creatures and we are all consumers of animals sacrificed to ensure the continuance of our fast-food consumer lifestyle. In the West, we have easy access to the consumption of far more meat than traditional society members could ever hope to see.

There are many other cultures, including those we would

consider 'Western', which recognize the hypocrisy in our denial to ourselves that we are eating the flesh of another creature. These cultures ensure, at least, that the animal concerned is dispatched in a humane and sacred way, rather than factory-rearing and then butchering them without thought in order to make a TV dinner we will eat without thinking that a real, live, animal has been involved in the meal.

In the Jewish kosher ceremony, for example, animals are blessed prior to their slaughter and the blood is then offered to god while its flesh is consumed by the congregation, the ceremony of sacrifice being what makes it sacred.

The Catholic Church sacrifices a lamb during the opening of each Holy Year, and there are even instructions for magical healing sacrifices in the Scriptures which followed the auto-sacrifice of Christ, such as this one from Leviticus 14 (4–8) which describes a method for the treatment of leprosy:

Then shall the priest command to take for him that is to be cleansed two birds alive and clean, and cedar wood, and scarlet, and hyssop. And the priest shall command that one of the birds be killed in an earthen vessel over running water. As for the living bird, he shall take it, and the cedar wood, and the scarlet, and the hyssop, and shall dip them and the living bird in the blood of the bird that was killed over the running water. And he shall sprinkle upon him that is to be cleansed from the leprosy seven times, and shall pronounce him clean, and shall let the living bird loose into the open field. And he that is to be cleansed shall wash his clothes, and shave off all his hair, and wash himself in water, that he may be clean. And after that he shall come into the camp, and shall tarry abroad out of his tent seven days.

Despite the stereotypes, blood sacrifice in Vodou is rare, and, when it does take place, it is entirely purposeful. There are few Vodou ceremonies which actually demand such a sacrifice. Those that do are when a vast amount of cosmic energy is being exchanged, such as when a new priest is being 'made' and the co-operation of the spirits is paramount. In most cases, the spirits will accept something much simpler, like cornmeal, an egg (Dambala), rum (Ogoun), or even water (La Siren).

It is, however, considered vital to feed the loa for, without new energy, they will soon become drained, just as a battery will run down if it is not recharged. But the loa do not take the body of the animal sacrifice or drink its blood, as is commonly imagined; they partake only in its life force. The roasted flesh, in fact, is often shared among the congregation as part of the ritual celebration – an act of social generosity given the incredible poverty suffered by most Haitians – unless the animal has been used in a purification or healing ceremony very similar to the one described in Leviticus. In this case, its body is disposed of in a sacred manner since, by absorption of negative energy, it now contains the illness of the person who is cured as a result of its sacrifice.

When sacrifices of any kind do take place as a stirring of the energy matrix, it is often because the houngan requires the presence of the spirits. When they appear, they make themselves known through possession.

POSSESSION STATES

The Western world is fixated on control: of itself, its citizens and, often, of other countries it can colonize or belief systems it can convert to 'the one true way'. We are concerned more than anything else by the idea of possession, where the control of the body is surrendered to another force and used by that entity for purposes of communication, interaction and trans-action without our acknowledgement or authority. For one thing, it would mean that the gods are real for if I, as an un-believer, can be taken over by a god entirely against my will, how else can I explain this? For another, it means that I might have to be responsible for my actions and passions during the time my body was out of my control.

In fact, the latter is not an issue in Vodou for no-one whose body is used in this way is held accountable for their actions – provided the possession is genuine and not faked. It is well recognized that spirit is moving through them and that they are not responsible – just as you would not expect to be accountable for your neighbour if you loaned him your car and he behaved with it in a way you personally would not.

The feeling of entrance into possession, before the darkness descends, can be a little unsettling for those not used to it. It is perhaps a little like we imagine drowning must feel, where all the power you have over yourself, all that you are, is taken from you and you are at the mercy of the waters in a thrashing sea. Or like wrestling with a god in a battle for supremacy between mortal and immortal. Inevitably, you lose. There is no time and there is no space in what follows, just the quiet peace of dreamless slumber.

During the time you are away, you are the vehicle of the gods – the *cherval* or horse which is ridden by spirit – and not conscious of any of it. The houngan at this time will use the opportunity to question the spirit which now occupies your body for information on current and future events and outcomes, to seek healing information and advice on other matters of communal concern, exactly as the shaman does in his time with the spirits as part of the shamanic journey. What emerges from you is wisdom beyond anything you are personally capable of and insights and information you could not possibly have known.

And then you come back, quietly, unharmed, cared for – and oblivious to all that has passed.

For those who are used to journeying or to possession states, meeting with the gods in this way can be sublime and beautiful, but for those unused to it, the feeling can be uncomfortable. Sheila, a young woman from the UK, described to me an episode of spontaneous possession she experienced one night.

'I absolutely did not believe in possession. I figured if it had any basis whatsoever, it was purely psychological. Then, one night I had a dream about Erzuli [the Vodou goddess of love and compassion]. She had a white kind of spotted leopard or jaguar with a black head, on a chain beside her. "I want to give him to you. Do you accept my gift?" she asked. I said "Yes, I suppose so" and she said "Are you certain? Because once he's yours, you can never give him away or give him back." I said, "Yes, I'm certain" and she handed me the chain. As our hands touched, I felt electricity or something pass from her hand to mine.

'I woke up suddenly and felt very strange. My head didn't feel like it was part of my body and I felt a tingling sensation travel all over me. I decided to get out of bed and get a glass of water and went through to the kitchen, filled the glass and drank. All the while I felt myself getting more and more detached from my surroundings. Then, all of a sudden, my legs became weak and nearly went from under me. The feeling of electricity in my body got stronger and stronger until it was all I was conscious of.

'None of this was pleasant. I didn't know what was happening to me and the experience was so jarring I thought I was going to die. Then I felt myself – my personality – almost drift away. It was pushing upwards, out of my head, and all of a sudden I heard a female voice say "This is what it feels like to be a god" and, in that second, I knew what was happening and I was so terrified you wouldn't believe it. I got frantic and desperately tried to regain control of my body before it happened.

'I could feel "me" slipping out and "something else" starting to come in. The sensation was from above, it was coming in through my head. The only way I could think of to stop my personality going totally was to count, to keep my brain working . . . 123451234512345 . . . I did that for about ten minutes and for some reason it seemed to work.

'I don't think I stopped the loa, I don't think anyone could, but I think the fact that I struggled against it so much convinced whoever it was to stop as I plainly wasn't ready for this . . . Allowing your body to be used by a loa may be a great act of kindness but I don't think I'll ever be that kind.'

Our Western worldview sets great store by the idea of self-control – our cities actually demand it (think of your last tube journey, your frustration and irritation and how you just managed to keep it bottled up inside) – so it is not surprising that we are disturbed when another entity begins to exert an influence over us. But not every 'possession' is like this, and relaxing into letting go becomes a simple and ultimately invigorating matter once we have allowed it to happen a few times. As the spiritist, Emma Restall Orr remarked in the Introduction to this book, 'ultimately, everyone is possessed by spirit'.[20]

Dreams, reveries, visualizations are everyday possession states, *inspirations* (literally, the entering in – in-spir-ation – of spirit), where we are able to receive information and advice which we may see as coming from our unconscious minds but which are, nevertheless, a gift from 'something other' than ourselves.

In Haiti, the arrival of the gods is positively welcomed and courted, and worshippers are more concerned that they will *not* be taken by the gods, so beautiful and enlightening is the experience. The difference between these experiences of possession can be viewed in terms of culture. In societies where absolute control of the self is not such a vital issue as it is in our 'city culture', and emotions can be freely expressed because no-one is concerned about 'making a fool of themselves' in front of others, possession is the most wonderful feeling imaginable.

My own experience of possession in Haiti was a quite magical one.

It was the second night of the *bat guerre*, a special ceremony within the Vodou initiation cycle, which lasts for three nights and immediately precedes the initiate's installation within the *djevo*, the inner sanctum of the Vodou temple where the secret, magical teachings are passed on to initiates.

The *bat guerre* is a battle for the spirit where the initiates kneel together before a large pillow called a *bila* which is stuffed with magical herbs. To the hypnotic rhythm of the Vodou drums, the initiates beat the pillow with machetes, matching the speed and beat of the drums, to release the herbal aroma into the air before them while, around the ritual space, church officials clash machetes as part of a mock battle to encourage the loa to appear and possess the initiates.

I had been worried when I entered the *bat guerre*, beneath a huge full moon, that I would be unable to become possessed since my way of contacting the spirits was so radically different from this and, indeed, on the first night, there had not even been an inkling that the spirits had noticed or taken any interest in me whatsoever. I had beaten the *bila* for hours, drunk the mildly hallucinogenic mixture of absinthe and local herbs offered to me, and listened to the drum songs, each one a signal call to a particular loa, all without any sensation of deep trance.

The second night had started in much the same way and, for some hours, I had no feeling that my consciousness was affected in any significant way. But suddenly the houngan was behind me, taking the machete from my hands, and pushing me beneath the *bila*, which is what happens when an initiate becomes possessed. The others will then continue to strike the pillow to seal the energy of the loa into the person who lies beneath it.

I was puzzled at first. I certainly had not felt possessed when the machete was taken from me, but now, as I lay beneath the *bila*, I felt my body jerking uncontrollably as new energy rushed through it, and my mind drifting off as strange and colourful images flooded my consciousness. Later, I would ask the other initiates what had happened to prompt the houngan to take the machete from me – how had he known that possession was about to ensue? 'Simple,' said the others. 'Your eyes were glazed and your body was swaying backwards and forwards so violently that you would have impaled yourself on the machete if he *hadn't* pushed you under the pillow.' I had felt none of it.

As the trance intensified, the outside world simply faded

away and I was taken by the spirits into the landscape of ancient Africa and introduced to the occupants of this strange spirit world, becoming only vaguely aware, what seemed like seconds later but was actually almost 30 minutes later, of the voice of Mambo Racine calling me back from the oblivion of my transported consciousness.

It must have been the night for possessions because immediately after my return another of the initiates was taken by the spirits in a much more dramatic display than mine. Ricardo, possessed by the spirit of the ocean loa La Siren, thrashed around the floor, screaming in ancient Yoruba, a language he did not, in ordinary consciousness, know at all. Those in the congregation who knew the language of the old world translated the experience of the loa who, pulled to Earth by the sound of the drum, was momentarily confused and lost, transported here from a battle she had been fighting for dominion of the oceans. Ricardo, when he resurfaced, had no knowledge at all of his possession and was quite amazed to hear that he had been speaking in Yoruba.

Not every possession is automatically taken as 'gospel', however. To be effective, the loa must be real and have things of value to communicate. If that is not so, one of the jobs of the houngan or mambo is to require the spirit to leave again, for he is the host of their incarnation here on Earth and has power of veto over their appearance and behaviour.

Mambo Racine offers guidelines used in Haiti for the detection of a phoney loa:[21]

- The loa appears as an ambassador for the person he or she has possessed and argues in favour of this person over a particular dispute or encourages those present to offer gifts to the one who is possessed.
- The personalities of the loa and their *chervals* do not differ. In reality, loa are recognized to have particular likes and dislikes, to express themselves in certain special ways and to behave consistently and in accordance with their own personalities over time and in whichever congregation they appear or people they mount

148

– in this sense the gods are very human! Each houngan will have a wide range of special clothes, foodstuffs, drink, and other ritual objects available for the exclusive use of the loa which appears so that he or she may be attired and fed appropriately.

A person possessed by Baron, for example, may wish to be dressed in black, including the characteristic top hat of this loa, and sunglasses with one lens missing, reflecting the fact that Baron is the spiritual energy of the crossroads, of life and death, and sees into both worlds. Baron likes to smoke cigars and to use highly suggestive sexual language, which is regulated by strict parameters and characteristics – he is never profane, rude or aggressive, for instance, but delivers his sexual references with quite sophisticated humour, puns and panache.

To watch a woman being genuinely possessed by a loa such as Baron is to watch a transformation of personality which immediately strips away the socialization into gender stereotypes we have all undergone during our childhood and subsequent development. One minute a demure and frail old lady is standing at the back of the peristyle where the ceremonies take place; the next she is drinking rum, smoking a cigar, delivering sexual jokes to the crowd and thrusting her pelvis towards you in a display which is totally out of character and the hallmark of a genuine possession state.

By the same token, men can become female loa, and even young children can take on the wisdom and attributes of someone far older, more knowledgeable, capable and worldly wise than themselves. There are stories of children as young as 10 being possessed by the loa and drinking an entire bottle of rum laced with the red hot chilli peppers which is the favoured drink of Baron. This child may never have touched alcohol before – and a bottle of rum is enough to make even a seasoned drinker drunk and ill, even without the chillies which usually make it undrinkable anyway – but when the possession is over, the child is not drunk or ill and can remember nothing of what has taken place.

- The person simply gets it wrong. Some loa are incapable of speech and must make themselves and their communications

149

known through gesture. Erzuli Danto, spirit of love, for example, never speaks in words but in clucking sounds, pointing at what she wants. Someone claiming possession by this loa and speaking aloud her messages in words would be instantly dismissed as a fake.

Another loa who never speaks is the serpent spirit, Dambala. A serpent cannot speak and does not have arms or legs, and so those possessed of Dambala will fall to the ground and crawl, sometimes exhibiting quite superhuman abilities, which is another trademark of genuine possession. In the middle of every peristyle is a centrepost which, like the world tree of the shaman, is the doorway by which the gods enter. A person possessed of Dambala may crawl to the centrepost and then begin to climb it, without using hands or feet, as a snake will climb a tree. It goes without saying that this is, of course, impossible for any normal person.

Anyone possessed by Dambala or Erzuli, who offers words of wisdom to the congregation or who, in the guise of a snake, begins to walk, is an obvious suspect.

- By trial. Some things are possible by humans only in the deep trance state which accompanies possession, or through the protection and patronage of the loa. The example of Luc Gedeon sitting in the flames of a fire and emerging unharmed is one example of this. Another is the *brule zin* rite of initiation into priesthood where, as part of the ceremony, the newly made priest sits before three cauldrons of boiling oil. The houngan plunges his hand into each of them and pulls out a piece of red hot dough which he places into the initiate's hand for him to mould, a gesture symbolic of the moulding of man by god and the creation of the priest as he is made in a new form.

I do not know the temperature reached by boiling oil but I do not recommend you try this at home in order to find out! But there is never any fear of injury to the houngan or the candidate; it is expected that they will be protected by their spirits and, having undergone this initiation myself, I can confirm that, despite all expectations to the contrary, burning oil really does not hurt when the spirits do not want it to.

'Sometimes there is a small gasp as the dough is placed in the person's hand,' says Mambo Racine: 'most times there is silence.'

Now that she is a priest, who has responded to the call of spirit, the mambo is under the protection of the gods and cannot be injured in this way.

Who, then, are these gods who bestow such superhuman powers on their children?

THE LIVING GODS OF VODOU

In the cosmology of the shaman, there are three broad energetic realms which may be travelled to – the upper, middle and lower worlds. This is somewhat simplistic, since in some traditions these realms are further subdivided according to the nature of the spirits who live there; and finally, all three 'worlds' also become one for many shamans, with 'pockets' of wisdom and areas of effectiveness scattered throughout them, rather like a city centre where you might visit the doctor's surgery to discuss health concerns, the police station to discuss a matter of authority or law, and the cinema for entertainment. Or like a library, which is divided into sections to make research and reference easier.

In the Vodou cosmology these spiritual specialisms are represented by the different loa who are expressions of 'an archetype formed of pure energy, directed into a specific channel . . . It is raw energy, awesome power visually and materially discernible', in the words of Migene Gonzalez-Wippler.[22]

In Vodou, as in Santeria, there is one god. In Vodou, he is known as *Gran Met* ('Great Master'), or *Bondye* (from the French, *bon dieu* – good god), an all powerful, all knowing and ever present force in the universe, broadly similar to our own Western notion of a divine being who is the creator of all things and master of all destinies.

The job of Gran Met is to hold the entire universe in

balance and to oversee all affairs and interactions between everything that is or can be. In the West, we say that our god knows the fall of every sparrow; so it is with Gran Met, who is aware of every action in the cosmos, and the reverberation of its energy and consequent impact on all things. His vast remit is to harmonize these forces to ensure the greatest good for all.

Because this job is so huge, and human beings just a small part of it, the supreme god of Vodou, much like our own, can sometimes seem distant and unconcerned with the world of humanity. This is not so – he is intimately concerned with human affairs but on a scale so huge it is beyond our comprehension.

Because Gran Met loves his human children, say the Haitians, he created the loa as his representatives so that we would not feel abandoned by god while he concerned himself with matters of the universal order. The loa, then, are both the children of Gran Met and parts of the same god-energy, just as every human child is both an independent being and a part of the parents who made her.

Each loa has its own personality and characteristics, likes and dislikes, just as any child, and there are sacred numbers, special colours, days, ceremonial foods, mannerisms and ritual objects associated with each.

People serve a particular loa – though any of them may make their presence felt to all of us at any time – and the loa, in return, serves the needs of his follower. As this suggests, there is an energetic transference and partnership between the people and the loa. Thus, the power and assistance of a particular spirit may be requested by wearing the sacred colours of that spirit, making offerings of preferred foods, and by certain ritual protocols such as sexual abstinence on the days held sacred to that loa.

In Haiti, there are three main groups of loa – the Rada, the Ghedes (or Gedes) pronounced *gai-dai*, and the Petro.

The Rada are ancient and gentle spirits, who once lived in Africa but who came to the New World in the 'hearts and minds' of the slaves during the days of transportation; while the Ghedes – 'the dead' – are more archetypal beings. Bawdy, humorous, mystical and keen to be of service, they are a curious mixture of the most sacred and profane. They may offer detailed advice, prophecy and healing even in the middle of the most sexually suggestive dancing as they possess the body of one of their followers. The Petro loa, meanwhile, are often seen as Western in origin, and are potentially very fierce spirits who are highly protective of their human followers (whom they see as their children) and aggressive toward adversaries. They offer the tough guardianship we can imagine the slaves must have needed in this New World against masters who treated them harshly and saw not their humanity but their economic value to the estate.

Broadly, then, we can see that each group has a specific type of activity for which it is responsible – the ancient and cosmic wisdom of the Rada; the magical intervention and good humour of the Ghedes; and the fierce protective force of the Petro – and each of the loa included within these groups also has a special role to perform, although there is some cross-over between them and their entire capabilities are very wide-ranging: always it is up to the gods to decide what they will be and how they will behave.

Some of the manifestations of Ogoun (Rada group), for example, are listed by Maya Deren as 'warrior hero; statesman and diplomat; politician and gangster; magician' as an indication of the various functions this one spirit alone may perform.[23]

Baron, meanwhile (Ghede group), is described by Deren as 'the cosmic corpse which informs man of life . . . the beginning and the end', responsible for both the crossing to death and, through his overtly sexual jokes, referring also to the regeneration of life through sexual union. He is a symbol, therefore, of life *and* death, like the t'ai chi mandala of the Buddhists, which is all *and* nothing, I *and* That, life *and* death, all at once.

Legba, finally (and principally, since he is the 'gate' through which all other spirits pass) is an example of the Petro loa. The divine trickster and keeper of the gate between the worlds, Legba is the means to all communication between the living and the dead.

EXERCISE: CALLING THE LOA

The houngan and the mambo have a developed relationship with their spirits and calling them has become a simple matter of practice. But, just like everything else, they have learned to do this over time, and you can learn it too. If you wish to try this for yourself, you will need either a rattle or some other way of making rhythmic sound; a stone and a piece of iron are also ideal.

Ensure you will not be disturbed for at least an hour. Begin by kneeling in front of your sound-maker and, using your voice, call to the spirits that you are asking to be present here, that you would like to develop a relationship with. In this way, you begin to open a channel to them.

The loa are archetypal forms of particular types of energy and are represented as gods and goddesses of 'love', of 'strength and endurance', of 'radiant wisdom', and so on, so it is helpful to have a particular loa or type of energy in mind for this exercise; otherwise it is like picking up the phone, dialling any number, and speaking to whoever answers – which may be rewarding, but not if you particularly wanted to speak to your sister in Oregon.

In this exercise, we are merely opening the channel to spirit, but in subsequent meetings you may require help with specific issues or questions so, again, it is a good idea to have a particular tutelary spirit in mind at this stage so that the right loa will know you when you next speak with them.

When you are ready, pick up your rattle or stone and

begin to make a regular beat. Vodou uses a three-beat: 1-2-3-pause, 1-2-3-pause. Keep this up as you close your eyes and relax, opening yourself to the spirits.

You may feel light-headed or even a little queasy as the energy of the universe begins to enter you. When you feel that a connection with a new type of energy has been achieved, begin to speak out loud, without any attempt to force or control what you say. Move around if that is what the spirits tell you, keeping up the beat if you can.

People enter the trance state with different levels of intensity. Some may feel only a little 'other-worldly', while others enter a deep trance where they are even unaware of their actions. If you know that you are susceptible to deep trance experiences, it may be helpful to have a friend with you who can supervise your actions and take notes of what you say and do; others use a tape recorder or video the event. In any case, it is helpful to have some method of recording what you say as you speak out loud, as you may find that some of it is forgotten when you return to normal awareness since – depending on your perspective – you are now speaking from a very deep and largely untapped pool of consciousness within you, or your body is the vehicle for spirit.

When you begin to sense that you are no longer connected to this other energy, bring yourself back to normal awareness by ceasing the rhythmic beat you have been working with, and then gently sprinkle cold water on your face in order to refresh yourself and wash away the last vestiges of the other energy. Sit down and be still for a while and then play back your tape or read through the notes taken for you. Do you connect with this recorded information?

It is important to remember that the loa operate on the basis of an *exchange of energy*. Now that they have entered your life and begun to help you, they must be rewarded, through sacrifice, for their efforts.

Ideally, you will create an altar for the spirits – which need not be elaborate – as a gateway between the worlds. On this altar, now place a plate of food – the same food you will eat at your next meal – with a candle in the centre of this, which will take the energy of this food to the spirit world. This, of course, is the true meaning of 'sacrifice' – to give of oneself in a sacred manner.

As your relationship with the spirits develops, they will tell you the specific foods they most like and you can adapt your offerings to them accordingly, as well as the ritual which surrounds your connection to them.

At the moment, this is enough to put the two of you in touch.

The loa typically live in the spirit world which the Haitians call Gine, which is something like the essence or 'energetic parallel' of primal Africa. Broadly, Gine corresponds to what traditional shamanic cultures call the otherworld, which is also know in Africa as 'the underworld' or 'the other land'. The loa may also sometimes take up residence in other life-forms, such as trees and stones, an animistic principle again reminiscent of shamanic belief, where 'everything is alive'. Trees seem to be important to the spirits of all cultures, and to those who seek communion with them.

Dr Brian Bates, looking at the British Celtic tradition in his paper, 'Sacred Trees', tells us that, 'human beings and trees were inseparable aspects of cosmic reality . . . seeing the familiar with new eyes is the gift of the shamanic journey. So the shaman climbed a "real" tree in order to undergo a journey. The tree formed a ladder to other worlds, other realms, other states, and climbing it physically was a metaphor for the journey from one realm into another'.[24]

The shaman, Christiana Harle-Silvennoinen, has also spoken of the importance of trees in Tuvan culture. Often, on a journey over land, a person will stop to make offerings to a sacred tree which is the home to a particular spirit – which means that short journeys can often take an interminably long time, but the gods must be honoured and respected!

It is not just trees: all natural things may provide homes for the spirits. In her paper in *Sacred Hoop* magazine, 'In the land of Song and the Drum', Harle-Silvennoinen includes an *algysh*, or power song, of the female shaman Kyrgys Kurgak, which illustrates this fundamental belief in the spiritual energy resident in all things and the shaman's power to control it: 'I can even subdue the sky . . . even forest taiga places. I am a shaman who knows even the beginnings of rivers, waters.'[25]

This belief in the power and spiritual energy of nature was very threatening to the orthodox religions – paradoxically, an acknowledgement perhaps of the fundamental truth it represented.

'Communicating with the Life Force of the natural landscape, divining the pattern of future events and performing healing incantations were forbidden by the Christian church,' says Bates. 'Edgar, one of the first Churchmen to hold high political office in England, urged the priesthood to stamp out the indigenous spiritual practices; to "forbid well-worshipping and necromancies and divinations and incantations and with sacred circles – and with Elders and also with trees".' St Eligius, in AD 640, ordered that 'no Christian place lights at the temples or at the stones or at fountains and springs, at trees or at places where three ways meet . . . let no-one presume to purify by sacrifice or to enchant herbs or to make flocks pass through a hollow tree or an aperture in the Earth, for by so doing he seems to consecrate them to the devil'. Another early Christian penitential states that 'no-one shall go to trees or wells or stones . . .'

Despite the obvious power of these places, we must not make the mistake of believing that it is the tree or the stone or the water itself which is to be revered or feared in any way – 'the loa *in* the tree is not the loa *of* the tree,' says Mambo Racine. It is the *loa*, the universal spiritual energy residing therein, which is being contacted and petitioned with these offerings. 'Ceremonies conducted at the foot of the tree are directed at the loa, not at any animistic principle of life energy pertaining to the tree.'

THE STRUCTURE OF THE UNIVERSE

The Cuban form of Vodou, Santeria, has its own pantheon of gods, called *orisha*, with hundreds of individual spirits, many of which are very closely akin to their Vodou counterparts and some – for example Chango, Oggun (Ogoun in Vodou) and Eleggua (Legba) – exactly the same.

The universe of Santeria derives from the ancient cosmology of the Yoruban Africans, who conceived of the world as a giant calabash, with the sky and stars, the realm of power (*Orun*) above, and the Earth (*Aye*) below. There is no division here between the realms: all is connected and becomes one great receptacle for all there is, the energy of the universe, man and spirits.

'The unseen world', according to Ekun, an American santero (priest of Santeria) 'is a sort of parallel to this one. The spirits and orisha exist here. Although our bodies live in Aye, the seen material world, there is also a spiritual part of us which exists in the unseen world and, when we die, we merely shed our bodies and the spirit of ourselves continues to exist in the spiritual plane.

'Humans are merely spirits in bodies. "Heaven is our home; this world is only the marketplace" as an old Yoruba saying puts it.'

Authors, Black and Hyatt, very recently, were among the first to publish a list of the orishas and their functions.[26] There are, according to some accounts, more than 400 of these divinities. Here is a selection of ten from Black and Hyatt's list:

Opin – guardian of sacred space
Iseri – master of herbs and healing
Wara – Eshu (or 'essence') of relationships
Elekun – the hunter

Arowoje – protector of those who travel the seas

Elebara – Eshu of power

Laroye – messenger of the love goddess

Ananaki – for remembrance of things past

Okoburu – 'wicked cudgel' in the Yoruba language; the divine enforcer

Aiyede – bringer of spirit messages

To use the power of these saints, a person about to embark on a sea journey, for example, would call upon the water spirit, Arowoje (Agwe in Haitian Vodou), for protection by performing the correct ritual actions to summon the loa, remembering that this is an exchange of energy and a sacrifice must also be offered in turn.

Whether we will ever truly be able to say, 'objectively' and 'scientifically', that the spirit of this cosmic entity then actually aids the person or whether the person is empowered more because she *believes* it to be true, the net effect is the same: a greater sense of ease and a feeling of protection. The spirits, in the form of the loa and orisha, are 'the soul of the cosmos', in the words of Maya Deren.[27] But whether they are aspects of our own soul, itself a part of and mirror to all things, or sentient fragments of the universal whole must perhaps remain a question of personal faith.

EXERCISE: CALLING FOR PROTECTION FOR YOURSELF OR A LOVED ONE

Ogoun

My particular *met tet*, or guardian loa, is Ogoun, the warrior spirit of Vodou. I have undertaken specific rituals of initiation in order to develop my relationship with this spirit-archetype but, even without these, you can get a sense of this loa by following the procedures used in the calling of the spirit.

Even though Ogoun is the 'warrior' loa and brings a

particular type of masculine or 'yang' energy, he is not an aggressive or violent spirit, nor does he work exclusively with men. In Haiti, women also are possessed by this loa, who is best seen as the spiritual specialist in matters of strategy and diplomacy, which can be represented generally by warriorship. One of his symbols – or power objects – is a machete and, because of his warrior nature, his colour is red. He is associated with iron and with fire and, consequently, with the traditional craft of the blacksmith – an interesting parallel to shamanism since, as Mircea Eliade has shown, many shamans were also blacksmiths and masters of fire.[28]

One of the 'foods' of Ogoun is rum and he will drink this from a red bottle when in possession of one of his followers. His Catholic counterpart is St Jacques, and he can also be represented by the image of St George, entering into battle with and then slaying the fire-breathing dragon with his machete-sword or lance.

To work with Ogoun, assemble as many of these power objects or symbols as you can around you in the ritual space and then follow the procedure outlined in the previous exercise, calling specifically to Ogoun this time, and asking for his assistance with a particular issue of protection. Begin to beat out the 1-2-3 rhythm as described above. Since Ogoun has an affinity with iron, this is an occasion when it is better to make the beat with iron on stone instead of using a rattle.

Again, as you enter trance, ensure that you have a way of recording the spirit information received, as advice will be given to you during the possession which you must have a way of acting upon afterwards.

When the trance experience ends, open the bottle of rum and make a salute with it to the four directions – East, West, North and South, in that order – then to the sky and finally, pour a drop of rum onto the Earth, before taking a swig of it yourself. Thank Ogoun for his help and review the information you have been given. Remember to leave a little food on your altar as an offering.

In many cultures, the connection with spiritual power is maintained through the charging of a necklace (or sometimes a bracelet) with the energy of the god. This is the purpose of the *maras* of India and Tibet, the *kolyres* of Haiti, the *beads* of Santeria, and even the rosary of Catholicism. These ritual items are simple to make and provide a constant reminder for you, and connection with, the power of the loa you have chosen to work with.

They consist of a length of leather or string with beads threaded along it in the colour of the loa you wish to maintain contact with. Since Ogoun's colours are red and blue, these are appropriate colours to use for this and, since he is also connected to iron, metal or silver beads might also be used. Ogoun is magically associated with the number five so, when you make this necklace, the beads can be threaded five red, five blue, one silver, for example, repeating this pattern until the length of string is complete.

Psychologically, whenever we remember that we are wearing this necklace or bracelet, or catch sight of it, we become conscious once again of our own spiritual dimension and our partnership with the gods, and aware of the energy within us, which makes us stronger. Spiritually, it means that our gods are always with us, protecting us throughout the day.

La Siren

Another protective loa is the mermaid spirit of the seas and water, La Siren, who is seen, in Haiti, as 'the Mother of All', according to Mambo Racine, who has a particular affinity with this spirit.

The belief in a spiritual entity represented by the mermaid is far from limited to Haiti. The shamans of Peru have a detailed understanding of three spiritual realms – the water world, the jungle world and the sky world (corresponding to the lower, middle and upper world of most shamanic traditions). The mermaid, one of the rulers of the aquatic world, is represented as a beautiful woman with a melodious and hypnotic voice who will lure men to the water in order to pass on her secrets (in a way similar to our own conception of 'the siren of the rocks' who draws mariners to her world by grounding their ships, changing the course of their lives and landing them in a different spiritual reality). In parts of West Africa, this spirit is known as Mami Wata, while in Ireland she is the Great Selkie, and in Santeria she is an aspect of the goddess Yemaya.

'In fact, our Mother is so universal that she is represented in all cultures on planet Earth,' says Mambo Racine. 'Every race on Earth which is in contact with the sea has an image of her.

'She is identified with women's affairs, with the moon and, of course, with the tides of the sea. Her colour is blue [other colours of the sea, such as the white of the foam, turquoise and light green, are also acceptable to her] and her number is seven [for the "seven seas"?] She loves seashells and combs.'

Mambo Racine has devised her own invocation to call La Siren for protection. It begins with a call to the spirit in Creole, the language of Haiti: 'Mami La Siren! Omio Yemaya, Yemaya Asesu, Yemaya Malewo, Yemaya Olokun! Yemaya Awoyo! Met Agwe Tawoyo! Metres Siren, Mam Kumba Bang, Mami Wata!'

This is a cry of names – La Siren, Yemaya, Mami Wata – by which this spirit is known. Equally, however, any English-language song associated with the sea or water might be sung quietly, or you can simply call for 'La Siren', 'The Siren/Mermaid'.

When you feel that you have been heard, take a seashell, a blue candle and a glass of salt water and, lighting the candle, pass the seashell over your entire body, always working downwards. Wash your hair with the salt water, scrub the shell with the remnants of the water, and then tie your damp hair with a blue kerchief.

Alternatively, fill a clear glass with seashells and salt water and a little blue food colouring and, lighting a candle before it, meditate on the reflections in the water for a few quiet moments.

To protect your house, steep fresh herbs, including basil, mint and rosemary, lavender and poppy seeds, in water for a few hours then, lighting a blue candle and calling to La Siren, walk around your house, sprinkling the water as you go.

'When you have done so, talk to La Siren and tell her you need money to run your house, and ask her to take charge of all your domestic affairs and your health. Praise her quiet strength, her depth, her raging power. You can offer her a bottle of champagne as well. Sing and dance all you want! Make any other special requests you have.'

Divining your own protective spirit
Although none of the loa will deny you if you are respectful and sincere, the best loa to work with, of course, is the one you feel most affinity with and who most cares for you (your *met tet*). Divination is traditionally used in order to determine this. If you normally use a divinatory method such as tarot cards, or rune stones, crystals, or the *I Ching*, then continue with these. Or you may choose to use the rock divination technique described in *The Journey to You*.

You will need to do a little homework first, however, as you need to know which loa are available to you. Images of the loa can be hard to come by in the West, but pictures of the Christian saints will also work since, during the days of slavery the images of the saints were used to mask their Vodou conterparts. When you have absorbed these and have their images in mind, begin the divination process, asking if the saints or loa you are drawn to are the ones who wish to work with you. By process of elimination, you will then be able to ascertain your own *met tet*

Once you have done so, begin your apprenticeship with this spirit immediately, calling to him or her and explaining your intentions and your needs. Allow yourself to remain open for the next few days and look consciously for signs and omens that your request has been heard.

THE ANCESTORS

As well as the loa, the spirits of the ancestors are ever present in Vodou and Santeria, just as in shamanism, and can be called upon for advice and assistance in more mundane and human matters. The national anthem of Haiti begins with the words, 'For the country, and for the ancestors, we walk united . . .' and there is a definite understanding that the spirits are all around us in our towns and cities every day. The dead are attracted to places of high emotion, such as graveyards, accident scenes, or even libraries and bars, places where mental or emotional energy is expended. They are all around us now in our city streets and, according to the shaman, the mambo and the houngan, can be called upon for help and intervention in our daily affairs, exactly as we have been doing in the exercises for 'calling the spirit', above.

In the Venezuelan form of Santeria, trance practitioners known as *bancos* act as the intermediary between the worlds of the spirits and people, using alcohol to induce trance or possessions, and tobacco smoke to cleanse the environment and to see remote events from the ancestral spirit world, while *babalaos*, who are somewhat like high priests, communicate with the orishas and higher spirits and act as oracles for their messages.

Emilio, a correspondent from Venezuela, defines the differences between the ancestral spirits and the orishas as follows:

'We live mainly in cities, so spiritual practices tend to become adapted to the limitations that urban centres impose. Santeria is [therefore] a mixture between African shamanism (Yoruba cult) and Catholic practice.

'Spirits tend to own some human behaviour – they could be jealous, vain, compassionate, and so on – while the saints [orisha] usually own very divine behaviour and are always good. One must be very careful when asking a favour from a spirit because then one must honour what is offered, otherwise the spirit could turn against you.'

This dual personality of the ancestral spirits, as both protectors and punishers, offering favours and retribution, is indicative of an underlying belief in an egalitarian relationship where the exchange of power is reciprocal, and the spirits must not just be taken advantage of.

In Haiti, this relationship between the living and the dead is respected and made evident in every daily interaction. Every family compound has its own graveyard, and in the city these tombs may be so elaborate that they resemble houses, complete with sitting rooms where the dead may entertain their guests who come to seek advice and to share gossip, memories and reflections on the day. In the villages, where money is a rarity, the tombs are often less ornate, though still the best that can be afforded, and would be considered grand in most Western countries, where the dead are concealed beneath the ground or reduced to ashes and kept in jars which take up even less space in our communal graveyards.

The rituals of death are elaborate and precise. People are normally buried with a Catholic ceremony, although this may have a very different meaning to Haitian mourners as a result of their different, syncretic, understanding of the rituals and symbols of Catholicism. A wake is then held for nine nights after the death, following which the Vodou ritual of *desounin* begins.

In *desounin*, the soul is removed from the body of the

deceased, and the guardian loa who has helped that person throughout life is set free. This guardian spirit can sometimes be inherited by another family member and, if this is the case, the loa will, at this time, declare the inheritor of his or her energetic power by possessing the person chosen. The loa then becomes this person's guardian and source of protection.

The soul of the deceased, meanwhile, will withdraw into the 'abysmal waters' beneath the Earth where it must reside for a year and a day. In this place, it is believed, the soul gains knowledge of its past life and the energetic patterns at play there, grows in strength and wisdom, and prepares for its return to the community. In a sense, then, the 'abysmal waters' of Vodou are not dissimilar to the Tibetan Buddhist concept of the *bardo* between life and rebirth, where the soul is given a karmic opportunity to achieve freedom and enlightenment, to become one again with the 'god-vibration' of the universe, or to be reborn in human or spiritual form.

It is also a lonely place, where the 'lost' soul is bereft of any sense of community or relationship with the living – a connection of primary importance in Haitian life – and so, one year and one day after the death, the houngan may perform the ceremony of *retire mo nan dlo* in order to remove the soul from this place by calling it up through a vessel of water and ritually installing it in a clay pot called a *govi*. This is then placed in the *djevo*, the inner sanctum of the Vodou temple, where it may be consulted on matters of personal and Earthly concern. There is an echo here of some shamanic practices, such as those of Mongolia where the soul of a dead shaman is called into the body of a doll called an *ongon*, which is then hung in a shrine to serve as a protective spirit for the community.

In Jamaican Vodou, the dead are served in a similar way. Here, the ancestral dead, known as *duppies*, are believed to rise from the grave for nine nights after death and roam throughout the night, visiting their homes and claiming the shadow of their belongings. In sorrow and disorientation following death, the duppy is also capable of evil and it is said that if one touches you, you will become sick and can even die as the spirit blows heat through you which causes you to go into convulsions.

One way to prevent this and to contain the duppy is to place ten or more seeds on top of the grave since the duppy can only count to nine and so cannot pass through the tenth seal. Salt sprinkled on the grave will also restrain the spirit.

In ritual ceremonies for the recently deceased, on the ninth night after death the duppy is welcomed to her ancestral status with a feast. Songs are sung and stories told in order to entertain her. She eats and is allowed to claim the shadow of the possessions she owned during life. Then she is spoken to by her surviving relatives and told that she has been honoured during this feast but must now pass on to the other-world and must not return. Her relatives will pray for her soul that it may rest in peace and never return to haunt them.

The spirit will then return to its grave and a cross is drawn with chalk over the windows and doors of the house to keep the duppy out.

In this tradition, it is understood that all people are a mixture of light and dark, good and evil, but in life these emotions and potentialities are much easier to control. The dead are no longer consciously responsible for their actions and can therefore do harmful things to the living, without even being really aware of this. Respect for the dead and instruction for them in their new status and the expectations of them in death are the keys to maintaining harmony with the ancestors.

Just as with the duppy, the spirit of an ancestor in Haiti may also return of its own accord, as was the case with Luc Gedeon and the spirit, Arapice La Croix. The ancestor does not have to be a member of one's own family in order to be effective. It is the fact that they have once been human and are now spirit which is of importance, since they can speak with a close understanding of the world of human beings but also with the power of spirit to see the future and the bigger cosmic picture.

Surprising as it may seem, there is much in this cosmology, and that of the shaman, which is shared with Western religions. Christianity, just like Vodou, believes in one male god who is sometimes distant from the affairs of humanity, and in a legion of angels who, like the loa, are his ambassadors and agents on Earth, maintaining a closeness to the human world and intervening in people's troubles to ensure that the good is served.

We read in the *Book of Enoch* of multiple dimensions of energy which can be visited by the believer, corresponding to the otherworld of the shaman. When, at the request of God, Enoch journeyed to these worlds and wrote of his experiences there, he described ten of these dimensions. The first contained the stars, the flowers, the stones and the dew. The second was a world of lost souls and fallen angels. The third was a land of light and shadows, a world of choice between divinity and compassionless existence, something perhaps like the 'abysmal waters' of Vodou where the dead must remain for a year and a day.

In the fourth stood the world tree, and the sun and the moon, which shamans would have no trouble in recognizing. For the Yagua Indians of the Amazon, for example, the sun and moon, along with the pole star and the evening star, are all separate realms in the land of the Great Sky.

The fifth heaven was a world for angels who had descended to Earth to marry human beings and, again, there are parallels with shamanism, where powerful shamans are said to have 'spirit wives' in the otherworld, whom they visit during their trance journeys, and with Vodou practices, where people may actually marry the gods in formal wedding ceremonies.

The akashic library was found in the sixth heaven, which contained all information on every soul who has ever lived. In the seventh was the experience of pure heart, where innocence and compassion reside. The eighth was the realm of the elements and the seasons, and the ninth, the celestial home of the zodiac. The tenth and final heaven was the realm of the divine, the final home of God.

In matters such as this, the difference between shamanism and Catholicism, or between the Christian Church and the Church of Santeria, is largely semantic. In all religions, as well as in our daily experience, we are basically talking about energy – the energy of the universe – which can be channelled, directed, used and exchanged in order to create changes in the world. It is only the 'spin', the cultural gloss we put on this energy, and the way we find of relating to it which turns it into a religion of any kind.

As the Amazon shaman, Viejo Itza, remarks: 'Energy. It is everything. We are energy. The Earth, those trees down there . . . the universe. Energy. That's all there is to it. The shapeshifter believes she can influence her relationship with the physical world. Therefore she can . . . it is only a matter of energy and belief. And one more thing. Intent.'[29]

What the shamans are saying here, and the followers of Vodou demonstrating, is that we all have the power to shift this energy, to change the patterns which have been created in our lives and to make something better for ourselves. The power of the cosmos manifests itself in the form of energy, which some call spirits, and they are our allies in this trans- formation – because they, too, want a better world for us and for themselves. It is in their interests too – for as soon as we forget the gods they cease to be, like a tree falling in a forest when no-one is there to see or hear. The tree may still fall but who will know or care?

But what exactly is this energy? And how can we use it in our daily lives, in our cities, in our work, in our relationships, our homes? What can we do to make a world where the sacred is remembered and, in turn, creates a more fulfilling life for us?

Let's take a look . . .

4

WORLDS WITHIN WORLDS: THE ENERGY BODY AND THE CITY

Do not adjust your mind, there is a fault in reality.
– graffiti in a London street

We wake to another rainy Monday morning in an overcast city, turn on the radio to hear of war and refugees, falling stock market prices, rising costs of housing, crime on the streets and disease in the fields.

The shaman wakes to a world of beauty. Not because her world is any different from ours; it is the same world with the same problems. But because her *reality*, her way of seeing the world is different. The shaman, just like our Western mystics and seers, *knows* that the physical world is an illusion, that our perception of the world and our enjoyment of life is merely a matter of attention and intention. What we choose to see and how we choose to feel is what creates our world. The rain may depress us, but then we notice the beauty of a single raindrop meeting other tributaries of rain on our window pane, forming little crystal rivers that reflect the light, casting rainbows into our lives. And then suddenly the world is different once again.

The core beliefs and *fundamental principles* of shamanism and Vodou underlie this ability to see beauty in all things with just a turn of the mind. What the shaman knows (and what we know too if we would just stop running for trains, buses, promotions, deadlines, council meetings, long enough to remember) is that:

- everything is alive, aware, sentient
- everything is connected
- beyond its material form and appearance of solidity, everything in the universe is energy
- because we are all connected to each other and to all other things, we can use this energy creatively to change ourselves and others, and the world itself. This very fact gives rise, for example, to the 'unexplained' phenomena of bodily healings of their clients by shamans, using only feathers or rocks, and the changes in reality accomplished by houngans and babalaos through incantations, spells and charms, all of which we will start to look at now.

As strange as it may seem, Western science is in full agreement that there is something going on beyond the atom which seems almost to suggest a mystical rather than a physical basis for reality, with purely energetic forces as the key.

Atoms, the matter we believe ourselves to be made of, are in fact composed mainly of empty space. According to analogy, an atom the size of an Olympic stadium would have a nucleus – the solid bit – only the size of a pea. What goes on inside the atom is mainly an exchange of energy. Furthermore, exactly *what is* going on is difficult to determine – so much so that the scientist, Werner Heisenberg put forward a theory he called the *Uncertainty* Principle to try to make the situation clear!

His basic 'solution' to the 'unknowableness' of the universe was the statement that it is impossible to determine the position *and* the velocity of any particle at the same time – which means we can *either* take a 'snapshot' of the 'reality' we perceive at any one moment *or* behave in the world, as we normally do, by making predictions based on the present situation. But we cannot do both since, by determining the property of one, we necessarily alter the other, our actions *now* affecting the outcome of what *would* have happened, rather like the divination example we looked at earlier, where the gods 'intervened' to offer protection to someone seeking personal safety. Every time we say 'Yes' instead of 'No', or vice versa, the whole world changes for us and for everybody else.

To put it extremely crudely, I can tell you right now that the box in front of me that I am currently tapping away at is a computer, but if you ask me to predict when I am going to need to replace it because its useful life is over, then it ceases to be a computer and becomes a jumble of circuits and electronics whose lifespan can be calculated.

In more scientific terms, whenever we look at any particle to determine its position, we can only do so effectively as a result of the light photons which bounce off it and bring us the information. But the action of these photons itself affects the velocity of the particle. Time slows down through the action of receiving information, so we cannot ever know where anything really is. In other words, we change the nature of reality every second by our own participation in it.

The paradoxes of this 'observer effect' have meant, over the years, that a completely new theory of reality has had to be developed to explain how the universe operates. Our best suggestion at the moment is that it resembles a giant and richly complex hologram where all things are connected and, fundamentally, can only be understood as the flow of energy. It is our own interpretation of the meaning behind this energy – the gloss or the spin we put on it – which actually *gives* it meaning. Everyone, and perhaps, every *thing*, alive is projecting their own personal reality onto the raw data of the universe and, through our collective projection, making reality what it is (or what we see it as).

If you compare this scientific summary with the beliefs of the shaman which introduced this chapter, you will see that all the elements are there: everything connected, all of it energy, the world as we dream it. Our scientists and our shamans are no longer adversaries, they are partners in the adventure to understand the universe.

In an earlier chapter I made the point that reality is a *political* decision, and the new scientific model bears this out. For what it says is that we all construct our own individual realities and there is no necessity whatsoever to accept the one we have been given by society. When our legal system tells us something is right or wrong, or our politicians make plans for our future, this is merely *their* projection of reality onto the raw cosmic data; a projection we have all of us, through habit, come to accept and have imbued with institutional power. By so doing, necessarily, we have given away some of our own unique and individual power. For our own perspective is equally valid. All that separates Them from Us is the power *we* have invested in *them* for determining what *our* reality will be and how we live our lives.

The theories of new science are explored in far more detail in *The Journey To You*, in Fritjof Capra's *The Toa of Physics*, and especially in Michael Talbot's excellent book, *The Holographic Universe*.[1] For now, let us just accept that energy is the key to reality so we can look in more detail at exactly what this energy is and how we can better employ it.

THE ENERGY BODY – INFINITY WITHIN US

The anthropologist and modern shaman, Dr Carlos Castaneda, has perhaps done more than anyone to increase our awareness and understanding of the energy fields we are all a part of, including the band of energy which is our own body.

Castaneda worked for years as an apprentice to the old Yaquí sorcerer-shaman, don Juan Matus, learning the ways of the Toltec 'seers', the 'men of power' who had mastered the art of engaging with a new reality in everyday life. In a sense the art of 'seeing' is like bringing the otherworld of the shaman into ordinary reality by allowing us to become fully aware of the totality and complexity of the real world by wiping clean our eyes and doing away with the habitual ways of seeing we have been taught to use from birth.

For don Juan, the ordinary world is merely one in 'a cluster of consecutive worlds, arranged like the layers of an onion',[2] and there is far more to be part of if we choose – the worlds of energy and potential.

The relationship between Castaneda and don Juan, while loving and supportive, was at best stormy. Don Juan seems to have regarded Castaneda as something of an academic buffoon, always relying on rational and intellectual Western scientific arguments to try to explain to himself what is essentially unexplainable from our analytical worldview, while, for Castaneda, don Juan was often difficult, cantankerous and a hard taskmaster. Nonetheless, this peculiar Laurel and Hardy relationship of the mystical yielded a dozen books of profound wisdom and insight into the nature of true reality.

According to don Juan, there are three energy fields which the human being is a part of (whether we are aware of them or not). He calls these the first, second and third attentions. He used the word 'attention' quite deliberately since reality is not physical and material but ethereal and energetic, so the way to enter new realities is not to search the planet or the cosmos for answers, but simply to become aware of these new dimensions as they exist in the world around us – to give them our attention.

The *first attention* is the habitual or socialized view of reality which includes all that we know (or think we know, given that reality is a personal matter) in ordinary life: that your name is Karen and you are a 25-year-old American woman who works as bank clerk in Lower Manhattan, for example.

Even everyday 'ordinary reality' varies, of course, culture by culture and across different times since no two cultures or periods in history view the world alike, which accounts for wars and territorial disputes. On top of that, we are all evolving, the world is changing, and different societies have chosen to adapt to its vicissitudes in different ways.

Even we, as individuals, are changing as our life goes on and our concerns and interests change. A career-driven American professional may not have much in common with an African Sangoma medicine woman, for example and, having built her world on the supremacy of money, which is one of the bedrocks of the Western dream, may struggle to understand the shaman when she tells her that money, too, is just a form of energy. One day, however, the career professional may give up her job to have children who, instead, will become the most important thing in her life. She may then reflect on the words of the medicine woman and realize that money *is* just an energy but that the energy of love she shares with her children is more precious to her and she is prepared to go without the luxuries of life as long as her children are healthy and happy.

The *second level* of attention includes all those things and potentials which our habitual view of reality causes us to screen from the world in order for us to define ourselves at all. At an obvious level, in order for you to respond to the name 'Karen', you have to be able to ignore the man across the street who mistakes you for someone else and calls out to you, 'Hey, Betty'. At a less obvious level, our worldview tells us that we are flesh and blood and nothing else, and so we accept this, never even considering that we might be more or different – creatures of spirit or energy or infinite potential. We can, however, come to know this new level of understanding through the employment of special shamanic techniques.

At the level of the *third attention* is all that we can 'never' know as such, but which we can certainly experience. The latter is, if you wish, the remit of the 'one god' of Vodou and of Christianity, the 'Great Mystery' of shamanic tradition – a reality so vast and complex that the human mind cannot contain it, but which acts upon us nonetheless in the order of the cosmos.

Each of these energy fields is infinite and they are all interconnected so that each of us may have an impact on any one, and each field also has an impact on us.

Despite the implication of this – that every human being has the ability to influence the entire cosmos – the powers and

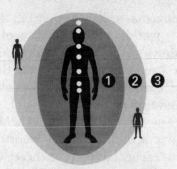

The Three Levels of Attention
**Representing the energy fields which run through us and
to which we are connected.**

1. **The first level** of 'personal space' and self-knowledge.
2. **The Second level** of transpersonal space where we
   are energetically influenced by, and can influence others.
3. **The Third Level** of 'cosmic' energy.

Also shown are the chacras – from the head down, crown, third eye, throat,
heart, solar plexus, sacral and root.

capabilities of human beings are, in a sense, finite. The gods protect us and do not want us interfering in their business, just as a parent would rather plug the stereo in for his child than have her playing around with electricity. But we certainly have an *impact* on the cosmos and can strengthen our ability to do so.

We have more control over the energy fields closest to us – the 'first attention' of the human field and the 'second attention' of the world we normally see as beyond us – just as when driving our cars we have absolute control over the environment we are sitting in, somewhat less over the road conditions outside, and probably very little immediate influence over the government's transportation policy for the country.

Do not be misled by the suggestion of limitations, however. Enhanced control over even the first of these fields can give us the power to change ourselves, to increase our health, wealth, vitality and power as we wish, to understand and interact more authentically with others and to live a fuller life. And, of course, as soon as *we* change, the world, by necessity, must change too.

Control over the second field of attention takes us into the raw energy and fundamental structure of the universe. And even the last of the fields, the third attention, the world of the gods, can be influenced to some degree.

1. THE ENERGY BODY – LEVEL ONE:
THE FIRST ATTENTION

Scientists can assemble a human body from spare parts and, through the use of sophisticated machines and biochemicals, even make it 'live' artificially – but they can't make it get up and walk and talk and think for itself. By the same token, once a body is 'dead', even though it looks physically the same as it did a second ago and is even still warm, it is nonetheless dead and beyond our control.

What is missing in both cases is some form of 'animating principle', which science may call energy and which shamanic cultures call the soul.

Some scientists will argue that they can now grow babies in test tubes who will, indeed, be able to act autonomously as normal children when they mature. But then the spiritists will say that the soul comes with the child because it has been allowed to develop in a more natural way than simply assembling the parts, and so the soul is able to incarnate.

Perhaps the argument is, for now, unwinnable, but the fact remains that some form of life force is present in human beings which enables us to act *as* human beings. A car needs petrol, a torch needs a battery, the human body needs a store of energy in order to operate.

All mysticism aside, the 'life force' we are describing here is what the shaman don Juan called the energy body.

Some people naturally have the ability to see this energy with their naked eyes; others can learn to do so. Our CAT scans, X-rays, and MRI machines can see it, after all, so why shouldn't we – or are we saying that only machines and not their creators are capable of seeing this energy? This would be a circular argument, since why should we build the machines in the first place to view an energy we didn't know or believe was even there?

Those who do see the energy body describe it as looking like a 'luminous egg', a cocoon which emanates from and surrounds the body, going beyond the physical self to a distance of some feet. The strands which make up this egg-like shape, which don Juan called 'luminous fibres', seem to come together at one central point, called 'the Assemblage Point' which is located between the shoulder blades at a distance of about 18 inches from the back of the physical body.

According to don Juan, the main aim of work with the energy body is to be able to move this point at will, for a change in its position also creates a change in our awareness, which means a new view of reality, and an increase in power. When the Assemblage Point moves you are able to do 'all kinds of good and bad things'.

The notion of the energy body has very credible standing in some scientific communities and is certainly within the remit of the new science.

Energy and auras

In 1939, Semyon Kirlian, on a visit to a hospital in Krasnodar, USSR, noticed that when glass electrodes were brought near to the body of a patient receiving treatment from a high-frequency generator, there was a short flash of energy close to the skin. Kirlian was curious to know what this was and decided to investigate.

He began to take photographs of bodies encased in an electrical field. In an early experiment he set up two metal plates, one containing a photographic film, and placed his hand between them. When the film was developed, his hand was surrounded by a luminous glow.

In another experiment, he placed the stem of a freshly cut flower between the plates and noticed that sparks of energy (or 'blood'?) were visible, emanating from the severed end; in another, the energetic ghost of the missing section of a torn leaf was captured on film.

As his experiments continued, Kirlian noticed that what we do with our physical bodies also has an effect on our energetic bodies. In a 'before and after' experiment, a man's hand was photographed and, this being Russia, he was then given a glass of vodka to drink. In the subsequent photograph, the image of the man's hand was far more intense and brighter.

'It looked, then, as if the Kirlians had found a method of photographing the "life field" of living creatures,' says Colin Wilson, who has studied this experiment.[3] 'The torn leaf phenomenon was in no way "psychic"; it meant merely that the electrical field of the missing portion still bridged the gap' – just as amputees often complain of itching or other sensations in the phantom limb.

The intensity of the energy image was also connected with health or illness so that a brighter image suggested a more powerful, healthy person, and a duller image someone suffering from a physical or psychological problem or, indeed, from the impact of daily life upon us.

The idea of an energetic aura to the human body is in no way new. The ancient Greeks, Hindus, Egyptians and Romans all depicted haloes around the heads of their gods and saints – as, indeed, do the Christians in their images of Christ – suggesting that powerfully spiritual figures are more intensely filled with this energy, which most religious tracts describe as a divine 'light'.

In the 1930s, Harold Saxton Burr, using sophisticated electrical apparatus, was able to show that the energy fields of trees varied according to the phases of the moon. Nowadays, of course, the notion of SAD – Seasonal Affective Disorder – demonstrates that human beings are also susceptible to fluctuations in the amount of natural light available to them, becoming listless and depressed when there is too little available: evidence that we too are affected by the changing energy of the seasons.

The world 'lunatic' is suggestive of our human connection with the changing energy of the moon phases as well. Early researchers noticed that the incidence of what they considered aberrant behaviour increased during the full moon, leading to 'irrational' and 'illogical' outbursts. Hence the term, *luna*-tic (Latin *luna* = moon). This is probably not so surprising when we remember that the human body is mostly comprised of water. We see the effect of the moon on the tides of our seas, the high and lows, ebbs and flows, and it is pretty well understood that the moon has an energetic effect on water – so why not on us?

Somewhat in support of Burr's observations, Dr Charles Fere recorded what he called a 'neuropathic aura' in his own patients, which he saw as offering a clue to their disorder. A hysterical patient, for example, would emit an orange light from the hands and head.

Commenting on this scientific activity, one writer, Dr Edward Aubert summarized the early research in his conclusion that human beings seem to 'live in a vast ocean of interlacing energies'[4] – which, of course, is basically what don Juan meant when he spoke of us occupying 'a cluster of consecutive worlds'.

It is not necessary to invest in massively expensive scientific equipment to become aware of the energy field of the human aura; that is merely our Western preoccupation with analysis. Edgar Cayce, in his 1945 book, *Auras*, says that

> *Ever since I can remember, I have seen colours in connection with people. I do not remember a time when the human beings I encountered did not register on my retina with blues and greens and reds gently pouring from their heads and shoulders . . . I do not even think of people except in connection with their auras; I see them change in my friends and loved ones as time goes by – sickness, dejection, love, fulfilment – these are all reflected in the aura and for me the aura is the weathervane of the soul.*[5]

The notion of colour-charting the energetic field of the aura is an interesting one and of value in shamanic healing and in our awareness of our own development and state of mind, since a change in our physical health is usually preceded by a change in our energetic state, which is characterized by alterations in the colour and intensity of the aura. Since the aura is also connected to our glandular and endocrine systems and corresponds to specific bodily organs, such changes in colour can provide useful early warning signals of our physical health and enable us to better adapt to or avoid the health-affecting stresses and strains of urban life.

By charting our personal energetic levels, we may not only be able to anticipate and ward off physical illness but, by refining the technique still further, come to understand through observations over time exactly what it is that precipitates an illness for us. By observing the colour emanations of others, we may also begin to better understand our relationship to them.

Colours of the aura

According to Edgar Cayce, 'the majority of people do see auras, they just don't realize it', and the emanations of the auric body, in terms of the colours they present to us when we are able to see them, do have a quite definite and particular meaning.

- **Red:** A strong red typically denotes a powerful and healthy body, strength of will, determination and passion. But it can also suggest excess pride or an arrogant personality, while light red implies tension, and very dark shades of red can reveal a tendency to anger or frustration.
- **Orange:** Bright orange is highly positive and suggests health, vitality and personal power. Duller shades, however, may suggest a personality who takes things to extremes, leading to over-ambition and selfishness, which is ultimately detrimental to health.
- **Yellow:** Generally implies optimism and well-being, the presence of spirit, and intellectual ability but, when pale, can suggest indecisiveness and an underlying sense of fear which may need

to be addressed if true personal power is to be fully achieved.

- **Green:** Usually means good health and the ability to heal the self and others, as well as a 'happy-go-lucky' soul capable of flexibility and adaptability, compassion, sympathy, and empathy with others. Darker shades, however, suggest dishonesty, or that we are deluding ourselves in some way.

- **Blue:** Indicates idealism, confidence, integrity and spiritual development. Dark blue may even imply saintliness and is certainly a sign of wisdom. Lighter shades denote potential which is as yet unfulfilled, possibly leading to frustration and inner tension.

- **Violet:** Strong shades denote the capability for love and enlightenment, while lighter tones may suggest a person on their way to spiritual fulfilment but, at the moment, perhaps, lost in confusion. Densely dark shades, tinged with black or grey, can indicate a person so full of their own spiritual worth that they may become tyrannical towards others.

- **Indigo:** Calmness and, often, psychic abilities.

- **Black:** Lack of awareness and insight. When it appears as a smoke in the aura, it is often associated with frustration and anger.

- **Grey:** According to Jonathan Cainer in *The Psychic Explorer*,[6] grey is indicative of depression and, in deeper shades, of fear, while greenish grey can suggest deceit.

- **Brown:** Can be associated with greed, but when it appears as a more natural colour can also mean stability and wholeness.

- **Pink:** Implies a sincere person at one with their emotions.

EXERCISE: SEEING THE ENERGY BODY

In order to test the colour theory of the aura and to benefit from it, you first need to refine your ability to see the energy body. This exercise will help.

1. Start by rubbing your hands together to warm them and to encourage an energy flow, then hold them out

before you to a distance of about 24 inches from your face, preferably in front of a plain dark or pure white background to ensure that your eye does not wander and there are no distractions around you. Allow your eyes to go slightly out of focus (shamans call this 'gazing') so you are aware of, but not staring at your hands. Widen your fingers slowly and you will become aware of a 'smoke' between them, perhaps sticking to the fingers as they are pulled apart. It may also appear as a misty outline to your fingers. This is one aspect of the energy body which surrounds you. Try to notice any particular colours which you can see in this 'smoke'. Refer to the list above to see what this might suggest about the way you are feeling right now. Does it seem to make sense to you?

2. Experiment by asking a friend to stand in front of you against the same background. Again, allow your eyes to go slightly out of focus. Don't look directly at your friend, but slightly past or above them. For some reason, the energy body always seems clearer to me if I fix my gaze at the spot just between the shoulder and the top of the head, as if I am looking at something just over the person's right shoulder. You will notice the same 'ghost' image of the person which is their aura. See if you notice any colours within it and check with your friend to see whether your interpretation of these colours ties in with their current mental and emotional state.

The energy body has its own centres of power, represented in Eastern traditions by the chakras, where particular energies are more strongly rooted. The word 'chakra' means 'wheel', these circles of energy appearing as vortexes of circular light of greater intensity than the energy body which surrounds them. Most of the colours discernible in the aura can be seen more clearly at these points.

The following chart identifies these points and the energetic meanings commonly associated with them.

Chakra	Position	Colour	Element	Focus
Crown	Top of the head	Purple	Ideas and images	Awareness and under-standing; ideals and spiritual development
Third eye	Centre of forehead	Blue	Light/enlighten-ment	Intuition and creative empowerment
Throat	Neck	Light blue	Sound	Communi-cation
Heart	Chest	Green	Air	Love and compassion
Solar plexus	Stomach	Yellow	Fire	Power, energy, the place of the will
Sacral	Lower belly	Orange	Water	Emotions and sexuality
Root	Sex organs	Red	Earth/grounding	Security and basic needs

Both shamanism and Vodou operate according to the principles of sympathetic magic, where like attracts like. So, for example, a need to enhance your material standing in terms of more money or better health (which, at its most fundamental level, translates into a desire to increase personal security) may be met by a greater focus on the root chakra, the centre controlling our basic needs for security and physical well-being. By bringing more of the colour red into your life, which is the colour of this energy centre – in your dress, the décor of your home, or by burning red candles, for example – and getting out more into nature where you can experience the 'grounding' power of the Earth, you are able to enhance the flow of these qualities towards you.

By the same token, according to the laws of magic, to increase health and vitality you would surround yourself with the colour yellow (solar plexus chakra), while dark blue (third eye chakra) and purple (crown chakra) are useful allies for developing intuitive and spiritual powers.

This like-for-like complementarity between need and solution is also one of the basic premises of the shaman's medicine wheel which, on the one hand, operates as a psychological tool, offering insights into the self and, at the same time, can be used as a means of personal growth and transformation by working with the elements and qualities associated with each of its four directions.

The basic concept at work here is that energy will use the channel of *intention* in order to manifest at a physical level. By focusing on what you need or desire, you create an energetic channel along which this power may flow – a little like rewiring the brain, as you would a house, to ensure that the lights come on where you want them to.

Even at this level, then, before we begin to use energy constructively in the world, you can perhaps get an idea of its diagnostic and healing potential in matters of self-awareness, well-being and personal development.

EXERCISE: FEELING THE ENERGY FLOW

Start with your hands together as if clapping, then pull them apart to a distance of about 18 inches. Start slowly to bring them back together, focusing all the time on experiencing the energy between your hands and gazing at the space between them, as you did in the previous exercise.

You will begin to notice that the space between your hands starts to get 'fuzzy', a little like the thermals that rise from the ground on a hot day and, at a certain point, you will also notice a slight resistance between your hands as they come together. It will feel somewhat more solid than air, though not of a material hardness. This is energy, which has mass and physicality to it.

Now that you are aware of it, try to focus this energy. Place a light object, such as a feather or a sheet of paper, before you. Start with the object reasonably close, and imagine, really 'see', a beam of energy coming from your hand and touching the feather or paper with the intention of moving it slightly.

This may take some time, so do not expect overnight success, but keep at it (I once watched a t'ai chi master push a man completely to the floor from the other side of the room using this technique alone – but he had been developing his power for thirty years!)

When you are able to see a definite movement, increase the distance between your hand and the object until you can make it move at will.

Over time, it becomes very powerful indeed.

How energy affects us all

All living things (and, to the shaman and the houngan, *all* things are alive) have their own particular field of energy which vibrates at a somewhat different frequency to that of human beings. Some of these energy fields are very calming and health-giving for humans; others most certainly are not. For those of us who live in the city and other urban conurbations, the distinction is important in terms of our health and also our capability for happiness in the world.

It is now well documented that people who live close to electricity pylons and other intense energy emanations are very often severely and detrimentally affected by them, leading to general ill-health and even cancers such as leukaemia. This is one of the problems of city living: we cannot always control where we live or the development that takes place around us, while above, below and around us, the energy of telephone wires, planes and satellites, cables,

186

cars and radio waves careers into us constantly.*

In my experience, the energy of most people is either very jagged, representing their deep disaffection with the stresses of modern life, or extremely low; the colour I most often see in the energy fields of those who visit me for healing is brown or grey bordering on black. I have also met people who exude a powerfully serene energy, with bright but not overbearing auras; they tend to be highly developed spiritually and are often healers themselves. They are rare indeed, but it is an absolute joy when you meet one of these people. I once loved a woman who could attract anyone to her, simply through the beauty of the energy she sent out into the world. There was nothing manipulative about it, she was simply *being* in the world and allowing her natural energy to flow. Walking through town with her was a nightmare! To cover a distance of a few hundred yards you had to allow at least an hour as everyone, perfect strangers as well as friends, seemed to want to talk to her.

Other life-forms emanate a grounding, calming influence.

---

* Sometimes the 'must have' fashion accessories of the modern world, as well as many other things where business and the system are involved, mask what can only be described as a violence and contempt for the people who are its consumers. On 12 June 2001, the *Daily Express* carried an article entitled 'When the Risks Are Hidden, We All Pay the Price'. This revealed that mobile phone companies are now 'quietly' patenting devices to protect phone users from the radiation that can lead to brain cancer. These companies have denied for years that mobile phone usage can cause cancer but, as writer Simon Hinde remarks, why would they bother with radiation-shielding devices (developed at cost) if there was no risk? As the article goes on: 'It also turns out, to nobody's great surprise, that airlines have long been aware that flying economy can kill you (through Deep Vein Thrombosis) . . . airlines have known this, or at least some of it, for ten years or more, and have kept it quiet . . . Then there is the tobacco industry, blithely insisting, in the face of a mountain of contrary facts, that there really is no link between smoking and cancer. The same syndrome affects government. Presented with the evidence of a succession of food crises, from listeria in cheese and pâté to BSE in cattle, ministers' and civil servants' first instinct was to keep the truth from the public. This need to lie, or at any rate, to conceal the unpalatable truth, is deeply ingrained in the culture of bureaucracies'.

This is the case with stones and trees, for example.

If you ever feel charged with energy, as if you might 'float away', which sometimes happens after a powerful healing or in situations of intense stress, it is always helpful to hold a stone in your hand, which has the immediate effect of bringing you 'back down to Earth'.

Trees are also great transformers of energy, including that of human pollution, and it is always restful to sit in the shade of a tree just to relax and allow your cares to be taken away by the embrace and shelter which the tree can offer.

Crystals, meanwhile, in contrast to ordinary stones, have a highly focused energy, like small lasers. This is especially true of quartz, which is always used with caution by shamans. Crystalline structures oscillate at different frequencies and so have different effects on the human energy system, but quartz is, perhaps, the most powerful of all and is even used in modern telecommunications equipment for its ability to harness, amplify, store and transmit energy-based information signals. It is one of the key crystals and should be approached with an air of reverence for its true power.

The following exercise, however, can be attempted by anyone, without fear, as an example of the curative abilities of even 'common' stones, which do not have the price tag of some of the crystals you will find in many new age stores.

EXERCISE: BALANCING YOUR ENERGY WITH STONES

Find yourself a dozen or so flat, round-edged stones, an inch or so in diameter, preferably white (it is always good to have these as part of your shamanic 'toolkit'). Lie flat on the ground on your back and place one of these stones over each chakra point and simply relax (see the chakra chart on p. 184 to remind yourself of where these points are located). After 15 minutes or so just of this, people generally feel far more calm and centred in themselves.

Or, if you need to work on a particular energy centre to help with a current issue in your life, place one stone at the appropriate chakra and hold another two, one in each hand. Spend about 15 minutes again, in relaxed awareness of the energy flowing to the place in your body where it is most needed.

The fact that all human beings have this energy field can lead to all sorts of complications in a city environment where space is at a premium and the concentration of people is high. Just think of the last tube journey you took.

Sociologists, psychologists and writers such as Desmond Morris, in *Manwatching*,[7] tell us of the importance of personal space for the 'territorial' human animal. Morris writes that every one of us is surrounded by an invisible egg-like demarcation space which goes beyond the human body to a distance of two or three feet in each direction (greater or lesser according to our culture and place in the social hierarchy) and that we grow uncomfortable when this is impinged upon.

What these writers are describing is the energy field which surrounds us. In shamanic terms, we are uncomfortable when this space is invaded since all types of energies can become attached to our own when other people's energy bodies enter ours. After a normal commuter trip, it is not unusual to feel dirty, irritable and frustrated after being herded together with hundreds of others, body to body, often for long distances, and this is by no means just 'normal' city grime; it is also due to our absorption of the negative energy of others. Just think back to a time recently when you were in a good mood and met a friend who was on a 'downer' and how your own mood changed, even without any conversation between you. Then amplify this a thousandfold to take account of the train ride home after the end of an average day at work.

One of the problems of modern living is the architecture of the urban environment and the sheer number of people around us.

- 59 million people live in the UK, 10 per cent of these in London alone, and the majority in other cities and conurbations. 274 million live in America, with 30 per cent in the country's cities.

- In India, a new baby is born every two seconds, despite the fact that 320 million people are suffering absolute poverty, and 186 million do not even have access to clean water. Of the 26 million children who will be born this year, 10 per cent will die before the age of one, and another 1.2 million before they reach the age of five.

- The largest city in the world, Mexico City, has 15 million people within its limits and another million in the suburbs. It is also the most polluted place on Earth. It is built on top of a huge underground reservoir, and the entire city is sinking under the weight of its huge population, at the rate of up to eight inches a year.

How can you be expected to retain a 'personal space' around you, or an intact 'energy body', with so many people impinging upon you every day? You do not need the statistics to know that the modern world is a crush and it usually feels bad after any day at work in the city.

One way of coping is to strengthen our energetic boundaries so that, while we may be caught up physically in the crush, we are protected from the energetic intrusions of others. Before we go on to look at techniques of energetic self-protection, here is one simple exercise you can use to build your own personal power so that the energetic grime of the city will have less impact upon you or you can recover from it faster.

Shamans do not believe in 'good' or 'bad' energy, *per se*. Instead, they believe that all ill-health and dis-ease is the effect of energy which is blocked or inappropriate to the system it occupies. The energy itself is just in the wrong place at the wrong time. This exercise, which enables its release back to the universe, is a gift to others who need this energy, so they can benefit from something which is unhelpful to you.

EXERCISE: TREE MEDIATION FOR CALMING AND CENTRING

Find a tree whose energy you feel comfortable with – oak trees work well for many British people since they are part of our cultural heritage and energetically connected to us. The tree may be in a park, a forest, a public garden or even in your own backyard. Sit down with your back to it, connecting physically with the trunk. Stretch out, relax. Bring to mind any problem or concern you are currently dealing with and then see it as a fluid entity, separate from yourself, which now slips from your body into that of the tree, flowing down through the roots or up through the branches, where it is transformed and released into the Earth or the air to a place where that energy can do most good.

Spend 15 minutes or so in this way and then, if you haven't fallen into relaxed sleep, thank the tree for its help with this transformation and return to normal consciousness.

There is a particular shamanic ritual associated with trees, called the Flowering Tree Ceremony, which you may also like to try. I am not certain of the origin of this ritual, but the person who reminded me of it recently had been taught it by Dr Michael Harner and it has a North American feel to it so it may originate with the shamans of North America.

The Flowering Tree Ceremony

Drop your grasping mind [forget the cares of the day and enter a light shamanic state of consciousness]

Seek the tree [find the tree that 'calls' to you, the one you wish to work with]

Give away to the tree [make an offering to the tree – a pinch of tobacco is a traditional gift]

Sit with your spine against the tree

Facing East, ask: 'What must I give away in order to clarify my mind?'

Facing West, ask: 'What must I give away in order to experience and understand my emotions?'

Facing North, ask: 'What must I give away in order to heal my body?'

Facing South, ask: 'What must I give away in order to know and travel my path with heart?'

Now, face the tree, sitting, and ask:
In the South, facing North, 'Who am I?'
In the North, facing South, 'What is my true direction?'
In the West, facing East, 'Where do I come from?'
In the East, facing West, 'Where am I going?'

Give thanks to the tree and know that your questions will be answered.

The alternative or adjunct to energetic revitalization offered by exercises such as the one above is to ensure that you are well protected before you enter the swirl and the crush of the city.

The Wiccan tradition offers an approach to energetic protection based on the visualization of your energy body surrounded by a mirrored substance which simply reflects any negative energy back to its sender.

To use this protective technique, visualize your personal energy field as an impermeable material, through which nothing will penetrate. You must truly *believe* this energy is real, and that this will work. Cast your mind back to the work of the Simontons with cancer patients and Vogel with plants and intention if you have any doubt. This ensures that you cannot be invaded by the excessive energy shrugged off by others. Depending on your mood and your sense of the energy directed towards you, you may then visualize it draining down into the ground where it is dispersed and can be re-used more positively (an *Earth* approach), blowing past you into the wind (an *Air* approach), up into the clouds (*Water*), or you may even choose to direct the energy back at the sender with equal or intensified force (a *Fire* approach). Whatever you choose, *know* that you are protected by your actions.

To add focus to your intentions, use whatever form of words aids you as a mantra or 'spell' to direct the energy you are dealing with.

The use of techniques and words of power such as these are known to shamans worldwide. In the shamanic communities of Peru, *arkana* ('defences') may often be given to a patient by the healer in the form of a song, like the one which the shaman Don Basilio sang over author Luis Eduardo Luna before he embarked upon a visionary ayahuasca journey in the rainforests of the Amazon.

'Arkana, probably from Quechua *arkay* (to block, to bar), indicates something that protects the individual so that no evil penetrates him,' writes Luna. 'It may be an animal spirit, a power song [*icaro*], or an invisible garment or armour [similar to the 'shield' we looked at above]. Lamista Indians explain this term as a 'seal' that prevents any penetration: they refer to *cuerpo selado* (sealed body), which is better than *cuerpo preparado* (prepared body) [presumably, since a prepared body implies a readiness for, or perhaps, expectation of, attack, rather than an encompassing seal which prevents any misuse of power against the person].[8]

In Peru, I had the opportunity to undergo just such a ritual of cleansing and protection with don Eduardo Guervera, a powerful shaman who lives and works just outside of Cusco, a beautiful and spiritual little town which is known in Peru as 'the navel of the world'.

I had managed to get myself into a disagreement some months earlier with an American Vodou practitioner whom I thought aggressive and arrogant. He felt the same about me. It had led to quite an argument before we finally parted company. The next day, I found blisters and raw red patches on my body. Such an occurrence is pretty typical in Vodou and represents a battle for power among differing houngans, so I suspected, not unreasonably, that my adversary had used a *wanga* to attack me. A wanga is a blast of 'negative' energy, if you like, which the houngan would define as a harmful intrusion into the energy body of the victim, and is sent as the result of a special magical ritual. The outcome was the blisters now affecting me.

I am usually pretty well protected myself so, while they looked ugly, the blisters I was carrying didn't cause me too much discomfort apart from some tenderness and itching. And so, busy with other things, I had simply ignored them and decided to extract the poison later but, being in Peru and close to so many powerful healers, I decided to visit don Eduardo instead. It was a good job I did.

'It is very grave,' said don Eduardo, 'and is affecting your energy body, spreading to your physical body, and will change your luck [your interaction with all things around you] for the worse unless it is immediately removed.'

Don Eduardo's healing ritual began with what felt like a reiki session as he sensed the energy of the spirit intrusion now within my body to diagnose its strength and effects. He then placed coca leaves, a sacred herb of the area, on my forehead and asked me to focus on the blessings I wanted to enter my life – 'without an atom of doubt,' he said.

As I stood with my eyes closed, calling in my intention, don Eduardo mixed herbs, seeds and ground crab shell together in a paper sachet he had created and infused with magical symbols. He then took the coca leaves from me and added them to the bundle, which he rubbed over my body in order to draw out and absorb the poison he had seen in me.

Standing before his *mesa*, his altar, he then called upon the saints and the Virgin and the local gods and spirits of the area to take away this unwanted energy, and placed the bundle in the flame of a candle standing there. The bundle exploded and burned up completely and immediately as don Eduardo continued with his prayers and invocations.

Next he began the blessing of a talisman, a Mayan cross, which he placed around my neck as a protective shield against further magic. 'You must never remove this – ever,' he said, before giving me further instructions for its charging and empowerment back in the UK.

Don Eduardo is an extremely accomplished healer and, needless to say, as soon as I returned to the UK, the blessings I had asked for began to materialize immediately. I was offered a completely new position at work which meant I never had to go into the building again even though my consultancy services were retained at more than full pay, which was exactly what I had had in mind for some considerable time. A woman I had admired for a while, but had not got round to asking out, contacted me out of the blue and asked me very directly if I would like to start a relationship with her. And the possibility of a TV documentary series which I had been working on for a few months and which seemed to have gone pretty quiet reactivated itself and became a definite offer of work.

Meanwhile, my old Vodou adversary had got himself into a whole heap of trouble through his continuing arrogance and had managed to upset a number of powerful houngans who were all now working together to 'teach him a lesson'.

A somewhat different, but surprisingly very similar, approach to personal protection is taken by the shamans of Tuva, close to Siberia, and about as far away as one can get from Peru in terms of culture and society. Here, as well as the use of power songs (called *algysh*), blessings are also frequently used in order to cleanse and purify the spirit and prevent the likelihood of attack, in a similar way to the *cuerpo selado* or the talisman prepared by don Eduardo. Instead of defending against spiritual or energetic intrusions, this is a pre-emptive action to ensure physical and spiritual strength and good fortune in life.

Here is the beautiful *algysh* of a shaman offering blessings for his children:

> *With golden hair you are my children.*
> *Let your mountain pass to cross over be low,*
> *Let your horses be fast,*
> *Let your food be satisfying.*

You are beautiful, my children.
Let your river crossing be shallow,
Let your path be fulfilled,
Let your happiness be complete.

My abundant children.
Let them sing their charming songs,
Let them carry out their tasks,
Let them have friends to be together with.[9]

Different again – and again, very similar – is the blessing offered by the Pueblo Indians of America:

Hold on to what is good
Even if it is a handful of earth.
Hold on to what you believe
Even if it is a tree that stands by itself.

Hold on to what you must do
Even if it is a long way from here.

Hold on to life
Even if it is easier to let go.

Hold on to my hand
Even if I have gone away from you.[10]

Blessings like these, talismans and energetic shields, all act as a focus for us: they remind us of our power and reassure us that we are protected and cared for. The power of belief may be all it takes for these symbols to work. Modern science is telling us so, and we look at some of the evidence later in this book.

The shaman's body
For don Juan, it is the energy body which gives us our awareness, pure and simple, along with our true ability to protect ourselves from others and to bend them to our own will – and

many other capabilities we normally take for granted as powers of the physical body.

In fact, the physical body (which is itself an energy form, our atomic structure being composed mainly of energetic space rather than solid material), particularly following socialization into Western culture, which is fixated on the material in all its forms, could really be just a robot going through the motions of living on automatic. There is very little that we actually need to pay real attention to – we even drive our cars on automatic pilot because the vast potential of our brains means that we do not have to be constantly alert to all that surrounds us. But if we were, we would have the power of gods compared to most people who simply go through the motions of living.

In the terminology of don Juan, the right side of the energy body – the luminous egg that we are a part of and that surrounds us – is where we fix most of our attention, typically a tiny percentage of our total selves, while the left side remains a vast untapped reservoir of potential.

Since the left side of our brains, the domain of intuition, psychic ability, natural healing powers, creativity and transpersonal experience, controls the right side of our physical bodies, perhaps it is not taking too much of a liberty with don Juan's description to say that one implication of getting more in touch with our energetic selves is that we have far more control over these intuitive abilities, with quite remarkable results, because we broaden our influence over the entirety of this luminous field.

An an example of this, *Positive Health* magazine carried a report recently of a scientific study into the power of reiki healing, the channelling of cosmic energy by one person in order to focus on and heal the physical illness of another through changes to their energetic field.[11]

In this experiment, one group was given healing by properly trained reiki healers, while another was healed by 'placebo' healers who had no training whatsoever in these techniques. The results for both groups were the same, and both positive: a demonstrable increase in health and well-being.

The implications of this study are twofold:

1. That the *intention* of the healer to help the patient is paramount, whether the healer is professionally trained or not. They must want and intend to help. In other words, *all people*, not just those 'officially' recognized as healers, have the power to heal others and themselves.
2. Secondly, none of the people healed were aware of who their healer was or their 'qualifications' or otherwise, yet all healed equally. The most critical factor was their own simple *belief* that they *would* be helped by the healer, as has also been demonstrated by numerous other placebo studies where 'reality' follows belief.

While I do not in any way wish to detract from the benefits offered by, and obvious power of, many very capable reiki healers, I do rejoice in the findings of research such as this. When I trained in reiki, I heard stories of people being charged $10,000 or more for their Master's qualification when, quite plainly, the most important factor in all healing, Western as well as shamanic, is the simple *faith* – of both patient and healer – that it *will* work (we look at some of the evidence for this a little later in this book). We need more healers, and a $10,000 fee is a sure way not to get them.

Cheyenne Maloney is a shamanic practitioner in Colorado, who works extensively with the energy body in order to realign the flow of energy in her patients and help them to overcome illness and dis-ease. She has been a student of shamanism for thirty-four years, following primarily a Toltec path, a healing tradition descended from the ancient Aztec and Mayan cultures. She works alone and also with a healing partner, Kathleen Bowman. While Cheyenne is primarily involved with adjustments within the energetic field of her patients, Kathleen is a powerful reiki healer who provides a strong anchor for the energies they work with.

Cheyenne works primarily with adjustments to the Assemblage Point, the bright vortex of energy which sits high in the cocoon of energy that surrounds the human body, and which determines our perceptions of the world and 'assemblage' of reality.

'A misalignment of the Assemblage Point will result in a range of energetic imbalances reflective of our physical, emotional, and mental health, the energy levels of major vortexes within the energy body – the chakra system – and the immune responses of the respective glands and organs with which they are associated,' says Cheyenne. 'At some point in our lives, every one of us will experience either accident, trauma, illness, drug addiction, depression, grief, pain or loss. Each of us will experience such things as an internal change in one form or another, often as a shift of perspective which may be experienced as an inability to return to our former lives. All of this is reflected by a deep shift in the position of the Assemblage Point, which leads to a new orientation in our lives and in our health. By realigning the Assemblage Point, these adverse effects may themselves be altered and the dis-ease thereby cured or eased. A proper adjustment of the Assemblage Point opens new doors of healing, perception, and empowers individuals with vitality, passion, self-healing ability, fulfilment and joy.'

In other words, and put very crudely, the way we perceive ourselves and the world around us affects our health and our well-being directly. If we can change the way we see and think of things, we can change our reality and heal our lives.

Cheyenne notes a number of quite remarkable successes among the people she works with (including sufferers of serious medical diseases such as hepatitis C, fibromyalgia, multiple sclerosis, cancers and AIDS), 'merely' as a result of working with the energy body to 'remould' it into a more positive and productive form – successes which have been borne out by clinical results.

Nancy, for instance, was diagnosed with hepatitis C over a year before she came for shamanic healing, and was exhausted and apathetic when she first began treatment with Cheyenne. Her Assemblage Point had slipped low into her solar plexus, and the hepatitis C seemed to have control of her life force. She had gained weight, which contributed further to her low energy level. She was unmotivated and struggling with her life.

Her first healing session involved basic shamanic soul retrieval (a technique where the shaman retrieves part of our energy-selves, or soul, which have been lost through trauma of some kind). This helped Nancy to restore some of her vitality and power for living.

In the next session, Cheyenne introduced spirit extraction work (a healing practice where the shaman powerfully visualizes the 'spirit' of the illness as a living entity and can then negotiate with it for its removal). In Nancy's case, the hepatitis C appeared as a large black snake wrapped around her ribcage, heart and neck.

Five months after her healing began, Nancy visited her doctor for her next series of blood tests. The results of those tests, in her own words, were 'Great news'. Her doctor had confirmed that 'my viral levels are undetectable'. She had started with a level of 1.2 million. The other good news for Nancy was that, during the course of her work with Cheyenne, she had been able, quite effortlessly, to lose 45 pounds in weight, which was a further boost to her energy level, as well as her self-confidence.

Another of Cheyenne's clients, Kristin, was diagnosed two years ago with fibromyalgia. At her first healing session she was in extreme pain and unable to sleep. She was also very thin, had not been able to eat much for two years and was having very difficult bowel movements.

The first session for Kristin was a soul retrieval similar to Nancy's, while the second was an extensive spirit extraction from her abdomen and solar plexus regions. Her Assemblage Point was adjusted to a position which would promote good health.

In the days immediately following this work Kristin became suddenly pain-free, with all abdominal pain ceasing after years of suffering. She also regained her appetite and was able to eat again. She had been unable to work for a long time, but now she obtained employment. Within a week, Kristin was gaining weight. She was eating freely, had been working every day and sleeping through the night. 'These results have held for the last few months,' says Cheyenne. 'What seemed at first like a hopeless situation has been reversed . . . Witnessing the healing of Kristin was like watching a miracle. She is a new person.'

Finally, there was Kalindra, a client who had discovered a golf-ball-sized mass in her right breast. She was alarmed and in subsequent days noticed that it changed form. It seemed very active, and she had put off a diagnosis out of fear of what she might be told. She stated categorically that she felt 'an inner knowing' that the mass was malignant.

Cheyenne and her partner, Kathleen Bowman, completed a large extraction of quite dark energetics which seemed to be a fully intact life-form, somewhat demonic. The energy was entrenched in Kalindra's hip bones with an extremely deep attachment at the underside of her right ribcage. The work was extensive, and, during it, Kalindra also spontaneously received a series of what seemed to be past life images, which indicated that she was once a warrior who had her right breast – the side of her current tumour – deliberately removed to facilitate archery.

'After the extraction, she felt filled with golden light and was very still for some time, crying while in touch with this light,' says Cheyenne. 'It was apparent that the mass was dissolving. When it came apart, it turned to liquid and melted throughout her body.'

Kalindra made an appointment with her doctor a few days later, but both a mammogram and a scan showed no sign at all of the breast mass which had been there for several months, and there has been no return of this mass.

As remarkable as these successes with the healing potential of the energy body seem, there is even more to the energy body than this, and things to be aware of, protect against, and powers to be discovered and applied. We will look at some of these in the next chapter when we consider soul retrieval and spiritual extraction, two of the shamanic techniques which Cheyenne uses so effectively. For now, perhaps we can just accept that a human being is not flesh and blood alone, but far more than this, with almost infinite possibilities for healing and empowerment at a deep energetic level. For me, one of the easiest ways to explain the potential of the energy body at this 'physical' level is to say that we are 'split' as human beings, between 'natural flow' and 'limitation', 'power' and 'disempowerment', or to say that we have two minds, which are the switches between true potential and socially or personally imposed limitation.

By 'two minds', I am not referring to the conscious and unconscious minds of Freud, Jung, and the other psychoanalysts. Rather, I conceive of the mind as a building with two rooms. One of these contains our socialized and limited selves; the side of us that is the child of the system. In this room reside both the conscious *and* unconscious aspects of our physical and mental beings. The unconscious also belongs in this room since it operates primarily in symbols, and we have been taught the meaning of these symbols by the system we live in. We can even buy books which will 'interpret' our dreams for us and tell us what all our symbols mean. According to these we do not even have an inner life of our own but follow a defined pattern of unconscious reality whoever we are and whatever our own unique experiences.

Certainly, there is a deeper knowledge available to us in the unconscious and a greater wisdom at play, but it is still knowledge within the framework of the world that we occupy. By the same token, whenever unconscious knowledge is made available to the conscious mind, it is filtered through the channel of language, a way of relating to the world which is extremely socialized (think back to the example of smoking and prayer which I used in the Introduction, where the phraseology of the question alone produced different responses).

Martin Prechtel makes the point beautifully in his wonderful book, *Secrets of the Talking Jaguar*,[12] when he tells us that in the Mayan language there is no real term for behaviour which relies on a future. For example, every time a person leaves home, she is not going out into the unknown but is already beginning the journey home again. As a result of their language alone, the Mayan people are much better able to Be Here Now, to be in touch with their joys and their pains, to fully experience life in the moment than we in the West will ever be, who are so fixated on the *analysis* rather than the *experience* of our current state, and far more concerned with racing into the future than being in the moment, and with a language of symbols that so well reflects this pre-occupation.

The second room we may enter contains our 'deep consciousness', which is a state beyond conscious and even *un*conscious awareness. This is the domain of spirit and of the emotions.

We can represent these rooms diagrammatically:

Content	1st mind: Room 1	2nd mind: Room 2
Connection to the universe is through . . .	The conscious and unconscious	The deep consciousness
Scope	Limited powers	Infinite powers
Aspects contained	Physical Mental	Spiritual Emotional
Orientation	Influenced by, and responsive to, social conditioning and imposed reality	Unavailable to conditioning. Learning is through self-exploration and self-awareness
Nature	'Rational'-ized and analytical	Energetic
Activity	Social and personal	Spiritual and infinite
Outlook	'I don't *think* I can do it'	'I *am* doing it'

In the first room are our human powers which can be moulded and curtailed most easily by the social conditioning of our worldview and, through this, by the view we come to have of ourselves.

An average child, told she is clever or beautiful, for example, will develop cognitively much faster, and act more beautifully (and therefore *become* more beautiful). The same child, told she is ugly and stupid, will also come to act that way.

Many years ago, I trained as a teacher and worked as a volunteer in the summer holidays, offering 'top-up' tuition for children from deprived backgrounds. One day, after setting the class some work to do, I noticed that one little girl had not even attempted the assignment, so I went over and sat with her for a while, and asked why she was not working. She looked up at me with eyes full of sadness and resignation. 'Because my mommy says I'm stupid and I can't do this,' she said. She had taken her mother's judgement of her as an *instruction* on how to behave and had filed this away in the first room of the mind along with all other limiting beliefs – which is what we all do since these aspects of ourselves are more open to influence from others; they have to be since our capacity to learn and to follow the instructions necessary for our own survival are also housed therein.

No-one was more amazed than this little girl when, after gentle coaching, she found that she *was* able to do the exercise I had set. It was as if her whole world had changed – which it had, of course – and a new doorway opened into the second room of her personal and infinite potential. I often wonder what happened to this little girl – because now she knew her mother was not god and that she, herself, had power over her own life. Such experiences *do* change us.

The powers we keep in the second chamber of the mind are far less available to influence from others since these are the things which, by and large, the system has no definitions for, does not understand, or does not see as important enough to bother with. These spiritual and emotional qualities therefore provide our primary escape routes from the dictates and definitions of an imposed worldview, and enable us to free our whole selves since the energy which comprises them is the same energy our limited selves also draw upon. By enhancing our spiritual or emotional powers we also boost our physical and mental powers, no matter what we have been *told* about the limits of our capabilities.

A good example of this is the mother who witnesses her child involved in an accident and lying trapped beneath the body of a car, who is able to rush forward and lift the car with her bare hands in order to free her child. Normally, of course, this would be impossible, well beyond her physical strength. But this mother is not using *physical* strength; she is lifting the car with the strength of her *emotions*, a power which is less affected by society's definitions of limitation and in that instant of anguish she breaks the barriers of social control so that she can reach her child.

Many people who experience a rush of power like this subsequently have a limited memory of their actions. It is as if they have been in trance during this time and, indeed, they have. We have an innate capability, it seems, to switch into a shamanic state of consciousness and to enter trance whenever we need to, and without the need to try, as if shamanic consciousness is a totally natural experience for all of us.

My friend, John, told me a story about a friend of his, called 'Manny', which illustrates this instant switching between states of awareness in life-and-death situations. Manny was a naval officer who served on a battleship during the Gulf War. Life on board ship was a strange mixture of brief bursts of action and long stretches of inactivity as the men waited for new orders to come through. During these latter periods, everyone would stave off boredom and keep themselves fit by lifting weights which they fashioned from the empty casements of unarmed torpedo shells. Each one weighed well in excess of 100 pounds and it became a contest between the men to see who could complete the most lifts.

Except for Manny, who could never even raise the casement off the deck. Although he kept trying, he failed miserably each time, and it became quite a joke among the men.

Then, one day, the call came for action and the men found themselves in the middle of a fierce sea battle. Suddenly they were under fire and they watched in horror as a torpedo from an enemy destroyer began winding its way towards them through the waters, on target for a direct hit.

At the last moment, through some fluke, the torpedo hit a wave as it sped towards their ship and, like a stone thrown from a beach, skipped off the top of the wave and bounced onto the deck among the men. Seeing the live shell among them, Manny rushed forward without even thinking, picked it up, then ran to the side and tossed it back into the sea, like someone throwing out the trash. His colleagues watched in amazement. Here was a man who couldn't even lift an empty shell casing, yet he had saved them all by lifting a live torpedo which probably weighed ten times as much as any casing.

But, of course, Manny wasn't relying on his physical strength this time – which he 'knew' was limited – he was acting from the power of pure emotion.

He then walked back to his colleagues in a trance, not really aware of what he had done and with no understanding of how.

There are many ways in which we can open the doorway into the second chamber of the mind and walk away from our own limitations. Dreams are one way of accessing this other world of potential. We all dream – in fact, we spend an average of ten whole years of our lives doing so – but many of us choose to ignore or make light of these messages from our deeper selves. In so doing, we waste a decade of our lives.

Yet, according to Dr Mark Solms of the Department of Neurosurgery, Royal London Hospital, dreams

tell us about our inner life in a unique way. The sleeping brain only has access to the parts of the brain that deal with emotions, personal memories, motivations and vision. The visual part acts like a cinema screen where the dreams are played out, while the emotional compartment, along with our personal history and the motivational part, work together to show us what is going on in our lives and how we feel about it. The rational or logical part of the brain is not working when we dream, so memories and emotions are completely uncensored.[13]

In other words, dreams are a highly focused means of accessing the 'deep unconscious' parts of our selves. Their messages may be in symbols or even 'code', but their wisdom is no less important to us. They have the ability to cut directly to the real heart of the issue and to bypass the analysis and rationalization which confuse or diminish the experience in waking life.

As an example of this, Dr Robin Royston, a psychoanalyst at Ticehurst House in Sussex, describes a dream reported to him by one of his clients who saw himself as being attacked by black panthers. 'At the climactic moment, one of the panthers jumped on him and he felt a sharp pain when its claw dug into his back. A month later, the man's wife noticed a new and unusual mole in the same spot, which tests showed to be a malignant melanoma – a very dangerous form of skin cancer – which he was able to have treated.'[14]

Dr Royston's view, based on evidence like this, is that our immune system (and perhaps other 'component parts' of the body), which knows about the state of our health and any problems beginning to emerge within it before we become consciously aware of them, can communicate this information to our conscious selves via the mechanism of dreams – which is not so different a theory from the shaman's belief that we have many souls within our body, each of them separate and aware, and each of them part of the whole.

'Predictive dreams about illnesses are typically acted out as a charade which only becomes obvious when disease has been diagnosed,' says Dr Royston.

Another way into the 'deep unconscious' parts of ourselves is through exercise and body movement. Martial artists, yoga students, dancers and athletes notice that strenuous physical activity often gives rise to a new sense of spiritual clarity and emotional stillness. They call it 'being in the zone', and it brings with it all sorts of benefits of bodily and spiritual integration which have led to more than a few gold medals over the years.

The spiritual practices of journeying and meditation can also help us to heal our mental and physical problems as well as developing spiritually and emotionally, as we will see in the next chapter. In all cases, we are allowing ourselves to become more fully in touch with the integrated power of our whole energy bodies, and the results speak for themselves. Here is a short exercise you can try to test the validity of this proposition for yourself.

EXERCISE: LIFTING FREE OF LIMITATIONS

There is a training exercise used in a number of martial arts traditions, called 'unbendable arm', which illustrates the difference between the use of strength (the physical body) and intention (the spiritual or emotional body) to achieve the objectives we set.

You will need to work with a friend on this.

Place your arm, as straight as you can keep it, on your friend's shoulder so that your forearm rests there, just below the elbow. Now ask your friend to bring her hands together in the crook of your arm and to press down on it in order to make you bend your arm. Use your physical strength to resist and notice how it feels and how long it takes before your arm is compelled to bend.

Now try again but, this time, forget about using strength and simply imagine instead that you are reaching for something behind your friend's head and that you are really stretching for this object or thing which is vitally important to you. Relax completely and allow that image to flood your mind so you really feel it.

Now have your friend apply pressure to your arm again and try to make you bend it. Notice how it feels to you this time and when – and *if* – your arm now bends.

Most people notice a considerable difference. Not only

is it easier the second time to maintain a straight arm but you may also find that you can keep your arm straight for longer or, indeed, that your friend is unable to bend it at all, no matter how hard she tries.

This is the power of the will, the non-rational mind, and the energy body, which is mobilized through your intention.

2. THE MYSTICAL POWER OF THE SECOND ATTENTION

When we shift our awareness and our energy more to the left of our bodies, our Assemblage Point moves, says Castaneda, enabling us to reconstruct the world around us in a different form. The result is that we become more whole and our powers begin to flow more readily throughout our entire system, leading to a greater integration of these powers and potential.

Scientific research using biofeedback techniques broadly supports this claim. Where people have been trained in laboratories to focus their attention in specific directions and to alter their brain wave patterns so that these become more fully integrated, quite incredible results of physical and mental control have been achieved.

In *Beyond Biofeedback*, Elmer and Alyce Green report that these techniques have shown that everyone is capable of controlling their body very precisely, including the 'automatic' survival functions of heart rate, temperature and respiration.[15] One of their experimental subjects, Jack Schwartz, was even able to withstand intense physical tortures such as burning and stabbing, without any sensation of pain – and, more interestingly, without any apparent injury – simply by controlling his brain waves to alter his sense of these experiences.

On a more positive and practical note, the Greens were also able to help migraine sufferers overcome their pain by physically altering the flow of blood around their bodies in order to deal with their discomfort. The Greens noticed that when sufferers experienced head pain, it always corresponded with a drop in temperature in their hands by as much as 20 degrees (subsequently medical science has discovered, but not yet explained, that during a migraine attack the blood vessels in the head dilate, while those in the hands contract, which would account for the cold sensation in the hands). The Greens used this fact, almost in the like-for-like approach of traditional magic, teaching people to control the blood flow in their hands, which had the effect of drawing blood away from the brain and relieving the head pressure. The result was fewer headaches for as many as two-thirds of subjects.

Just as interestingly, those who failed to control their pain, the Greens discovered, were either 'sceptical of the training, suspicious . . . or very self-determined'. They either wanted to prove that the technique was ineffective – again, paradoxically, an example in itself of the mind's power, since this act of will also worked! – or were simply trying too hard and were unable to relax sufficiently for the process to work.

What was important, said the Greens, was a *casual* intention to warm their hands and thereby redirect the blood flow from their heads – along with *faith* that the technique would work. This combination enabled their subjects to develop more effective alpha rhythms in their brains, which are associated with mental relaxation and the spread of energy throughout the system (and also, incidentally, with the trance state achieved by the shaman during the out-of-body experience of journeying); from there they could achieve the desired results.

'Most civilised people are so tensed up that they cannot go into alpha rhythm states for more than a few seconds at a time,' says Colin Wilson, before 'some anxiety "starts up the engine".' However, 'biofeedback research has shown that nearly all diseases are "psychosomatic" – caused by either "stress" or the body's failure to deal with the illness because the mind is not co-operating. There has even been startlingly successful cancer treatment by persuading the patient to mobilise his forces, often by a kind of visualization.'[16]

In the West, we are trained only to use and pay attention to the more rational side of our brains and, fairly obviously, are most of the time running at only 50 per cent of our true capacity at best. When both the right and left sides of the brain are used together, however, biofeedback demonstrates that we have quite remarkable powers at our disposal. In some cases, this has even suggested natural and innate powers of telepathy, precognition and distance healing. Cleve Backster, inspired by the work of Dr Marcel Vogel – whom we met earlier in our discussion of the curative energies of plants – conducted an experiment in London in 1974 where an Indian healer, Tommy Wadkins, was successful in sending healing energy across the Atlantic to a glaucoma patient meditating there. Details of the full experiment can be found in Tompkins and Bird's *The Secret Life of Plants*.[17]

The shaman and the houngan are concerned not just with the increased physical and mental powers resulting from this energetic shift, but with the transpersonal capabilities which also result. By going beyond the material body into the world of pure energy, they are able both to enter the energy fields of others, human and otherwise, and to communicate with and through non-physical beings and spirit entities.

A number of recent research reports demonstrate that it is not just advanced spiritual practitioners who have this power – we all do.

In one intriguing study, Dr Mitch Krucoff of Duke University Medical Center, North Carolina, decided to see what would happen when he asked religious congregations to pray for a sample of people undergoing heart surgery. He divided his sample of 150 patients into groups of 30, one group of which had their names forwarded to religious organizations around the world where worshippers agreed to pray for them. Patients' names were sent to Buddhist monasteries in France and Nepal, to a Carmelite nunnery in Baltimore, to the Wailing Wall in Jerusalem, and to American congregations of Moravians, Baptists, Unitarians and Christians. All patients were monitored during invasive surgery, which took place during the time of prayer.

The research team, which collected data on patient blood pressure and heart rate during the procedure and during their subsequent stay in hospital, found that those people who had prayers said for them did 50–100 per cent better than those who were not prayed for in terms of general levels of health and faster recovery times. A second group, who had been treated with relaxation techniques and taught to use visualization and guided imagery, did 30–50 per cent better than those who did not use these techniques. Those who received standard medical treatment did worst of all.[18]

Prayer, the expression of blessing through the transmission of energy to another person, was shown to work as a form of spiritual healing, and it did not take a shaman or a houngan to perform this, simply the action of a person with genuine compassion for another entering the energetic space between them through the power of intention to heal. In this sense, *faith* rather than medicine was the key to a healthier future and a faster recovery from illness.

The power and the energy of faith can also be used for self-healing, according to a study by Dr Harold Koeing reported in the *International Journal of Psychiatry in Medicine*, which found that blood pressure was 40 per cent lower among people who attended a religious service at least once a week and who prayed each day.[19] The study, which followed 4,000 Americans aged 65 for a six-year period, noted that 'this was a large and clinically significant difference' to the rest of the American population, one third of whom suffer high blood pressure.

A second study by Koeing found that open-heart surgery patients who had a strong faith which they had called upon during their clinical treatment had a mortality rate one third lower than those who did not. His findings, from a sample of more than 1,700 patients, support those of a thirty-year study of 5,000 people by the Human Population Laboratory at the University of California, which show that people with strong faith have a 25–30 per cent lower mortality rate *from all causes* than those without.

The *American Journal of Psychiatry* also reported findings by another university research team which show that faith can conquer depression and its symptoms. The team studied the emotional well-being of just under 100 people for around a year. All of them were over the age of 60 and had a strong faith, but had been diagnosed as suffering from depression following a stay in hospital.[20]

During the course of the study, 54 per cent recovered from their depression and, the stronger their faith, the faster they recovered. Using a scoring technique based on a questionnaire developed by Christian and Jewish religious authorities, the researchers showed that recovery from depression takes place 70 per cent faster for every 10-point increase in the depth of the patient's religious belief. Church attendance had nothing to do with this. Rather, it was a 'sense of hope that things will turn out all right regardless of their problems' which was the key to recovery, a sort of pure faith where 'beliefs may bring comfort and facilitate coping'.

So much evidence about the positive power of faith and spiritual belief has now been accumulated that *Time* magazine ran a feature on the whole subject in its issue of 24 June 1996.[21] Highlights from their report include:

- A study of 20 severely ill AIDS patients, by Dr Elizabeth Targ of California Pacific Medical Center in San Francisco, who split the group equally and arranged for half of them to be prayed for. She described the results as so 'encouraging' that she was proceeding to a follow-up study with 100 patients.
- A 1995 study from Dartmouth-Hitchcock Medical Center in California which found that faith was the strongest predictor of survival among 232 heart surgery patients, who had a three times better recovery rate than non-believers. Those with strong faith and who also took part in religious social events had a fourteen-fold advantage over those who lacked faith or were not committed to it.

213

- A thirty-year study which proves that religious believers have significantly lower blood pressure than others, even when adjusted for smoking and other risk factors.
- A 1996 National Institute of Aging study of 4,000 people in North Carolina which showed that those attending religious services are physically and mentally healthier than others.

Many researchers believe that religious experiences and faith have a neuro-anatomical basis similar to that of the placebo effect, say the *Time* reporters. 'Decades of research show that if a patient truly believes a therapy is useful – even if it is a sugar pill or snake oil – that belief has the power to heal. In one classic 1950 study, for instance, pregnant women suffering from severe morning sickness were given syrup of ipecac, which induces vomiting, and told it was a powerful new cure for nausea. Amazingly, the women ceased vomiting.'

Most people now do believe that prayer itself can have a highly positive effect on their health. A 1996 *Time*/CNN poll of 1,004 Americans found that 82 per cent believed in the healing power of prayer, and 64 per cent thought doctors should pray with their patients on request. Moreover, even our conservative medical educational institutions are now recognizing these effects. A study by Stanford University's Dr Wallace Sampson of every American medical school shows that many are now introducing courses on holistic medicine, with titles like Caring for the Soul. 'The majority, 10 to 1, present the material uncritically,' he says.[22]

What studies like these show is that when we move beyond the prescribed limitations of the mind and body and into the energetic realm of the possible, 'miracles' can become everyday occurrences as long as we retain our belief in them.

It is this sense of belief focused on a definite outcome or purpose – what shamans call *intention* – which anchors us in the realm of the second attention and makes miracles happen by enabling our energy to work for us.

The voyage beyond the body

For the practitioner of Vodou, the chief expression of faith is spirit possession where she literally gives over her body to another energetic force, so that her energy body is entered and controlled for the duration of her trance. The spirit entity which activates her is then able to bring the energy of the gods into the material plane.

As Priestess Miriam of the New Orleans Voodoo Spiritual Temple puts its: 'Voodoo is a religion of the universe. The way it works is through the energies and intelligence which are directed and manifested of ourselves and our universe.' We are equal partners with the spirits in enabling and allowing these intelligences to work through us. Or, if you prefer, we are all of us innately and powerfully able to manipulate the energies of the universe, since we are all part of them. Our heightened sensitivities and awareness during spirit possession and trance, and the faith which goes with them, makes natural telepaths and healers of us all.

In Haiti, this partnership with spirit is made very clear in the healings which take place during spirit possession. Just outside of Jacmel, I watched Houngan Yabofe treat an elderly man who was convinced that he was the subject of malevolent spiritual attack from a *bokor*, a malign sorcerer, and had become ill and depressed as a consequence.

Yabofe's first action was to call one of his partner spirits, Gran Bwa, the great healer and loa of nature and the woods, and to allow this entity to possess his physical body. Gran Bwa then set to work to heal the patient. He sat the man down and began to rub his body with live chickens, one in each hand, which would absorb the negativity that had been injected into the energy body of his elderly visitor, just as don Eduardo in Peru had used seeds and shells to do the same job for me. Later, the chickens would be sacrificed in order to release this energy, as don Eduardo had burned the packets of seeds he had used. Normally, animal sacrifices contain a practical component as the meat is eaten by the people of the congregation, their life force only being offered to the gods,

215

but in a healing such as this they are considered 'contaminated' and must be ritually disposed of. Gran Bwa then went on to prescribe healing baths and herbal tonics before returning Yabofe to his body.

In another healing, the *eggun* (personal spirit) of a Palo priest worked with a woman suffering a machete cut to her hand. Having spontaneously possessed his human host, the spirit called for an orange, cornmeal and white cloth, and proceeded to rub first the juice of the orange and then the cornmeal into the wound before binding it. The next day the patient, who before could not bend her thumb and thought she had severed the tendon, was able to move the thumb and reported that it did indeed feel better.

Interestingly, this spirit had only been working with the priest for a few months and was considered to be on a 'probationary year'. As soon as he returned to his body, the priest asked immediately that his patient monitor the condition of her hand and tell him if the healing proved ineffective since, if the spirit could not heal, it would be considered a braggart and of limited value, and so returned to the spirit world as part of a ritual 'exorcism' of sorts.

The shaman's partnership with the spirits, however, is not expressed through possession, but as a journey out of the body, to meet with the spirits in their own domain. In some shamanic cultures and, very often, in the core shamanic practice adopted by the West, it is common to adopt a particular bodily position in order to deepen the trance state that is required for journeying. Dr Felicitas Goodman has argued convincingly that these trance positions work by opening particular neurological pathways in the body and thereby facilitating the shaman's entry to specific places with the energetic matrix of the universe. The Jivaro posture is thought to be especially useful for journeys to the lower world of the shaman's cosmology. The position, described in Harner's book, *The Way of the Shaman*,[23] is to lie on the back, legs straight out and feet slightly apart, while the left arm covers the eyes and the right arm, fingers outstretched, remains at the side, exactly as we have been doing in this book.

In other cultures, however, Haiti included, this immobility is anathema. Christiana Harle-Silvennoinen says of her experiences among the Tuvan people, 'rarely did I observe Shamans just standing or sitting and beating their drum. Song and movement were actively and equally involved in the Tuvan Shamanic ritual . . . Prior to this I thought I could only sit, stand or lie during the journey even though I felt to do otherwise. It has taken me several years to figure out why I thought this . . . I had to trust that those feelings of moving, of singing and what I heard and saw, moving as I did during the journey were correct.'[24] The solution is to trust your spirits and your instincts, so from now on continue to use the Jivaro position if you like, or simply move or lie in whatever posture feels most appropriate to you.

The typical shamanic journey in the West takes around 20 minutes, but this fixation on time can be misleading. In the otherworld of non-ordinary reality, the passing of time as we are used to it has little meaning and so the shaman may actually be away for years in non-ordinary reality while only minutes have passed for us – like the experience predicted for deep space astronauts where the journey may last a few months for them while, due to the peculiarities of time and space, centuries may have passed on Earth.

Almost always, the shamanic journey is conducted to the sound of the drum or rattle, whose hypnotic beat deepens the level of trance and acts as a channel for the spirit, just as it does for the congregations of Haiti where the drummers call to particular spirits according to a precise drum rhythm which is a summons only for them.

Scientists have discovered that the rhythmic beat of the drum – at 220 beats per minute – acts as a stimulant for the release of certain neurochemicals in the brain, which activate the areas responsible for dreaming and for visions. Very recent research from California has also determined that the very experience of group drumming and of the rhythms produced can, in itself, be healing, helping patients to combat serious illness such as cancer simply through the effect of the drum on the body.

The shamanic journey is always a mission, an action of purpose, and a clear and unambiguous statement of intention at the outset is vital for guiding the shaman on his voyage. It is this which acts as a signal to the spirits who can best serve him on his journey and which ensures that he reaches the appropriate destination in an entire universe of infinite possibilities.

During his time away in the otherworld, the shaman will meet with sentient energy forms, perceived as spirit allies, which may take a variety of forms and appearances. All will offer insights and information into the problem he is working with but the shaman remains the final arbiter on this advice and will choose whether to accept it – the spirits offer help, not prescriptions – though often it is wise to do as the spirits suggest. They know us better than we know ourselves, say the shamans, as we were once members of, and all of us born from, their world.

EXERCISE: FINDING A SPIRIT HELPER IN THE UPPER WORLD

This is a journey to the upper world of the shaman in order to connect with one spirit entity who will act as a guide and source of illumination and insight for you in future.

Use the Jivaro posture for this journey if you wish. Alternatively, sit in a relaxed position, close your eyes, and allow your head to drop forward in meditation; or, as other shamanic traditions do, move around, swaying to the rhythm of the drums, keeping your eyes closed throughout.

See before you now the world tree of the shaman which connects all three of the energetic realms and, when you are ready, begin steadily to climb this. If you are standing, you may find it helpful to make the movements of climbing in ordinary reality too.

At the top of this tree you will find that the clouds have a rather pliant quality, as if you have reached a membrane of sorts which separates the worlds. You need to experience passing through this threshold in order to be sure that you have entered the otherworld.

Once you are through, notice how the upper world feels and looks different from the lower and middle worlds you have previously visited. The landscape here is somehow less dense, more ethereal and weightless.

Begin to explore, keeping in mind your intention to meet with a spirit helper and guide in this place. Follow where your instincts lead you on your journey and, in particular, look for gardens in this world. In my experience, on this initial journey to the upper world we are often met by our spirit helpers in peaceful and beautiful garden landscapes. Notice how this garden looks, too, if you find your spirit guide there as, over time, its appearance will tend to change: this, I believe, is a reflection of changes within ourselves.

Once the connection is made with your guide, state your purpose in being there and ask that they help you on this and future quests for greater understanding. Then let them lead you. You will find that they are most gentle and welcoming and you may even feel that they have been waiting for your arrival for some time.

Spend as long with this helper as you wish. When you are ready to return, say your goodbyes and offer thanks for their warmth and wisdom, then retrace your steps back to ordinary reality. Open your eyes and make a note of all you have learned in this other world.

Westerners, of course, are sceptical of the notion that other dimensions, worlds of energy, exist and that we can somehow journey to them. Our every waking moment is, after all, intensely focused on controlling our world, our environment and our behaviour, and this is especially so in the cities where most of us live, controlled (seemingly) as they are by the clockwork mechanics of train timetables, tax demands, electricity bills and the route walks of traffic wardens. 'Control' is a big thing in our lives, and to relinquish this to a spirit entity which may not even exist is difficult for most people: it implies the undoing of every scrap of socialization we have been exposed to until now, and all that we believe in. It means that we must *trust* instead of looking for objective 'proof' as part of our socialized desire to analyse and 'understand', and allow ourselves to flow in the world rather than reaching habitually for the control button.

Yet there is significant scientific evidence that the heightened awareness which results from the trance experience can have massive effects in increasing our own powers of intuition and psychic ability, and even the act of relaxation can have considerable benefits in terms of brain integration and the capabilities which result – whether or not we believe in the spirits. All we need do is believe in ourselves.

The case of Judy, who came to see me for shamanic healing in 1998, is an example of the ability of spirit – or, if you wish, of intuition – to offer wise insights into our human problems, and also illustrates the structure of the shamanic experience.

Judy had suffered with asthma since childhood; it had grown increasingly worse over time and was severely limiting her capacity for life. She had seen many doctors over the years, none of whom could offer any real clues to her problem or its long-term solution. She had had this problem for as long as she could remember, she explained, and now, at the age of 35, she wanted a different life before it became too late for her to really feel she had lived it at all.

I decided to take a shamanic journey for Judy in order to understand the root cause of her health problem, and what was necessary to fully cure it.

The otherworld was cold and stormy. Wind and driving rain lashed at my face, and I found myself standing on a clifftop, part of a wild coastline. Out at sea, the waves rose and fell erratically, steep mountains and deep chasms opening up in the grey blanket of water below me.

In the middle of this turbulence a ship was tossed and buffeted by the storm. It looked damaged and in trouble. As I continued to watch, it was hit across the side by a massive wave which rocked it and then dropped what must have been tons of water directly on top of it. I heard cries from the men on board and then panic as the mast splintered. Careering wildly, the ship began to sink.

As she went under, I heard a scream from my right, which shocked me from my reflections on the chaos I had just witnessed. Turning, I saw Judy standing a little way off from me: not as she is now but as a young girl, aged six or seven, but undeniably Judy. She moved forward to the edge of the cliff and, before I could reach her, threw herself from the top. Her body hovered for an instant, caught in the powerful crosswind, and then plummeted to the rocks below where she lay, crushed and broken.

But as I looked down something else, some spirit, a ghost-child, rose from her broken body and began swimming out to sea until she reached the exact place where, moments before, the ship had sunk beneath the waves.

The figure of a man rose from the water and held her, not in a threatening way but in a loving embrace. Then the ghost-child and her father sank into the water.

The storm had blown itself out, leaving no trace of the events of moments before. No ship, no child, just a still, calm sea.

I returned from my journey and told Judy what I had seen. He reaction was emotional. As a small child, she said, her family had lived near the sea and her father had been a fisher-man. He had died at sea. Judy had idolized her father and felt as if part of her had gone with him. It was around this time that her asthma had begun.

Judy and I agreed that, in order to gain full control over her life, she needed to make her peace with her father and to let his spirit go so that she could untie herself from him.

At our next meeting, we journeyed together to the other-world. I stood beside her as she returned to the clifftop and, as a young girl once again, relived the storm of that night. This time, however, instead of throwing herself into the sea, she watched as her father's boat floundered and then called to him, asking him to come to her.

Suddenly, her father was at our side, a strong, good-looking man who radiated love for his daughter. 'I'm so glad you're here,' he said, even before she had time to speak. 'I have loved being with you, but I have always known that at some time you would be ready to live your life on your own and to make your own way in the world. I love you and will always be here for you if you need me but I understand that you have your own life to lead. Goodbye, Judy.'

'It had always felt like a betrayal of my father's memory to let him go, but I know it's OK now,' said Judy.

As I write this, it is nearly two years later and Judy has not had a single asthma attack since this experience. As a result she has had the confidence to expand her normal world into activities she would never have thought about before.

How can it be that a journey into the spirit world can solve physical problems such as these? What goes on in the otherworld to make such 'miracles' possible?

Peter Cloudsley, a student of Peruvian shamanism, tells us that in Andean shamanic healing all

> illness is believed to originate in the non-material world, but it is only when it assumes a physical manifestation that it is forced into human consciousness. For example, the energy of strong resentments or jealousy [or of attachments like Judy's] . . . may cause a common ailment referred to as dano or harm. The harm may or may not be conscious or intentional. In the course of a mesa [a shamanic healing ritual] it will become conscious and thereby the origin or cause of the illness, which is unique to each patient, is discovered. Forgiveness may play a part in a case of dano. In Western medicine, on the other hand, symptoms are identified and treated in a standard way and little is asked about the individual patient. In Andean medicine, the patient's story and what he thinks may be wrong with him are significant.[25]

Perhaps, in a sense, we all actually know the cause of our illnesses and dis-eases and merely need a route to making them conscious so that our minds and bodies can find the right solution for us.

One of the interesting things about shamanic healing is how often the healer is contacted for help by people who present with exactly the same problems as the healer has herself experienced in her own past. The shamanic archetype talks of 'the wounded healer' who is able to help others because the shaman has herself experienced their pain and found a solution to it in her own life. Clearly, this has more to do with 'synchronicity' or energetic attraction than scientific probability.

Often also, during the healing journey, it is not just the client who is helped, but the shaman who gains by learning some remarkable new information about the dis-ease she is treating and, indeed, the nature of life and reality in its wider sense.

In early 2000, I was asked to assist with distance healing for Jennie, an American lady suffering from hepatitis C. On my journey into the otherworld, I found Jennie in a dark panelled bedroom, which was very oppressive. She seemed initially very resistant to the healing itself and asked how I thought I could help her. I told her that I would journey into her body to meet with her virus and see what could be done.

I entered through her mouth and noticed that it was filled with stringy white, cobweb-like material, and wondered if she also had a throat infection or problem of some kind in this area. My spirit helpers and I spent a while cleaning the cobwebs away with salt water, and then continued into her chest cavity where we met with a tribe of virus-people, who looked like large black beetles. They stood on their hind legs so their legs and bellies were exposed.

My first realization about the place of us all in the world came as I explained to the leader of these entities that, although he could have no possible knowledge of it, he was occupying space within a much larger living body (Jennie) and that his presence there was harmful. What I realized was that this is very much the same situation we are in as human beings

– part of a vast living system (the Earth) and equally harmful to that system by our crazy actions of atomic and chemical warfare, pollution and environmental destruction. Just like Jennie's virus, we really only have two options: modify our behaviour or leave the system for somewhere more conducive to our own needs and predilections. The alternative is that the host (in our case, the Earth; in theirs, Jennie's body) dies and we die right along with it. Eventually, all destructive behaviour must also become self-destructive.

The virus agreed to leave if I could find a more suitable environment for his people. That was the point of my second realization – that there had to be a sacrifice here. To help Jennie, someone or something else was going to have to accept this virus since the virus people are living entities too and have as much right to life as anyone else.

Making this choice of a new host body was not a comfortable situation for me (and, of course, it is the same situation that god is faced with every day – how do you put a value on a life, whatever form that life takes? How do you choose one person to suffer and one to be well?), but I knew I had to do it and so transported the virus to a 'suitable' new host body.

(I was once explaining this journey on a religious radio programme, and the interviewer pointed out that Christ himself was also in this position once, where he had to cast out an illness, which he perceived as a demon, from the body of a young woman, and transplant it into the body of a pig – so at least there is a Christian precedent for doing so.)

In the new host, the virus and I agreed on the places to avoid in the body so that least harm was done, and I returned to Jennie, who looked more alive now. Still in my journey, I took her to the window and threw it open to let the sunlight in, then took her in my arms and flew her to the ocean, where I bathed her in the waters, before returning her to her room, which was now suffused with a blue healing light. As I was leaving, I just noticed the door of Jennie's room opening and someone else enter, but did not stop to notice who. It was a good journey.

There is an interesting twist to this story, though, since it was actually taken with a number of other people who journeyed independently from other locations in the world to help Jennie in her healing, none of whom, like me, had ever met Jennie face to face – and yet the correspondence between the journeys was quite remarkable. One healer reported, for example, that 'in dialoguing with the virus, two things became apparent: first, that the virus had found a willing and accommodating host, and secondly, that Jennie was unwilling to engage with that part of herself that had allowed her to succumb to the virus'. This is similar to my own impression of Jennie's initial reluctance to engage with her own healing.

This healer goes on to say that in conversation with the virus, there was a realization on both their parts that 'It was in the virus's interest to keep Jennie alive so that its home site remained undisturbed. This formed a congruence of intention between us: we both wanted Jennie alive. The next task was to separate the virus from Jennie.' This comment reflects my own realization that the virus and its host both had an equal right to life, but the only way for both to survive was through Jennie's good health.

A third healer reported meeting the virus, which appeared to him as 'a black water bug with two thin black arms pointing upward and another two pointing down'. I had seen the virus as a beetle-like form standing on its hind legs.

When I had left Jennie, she was bathed in a blue light and I had also seen someone else entering the room. Another healer, who began her journey report with the observation that she felt that someone had just left as she arrived with Jennie, described her as surrounded by 'a very light blue luminescent egg-shaped field. I thought it was strange that her energy was so glowing.'

Finally, the last report from the journeying group described 'a quite large energetic restriction at Jennie's throat chakra' (I had seen her mouth and throat as covered with a cobweb-like stringy material, which would also suggest an infection or disease in this area). The healer suggested that this might be due to 'a "stifling back" of creativity – she needs to express and be able to say things she has not said' (which, again, ties in with my perception of Jennie's reluctance to take an active part in her own life and healing). The healer goes on to describe her meeting with the hepatitis C virus, which she sees as 'thin grey sheets of energy, cobwebby and shadowy' – cobwebs again – which then turns into a 'great creature with wings' – like a beetle perhaps?

In removing the virus, this healer also had the impression that '"they" did not have particular attachments to where they lived, they were just trying to find a space to live in' – rather like my own perceptions. And the virus was also just as helpful: 'He was very amiable about being moved and showed me that the tensions of misaligned energies within the energy field tend to beckon or call to viruses, and how imbalances indicate a place where it is very easy for them to "set up house".'

The consistencies in these reports are quite remarkable and are evidence, for me, of the existence of some other form of very real and very independent energetic universe, occupied by aware beings with valuable and consistent teachings to offer.

But perhaps the last word should go to Jennie herself, who emailed the journeying group via a friend a few weeks later. This is what she had to say about her own healing experience.

'I'd been unaware of the date of the journey, but during that time I had the feeling that someone else was in the house, in my bedroom, etc. – when my friend forwarded your journeying reports I understood why!

'It was extremely interesting the impressions that were picked up regarding my throat chakra and mouth as these two areas have been challenging me not only physically (frequent mouth lesions/infections from the Hep C treatment and former thyroid cancer) but also metaphysically. I keep my mouth shut rather than expressing a valid opinion.

'Good take on the bedroom – it *is* dark. The sea has always been a healing place for me and I have moved my sea shells into the bedroom as a constant and subsconscious reminder of my sea bath.'

Another example of the surprises to be found in the other-world is the case of Honesty, a young girl born with a rare condition which meant that she was without an immune system. According to her grandfather, Honesty had 'had to take injections that boosted her immune system until it stayed up by itself. But she has had a fever and sores on the back of her throat for the last four days and the doctors have been giving her antibiotics in an IV but they have stopped the treatment now and she is still sick and has a fever.'

In my healing journey for Honesty, she appeared quite an angry, frightened child, not at all the way I had imagined her from her grandfather's description of a 'happy, smiling child'.

I entered Honesty's small body in the same way I had done for Jennie, and tried to locate her immune system in order to strengthen it. I couldn't find it. At first I thought that was because it was so depleted but one of my spirit helpers had a quite different view: 'There is no such thing as an immune "system",' he said. 'All immunity comes from the life force, a desire to live. Immunity is an act of will.'

I was amazed that someone as young as Honesty could have already given up the will to live, and began looking for what might have caused her to become so afraid and angry at the world. At that point I was catapulted into her future and found her at a roadside. Something had happened to her at this point which was quite traumatic, but which should not be repeated here.

What was interesting was that this was an event in her life which had not yet even taken place, but it was having a very real impact on her in the *present*. It seems that we are born with some knowledge or awareness of our destiny, the course of our lives and the pattern our life will take, as if we know our purpose in being here, right from the very start. It was the knowledge of this future event and the devastation it would have on her which was making Honesty fearful of attachment to the world.

Knowing this, I set about changing the outcome of this possible future so that it would no longer occur in Honesty's life, by altering the event itself and thereby changing the energy patterns associated with it. This event would now never happen and, since all things – past/present/future, there/here/everywhere – are energetically connected, the effect of changing this possible future should have the effect of curing Honesty's illness in the present.

Whilst this healing was progressing, a number of others were also working for Honesty. Many prayed, others journeyed, some offered blessings for healing and empowerment. A few days later, we were all delighted to hear from her grandfather that Honesty's fever had broken, her sickness had dissipated and she was feeling much better.

'The update on her condition is very favourable,' he wrote. 'Her fever completely left on Monday and the sores in her mouth are slowly going away. All in all she is much better.'

Remarkable, isn't it, that so much can be accomplished at a non-physical level? And yet, this is the world of the shaman and the results which he sees all the time from his work in this other reality.

The key realization for me from Honesty's story was just as remarkable – that future events, of which we *do* have 'residual' knowledge from the time of our birth, can have a profound effect on our lives in the present. It is almost as if our time here is purposefully leading up to an enactment of the significant event we have chosen.

In this sense, an illness or dis-ease can be a remarkably healing event, giving us access to a deep pool of knowledge – an echo of events to come – which can enable us to change the future to live a better and more fulfilling life now if we only listen to the message of our illness. We all have the right to change our minds, whatever outcome for our lives we originally chose! There is nothing fatalistic about shamanic healing work – the future is there to be changed (as is the past), just as much as the present.

As a final example of this incredible healing potential of the transpersonal world of the second attention (one which has nothing to do with human healing, but with the healing of the spirits themselves), I read an account recently of how a shamanic practitioner in America had intervened to prevent the onslaught of a major forest fire, 'simply' by working with the spirits.[26]

The fire had been raging for days and the emergency services seemed powerless to stop it. Since it had not rained in weeks and showed no sign of doing so, the ground was dry and easily caught fire. This particular practitioner lived near to the area affected and, while probably not close enough to be in serious danger, was certainly able to watch as the flames and the smoke got nearer.

One morning she awoke to an inspiration. The spirits of the forest, she realized, had been battling with the spirits of the fire for days in order to stop the oncoming conflagration. 'The forest spirits must be thirsty in the face of all that heat and dust,' she thought. Stepping outside, she offered a simple glass of water to the forest spirits. Tipping it into the Earth at her feet, she voiced her thanks and prayers for their success.

In that moment, the skies opened and a thunderstorm began, though there had been no forecast of rain. With her simple, beautiful gesture and her acknowledgement of the connection between all things, she had caused the universe to answer her prayers and respond in kind. The forest fire was extinguished naturally within hours.

In the Western world, we find it hard to believe that the shaman can actually voyage in such a way, beyond the body into a real other world where she is able to connect with another at a deep, energetic level. We have all been conditioned to consider only the primacy of the individual and the world of mind, exemplified by the fashion of psycho-*analysis* – that word again – but there is plenty of scientific evidence to support the shaman's claim. The 'Philip' experiment referred to earlier is a case in point, where a group of people were able to create a ghost, an autonomous energy-being, through the power of their intention; while in quantum physics, scientists talk of particles of matter which themselves cease to exist and then reappear, 'ghost particles' which have a new life beyond the material.

And if all of this can be accomplished with healing and with the containment of natural disasters such as a forest fire – and if even subatomic particles seem capable of entering into the 'otherworld' dimension – then, surely, with enough of us working together and a concentration of will and intention behind us, we should also be able to change the system and the cities we live in to create a less stressful and more enriching world for ourselves and for others.

Scientific evidence for other worlds

In December 1999, the British television science programme, *Tomorrow's World* reported on new experimental findings about multiple personality syndrome (MPS), the condition which manifests in some people who are able to switch mentally, though usually not in a controllable way, between independent personalities who have a separate life, memories and experiences, all of whom reside within them. These personalities are able to take over and control the body, in a way not dissimilar to the possession states of Vodou, where the gods ride the body of the follower for a while.

Multiple personalities were seen in the past as a mental disorder, an aberration of the mind which created the illusion of a new personality. This new evidence, however, suggests that something else may also be going on here: brain scans of MPS sufferers have shown that different areas of the brain actually spark into life when the new personality takes over, proof that something 'real', something physical, not imaginary, is taking place.

One person in these experiments was often taken over by an older version of herself, who was able to act from a deeper place of wisdom based on experiences the host body had not actually had – much as Honesty, the young girl I referred to earlier, was suffering illness *now* as the result of an event from her *future* yet to come. In the MPS experiments, this future personality or older self had its own signal in the brain as its trademark area was activated during the 'possession'.

How is it possible for us to 'become' a person from our own *future* who is able to interact with the world we are part of *now* and to apply insights and information we have not yet had to the world we are currently living in?

The shamanic explanation is that our consciousness, our spirit, exists in an immaterial world – the Infinite Now – which is unbound by constraints of time and space. In effect, we journey to ourselves and consult with a wiser entity – our own possible future self – which truly *exists* in the external energetic, spiritual dimension. This entity is able to enter the world of the person seeking its answers and have its independence registered and verified by scientific instruments. This is essentially no different from the possession states of the houngan or the deep trance of the shaman. According to the evidence, it is a real change, a new physical self, with its own brain-reality and patterns which takes over. These personalities are real and we can meet them.

If the scientific evidence starts to look interesting, the anecdotal evidence for the existence of another, quite different world at this transpersonal level is compelling. One woman skilled at journeying beyond the body decided to use her talent to find her dream house, since she and her husband were planning to move soon. Each night before she went to sleep, she would will herself to 'astrally project' during the night in order to look for the perfect house for them (a technique shamans know as 'lucid dreaming').

After some time, she discovered the house that would be ideal for her and her family – the only problem was that she had no idea where it was in ordinary reality. Then, one day on a house-hunting trip in London with her husband, she came across the details of a house which perfectly matched the description of the one she had seen in her dream journeys, exactly as she had seen it. She had found her 'dream' house.

There was some bad news, too, however. According to the estate agent, the house was haunted.

Despite this, the woman and her husband were not deterred and, in fact, were pleased to discover that the house was on the market at a very competitive price because the owners wanted to get away from it and its ghost, and so they met with the seller.

As soon as they entered the room, the owner blanched and screamed. 'You're the ghost!' she said, pointing at the woman who had come to buy her house. Her journeys beyond the body to find the house of her dreams had been so successful that she had actually been witnessed by the owners, who had seen her around the property and decided to sell it because they thought it had a ghost. The 'lucid dreamer' had haunted her own future home.[27]

In this context, it is worth pausing just to ask ourselves how many 'ghosts' may actually be the energy bodies of living people, such as shamans in flight, or those skilled at astral projection – or even our own dreaming selves!

Harold Puthoff and Russell Targ of the Stanford Research Institute have carried out a number of studies into out-of-body experiences such as these. In one experiment, subjects were asked to lie on their backs on a bed and to identify a number of geometric shapes on a shelf high above them, which they could not possibly see from their prone position. The only way they could know what these shapes were was to journey spiritually outside of themselves and take a look.

One subject was so successful at this that he was given an additional assignment – to describe the physical features present at a geographical coordinate of longitude and latitude at a point unknown to him on the planet.

At first, during his journey, he saw it as a mountain but then immediately modified his opinion and described it as an island – both of which descriptions, unfortunately, could only be wrong since the location chosen by the experimenters was an empty stretch of water in the Indian Ocean. They decided to look into the matter, however, and, much to their surprise, found that there *was* an island exactly at these coordinates, complete with a mountain range. A sketch of the island made by the subject was later compared with an aerial image and found to correspond with it almost exactly.[28]

It seems at least possible that the shaman's journey is more than just fantasy. And, if that is true, then what of the spirits they meet there? There must at least be a possibility that they are real too.

In fact, it is more than a 'possibility'. Scientific research conducted recently in the village of Scole in Norfolk, offers incontrovertible evidence for the survival of the spirit beyond physical death.[29] The research team, which often included visiting scientists of various academic disciplines, including professors of engineering, psychology, mathematics and astrophysics, was able to make contact with a group of scientists in the spirit world who wanted to experiment with a new form of spirit-energy, rather than the more traditional mediumistic ectoplasm (a form of spiritual emanation from the medium which then takes on physical form and is used by the spirits to create solid objects as proof of survival).

The reason for moving away from the use of ectoplasm, said the spirit team, was because: 'The traditional methods had not worked in convincing people of the reality of survival . . . the team thought they could replicate the same effects with energy. The spirit team said this new energy was much safer and easier to use for a larger number of people . . . They also showed how so much more could be achieved using this new creative energy.'

The experimentation with this new form of 'creative energy' lasted five years between 1993 and 1998, after which the Scole team produced guidelines for working with this energy which, they claim, enable anyone to replicate their results.

During the experiments themselves, the team received more than seventy apports (physical objects transported from the spirit world), including a comic seaside postcard with the message 'If living, please write – if dead, don't bother!' (the spirits have a sense of humour), sacred ash from the funeral pyre of an Indian holy man, and an original copy of the *Daily*

233

Mail newspaper dated 1944. They also recorded lights which moved around the room and voices from the spirit world on the recording equipment they kept with them during these experiments.

Even more remarkable are the photographs they took, which are published in the book, *The Scole Experiment*, by Grant and Jane Solomon. According to the writers, much of this 'photography' was created by the spirits themselves, without the use of a camera, simply by 'influencing' the film itself. 'This work advanced to the stage where the spirit team's "photograph department" could put faces, glyphs, handwriting and diagrams onto rolls of unopened film, which were simply placed on the table during experiments, still in their factory-sealed packaging.'

Once developed, the films showed a range of very clear images, including faces of the dead, writing which is immediately legible and easily read, and images from history, such as a picture of the River Seine taken from Notre Dame Cathedral in 1944. Other images were of Greek lettering, poetry written out by hand in the German language, electrical diagrams with instructions for creating a device for communications, and X-ray pictures of a human hand.

If the Scole experiment results are not shown to be a hoax, then they offer the clearest scientific evidence I have ever seen for life after death. And there is no reason to suspect that any form of hoax or trickery was involved. As the authors of *The Scole Experiment* remark:

> As the project progressed, it appeared that a number of other groups were beginning to get similar results to those achieved during the early days at Scole. This brings us on to perhaps the most convincing aspect of the Scole Experiment: transferability. Hundreds of groups throughout the world have begun to experiment along similar lines, all following the instructions in the Scole group's A Basic Guide booklet . . . many of these groups are reporting consistent results.

For me, however, it is not the physical evidence of spirit existence which is most convincing, even though it is dramatic in itself, but the messages the Scole spirits bring, many of which are borne out by my own experience of this immaterial world. In *The Journey to You*, for example, I described a journey I took from a point after my own death so I could see for myself the destiny of all human souls; why we are and where we go after death.

I was shown a reality where we are as points of light in the darkness, each one fully conscious, travelling through space and able to choose our next incarnation from any point of our awareness, according only to what interests us most at the time. Strong emotions, and especially love, are what trigger our interest and cause us to reincarnate at any particular point in time and space.

I must have taken this journey in 1997 or 1998, towards the end of the Scole experiments. During this time, the spirits themselves had a similar message to impart to the Scole experimental group.

'Our spirit selves are really travellers,' they said, 'and the point at which you are now is the place to which you have decided to travel . . . Love is the key word. Love makes things happen. Love is a very creative thing. True spirit energy is a creative force.'

They go on: 'We want to awaken in all mankind the truth and help people to find it in their own way; to awaken the desire to question; to look deep within themselves. There they will find something wonderful: the spiritual self. No-one else can do it for you.'

If you want unequivocal evidence of life after death and the existence of the spirit world, I suggest you buy a copy of *The Scole Experiment* and see for yourself.*

---

* If you would like to try these experiments to see if you can produce the same results for yourself, you can get a copy of the group's guidance booklet by writing to The New Spiritual Science Foundation, Street Farmhouse, Scole, Nr Diss, Norfolk IP21 4DR. There is also a web site at www.psisci.force9.co.uk.

Exercise: Journeying for Guidance to Your Own Future Self

In the worlds beyond the atom and the energy-domain of the shaman, time and space are meaningless concepts. In this journey, you will voyage into your own destiny to meet with the spirit-essence of the person you may choose to become in one possible future.

When you meet this person, you will be able to ask them for any guidance you wish about any current matter of concern in your life, and to see the outcome of any decision you may choose to take about this.

Begin by closing your eyes and relaxing and, as always, by stating your journeying intention. Express it out loud two or three times, in whatever words are appropriate to help you anchor your purpose on this journey. If you are using a drumming tape, begin now.

This will be a middle world journey, so simply allow the essence of yourself to blend with the elements around you, spreading out into the energetic realms of non-ordinary space beyond our own world.

Call for your spirit helpers and ask for their advice on the issue which concerns you, requesting all the clarification you need at this time. Ask for advice on the options open to you, and to be shown how your future looks, should you decide to pursue any of these.

You have a further option too, which is to change this future, since your behaviour now will transform the whole configuration of energy of which you are a part. When you are happy that you have identified the best possible future for you, ask your spirit helpers what you can do now to ensure that this particular future unfolds for you.

If you are given a ritual to perform in answer to your question, a power object to craft, or a healing song to learn – all of which are typical responses from the spirits, who tend to operate on a symbolic, though usually quite practical, basis – be sure you have all the details before you return.

When you are ready to come back, retrace all the steps you have taken into the otherworld and ensure you are fully back in this one before stirring. Normally, a lot of energy will have moved during this journey, so be sure you are ready before making any dramatic movements.

Reflect on the information you have received in answer to your question. Does it 'make sense' to you – not necessarily on a rational level, but maybe in terms of a bodily feeling? Perhaps it is worth trying it out to see if it works in practice.

In core shamanism, we are taught that as soon as the journey ends we must write down our experiences immediately, and this *is* helpful since the act of writing them down can often reveal new insights into their content. We also begin, in this way, to create a personal map of the otherworld, and to understand its terrain.

In truth, however, it is the powerful, unconscious resonances that usually strike a deeper chord as the journey enters our dreams and reveries and our deep conscious minds continue to work on the content. The energy body will also be incorporating the new energy returned during the shamanic voyage. A dream diary is often a useful tool at this point and will help you to see the bigger pattern of what your whole-body experience is telling you about yourself.

Lucid dreaming
In addition to conscious journeying and possession states as a means of spirit consultation, shamans refined a technique known as lucid dreaming, which facilitates out-of-body experiences, spirit guidance and practical journeying during sleep. This is the technique used by the London househunter

I wrote about earlier, who was so good at it that she ended up haunting her own future home.

The method takes a little practice but is achievable since the same energy fields are involved, the human and the transpersonal, enabling you to connect with another or to visit a distant destination without needing to do so physically.

In the second energy field, the transpersonal, every one of us has an energy body 'double', says don Juan. It is this energy body which is separated from us during the act of dreaming and which we use purposefully by guiding its actions with the power of our intentions.

An American mambo told me a story of her early experiments in using this dream-body. She and a friend some distance away arranged to dream together on a specific night every week and to share adventures this way, and then phone each other the next day to see if they had had common experiences during sleep.

Their procedure was to ensure they were both asleep at a specified time and to *intend* that, whatever their dreaming adventures, they would be joined in them by their friend. Both would start out in the dream at a specific and pre-determined landmark known to both of them in ordinary reality, by holding the image of this place in mind as they began to drift into sleep. Any commonalities of dreaming experience they reported the next day would be verification of real contact during sleeping awareness.

One night, having gone to bed and begun to dream at the appointed time, the mambo was surprised to see her friend driving along a particular American highway, since this was nothing like the dreaming destination they normally started from. Even stranger was the fact that the highway scene was interspersed with images of a tropical beach. When she awoke, the mambo dismissed the experience as too 'jumbled' and unlikely to have been a real lucid dream: her friend would have been asleep in bed at this time, not driving, and the beach scene in any case seemed only to be nonsense.

She phoned her friend next day to tell her about this strange image and to share a joke about it. Her friend, however, reported that she had been late home from work that night, so had not been able to take part in the dreaming exercise. Instead, she had been driving home – on the exact highway described – at the time and, realizing she was late for the dreaming experiment, had held up and focused on the only thing she had to hand at the time – which happened to be a tray with an image on it of Malibu beach.

'I was so shocked at the accuracy of what I had seen that we decided not to do any more dreaming for a while,' the mambo laughed.

The dreaming body can be used for practical and useful purposes as well as experiments like this. Many years ago, a girlfriend of mine had to leave my house during the early hours of the morning in order to drive back to her own home. I lay in bed and watched her leave before falling asleep.

Half an hour later, I was surprised to hear the front door open downstairs and footfalls on the stairs. Then Annie was walking towards me again across the landing, looking concerned. As I sat up to ask what was wrong and why she had returned, she simply vanished in front of me.

Realizing that I was actually still sleeping and that this was a dreaming message, I woke myself, got out of bed and dressed quickly. Getting into my car, I followed the route Annie would have taken home. I found her on a dark country road about 10 miles from my house, where her car had suffered a puncture and was sitting almost in a ditch at the side of the road. She was shaken but uninjured. 'Thank god you're here,' she said. 'I was praying you would come.'

How can we use this capability for dreaming in a practical way? Apart from examples like the one above, I wrote in *The Journey To You* of how I was able to use dreaming to write a chapter of the book, suggesting that we can carry out useful work with this technique even while we are asleep. We might also use it to check on loved ones to ensure that they are safe and well, to visit libraries to learn new skills, for research, and for advice on healing and empowerment through dreaming consultations with great healers and spiritual leaders who are alive in this world or the next. A number of major scientific breakthroughs throughout history have been put down by their creators and discoverers to the impact of a dream or even a waking 'reverie', a daydream of sorts.

A friend of mine, Robert, through lucid dreaming, was able clearly to predict almost exactly a situation of conflict which he would be a part of in a foreign country, 1,000 miles from his home and a month or so after the dream itself. In this instance, since he was not the main character in the drama which was to unfold, he could watch as the event took place, just as he had seen it in his dream. In other circumstances, with advance knowledge such as this, it would be possible to avoid the situation altogether and ensure that the problem never took place at all.

The key difficulty with dreaming is one of belief, of convincing ourselves that it is possible. Once we can do that, the dream-body seems naturally to know what to do. To begin dreaming, lie comfortably in bed as normal and, just as you feel yourself slipping into the meditative state between wakefulness and sleep, send a precise and deliberate command to your deep conscious self that tonight you will dream and that you will be aware you are dreaming and in control of your actions during the dream itself.

When you recognize during sleep that you *are* in a dream, you must then separate yourself from the dreamer so that you can control your actions. The simplest way to do so is to pull back your energy from the character you are in the dream and to position yourself a few feet behind and slightly above this person. You are then able to see as they see and to guide their interactions with others.

EXERCISE: THE PRACTICE OF DREAMING

Arrange with a friend to set up a dreaming experiment. Agree that you will go to bed at a pre-determined time and that you will meet at a certain place in the dreamscape.

Notice the interactions between the two of you and what is said and done, as well as the environment around you and the landscape you are in. Are there any distinguishing landmarks, signs or symbols visible to you which you can use later to confirm your experience?

The next day, meet with your friend and discuss your separate dream experiences. What do they have in common? Did your friend see the same landmarks as you? What did you speak of in the dream – can you both remember the content?

The shaman, don Juan, warned that this energy body, which he called the 'double', can sometimes become separated from the physical body in ordinary reality and that for the two to meet is highly dangerous, sometimes even resulting in death.

Personal experience suggests that this is a rather over-dramatic conclusion. Many years ago, in Glastonbury, a friend and I were sharing a coffee in a restaurant, having just returned from the Tor, when in walked her exact double and sat at the table next to us. My friend became extremely uneasy and we left. No sooner had we stepped outside than the same *doppelgänger* rounded the corner in front of us in a car, narrowly missing my friend. The episode was unpleasant, yet we both survived.

The shaman, Ken Eagle Feather, tells how he was sitting on an aeroplane one day and, looking across the aisle, found himself staring directly at his own double. The situation was eerie but, again, no real physical harm arose as a consequence of it.[30]

It is my feeling that such non-deliberate separations of the physical and energy body arise primarily as a reaction to stress or trauma of some kind. My friend in Glastonbury had recently had an emotional upheaval in her life, for example, and Eagle Feather reports that his own experience arose during a time of frequent travel in connection with his lecturing work. One of the key characteristics of modern urban life is exactly this type of emotional and mental stress, so it may be that strengthening the energy body through lucid dreaming exercises such as the one above can itself be a form of healing and self-protection.

Other dreamings

There is another way in which shamans use the term 'dreaming'. They talk of all things, natural as well as man-made, and places as well as objects, being alive and having their own dreaming, their own expression of consciousness and involvement in the reality around them. In *African Spirits Speak*, Nicky Arden tells of her initiation into the healing practices of the Sangomas, part of which involves a test of the candidate's psychic abilities by identifying and then locating a hidden object which the teacher is merely thinking about. The candidate must tune in to these thoughts and then find the item in question.[31]

In one such exercise, having correctly identified that the hidden object was man-made, worn around the wrist, metallic, and made a ticking sound, Nicky was thrown completely when she asked 'Is this thing alive?' and received the answer 'yes'. Having gone on to determine that the object was, indeed, a wristwatch, she asked how it could also be 'alive'. Because all things are alive, was the response: your car, your clothes, your cooker, your computer: it doesn't matter that they are all man-made, they are all composed of energy and have a dreaming of their own.

All places also have a dreaming – which explains why you sometimes feel energized and at peace in one location and ill at ease in another or, when looking round for a new house, you sense that somewhere feels good while another makes you uneasy, though you cannot rationally explain why. The Chinese system of feng shui was designed to work with just these energies, to determine which are advantageous for you and which are out of resonance with your own energy, so you can take corrective measures in order to bring the two more into line.

Shamans maintain that we feel and function better in places – called personal 'power places' – which are in resonance with our own energies. Such places are everywhere. In every situation, even in a square metre of space, there will be one particular spot which is more beneficial for you. If you find this place at work and then move your desk there you will be able to perform more effectively and with less draining of your energy; finding this spot at home will mean you are more relaxed and healthy. In both cases, creating such a space will always bring mental, physical and emotional benefits. We will look at how to do this in a later chapter.

EXERCISE: FINDING YOUR PERSONAL PLACE OF POWER

We are conditioned when we enter a new (or even a familiar) environment to simply respond to it automatically, to sit where we are told, to work at a desk which has always been positioned in a certain place, and sometimes – as with the crowded train journey to work or the last remaining table in the restaurant – we do not seem to have a choice at all. Our response is to shut down the sensory mechanisms which alert us to our surroundings and the energy flows between ourselves and the environment in order to 'make the best of things'. Unused, these psychic tools become blunted over time.

If you practise quiet stillness as you enter a new place, however, you will soon begin to sense this flow again.

Try to detach yourself from your surroundings – in this experiment, wearing a blindfold may help you to develop this skill as you are then forced to rely on senses such as hearing and smell which you do not normally use – and empty your mind of expectations and judgements. Remain still for a while until you begin to become aware of your body's sensations of being in this place, then start slowly to move around your environment. Note if you feel heat or cold, a sense of calm or foreboding as you reach new areas of the room. When you have eliminated any places that cause you to feel uncomfortable, refine the list of those that make you most at ease until you find the one spot most appropriate for you and in tune with your own energies at this time. This is your personal power place.

Some areas of the city, as well as rooms and buildings, have their own power places where you will feel more refreshed and revived if you rest there during a lunch hour perhaps. Research into ley lines and geopathic stress suggests that a giant energetic grid criss-crosses our land like the meridians of the body and the synapses of the brain. Since energy ebbs and flows, some areas of this grid will pull your energy from you while others will enhance your power.

When you are able confidently to find your own power spot in a compact and enclosed space, begin to experiment with more open spaces such as city streets and parks. Initially, this will take more concentrated effort since there are more distractions which must be filtered out, but eventually you will be able to accomplish it and then to move through the energy web of the city with ease.

Shamans would say that these places of power had their own 'dreaming' which you are connecting with as the energy fields between you merge. Those places or people you feel most comfortable with share a common dreaming with you; in those where you feel least at ease your individual dreamings are out of resonance.

Eagle Feather describes the difference between these two fields as either 'Natural' (*in* resonance) or 'Forced' (*out* of resonance with ourselves and with nature). Natural fields are those where individual energies are comfortably aligned with the social order of ordinary reality (you work at your job because you enjoy it, for example), while Forced fields require a curtailment of individual energy and a sucking away of personal power in order to feed the social situation or system with an investment by the individual based on need or control (you work at a job you hate only because you need the money, for example).[32] Forced energy fields are, in my experience, implicated in every form of ill-health and dis-ease, whether physical illness resulting from stress or overwork or emotional illness caused by a domineering or abusive personal relationship.

Eagle Feather proposes the difference between Forced and Natural fields as follows:

Life is based on . . .	Forced	Natural
Worldview	What *should* be	What *is*
Way of the world	Rigid	Fluid
Values	Judgmental	Accepting
Relationship of the individual to the system	Social conditioning and expectations are central	Self-actualization is valued
Individual contribution	Habitual; repetitive	Innovative; creative
View of 'life beyond the physical'	Dogmatic	Embracing of mystery
Development of society and individual	Static	Evolutionary
Reality	Imposed by the cultural worldview	Defined by personal experience

The differences between these two ways of relating to the world are, more or less, those between a spiritual worldview and the more mechanical life we face in the cities of our modern, urban world. They also reflect the differences described in an earlier chapter between the 'global' and 'personal' views of the post-modern world, where more people, according to research, want a new way of relating to the world. This 'new way', paradoxically, is really a return to the Natural and ancient values of honour and integration rather than the Forced 'Me-Generation' perspective of the late 20th century, which we are now getting thoroughly – and literally – sick and tired of.

By participating in any worldview, says Eagle Feather, 'we gradually align our energies with that of the world. As a result, we actively condition ourselves to what we can and cannot perceive [and achieve] . . . the downside is that we expand our snapshots into ultimate truth, thereby leaving other worlds [and other potentials and possibilities for ourselves] out of the picture . . . But worldview is not truth; it is technique.'[33]

In other words, it is not just people or places which have a dreaming nature. Collectively, our entire society has a dream of itself which, through conditioning and socialization, we are required to subscribe to. We learn as children to focus our energy in a particular direction in order to make sense of the world, and the easiest for us to absorb is the dominant cultural dream, passed on to us by our parents, teachers, and the TV programmes we are encouraged to watch. Thus, the worldview of our society becomes self-fulfilling.

We refine this worldview as we bounce off the perceptual framework of others who are our guides and tutors in life – our fashion-conscious friends, the latest rock star hero, employers, government demands, laws, rules and regulations – until our raw energy eventually becomes honed and refined in line with the prevailing social consensus. We then assume that this one selective reality is the only *possible* reality and so the world turns unchallenged.

Some deviance from the social world is tolerated, if not encouraged, as long as it is not too dramatic or if it serves a cohesive function in itself. For example, murder is penalized in times of peace but encouraged and institutionalized in wartime and even bolstered by the prevailing religious and ethical system which will reward with honour those who fight 'for God and Country'.

But the simple fact is that there is no 'reality gene' in the human body; there are many realities open to us and many different people we can be or still become. The reality that we subscribe to is most often simply the one which has been handed to us.

The consensus dream versus the Second Attention

An American priest of Santeria, who is also a graduate of Harvard and a clinical psychologist, gave me a different perspective on this conflict between consensus and true reality when he described an episode from his own initiation into the faith.

As part of the ritual of initiation he was required to sit in silent isolation for days and merely to stare at the wall a few feet in front of him. 'I imagine I had what psychiatrists would label as a "psychotic attack",' he laughed. 'Ordinary reality stopped being meaningful and all sorts of unusual and spiritual events began to take place.

'I was part of an entirely separate reality and it was plain that there were far more dimensions to the "real world" than the one single and simplistic view we learn from social convention. When this reality is stripped away, the gods are entirely visible to us but, of course, we have never been given the tools to handle this experience or the opportunity even to see it. The test then, which is the same test for all initiates into any spiritual field anywhere, is to handle what we find out for ourselves or to risk complete mental collapse.'

How this 'other reality' can sometimes manifest is exemplified by this man's experience at a recent *misa* (seance) where a healer was ministering to a small child. 'As I looked at the child, the image of a car crash popped into my mind,' he said. 'Then, all of a sudden, the healer began to beat the shit out of this kid for no reason at all that I could see. I asked her later why she had done this and she said that the child would be seriously injured in a car accident when she was 19 – just as I had also seen – and by beating her now, she was preventing the accident from taking place by "pre-living", in a less intense form, the injuries that would arise. She was altering the flow of energy which was drawing the event to the child.'

The notion that two separate people can look at a child and see the same future event in her life and that the future can be changed by dealing with its energy now is entirely alien to the linear-scientific worldview that is the Western description of reality. And, of course, in a sense, it is untestable: if the car crash does not take place when this child reaches 19, do we say it has been prevented by the healer's intervention, or that it would never have happened anyway and the healer's actions were just for show? The Western model has tended to go down the latter road – and yet the former is an interpretation which is now very much supported by leading-edge research in quantum physics which demonstrates that, at a deep level, even separate particles across great distances are aware of each other and responsive to the other's movements. Merely by observing their interactions, without doing a single thing to deliberately change them, we already change the flow of energy between them and so alter the future of their relationship.

By being aware of someone's future (or our own) and changing its course now, perhaps we can also change their lives (or ours) in the same way.

Another way to improve your circumstances and to feel greater peace and joy in life, therefore, is to understand the dreaming of another person, thing, or the society in general, and then either to change their dream or change your own in order to adapt to, or find a way to live in peaceful dissonance with, theirs.

To put this a different way: every part of our human experience, every memory, every event, is stored within our energy bodies. The energy expended by subscribing to the conditioned social reality we are a part of in our urban world can cause us pain and distress as well as, in some ways, making it easier for us to be part of society. Our attachment to a bad childhood, for example, will have an effect on our image of ourselves right now – 'I must protect myself by hiding from others because I am unlovable' or 'I must aggressively defend myself whenever I am challenged because I know I will be punished if I do or say something they do not like' – and this, in turn, determines our behaviour. In fact, it is never too late to have a happy childhood: we just need to see ourselves in a new light now.

The shamans have a way of making this very simple. Instead of focusing on what is negative in your life, they say, and expending time and personal power in 'addressing' childhood and other issues so we can 'deal' with them, we can choose instead to ignore the negativity of the past and fill our present lives with joy. Since the energy body can only contain a finite amount of energy, if we fill ourselves with light, the darkness is automatically made brighter. Instead of years in therapy when we talk about the hurts of the past, we will ourselves make more positive and life-enriching choices *now* so the past ceases to be a matter of real concern.

It sounds simple – and, in fact, it is. Modern psychology, in the form of Neuro-Linguistic Programming (NLP), says practically the same thing, based on years of research into how people actually do think and operate and how our minds work. 'When asked about their goals, most people respond by saying what they *don't* want rather than what they *do* want,' write Harry Alder and Beryl Heather in *NLP in 21 Days*. 'The brain actually works in such a way that negative terms can have the completely wrong effect. Parents sometimes tell their children what not to do ("Don't trip", "Don't spill it", "Don't do so-and-so"), only to find that they seem more inclined to do the very opposite . . . The negative thought becomes self-fulfilling.'[34]

The brain, however, can only really handle about half a dozen ideas or 'thought-streams' at a time. The solution, therefore, is to flood the mind with positive images, ideas, affirmations and experiences, so there is no room left for the negative. The strategy is simple: in the most basic words possible, 'forget the past and instead start living for today – with *conscious, positive intent*'.

Ultimately, to achieve any objective and move out of the past or the shadow of our social conditioning, we must first put ourselves into a place of mystery, a place unfamiliar to us, where the old rules have no currency. This can be as simple as a minor life change – for example, if you are a person used to saying 'no' to things, try saying 'yes' instead, *whether you 'think' you want to or not*. This agreement to take part in something you would normally avoid does not have to be a deeply mystical experience or a major life-changing event. I know a man who was highly resistant to dancing in public and would always say 'no' when his wife asked him to dance with her. He had never had the confidence to say 'yes' because he had always been taught that dancing was not a thing men did; it was a frivolous and pointless activity for girls.

One night, on a whim, however, he said 'yes' to a dance and, through the feedback he received from his friends, discovered not only that he was a wonderful dancer but that the accepted reality he had been carrying around (that dancing is not manly) was wrong!

Now he and his wife go to dances all the time, their relationship is improved, and his confidence has increased dramatically. Something as simple as dancing – having the nerve to put himself forward in public – has changed his whole life. By placing yourself at the centre of the mystery, you are freed because when you are no longer sure of something and the rules are changed, the old limitations are eroded too. From mystery comes mastery.

But first of all, of course, you have to become conscious of the dream of reality you are currently living by.

EXERCISE: UNDERSTANDING AND CHANGING THE DREAM OF ANOTHER

It is often easier to get feedback on ourselves from others than to spend hours in introspection [which also lacks the validation of another]. Here is an exercise you can do with a friend to tune into and understand the dream of the world, and of your life, that you are both living by.

Relax and close your eyes. Ask your friend to sit with you and quietly allow an image of them to come into your mind. What you see or hear or sense might be a colour symbolic of your friend's mood, or a shape or scene or feeling. Whatever it is and no matter how unusual it seems, keep that image in mind as representative of your friend and begin to work with it. What is this image telling you? If you were this image, how would you feel and how would the world seem to you?

Open your eyes and share the image with your friend – how close is your assessment to their current feeling and disposition?

Now close your eyes again and, calling the same image back to mind, begin to change its key components. If your image is of a dark cloud hanging over that person, for example, see it blown away by a light breeze and the sun come out and shine upon your friend.

Now ask again how they feel and see if there is any significant change in their mood.

You can also use this technique with objects (which we are typically told are not conscious or aware) since all things are alive. I once had a CD player that kept sticking and slipping when I tried to play certain discs on it, which was highly frustrating and usually resulted in a battle of wills as I was determined to listen to the CD I had selected, while the CD player seemed equally determined that I wouldn't.

Eventually, I sat down in front of it and closed my eyes in order to enter its dreaming. Above the CD player I saw a grey mist of gloom and, in the middle of it, a smiley face with a downturned mouth.

Exploring further – as unlikely as this may seem – I was able to ascertain that the player itself did not like the music I had selected, feeling it was too loud and raucous.

With this information, we were able to reach a compromise – I put on a quiet, soothing CD first and left the room while it played since I did not want to listen to it at this time and, in exchange, the CD player played my selection faultlessly when I returned to the room immediately afterwards.

This sounds incredibly far-fetched – except that, once again, there is a body of scientific evidence to support the possibility of sentient machines. In *March of the Machines*, Kevin Warwick, Professor of Cybernetics at Reading University, reports on experiments he has conducted to test just this hypothesis and to see how far machines are capable of 'artificial intelligence'.[35]

The human brain is a vastly complex organism, containing some 100 billion neurons, but Warwick found that when he built robots capable of movement, with a neural network equivalent to even just 100 neurons, and left them to wander at random, a natural leader seemed to emerge and, after a while, all the other robots began to follow him. Their walk was no longer random, but followed the course set by their chosen leader.

There is even a suggestion in Warwick's book that machines can sense our emotions and, if treated harshly (for example if a faulty TV is hit, in an attempt to get better reception), will respond to the emotion of the person almost as if they had a personality of their own.

What the scientists are now discovering, the shamans have always known.

In the Second Attention, then, we can enter a transpersonal space, beyond the body, by 'taking ourselves outside' of our body's confines to enter the energy space and reality which connects us all. We can then commune quite easily with the reality experienced by another person – or even a machine – by using techniques such as the out-of-body journey, lucid dreaming, freeing the body's double, and so on.

But what exactly is it that is freed from ourselves in order to make this journey into the other-space?

The answer is – our soul.

Western spiritual practice, typically, sees the human body as having one soul: an animating principle which is the spirit or energy parallel of our physical selves. Spiritualists talk of a golden or silver cord which is attached to the soul at the navel and enables our spirit to roam free from us while still remaining connected to the body so we can return to ourselves when our out-of-body journey is over. The soul may journey at night as we sleep, to meet with others and to share experiences which we call dreams. As long as it remains attached to our bodies and the cord which connects us stays intact, there is absolutely no danger in this and, in fact, we can receive profound wisdom during these out-of-body states.

The shamans have a rather different and more sophisticated view of the soul, however, as do the houngans and mambos.

For the shaman, the body normally has more than one soul. The Amazonian Yagua, for example, believe in five different souls, all of which survive beyond death. The *hunitu* soul appears when a baby first begins to walk, and is located at the top of the head; it gives the body the ability of movement. The *hunisetu* soul is found in the pupil of the eye and is concerned with spiritual vision. Both of these are involved with the spirit–body connection; they are what make us spiritual beings. They may both leave the body during sleep (and *we must therefore be careful as we dream*, since they can be captured by magicians or by the spirits of plants and animals, leading to madness or death if not recovered quickly). The other three souls, situated between the chest and the stomach are, collectively, called the *ndenu mbayau*, and really only become powerful after death; they are, if you wish, the animating principles of the dead, just as the first two souls are an animating force for the living.

Vodou tradition speaks of three souls, called the *ti bon anje* ('little good angel'), *gro bon anje* ('big good angel'), and the *met tet* ('master of the head'). One way of understanding the first is to view it as the ethical soul, the force which allows us to differentiate between right and wrong and to act from a sense of morality and compassion. The *gro bon anje* is the spirit connection within us, which links us to the infinite so we may understand the will of god. The *met tet* is our specific link to the gods, literally the loa who inhabits, protects and drives us throughout life. The *ti bon anje* is, in this sense, an aspect of the First Attention (our human occupation of the world); the *met tet* is an aspect of the Second Attention (our occupation of wider, transpersonal, space, where we can access the energy we must call upon when we wish to act stupendously or remarkably in life); while the *gro bon anje* is our human participation in the Third Attention (see below), our spiritual-genetic memory of our original connection with the universe and with god.

For the Guatemaltecan Indians, there are many souls in the body and one of these, in particular, is a healer. It is this soul that makes the journey of diagnosis and healing during shamanic interventions in the welfare of the community.

If any of this sounds strange, we need only remember that in Western culture we also differentiate between the spiritual and emotional aspects of the body's component parts. The brain, we say, is the seat of reason and of thought, while the heart is the centre of our feelings, the solar plexus is where our will resides, and our back and shoulders are where our motivation lies (as suggested by expressions such as 'put your back into it' and 'shoulder the weight'). Even these definitions are not fixed, however; until just a few hundred years ago in England, illness was seen as the result of 'humours' spread throughout the body – *sanguine* in the blood, for example (a notion similar to those of some shamanic cultures, which see the soul as residing in the blood and so spreading throughout the body) – while in the literature of the Middle Ages the power of reason and thought was seen as coming from the heart rather than the brain.

It is apparent that the idea of the soul cannot be laughed off or dismissed as easily as some people think, and nor should we be too quick to accept the modern idea that we have only one soul. The reality may be that we have many.

It is very easy to get a sense of your own soul – or souls – and where they may reside in your body, as the next exercise will show.

EXERCISE: SAYING HELLO TO YOUR SOUL

Relax, close your eyes, and breathe deeply. Ask yourself which part of your body feels closest to spirit, which feels most 'aware', which feels most ancient and wise within you, which has most knowledge of you, your health, your lifepath, your sense of self; which holds most power for you.

Let your attention be drawn to each part in turn and get a sense of how each of these parts looks and feels, and of what it knows. Ask questions of this part, specific to the information it has about you and your potential, and understand that you can always return here if you need guidance or support in your life.

If you got a sense of consciousness or soul which was part in and part outside of your physical body, as many people do, that is perfectly natural since these souls are part of the energy body, which exists in transpersonal space, like a cocoon that is both within and without us.

See these soul parts now as one whole field of energy connected in all of its aspects. This is the 'one soul' which the spiritualists talk of, though actually it is more than one soul, it is a series of 'spiritual specialisms' which can be consulted independently as well as used together as a single animating force in your life.

Open your eyes and return from your journey. If you wish, draw a picture of your body and map the consistent parts of your soul onto this so you know where to return for future information on specific issues.

3. THE ENERGY MATRIX –
THE THIRD LEVEL OF ATTENTION

If the first level of the energy web we are a part of is focused on the body in the widest sense of a physical, mental, emotional and spiritual entity and its connections with the wider environment, and the second level involves our 'soul-selves' in transpersonal interactions, then the third level is the entire field outside of ourselves, of which everything in the universe is a part. We can see these energy fields as circles within circles, widening out from the self to encompass everything that is.

The first level of energy can be described as the *somewhat known*: this consists of the abilities we know ourselves capable of as well as our potential for learning to use these abilities more effectively, while the second level is the *knowable*, the space beyond ourselves that traditional spiritual practices can enable us to connect with. The third level is, in a sense, the *unknown and unknowable*. We feel its energy since we are intimately connected to all three zones and we can journey intuitively into this realm to explore and learn from it. The problem is in describing it since there are no words to do so. This is what is meant by *unknowable*: the sense that the information we receive can never be rationally processed using our normal faculties.

Castaneda's distinction is between the *tonal* and the *nagual*. The *tonal* is all that we are aware of and can describe to others, while the *nagual* is the cosmic mystery which can never be expressed in words since, when we do so, we bring it into the realm of the known and the very mystery which is at its core is destroyed in words.

What we can experience in the realm of the *nagual*, however, can radically alter our perception of reality and our conception of our place in the world. It is in this place that the very heart of truth, the 'what is-ness' of our combined consciousness, the essence of pure reality, is to be found in the intricate web of energy that is the source of all being.

Sir John Woodroffe in the foreword to that guidebook and route map for departed souls, *The Tibetan Book of the Dead*, tries to paint a word-picture of the nature of this realm when he describes it as a void of 'consciousness freed of all limitations', but even he recognizes the problem of using language to explain what cannot be explained when he says that this void 'cannot even strictly be called Nirvana, for this is a term relative to the world and the Void is beyond all relations'.[36]

Those who travel to this realm sense the ultimate, irrational, experiential truth of raw, undefined and limitless energy which is true reality, quite beyond the consensus descriptions we then apply to this flowing sense of life laid bare. It is a humbling and awe-inspiring experience to journey here, like meeting with god and having her secrets revealed quite openly. It feels a sharp contrast to the trivial concerns and brittle harshness of mankind's limitations, and our mindless fixations on meaningless pursuits as human rats running mazes of our own making. To be a part of this realm, even for an instant, is to redefine your life and see your place in the whole cosmic order, at once everything and nothing.

Those who make this journey must exercise extreme caution as they are literally moving beyond time and space, life and death, and all known sensations and points of reference, and it is a journey not recommended here.

When you enter this place of the Third Attention, you must also be careful not to bring anything back with you on any account – a mistake I once made and immediately came to regret.

I was 19 at the time and living temporarily as part of a shamanic community near Wales, which was inspired by the works of Timothy Leary, Gordon Wasson, the modern 'psychedelic shamans' like Terence McKenna, and the ayahuasca shamans of the Amazon, who use teacher plants to facilitate specific shamanic experiences in non-ordinary reality.

Whenever one ingests a psychedelic substance, the nature of 'reality' is changed, freeing the mind to connect with new, different and bigger aspects of the self and to see the wider picture of the universe we occupy. As Albert Hoffman, the scientist who discovered LSD, said of his own research into this particular psychedelic: 'Of greatest significance to me has been the insight that I attained as a fundamental understanding from all of my LSD experiments: what one commonly takes as "the reality", including the reality of one's individual person, by no means signifies something fixed, but rather something that is ambiguous – there is not only one, but many realities, each comprising also a different consciousness . . .'[37]

On this occasion we were working with psilocybin ('magic') mushrooms, our native equivalent of the teonanacatl family of mushrooms which the Mazatec shamans of Mexico revered as sacred healing food, the 'flesh of the gods', when suddenly I found myself beyond the normal landscapes of the shaman's otherworld, away from my friends, and within the energy matrix itself.

At first there was only darkness, like a death of consciousness where I was aware of my surroundings but had absolutely no sense of emotional attachment to anything, no fear of the dark, no experience of peace. Before me in the distance, and moving closer, was a huge orange grid of pure, pulsating energy emitting a sound like the hum of electricity or white noise, which I both heard and experienced. As it came closer it also seemed to become a part of me, and I of it.

And then I *was* within and a part of it. I was all things and all things were me. I was tiny and of no significance, but I was also a central part of everything, *the* most important part of everything, the one single thing that held everything together. And I was not alone.

I was aware of other consciousnesses, other disembodied awareness, all of which were also everything and nothing, crucially important and of no consequence, and I understood that we are all connected and all vital conduits for this flow of energy – indeed, we *are* the energy itself. I couldn't say that these other consciousnesses were human entities; they might just as well have been animals or plants or thought-forms from the first human awareness of perceptions and emotions, the first separation of 'I' and 'That'. It didn't matter: we were all equally precious and all equally pointless in the sense that things 'just were', everything 'just was', there was no reason, only *the* reason itself.

Reflecting on this experience later, I would see it as one of the most humbling and empowering, meaningful yet un-explainable visions I have ever had (or, rather, been a part of, since I did not just 'have' the vision but was myself an aspect of it).

My fundamental mistake at the time was one of simple human arrogance. Some part of me must have wanted to stay in this experience for ever and remain part of this vast ener-getic flow and I remember thinking that it must be possible to do so, that I could somehow *control* the vision (since, after all, it was *my* vision – wasn't it?) and remain there as long as I wished. In that second, I was thrown out of paradise.

It was like being vomited out through space and time, back through the darkness. So repugnant must my human ego have been to this energetic entity I was one with that it just wanted me quickly out of its 'body', as we would want a virus gone.

As I hurtled through this dark dimension I was aware of things sticking to me, of areas of resistance in the fabric of the blackness. Then, with a jolt which felt like my heart being jump-started, I was back in my body again and aware of my thoughts and mental associations. Thinking the experience was over, I opened my eyes.

There in front of me, less than four feet from where I was sitting, was the most repulsive being I had ever seen. It had a human shape but it was grey and bloated, its fingers pointed, its eyes glaring. I thought it similar in form to a man who had drowned and whose flesh had become sodden with water, who had been buried in the earth and then exhumed some months later, for its skin was hanging off it in parts and its stench was dreadful. I had the feeling that its repugnance to me was on a par with the sensations I must have created within the energy matrix with my presumption that I was all-powerful and able to control the consciousness of the universe in some way.

I tried to remain calm, to put aside my perceptual prejudices, and to will myself to relate to this entity as I would any other person or thing, regardless of their appearance, for I had no knowledge that it was malign; rather it seemed interested in me and, if anything, slightly irritated to be in this place, as if its essence had been stuck to me as I flew through the dark world, and it had been dragged away from its own environment into this one, unfamiliar to it.

As it began to move towards me, rotten arms and hands outstretched, however, I could no longer maintain the calm I was fighting for. I closed my eyes tight and rubbed them in order to shut out and erase the vision in front of me, just as people do in the movies when awakening from a bad dream.

In the movies it works, of course, but when I opened my eyes again, rather than disappearing, the creature had moved closer, its hands about to cradle my head, its face less than a foot away from me.

As objective and non-judgmental as I wanted to be, I wasn't about to hang around to see what happened next. I got up as calmly as I could and walked from the room into the open air, then took myself on a long walk in the countryside. When I returned an hour or so later, the entity was gone. I still have no idea how or where to, or if it returned to its own world. It was incredibly irresponsible of me to bring this entity back and then leave it abandoned and a free agent in our world, but I just didn't have the powers at that time to deal with it. I often wonder about its fate.

Castaneda mentioned a similar, but altogether more pleasant, experience when he talked of his meeting with the entity he came to call the Blue Scout.

He first met this entity during an otherworld journey. Castaneda calls such entities 'inorganic beings' from other realities, and says that they are as attracted to human energy and as curious about us as we are about them. Just as we send probes into outer space and direct radio signals at the stars to try to contact our distant relatives there, or seek also to explore our own inner space, so these inorganic beings send adventurers and explorers, which Castaneda calls 'scouts', into our world in order to discover more about us.

When Castaneda first encountered this being, he saw it as a blue flame (hence 'Blue Scout') and had the sense that it was lost between worlds and in distress. He had been warned by his mentor, don Juan, never to interact with these beings and so ignored the entity on this occasion. However, from a mixture of curiosity and compassion, he could not help returning at a later date: this time the Blue Scout presented itself as a small female child softly crying, lost and alone. Castaneda says he made a deliberate and conscious decision to return with this entity to our reality so he brought the Blue Scout back with him. Literally. The entity he returned took human form and is still alive here on Earth.

Don Juan was furious at the irresponsible actions of his student and told him that he would now have to be personally responsible for this entity throughout his life. Castaneda took his duties seriously and acted as the parent and guardian of the Blue Scout until his own death a few years ago, whereupon the Blue Scout, according to some reports, simply vanished from public life, although it is likely that she is still here amongst us.

Incidents like this are suggestive of the vast potential of this third field of energy we are connected to – and also of its dangers, of course. You need to understand the risks of electricity as well as its benefits before you can use it purposely and practically to assist you in daily life.

THE STRUCTURE OF MAGIC AND THE NATURE OF ENERGY

We have looked in some detail at the nature of energy and its three expressions as fields of attachment to ourselves, and have touched upon the applications of these energy forms in daily living and in the spiritual-energetic practices of shamanism and Vodou. How, briefly, can we use this energy in our lives? Let us take a quick look at the principles for doing so now, before we move on to consider some of the specific practical applications of energy work in everyday life.

Imagine you have an accident one day and manage to break your leg. You hobble to the nearest shaman healer or houngan and ask her to help you. What do you suppose she would do? Smudge you with cleansing herbs? Pray? Prescribe a magical healing bath? Conduct a soul retrieval? Rub your injured leg with feathers to extract the pain and then ritually burn them? Work a magical ritual or *wanga* for you?

The answer is, if she has any sense at all, and if she is a bona fide healer, she will drive you immediately to the Accident & Emergency department of the nearest hospital to get your leg fixed and plastered. Only later, when your leg is set and the painkillers are at work, will the houngan want to know the circumstances of your accident to see whether a loss of spirit has caused it or, perhaps, if evil magic is being worked upon you.

For the shaman, there is no smoke without fire. In the whole context of the flow of the universe and the energy which holds it, there must have been a reason for you to be there, at that place where you tripped and fell; there must have been something to trip over. So what was it that took you to that place of potential danger, why weren't you aware of the hazard and why didn't you see it coming?

The energetic healing, however, is only one aspect of your problem. You still have a broken leg, and there are urgent practical actions which need to be taken too – like getting your leg fixed – before the other things can be looked at.

Working with energy is very much like this. By becoming more in tune with the powers that surround us, and aligning ourselves to them, we can achieve remarkable control over ourselves and our environment. But it is an illusion to believe that we can then *ignore* the world around us. Instead, we must take the energy which is now within our power and apply it *to the world* in order to achieve results and ensure the materialization of the good things we desire for ourselves. In other words, we must first find the energy we need for our works and then focus it on the result we want so that the energy flow is directed beneficially and appropriately.

Sometimes this requires straightforward mundane action as well as esoteric magical practice. We cannot simply will good things for ourselves and then sit back and wait with no need for further effort or involvement on our part. We live in a physical world and to attempt to influence it solely by ethereal and spiritual means is, frankly, wishful thinking.

In Haiti, Greg, one of our party of Vodou initiates, had lost his job just before he left the States, so one of the mambos taught us how to petition the spirits for better prospects, a more fulfilling job or the receipt of more money. Using a *wanga* similar to the one she showed us, she had, she said, been able to accumulate a large amount of money in a short time, which just continued to flow towards her from the most unexpected sources, such as the repayment of a loan made some four years previously, which she had long since forgotten about. Others who had used this *wanga* had achieved the same results.

To help Greg find a new job, the mambo advised him to write a letter of request to a particular loa with whom he had an affinity and to use this as part of a specific ritual, then to make an offering to the spirit in the sure knowledge that the request had been heard and would be answered.

'Then,' she said, 'get off your arse and get your résumé out there in the market!'

Sitting back and waiting for job offers to come out of nowhere might well have produced the desired effect for Greg. But giving the spirits something to work with – such as an announcement to employers that you are available for work – is likely to deliver a better result faster!

Exercise: petitioning the spirits

This exercise is based on the one taught to us in Haiti, which would help Greg to find a new job. It is a very practical technique for modern living where money and work, stressful as these can sometimes be, are also necessities for survival.

Write a letter, just as if you were writing it to someone, such as your GP or solicitor, who is known to you but whom you would nonetheless address fairly formally and with professional courtesy and respect, detailing quite specifically the request you are making.

If you are looking for a new job, for example, and need to make £50,000 a year, say so, and add the words '*at least* £50,000' so the spirits know what the bottom line is for you but also have room to manoeuvre in bettering your life, and so that you do not end up limiting yourself with your own expectations by putting false ceilings on your worth.

Also tell the spirits what time frame you want this job to appear in – if you need it in six months but do not say so, you may end up getting it in six years, or even six days. If there are any other specifics you need to mention (the type of industry you want to work in, the company you want to work for, etc.) remember to state these too.

Fold the letter *towards you* to attract these things into your life (you fold *away* from you to repel something, such as a negative situation you are faced with), at all times intending and believing that your request *will* be answered ('without an atom of doubt'). Place the letter on the table in front of you and next to it light a candle, whose energy will carry the petition to the spirits.

The loa work on a quid pro quo basis – there must be an exchange of energy with the universe in order for any magic to be effective – and require something in return. You can satisfy this requirement by making an offering of food to them; a plate of the same food that you eat at your next meal should suffice.

When the candle has burned down, put the food, the remnants of the candle and your letter itself into a bag and take it to the woods. Bury it among living, growing, things. And then – as the mambo says – get off your backside and get your CV out there too.

In the words of Maya Deren, it is true that 'a man may be strong and powerful because the loa have made him so, but it is the man who makes the magic, not the loa'.[38]

Of course, getting a well-paid job is one thing but if you have to work like a slave in it and have no time for the enjoyment of life, you will have achieved very little, so you may wish to write a second letter in the same way and repeat this ritual, but this time asking for a little luxury and fun in your life as well.

As you can see from the exercise above, the principles of working with energy are in many ways similar to those of natural magic, which Sir James George Frazer, in his classic book on tribal magic, *The Golden Bough*, has reduced to two essential principles, which he calls the Law of Similarity and the Law of Contact.[39]

The Law of Similarity
The Law of Similarity suggests that 'like produces like' so that a similar form or representation of the object or person to be worked upon can be used in place of the original and the effect produced will be the same as if the actual object had been used. For example, in Andean shamanism, Peter Cloudsley tells us that 'a leaf that has the shape of a kidney is assumed to be good for curing those organs'.[40]

The vegetalista shamans of the Amazon (healers who work with the magical powers of plants) use this principle in their work. Luis Eduardo Luna, in *Ayahuasca Visions*, mentions one shaman, don Pascual, who taught him of the importance

265

attached to the shape of plants, as well as other features, which all offer clues to their curative powers.

If, for example, a flower had a shape resembling an ear, then they [the shamans] would use it for ear diseases. If the root of an epiphyte looked like a spider, then some part of the plant was used for spider bites. A small bush found at more or less equal intervals would be thought to jump like a dolphin, and therefore would be used as a remedy for an illness thought to be caused by the dolphin. During his training, the neophyte scrutinises plants, animals, and nature in general, trying to find clues and analogies that reveal their properties and how they can be used. There is a remarkable similarity with the ideas of Oswald Coll, a Paracelsist physician who, in his book, De Signatura Rerum (1608) proposed that by contemplating the body of plants, one would be able to discover their hidden virtues.[41]

In Peru, shaman Antonio Montero Pisco uses the deep red-purple juice of the pokeweed to cure excessive menstrual bleeding in his female clients. Here, it is the spirit of the plant, its herbal properties and the association between its natural colour and that of the menstrual blood itself which carry the magic. Montero also points out that ultimately it is the patient who cures herself through an act of her own will – she must 'intend' strongly to become well and, through this, will change the energy flow within her own body, in much the same way as migraine sufferers helped themselves by altering their own blood flow, in the case we looked at earlier.

'Practitioners need to understand that medicine by itself does not cure,' says Montero in a *Washington Post* article written about him during a 1999 visit to the United States. 'People heal themselves by having faith in the spirits and the healing power of plants.'[42]

By the same token, in the New Orleans Voodoo tradition, the practitioner may use a doll (the much-hyped and misunderstood 'voodoo doll') to represent and symbolize a person he is working with and then produce an effect in the doll which will be transferred to the person concerned. Normally, the practitioner also requires some personal items, such as hair, fingernails or an item of clothing from the individual in order to strengthen the energetic attachment between the person and the doll, though this is not always necessary. Indeed, with modern technology it is feasible to use a web cam to broadcast a live image of the person concerned, or a video of them or a jpeg image sent down the line. As long as that person can be represented in some way, the magic will work.

People tend to believe, through the influence of Hollywood, that voodoo dolls are used only for malevolent purposes but this is far from the truth. A person suffering from an illness may be represented by a doll which is then 'healed'; the effect transferring itself to the person suffering the illness through the sympathetic alliance established by the will of the magician.

One practitioner I know in New York claims considerable success with this method and has used it to cure people of a range of problems by carrying out massage, energetic cleansing by burning special herbs and oil and, in some cases, even surgery on the doll. By the same token, someone seeking promotion at work can be helped by working with the doll to symbolically enhance its 'status'. According to this practitioner, he had been successful in achieving promotion for an army officer with a single stripe by sewing a second stripe onto the arm of a doll made for him as part of a ceremony. I can only imagine what his superior officers would have done if they had discovered this soldier's methods, but to me it is a good example of the creativity and ingenuity we require from our armed forces!

Hoodoo practitioners, the root doctors and magical herbalists of the American South, also use the Law of Similarity in their work, using plants and herbs which, by their very name, as well as their appearance and pharmacological actions, are thought to bring power to their client.

Two of the most popular items which can now be bought from magical supplies shops (called *botanicas*) are Lucky Hand Root (salep root), which has the physical appearance of a five-fingered outstretched hand and is said to be good for drawing luck, particularly in gambling and games of chance; and High John the Conqueror Root which, as the name suggests, is used for drawing in power and success in situations of personal mastery, financial and business undertakings.

Others include Devil's Pod, a seed pod of the aquatic Asian plant, *Trapa bicornis*, which has the appearance of a horned devil and is typically placed in the doorways of houses, facing outwards to ward off evil; and even Irish Moss which is used to imbue its owner with 'the luck of the Irish' and bring good fortune in all matters of money and chance.

Most of these herbs can be purchased commercially, along with *gris-gris* bags which contain a mixture of herbs, seeds and power objects to bring success in a variety of matters and concerns – such as Love Me oil, Reconciliation crystals, Peaceful Home powders, Steady Work crystals and Money Drawing oil – or for protection against the evil 'tricks' or unintentional actions of others. Hot Foot powder, for example, is said to drive away an enemy when sprinkled in their yard, while Fiery Wall of Protection oil offers protection from the evil eye, from violence and from *susto* (soul loss), while Bend Over crystals will enable you to subjugate another to your will.

The principle of Similarity is used in herbal healing work in Haiti. To prepare us for a very vigorous and demanding ceremony, where we would be required to handle flaming materials with our bare hands, we were given a herbal mixture to rub into our palms, the main ingredient of which was a plant seen as having considerable magical properties of empowerment and strengthening. Its name, translated from the Creole, was 'I Can'.

The Law of Similarity is also used in Vodou for the casting of certain spells and *wangas*. A priest of Palo taught me the following spell, which is used in order to 'keep someone sweet' and loyal within a relationship.

EXERCISE: KEEPING SOMEONE 'SWEET' TOWARDS YOU

Take a jar of honey, five sticks of cinnamon and a photograph of the person concerned. If you can also get some of their pubic or underarm hair, so much the better.

Write their name on a piece of paper and yours over the top of it in a slightly thicker pen and then wrap the cinnamon sticks with their photograph facing *inwards* (towards the sticks). Wrap the paper with the names facing *outwards* (away from the sticks). Wrap both in yellow and white thread and, if you have it, add any hair or other personal items to the bundle. Finally, add a length of yellow thread tied with five knots. Place the entire bundle in the honey and tighten the lid.

Keep this jar in a safe place and do not dispose of it until you want the relationship between the two of you to end.

Here, sweet things such as honey are used as an item of 'Similarity' in order to 'sweeten' a person towards you, while the use of their personal effects creates the energetic link with them. Their photograph and hair *is* them and when this is immersed in honey and linked to you through your name, the effect is transferred to them.

Because Similarity works without boundaries, it is also possible to heal someone at a distance, using a representational item which *becomes* that person in order to close the gap between the two of you.

A few years ago I was asked by Miriam, a young woman in Sweden, to help with a problem she was having of constant severe tiredness and chronic loss of energy.

Fearing that she might be suffering from something like ME (the so-called 'yuppie flu'), she had visited doctors and been tested a number of times, all without result. Her doctors could find nothing wrong with her, yet *she* knew how she felt and her condition was now quite debilitating, leading frequently to time off work and ensuring that her social life was practically non-existent.

Since I had no plans in the near future to visit Sweden, Miriam and I agreed to work together by email.

I asked Miriam for a brief outline of her life and, learning that she liked to write poetry and short stories, for a few examples of her writing too. All of this was useful in forging the link between us which is important for energy work and the practice of sympathetic magic.

Then, at an agreed time, we lay down together in our respective countries, she to meditate quietly and I to undertake a shamanic journey of soul retrieval (see next chapter) on her behalf to establish the cause of this illness and the method of its cure.

Through the technique of soul retrieval, I was able to recover Miriam's lost energy, and with its return, the healing for Miriam could begin. But what got us to this point at all was the Law of Similarity. By developing a rapport with Miriam at some distance, through her poetry and writings, I could get a real sense of her and an energetic connection was firmly established between us.

The Law of Contact

The other principle operating in energy medicine and magic is the Law of Contact, which states that energy can be transferred from one place to another via an object which has been in contact with both.

'An example of contact magic is afforded by the belief that if toe nail clippings are carelessly discarded, they can be used to harm the person of whom they were once a part, or if a piece of clothing were lost this could bring bad luck,' says Peter Cloudsley, writing of Andean shamanism in the *Journal of Museum Ethnography*.[43]

This is also the principle used by Yabofe, the Haitian

houngan-healer who uses a live chicken, which he rubs over his patient, to transfer illness from that person and into the chicken, which then becomes its carrier. By killing the chicken, he then releases the energy of the illness.*

In Peru, guinea pigs are used in place of chickens in healing rituals called *sobada de cuy* in Spanish, or *caypa* in the Quechua language. Live guinea pigs are rubbed over the body of the patient to absorb the illness and, invariably – and also quite interestingly from our Western perspective – the animal itself will die of 'natural causes' during the course of the ceremony itself. It will then be cut open and the state of its internal organs used to diagnose the patient's problems as well as the outcome of the shaman's intervention. Often, the similarity between the presenting problem of the client and the condition of the guinea pig's internal organs is quite pronounced, such as a blackening of the kidneys or an engorged spleen.

In a variation on this healing practice, the guinea pig is touched lightly to the patient, just enough to allow the transference of energy from one to the other, and various herbs are then offered to it. In the words of Peter Cloudsley, who has witnessed many of these healing rituals, 'if it nibbles or just sniffs at the herbs, these are not considered to be strong enough, and other herbs will be tested until the guinea pig eats some of them, thereby signalling the appropriate one to be used medicinally [on the patient]'.[44]

In either case, it is contact with the patient which is important for both diagnosing and then suggesting an appropriate healing approach.

Some shamans even undergo the extreme practice, when working with a patient and using this principle of contact, of exchanging clothes with the sufferer. The shaman then takes

---

* Since energy is neither good nor evil but neutral and ambivalent, it is actually incorrect to refer to the release of an 'illness'. Instead, the energy trapped within the patient's own energy body, which is detrimental to his health, is transferred to the chicken and then, through sacrifice, allowed to return to the universal 'pool' to be drawn from by others who can put it to more productive use.

on their illness herself through magical association and fights it within her own body, while the patient is steeped in the powerful health of the shaman by wearing her clothes. By doing so, she is effectively protected or even temporarily cured, and then fully healed when the shaman releases the illness from her own body.

The English magician, Aleister Crowley, defined magic as the ability of a person to deliberately create changes in consciousness. In other words, since 'reality' is what we generate with our own minds through a projection of our intention onto the cosmos, by changing ourselves through traditional healing methods and ritual performances of this kind, we also change our experience of the world.

'If one were to ask "Does this ritual cause that thing to happen?", the answer would be in the affirmative,' says Maya Deren, who studied healing and the use of ceremony extensively in Haitian Vodou.

> *The primary effect of such ritual action is upon the doer. That action reaffirms first principles – destiny, strength, love, life, death; it recapitulates a man's relationship to his ancestors, his history, as well as his relationship to the contemporary community; it exercises and formalises his own integrity and personality, tightens his disciplines, confirms his morale.*
>
> *In sum, he emerges with a strengthened and refreshed sense of his relationship to cosmic, social and personal elements. A man so integrated is likely to function more effectively than one whose adjustment has begun to dis-integrate, and this will be reflected in the relative success of his undertakings.*
>
> *The miracle is, in a sense, interior. It is the doer who is changed by the ritual and, for him, therefore, the world changes accordingly.*[45]

At the root of both shamanism and Vodou is the belief in personal, communal and cosmic energy – the First, Second and

Third level energy fields we have discussed. By changing any one, we transform our relationship to the whole.

SELF AND THE CITY

The city does not exist in isolation, as an independent entity with no connection to ourselves. On the contrary, as an aspect of our dreaming, it is an entity we have created in our own image and it is intimately connected to our worldview. Its energies cross the three fields we operate within. It has an effect on the people who live within it, for the transpersonal community created by this mingling of energies and souls, and on the cosmic order itself, since our communal dream, represented by the shape, structure and morality of the modern world which is symbolized by our cities, also has an impact on the nature of the universe that we see ourselves as a part of. This, in turn, has implications for our behaviour towards our fellow humans and the planet which is our home.

We have created a modern world of extremes and paradox. We want to get from A to B as quickly as possible, since only the start and the destination are respected in the Western equation, and we don't care what we have to do in order to get there, either, including giving ourselves over to others and to systems so they can control our journey, or seeking to control others so they can bolster us.

The problem is that by doing this we are giving away our energy, and sacrificing huge chunks of our lives. There is a popular truism treated almost like a joke, though it is deadly serious: 'No-one on their deathbed ever said I wish I'd spent more time in the office.' Yet I know people who spend 14 or 15 hours, often more, in every 24-hour day, in the office or on company business. They desire nothing more than to leave their jobs and even have the money to do so, but they are afraid to resign because then they would be on their own, undefined by the roles they currently occupy.

I know other people who tell me they would love to escape the city before there is nothing left of them, yet they refuse to leave for fear of what might really wait for them in the unknown darkness of the rural idyll which serves them as a dream. They are scared to take a chance on life and so they will die without really having lived.

Yet, when our energy is out of resonance with the people around us and the environment we occupy, our very souls are at risk. Shamans call such dangers 'spirit intrusions' or 'soul loss' and by this they mean a very real state of suffering and ill-health. In the words of D. H. Lawrence:

> *I am not a mechanism, an assembly of various sections*
> *And it is not because the mechanism is working*
> *wrongly that I am ill.*
> *I am ill because of wounds to the soul, to*
> *the deep emotional self* [46]

We will look at these conditions in the next chapter and then see what we can do to help with our recovery and self-protection.

5

SPIRIT INTRUSION, SOUL LOSS AND ENERGETIC SELF-PROTECTION: HOW ENERGY CAN HEAL OR HARM US

Shape without form, shade without colour,
Paralysed force, gesture without motion;

Those who have crossed
With direct eyes, to death's other Kingdom
Remember us – if at all – not as lost
Violent souls, but only
As the hollow men
The stuffed men.[1]

Look up at the stars. The space between this planet that you stand upon and the others in the sky is the same distance that separates each atom in this book you are holding.

Why does the book not fall apart? Why does the sky not fall?

What holds it all together is the energy between the atoms, and this energy may have unlimited potential. You need only look around you, at the world of nature, to see evidence that such energy truly does exist, and the remarkable things which can be achieved with it.

Australian Aboriginal shamans use quartz crystals for healing, aware that the natural vibrations of the crystal are amplifiers of energy and can hold the expression of any energetic form within them. Crystals are used for healing, in order to absorb negative energy.

But this is no great achievement – a simple arachnid knows the truth of this too. There is a spider which builds around it a fortress of crystals and then weaves a single strand of its web across the top of each. When its prey touches the crystal, the vibrations of its movements are amplified by the crystal and alert the spider to its presence much more effectively than a fully woven web could do. But more than that, the energetic emanations of the crystal tell the spider the nature of the prey, its size, exact location, and the best way of tackling it. It is *as if* the spider has an affinity with the crystal and can tune in to its prey by using it in this way.

The torpedo ray is another case in point. One sixth of its body weight is taken up by specially adapted muscles which can dispense an electrical charge of high enough voltage to stun a fully grown man, and certainly enough to kill its normal prey. The ray is an excellent hunter because not only can it generate electricity within its living body, it can also detect the electrical signals of other living things and so is able to zero in on them with lethal accuracy.

Electricity is just another form of energy. How can creatures of flesh and blood generate electricity within themselves? They can do so because, at another level of awareness, we are all composed essentially, and first and foremost, of energy.

Talk of shamans and distant lands may make this fact seem exotic in terms of its usage and healing potential, but it is not. At an innate and intuitive level, we all understand that this energy exists and can be used. Our ignorance of it is a modern invention and a consequence only of the predominance of scientific thinking within our culture, and our acceptance of this as our consensus worldview. Even our recent ancestors knew better.

In medieval England, for example – just a few hundred years ago – abbeys like St Mary's Spittal were also hospitals. The sick were given beds in wards around the abbey so that they could see and share each prayer, each psalm and each song from where they lay, the abbots recognizing that healing did not just depend on medicine but on energetic exchange, the healing power of prayer, and connection with the spirit.

The Middle Ages was the last time that Western countries truly practised holistic medicine which cared for the body, the emotions and the soul at one and the same time. After that, science and systems began to take over and we lost ourselves. We lost faith in our instinctive, natural knowledge of spiritual healing and sacrificed ourselves to a belief in an exterior wisdom based on rationality and theorems and a world which can be 'proved'.

The pendulum is now returning and we are once again discovering that faith in ourselves is the final answer to all our problems.

While we wait for the pendulum to complete its swing, however, we must continue to live in the rational world of the city. But, even here, we can at least develop a deeper sense of connection with our environment and the spiritual energies which occupy these city places. In so doing, we will come to better understand and so protect ourselves from the loss of self associated with modern living, as well as recovering the sense of the sacred in our lives that is so much missed and so pined for in today's world.

If we do not do so, we are vulnerable to the chaotic energies which surround us and to the deliberate or accidental actions of others which can have an effect on our well-being, as well as to blind faith in a system which may well end up killing us – and this is no exaggeration. Nick Williams, in *The Work We Were Born To Do*, quotes a study by the World Watch Institute which estimates that it would take six years and $456,000 million to clean up our environment completely and repair all the damage we have done to it so far – which, in Nick's words, 'seems like a lot until you compare it with the $625,000 million spent in *one* year on arms worldwide. We have the money, we lack the will.'[2] And we lack the will because – and only because – we have never realized that it is *we* who have the power over the system and not the other way around, so enamoured and enchanted have we been with the city's pronouncements of its grandeur and the alluring sparkle of its hypnotically bright and shiny lights.*

In this chapter we look at the impact of the urban world upon us, at some of the ways in which we can defend ourselves against it and, indeed, focus our attention and intention in order to improve our own happiness.

THE NATURE OF ILLNESS

'The problems of our time are interconnected: poverty, over-population, environmental degradation, debt and violence are all facets of a single crisis,' writes Peter Cloudsley, in his study of Andean shamanism[3]. 'Although we know some solutions, a radical change in perception, thinking and values is what is needed. Seeing the world as insoluble or dealing with problems in isolation is part of a mental predicament which, in older societies, was the domain of the shaman. A shaman can help us see through the partial and unsustainable solutions preferred by politicians.'

A radical change in perspective is *exactly* what is offered by the houngan, the mambo and the shaman, who see not just physical but spiritual problems as the underlying cause of every bodily and mental health problem, and those of society

---

* Our attachment to work is an example of how life experience affects the energy body, and the contradictions inherent in our system of living. As a way of earning a living and giving us an identity in the world, work brings us the benefit of income and status within the system – as well as killing us. A study reported in the *Daily Mail* on 30 April 2001, shows that high work-related stress loads are now proven to lower the number of the body's antibodies which fight bacterial and viral infections. 'Pressure on managers is increasing,' says the report. 'People in senior positions no longer have the job security of 20 years ago . . . companies have become too lean and too mean.' As long as we acknowledge the contradiction of working for a living in a way of life that is killing us, we may at least be able to find a strategy of coping. An informed life, where we understand the pros as well as the cons of our decisions is, certainly, a life with more personal integrity than one which merely 'follows the company line'.

as a whole. For these healers, individual or social dis-ease arises from two specific causes: spiritual intrusions (perceived as energies foreign to a person which have been introduced into her energy system, where their detrimental impact is experienced as illness); and soul loss (where certain traumatic events or wilful actions result in a severe loss of power which, once again, will ultimately create illness). These two are behind every single manifestation of illness or lack of harmony, whether individual or at the level of society itself.

Among the Yoruba people of Africa, for example, someone reporting feelings of emptiness and lack of connection with, or engagement in, the world around her will be diagnosed as a fractured person whose soul has become separated from her body, resulting in a weakening of the spirit. By her subsequent interactions with others, her way of relating to the world, this spiritual illness is spread until, eventually, the whole society may become sick.

In attempting to discover when this loss of soul took place for the individual, the shaman will often ask the patient, 'When did you stop laughing? When did you stop singing and dancing?' For the shaman knows that a whole person, integrated and healthy in herself, is naturally joyous; it is only when the soul is wounded that the singing and the laughter stop. Once she has established this information, and identified its cause, the shaman is in a position to introduce a creative healing programme which will not only cure the patient, but will make its impact felt by association on the entire social system.

The feeling of a spiritual intrusion or a loss of soul is one of disinterest, of watching the world go by, with no desire or ability to involve oneself in it. In a sense, it is the essence of the socialized Western life, where we become content, and yet frustrated and unfulfilled, with a life handed to us 'on a plate', with no obvious way out. In extreme cases, the sufferer, finally, is unable to cope with 'normal' life and, in the most serious, may even simply give up on life, with no physically obvious or even circumstantial reason for this. It is like that mysterious phenomenon of 'dying of a broken heart'.

In some cases, tribal (just like contemporary city) rivalry and power struggles deliberately introduce an intrusive energy to a person's system.

Bon Houngan Yabofe is explicit and deliberate in his protection of the people in his *lakou* (the houngan's compound) from attack in this way by rival houngans who would like nothing more than to injure the people in his care through evil magic, in order to undermine his power and demonstrate to others their greater strength, thereby increasing their own power base and the size of their spiritual congregation (and, of course, the financial income they can generate from it). The shaman, Malidoma Some, talks of a similar situation among the African Dagara, where special magical darts, invisible to normal people, are often left on the ground in the path of an enemy so that they embed themselves in his energy body when he walks over them. They must then be removed by the shaman or else the man so attacked is certain to die.

The practice of spiritual attack in this way seems almost universal and appears in the literature pertaining to most tribal peoples. The shamans of New Guinea project the energy of bone and teeth splinters into their enemies in order to do them physical damage. Among the Aborigines of Australia, death is natural only in the very old or very young; all other deaths are considered unnatural and can be avenged using magical techniques to project bone fragments into the spiritual body of the presumed assailant. All the shaman need do is adopt a particular posture (known in the West as 'bone pointing posture') and *intend* to harm her adversary, and the dart will find its mark. In a similar way, the Wana shamans of Sulawesi use sharpened bamboo to attack the energetic parallels of the body's vital organs, while the Eskimos of Alaska use the magically reanimated sinews and skin of dead animals which they set against their rivals.

The situation is not so very different in Western cultures. We talk of people 'looking daggers at us' and observe that 'if looks could kill' we would be in trouble from our rivals and competitors – an innate recognition, perhaps, of the harmful power of 'the evil eye'. These expressions, like 'old wives' tales' and folk medicine, are often an unconscious acknowledgement of a spiritual fact. Looks can, in fact, kill. It happens in traditional societies all the time. Just because we have forgotten does not make the action itself any less lethal.

Vodou priestess, Mambo Racine, who also has an MSc in molecular biology and is involved in traditional and Western healthcare in America and Haiti, is well placed to offer an interesting cross-cultural perspective on this.

'There is a whole list of illnesses in Haiti to which Americans do not fall prey [simply because] we name and define our illnesses differently and behave differently.

'In Haiti, a person who has received an insupportable insult, for instance, can "have *sezisman*", *sezisman* being shock, seized-up-ness, paralysis with rage, in which case the person lies down, refuses to speak or eat, weeps, or, more frequently, is completely unresponsive. This condition may last anywhere from a few hours to a few days.

'A person who witnesses something horrific is also expected to be at risk of *sezisman*. When I was a UN Human Rights Monitor and viewing cadaver after cadaver left by the Haitian Army, people would say, "Now go home and lie down or you will have *sezisman*". After viewing one particularly vile massacre scene, I went home and followed the cultural model I had been shown. I lay down, curled up, and went incommunicado. "Ah-hah! *Sezisman*!" said the people [and] I was then the recipient of massage, herbal teas, cuddling and general cheering up.

'In the USA, I would have said, "I'm stressed, I'm traumatized" and got the same kind of treatment, more or less. I would not declare and manifest the symptoms of *sezisman*. That is how belief shapes manifestation, if you will.'

Michael Harner, from his study of indigenous shamanic practices, has suggested that 'the concept of power intrusion is not too different from the Western medical concept of infection' and, just as we discussed earlier

> *the patient should be treated both for the ordinary aspect of intrusion (i.e. infection) by orthodox material medicine and for the non-ordinary aspect by shamanic methods.*
>
> *Power intrusions, like communicable diseases, seem to occur most frequently in urban areas. From an SSC [shamanic state of consciousness] viewpoint, this is because many people, without knowing it, possess the potentiality for harming others with eruptions of their personal power when they enter a state of emotional disequilibrium such as anger. When we speak of someone 'radiating hostility', it is almost a latent expression of the shamanic view.*[4]

These are not 'primitive', tribal views understood only by the Indians of the rainforest, cut off from 'civilization', or the plains Indians of a few hundred years ago whose 'superstitious' beliefs have been surpassed by the effects of modern technology; these are problems of the city. Even today, in modern New Orleans, Voodoo practitioners and root doctors (experts in the magical and spiritual effects of plants) possess the power to send *haints* – disembodied spirits – after and into people, to do harm or to heal. The *haint*, which may be the spirit of a person, a plant or an object, is given intention and purpose by the practitioner and will then carry out his instructions to enter the body of a sick person to do battle with and defeat the spirit of the illness which lives there, or to act out some more nefarious purpose.

As recently as June 2000 the Reuters news service carried a story from the *East African Standard*, in modern Kenya, of a businessman who was arrested in Nairobi for sending spirits to attack a group of schoolgirls at Itokela Girls Secondary School, after his own daughter left the establishment.[5]

The pupils marched to the District Commissioner's office to protest about the invasion of the school by ghosts who seemed to take delight in tormenting them, throwing the girls around and pushing them to the floor, Reuters reported. 'The man apparently agreed to meet the cost of exorcising the spirits and of a ghost-buster named Ntingili, who retrieved shells and other witchcraft paraphernalia from the school grounds', after which the attacks mysteriously ended.

Deliberate spiritual attacks like these – even in our modern cities – along with the 'emotional disequilibrium' Harner speaks of often result in illness for the victim, including soul loss (where emotional and spiritual problems lead to an erosion of our personal power) and soul theft (a form of energy draining, where this power is taken from us by another, either through deliberate intent or as a by-product of our other, sometimes even loving, relationships with them). These aspects of dis-ease (all of which we look at later) essentially create a loss of balance in the body so that our energies are misaligned or depleted, creating an energetic vacuum where dis-ease can enter, or such a loss of power that we are unable to fight infection.

As a result of her Western medical training and her experiences among the shamans of Ecuador, Dr Eve Bruce of the Dream Change Coalition offers an authoritative comment on the nature of illness, from both a Western and a shamanic perspective. Her conclusion, too, is that all dis-ease is a signal from the body of a profound need for balance which we can even, if we wish, interpret as a 'gift' of understanding and wisdom from the body itself.

'Healing is returning to balance and, no matter what the body does in disease, there is always a spiritual reason,' she says. 'I often ask the people who come to me for healing, "why do you have this disease?" or "why do you have this injury?" Those from industrialized nations have difficulty with this question. They answer in physical terms, often telling me about the situation surrounding the time and place of the injury, the events leading up to the disease, the predisposing factors such as genetics and lifestyle. These physical factors are the basis for modern medicine. This is what is learned in the training of doctors. Yet these are all answers to *how*, not to *why*.'

Eve's own medical credentials are impeccable. A prominent plastic surgeon in the Baltimore/Washington area, she is dual board-certified in plastic and reconstructive surgery and in general surgery, and a member of numerous medical societies, including the American Society of Plastic Surgeons, the Lipoplasty Society, and the esteemed American Society of Aesthetic Plastic Surgery.

She is also the first non-Quechua woman to be inducted into the Circle of Yachaks, the Birdpeople shamans of the high Andes – and she understands the importance of asking for the 'why' of a dis-ease as well as the 'how'.

'There is always a *how*, a mechanism – an unsteady ladder leading to a fall, a biochemical dysfunction leading to diabetes, an overgrowth of autonomous cells leading to cancer. These are the messengers in the physical world, for it is the physical life that is under question. *Why*, however, is a different and very important question, for we are spiritual beings in this physical world. We are given messages, even gifts of illness – for disease and injury *can* be gifts. Sometimes they may be re-routing opportunities, messages from spirit to be listened to carefully.'

Our dis-ease, in other words, is not something to be shunned or feared or 'overcome', but a chance to understand more deeply the patterns of our lives, our need for empower-ment, the nature of our selves.

'Our physical, emotional, and mental bodies are connected to our spiritual bodies; they are not as separate as the Western world likes to think. When there is an imbalance – a dis-ease if you will – there is a reason, a message. It is a gift, and a time to journey, to ask your spirit guides for answers. An illness is a wonderful opportunity to re-evaluate, to become quiet, and to listen. When the message is not listened to, even if a "cure" is obtained, the same energy pattern will recur, with a shapeshift back to dis-ease again. If the first message did not get your attention, the second may be much more severe.'

SPIRITUAL INTRUSIONS AND THE MEANS
OF THEIR EXTRACTION

I have a good friend who is particularly sensitive to the energy emanations of others. Standing next to another person at a party or even in a queue at a shop counter, he is often able to pick up on the feelings of that person to the extent that he will sense their emotions and their pain. This used to result in headaches, sickness and other feelings of distress without any obvious origin – he had no idea why he was feeling like this – until he became aware over time that the sickness he was feeling was not his own but that of another. Then he was able to defend himself against this pyschic intrusion. In the city, such experiences are the basis of modern life.

There is no physical link between us as human beings, no common material space that we share, yet perhaps we have all had times when we could pick up on the emotions or the physical sensations of others. What enables us to do so is the *immaterial* space we share as our energy bodies brush up against one another and our personal energy is transferred.

Even quite innocent exchanges can result in such 'spiritual contagion', but the effect is heightened when negative force is added to the transferral through anger, irritation or ill-will towards another, and still more so when one person seeks deliberately to cause harm to another.

The result of such intrusions can be plainly seen by the shaman in his special state of trance consciousness as an unwanted object or entity in the spiritual field. In traditional societies as well as contemporary shamanic practice (and even in the bodily sensations of some sufferers who are non-shamans), this entity will be seen or sensed as a frightening and repulsive life-form, often a crawling insect or a malignant black shape, just as I saw a virus in the form of a black beetle in the case study I reported earlier, and the illness of one of Cheyenne Maloney's patients, whose dis-ease had taken on the appearance of a large black snake in her energy body.

'An illness has a spiritual identity,' says Sandra Ingerman.[6] 'This means that when I journey into a client's body to look at illness, it will actually have an identity. It will look like a fanged reptile, or an insect, or some dark, sludgy material. The illness will show itself in a form that is repulsive to me.

'Some of the modern work being done with imagery and healing correlates with what shamans have always seen with illness. For example, when patients with cancer draw what their illness looks like, they often draw fanged reptiles and insects. People see on their own what classical shamans have always seen.'

To test the truth of this, you have only to think back to a recent illness or localized pain of your own and ask yourself, if you were to express this as a thing with its own identity, how would you describe it? What would it look like? And what would it have to say to you? For, as Eve Bruce pointed out, an illness has a message or a gift for us – the seeds of our own healing – and often 'the messages of illness are very literal and very simple. Most modern diseases are from loss of connection . . . As children we were all connected to nature and to spirit. As we became disconnected, our bodies became blocked and imbalanced and disease then occurred over time.'

When I have asked my own clients to meet with their disease and to get a sense of its appearance, I am often told that 'it feels like a bee sting' or 'like an army of ants crawling all over me' or like 'a snake writhing in my stomach'. It seems entirely natural to use word-pictures such as this and the richness of the description makes the effect of the illness easily understood by others.

But these are not just 'word pictures', they are very real and highly dangerous intrusions.

One of my shamanic teachers, Howard Charing, described how he worked with a client one day to extract malign energy from him by sucking it with his mouth from the energy field of his client and then spitting it out – a technique used by many traditional shamans. As he entered the shamanic state, he saw his client's body covered in vile, thick

286

black leeches, like ribbons of dark pus filling slowly with the life force of the person they had attached themselves to.

Howard began to pick or suck them from the energy body of his client, one by one, a process which took hours. When he had finished and the client had left, and feeling himself filthy and anxious to get rid of all sensation and memory of the experience, Howard got quickly into the shower. It was only a few minutes before he was violently sick. 'Oh god, why do I have to do this work?' he moaned. To which the spirits, with dark humour, answered him, 'Well, somebody's got to do it!'

EXERCISE: SEEING YOUR PAIN

Relax, close your eyes, and begin your drumming tape. Now, casting your mind back to an accident or injury that you suffered in the past, allow an image to emerge of the shape and form of this pain. See it before you in the landscape of the middle world.

What does it look like? How big is it? What colour is it? Does it have a name, a history, a future? Is it alone or does it have a wider context? Where is it in relation to you? What is its relationship *to* you?

Approach the pain-image and ask it its purpose in visiting you when the injury first occurred. In the wider context of all the events in your life at that time, what can the pain-image tell you of the reason why that injury took place at that time?

When you have understood the reason for its part in your past life, tell the pain-image that you now appreciate its purpose and accept the information that it so dramatically made you aware of, and then ask the pain now to leave you since you have embraced the wisdom it brought and can work with this. There is no need for it to return, or for a similar injury in the future.

Now begin to work with the pain-image so that it can dissipate. If the image appears to you as a large, black snake, for example, begin to change these elements. Allow the image to become smaller, to change its colour to the healing tones of green and blue, let it become a stick instead of a snake, and then pick this spirit-stick up and throw it away, or transform it so you can keep it with you in the otherworld as a protective talisman against further harm.

Return to ordinary consciousness and, if you wish, draw the pain-image as you originally saw it. How does it compare with what shamans have traditionally *seen* in the otherworld when they have been involved in spiritual extraction work for their clients?

Be sure to write down what the pain-image told you of its wider purpose so that you are aware of the instances in your life that are likely to attract similar events. This will serve as a warning that you need self-protection.

While spirit intrusions can occur as a result of the deliberate actions of others, it is more usual that 'a person doesn't even know they are attacking you', as Eileen Nauman points out in her book, *Soul Recovery and Extraction,*[7] which, perhaps, makes it even more dangerous.

> *And then, there's those who do it on purpose and consciously . . . Often, in dysfunctional family dynamics, we see prana-guzzling [the over-control of another which leads to the theft of their free will and vitality] from a parent to a child or vice-versa. This is where pieces get taken from everyone involved in this psychic dance of unhealthy patterns.*
>
> *It can be a co-worker where you have your job. Or your boss. It could be the type of job you're in, such as a nurse in a hospital, a police person, a fire-fighter or any activity where there's high drama linked with life–death situations.*

Or, it's someone who doesn't like you – and you may or may not know it . . . Inevitably, we all make enemies by simply being alive . . . Just by standing your ground and staying in your own, personal balance, you can make people angry at you. You can be attacked just because you're breathing . . . A psychic attack can happen to any of us, anywhere. So, we must be aware and be prepared.

One of the best defences, she says, is to remain unattached and uninvolved emotionally in energetically hazardous situations like this for 'If you can shift yourself into detaching emotionally from those who don't like you (and never will), then you are stopping the giving or frittering away of your energy to them. You can literally, bleed yourself dry over an issue, person, circumstances – and you're haemorrhaging yourself!'

This is an important point. Just as our personal power is the last arbiter when it comes to whether we heal ourselves or not, so our own perspective on events is the most important in whether we give away our power and suffer those problems in the first place.

Dr Stanley Krippner, Professor of Psychology at America's Saybrook Institute, and co-author, with Dr Alberto Villoldo, of *The Realms of Healing*, has made an extensive study of healing practices among the Afro-Brazilian traditions, and concludes that the power of our thoughts alone – whether positive or negative – can have a profound effect on our health. When we accept the psychic emanations of others, pick up on their negativity and – crucially – if we then allow these to be absorbed within us or to consciously or more subtly find ourselves in agreement or resonance with them, we are wide open to injury.

Some of the more sophisticated of the Brazilian practitioners have told Dr Villoldo and myself [that] the worst black magic is the black magic we commit against ourselves. It is the sorcery that hurts ourselves when we think negative thoughts, or we hold onto a destructive self-concept, or when we allow ourselves to say negative, hostile things about ourselves and the people around us, and those sentences go over and over in our minds. It is no wonder, then, that people get stomach aches and backaches and headaches with those negative thought images going around . . . If you want to call this a malevolent spirit, fine. If you want to call it negative thinking, fine. But either the spiritist or the psychotherapist, or both of them, really have to approach that negativity and get rid of it if the person's going to recover.[8]

His conclusion is entirely borne out by a South African friend of mine, Jane, who has experience of the medicine men and witch doctors of her country. There, she says, the witch doctor may sometimes send his own helping spirit to do harm to another on behalf of one of his clients. This is particularly so if the client is suffering from the effects of spiritual attack from an enemy and can be saved only by a reversal of the 'bad medicine'.

Then, the witch doctor's helping spirit, charged with intention, changes its own form and becomes a *tokolosh*, a 'devil-spirit' whose intention is to harm another. The *tokolosh* have a particular form and shape. They are small, gnome-like demons with big oval eyes and high foreheads (not unlike the descriptions some people offer of space aliens), which enter the home of their target while they sleep and, creeping into their bedroom, will crawl into their sleeping souls and make their malevolence felt through sickness and eventually, death.

Once infected there is no cure – and the victims *do* die.

What kills them is belief, exactly as Krippner says. They *know* they are going to die – and so they do. In considering the reason for this attack upon them, trying to reason it all out, they are also brought face to face with their own indiscretions and guilty feelings, and this guilt, eventually, may also be what kills them.

Krippner's own experiences among traditional healers have led him to conclude that, in situations like this, there are four crucial ingredients to effective treatment. To my mind they are equally valid for traditional and modern medical settings:

1. The healer, the healing environment, and the treatment itself must all build upon and support the healing expectations of the patient.

2. It must empower the patient to help himself. Without his co-operation there can be no success at all. The point is also made by Maya Deren with reference to healing in Vodou, when she says that therapeutic actions are not 'executed by the priest but must be carried out, in major portion by the patient himself under guidance of the priest. The patient must himself straighten out his difficulties with the loa. In other words, the patient treats himself, and this is another boost to his morale. Almost inevitably, no matter how ill the person is, he must take part in the rituals relating to his treatment.'[9]

3. The charismatic qualities of the healer are also important as he must generate faith in the patient that his personal power and methods (whatever they are) will be sufficient to ensure a cure, whether by direct action or supplication to the gods, with whom he must therefore be seen to have good relations. In this sense, *all* medicine is faith healing.

4. The healer and the sick person must share the same worldview. A Western sceptic is unlikely to respond to shamanic healing (or, indeed, to homoeopathy or acupuncture) as effectively as a believer in the approach; their systems of belief are simply too dissimilar for the treatment methods to have the emotional impact and meaning necessary to engage the body's own powers of recuperation. They may, however, respond perfectly to the Western medical approach which, of course, has its own dramas, symbols, and rituals of treatment, in no way contradictory to the first 'law' of healing that the patient cures herself.

'Sometimes a technique can work if only one of those four is present [but] the more of those four that are present, the more quickly the person seems to recover,' says Krippner.

Some healing ceremonies in traditional societies, which display all of these qualities, not only last for days, but are highly complex and intense. One North American ceremony takes a total of nine days to perform, with complicated and involved chants and ritual performances at all stages. A single healer cannot handle the entire event; instead the whole tribe takes part – which, of course, provides a further powerful expression to the patient of his value to the community and their love for him. This, in itself, is a great healing, irrespective of the magical content.

In my own urban healing practice, I find that the most important thing to achieve is a shift in the worldview of my clients so that they can come to recognize their own potential for self-healing and re-establish a connection with their power. For, in any healing – whether it takes place in a tribal hut or a modern teaching hospital – the person who ultimately performs the healing is the patient herself. She must believe unequivocally in her own ability to heal.

Jennifer was a client of mine who had found herself on the wrong side of a powerful community of witches and had been told that one of them had directed malevolent magic towards her. Her case is interesting because it illustrates how the power of belief can influence susceptibility to dis-ease and how the shamanic practitioner might then go about the healing process.

Jennifer had started to feel tired and ill as soon as she had heard about the curse which had been levelled against her. She had 'bought in' to it mentally and emotionally and now her body was responding physically to her beliefs.

It is important that the healer accept unchallenged the sufferer's description of her circumstances and the reason for it, without question or contradiction, since this is her fundamental and undeniable truth. Then, of course, once these circumstances are changed, the client must necessarily change too and become whole and well again since the circumstances which the patient herself defined have now been positively and demonstrably altered.

This is one of the central differences between this aspect of traditional healing and modern psychotherapy. The latter often takes as its central philosophy the standpoint that the client is wrong, mistaken or misguided and is there to be 'cured' – or is sometimes even beyond 'cure'. Why else would they be there?

NLP founder, Richard Bandler, has seen the same thing many times in the modern psychotherapeutic context. 'I gave a lecture at an analytic institute in Texas once,' he says.

Before we began, for three hours, they read research to me demonstrating basically that crazy people couldn't be helped. And at the end I said 'I'm beginning to get a picture here. Let me find out if I'm right. Is what you are trying to tell me that you don't believe that therapy, the way it's done presently, works?' And they said 'No, what we're trying to tell you is that we don't believe that any form of therapy could ever work for schizophrenics'. And I said 'Good. You guys are really in the right profession: we should all be psychiatrists and believe that you can't help people'. And they said 'Well, let's talk about psychotics. People who live in psychotic realities and blah blah blah' and all this stuff about relapses. I said 'Well, what kind of things do you do with these people?' So they told me about their research and the kind of therapy they had done. They never did anything that elicited a response from these people.[10]

Shamanic healing does not achieve this shift through debate and discussion; instead, it goes straight to the heart of the problem with definite action since, the sooner the negative conditions are changed, the sooner full health will be restored. The Haitian model of healing is, once again, typical of this approach. 'The Houngan's main job is to discover the non-physical or unnatural cause,' says Maya Deren. 'This may be either an act of aggressive evil magic against the person or a punishment for his failure to serve his loa properly. In either case there exists the possibility of a resolution through *action* . . . it is an accepted fact that activity, hopeful activity, is the only thing which can prevent demoralization and can rehabilitate.'

The way the healer goes about this is to change the flow of energy surrounding the precipitating event through an action which 'exercises the will, tighten's one's forces, focuses the personality into an integration'.[11]

My client, Jennifer, had had enough of 'magic' so the first treatment I prescribed for her was a gentle (and non-threatening) cleansing bath, the effect of which is to release unhelpful energies and reinvigorate the life force, but to Jennifer it would look like a herbal cure of sorts, which was well within her own belief system.

If you would like to try this bath for yourself, here is the formula:

EXERCISE: THE CLEANSING BATH

Add lavender, poppy seeds, watercress, aloe vera, fresh lettuce, cucumber and rosemary to bath water which is as hot as you can bear, along with blue food colouring to lighten the water to a pale blue, and quartz crystals if you have them.

Bless the water before getting into it. A powerful affirmation in your own words of the curative powers of this bath is ideal, but even holding your hands over it and saying 'Bless you' is better than nothing. Light a candle and turn off the lights so that the atmosphere is soothing, then get in and soak for 15 minutes.

After this time, stand and, naming your problems, illnesses or fears, squeeze the water and herbs over your entire body, working from the head down, and paying special attention to the top of the head, forehead, back of the neck, insides of elbows and knees, the pulse sides of the wrists, the heart, genitals, ankles and the soles of the feet, all of which are typical targets for magical attack. Remember always to work *downwards*, never up the body. Keep naming your problems as you do this.

Repeat the process exactly and in the same order of washing, now using seashells if you have them or, if not, natural stones (not crystals) gathered and cleaned in salt water beforehand or even, if needs must, a hard sponge. Then lie down and soak again for a further 15 minutes.

At this point stand and make three complete revolutions in an anticlockwise direction, the direction of removal and decrease. Clap your hands loudly, or make some other big noise and immediately get out of the bath, turn on the lights, do all you can to dramatically change the atmosphere you have created. Importantly: as you step out of the bath, shout 'Now I am free' or 'I am healed', or whatever other words seem appropriate to you, in order to confirm the change which has just taken place in you.

Let the water out of the bath, being careful to insert a strainer first to catch the herbs, then gather them together into a bundle. Later you must walk to the nearest crossroads and throw them there to dispose of them. (If this is truly impossible for you, throw them down the toilet; or, throw them, tightly and securely bound, into the rubbish and put it immediately outside the house. Whatever happens, get rid of them as soon as possible.) If you have used shells or rocks, scrub them in salt water again before returning them to where you found them.

Let your body dry naturally and leave any herbs in your hair or on your skin to dry there. Then lie down and relax. There should be no sex that night and, preferably, no interaction of any kind with any other living being, animal or human, until the morning.

Next day, take another, ordinary, bath or shower to remove the remains of the herbs from your body.

The next time I saw Jennifer, we agreed on a spirit extraction.

One of the traditional means of extraction is to suck the intrusion from the energy body of the patient. With this method, the shaman locates the point of unhelpful energy in the client's body, through her entry into the shamanic state of consciousness, and then uses her mouth to suck the intrusion out. She then spits it into a bowl at her side. Sometimes she may also keep an object, such as a stone or a piece of wood, in her mouth, which becomes the receptacle for the energy which is removed. She will then disperse this energy safely by burning or burying the object she has used.

If you have seen the Tom Hanks film, *The Green Mile*, you have also seen this form of extraction in operation, in the scene where the main character removes the cancer from the prison governor's wife by sucking the intrusion from her body. When he later releases this, it takes the form of a swarm of flies which stream from his mouth, exactly as the shamans might describe or depict this illness.

In Peru, the ayahuasca shaman, Javier, also used this technique to suck 'spirit poison' from his patients. Instead of stone or wood, he would take a deep swig of water before he began the sucking treatment, continuing for maybe 15 minutes at a time before he spat the poison away in a spray of water.

In Western societies, unused to such physical contact, procedures such as this are sometimes unnerving for a client. So, instead, with Jennifer, I used another method of extraction, which employs a feather like a surgical instrument to 'dip into' the energy field and cut away the negative influence. Feathers are remarkably sensitive instruments for healing. As far as I can tell, they are attracted to fluctuations in the energy field and, where its normal intensity is dimmer, will dip towards this place, as if being dragged into a black hole. The reverse also seems to be true: they are repelled where energy is unusually strong and out of line with the rest of the body.

Jennifer's illness appeared as nuggets of blackness, like small pieces of coal or ash, which peppered the area of her left shoulder. I passed the feather along her body, a few inches above her skin, within the field of energy that surrounded her. As it reached her shoulder, the feather began to dip as it was pulled towards the hole in her energy field. I was then able to remove her spirit intrusion, using the tip of the feather to pick it away, sometimes in long strands which stretched out from the body and could be wrapped around the feather; sometimes as hard pellets.

Shortly after this, Jennifer recovered fully.

Psychic or bare-hand surgery, the use of feathers and of sucking, are all typical shamanic extraction methods. In her experiences among the Siberian shamans of Altai, meanwhile, the Russian psychiatrist Olga Kharitidi discovered another variant of the extraction ritual, where the shaman used melted wax to absorb the patient's negative energies, circling the patient and chanting spells and incantations to chase the illness out, while the patient entered a state of trance.[12]

When the spirit intrusion was extracted into the wax, the shaman poured the hot liquid into a bowl of cold water. The strange shapes made by the wax as it hardened enabled the patient to see the shape of his own illness made solid in the water, with the certainty which accompanied this that the disease had indeed been removed.

In a sense, this is exactly the same reassurance the dentist offers when she shows us the rotten tooth she has just removed, or the doctor who gives us a jar of kidney stones to take home after our operation. Here, however, as with all extraction, we are dealing with the energy body and with spirit, as well as the client's own belief system.

A CONVERSATION WITH PARALYSIS – A BEAUTIFUL SPIRIT INTRUSION

In all the times that I have worked with spirit intrusions, such as Jennifer's, I have only ever met one (cancer) which actually wanted to hurt anyone. Most of them, even those sent deliberately as an attack by another person, are rather beautiful spirits with their own gifts to bring and are often quite unaware of their harmful effects and disturbed to hear that they may be hurting someone by their presence.

Sometimes, the circumstances surrounding their arrival are sad ones, where both the human host and the spirit itself feel alone and distressed, and the intention behind the intrusion – albeit misguided – is one of healing and completion. The sad fact is that this rarely works for either party. Both continue to feel displaced and wounded since they remain out of resonance with each other. It is like finding yourself lost in the city one day and having to take cover from the rain in a doorway until you can get your bearings and find your way home. The doorway is functional and offers you temporary protection, but it is still your home that calls you.

Dianna came to see me suffering from facial paralysis which she said she had had for seven years and which had affected one side of her face. She had become almost blind in one eye, and in moments of stress that entire side of her face would freeze. She also suffered terrible headaches which made her sick, as well as a ringing and occasional deafness in her ears. The doctors had suggested some form of multiple sclerosis, though there seemed little evidence for this. Moreover, Dianna was convinced that this could not be the full answer because sometimes the paralysis would leave her for days at a time, returning only when she had to face another stressful situation. *Face* another stressful situation. There appeared to be a psychosomatic component to the problem too.

Dianna explained that the onset of her illness had coincided with her pregnancy and the birth of her son, along with the break-up of her relationship with the father, which happened at the same time. She had felt guilty about bringing a child into such an unstable world and was alone and unsupported during the time she was carrying her son.

Her sense of loss and abandonment had, in shamanic terms, created an opening for a spirit to enter and occupy the void in her energetic body.

I guided Dianna into a light trance and asked her to go

inside herself to find an image which represented the spirit entity, Paralysis. She found the being in a clearing in a wood, near a lake. I then asked Dianna to act as intermediary so I could talk with Paralysis directly.

The story of Paralysis was as moving as Dianna's own. Paralysis had lived in a lake as an essential, an Earth creature or elemental, in the form of a mermaid who had enjoyed the community of other creatures, where she felt safe and loved. Then, one day, something vast and unknown had been dropped into the lake, all but destroying the community there and, in the explosion that this vast thing created, Paralysis had been thrown clear of the lake and had become disorientated.

Feeling frightened and confused, she had wandered at the shore for days until a 'sad lady' (Dianna) had appeared at the lakeside, with an empty place within her. Paralysis, now without a home, saw an opportunity to help the sad lady by filling the emptiness inside her, to their mutual benefit, and so climbed into Dianna's womb where she had remained for the last years of Dianna's illness. (In fact, Dianna had also had problems with her womb which may or may not have been associated with her other physical illness.)

Paralysis had no intention to hurt Dianna and agreed willingly to go back to her own home in the lake if we would only show her how; she thanked Dianna for providing her with a safe living space for the time that they had been together. Dianna was very moved by this story but also willing to return Paralysis to the lake and to let go of this entity who had become a 'companion' of sorts to her.

I drummed for Dianna, then, as she journeyed back to the lake with Paralysis. When they reached the shore, the Dianna lying on the blanket before me raised her arms, lifting the little Paralysis soul into the air, and blew through them as I had showed her, to let the spirit go.

The next morning, I was awoken early by the phone and then the answermachine clicking in before I drifted back to sleep. When I later listened to the message, it was Dianna, excited and overjoyed at a dream she had had that night, one which had woken her at 3a.m. and refused to let her sleep again. I called her back.

Her dream self, she said, had gone back to the lake to check that all was well and had found Paralysis happily swimming there. They met as equals, as friends, each remaining in her own world but smiling at one another through the thin lace which divides our separate worlds.

Dianna had asked Paralysis what her life was like before the two of them had met, and why Paralysis had chosen her those seven years ago.

The answer she received had stunned her – 'Dianna, I didn't come to you seven years ago,' she said. 'It was *twenty-seven* years ago.'

Immediately, Dianna was transported back to a time in her life twenty-seven years before when she had found herself on a hospital trolley, bleeding profusely as she miscarried her first child. The screams and moans around her, the clinical smells of antiseptic and gas, the harsh lights and grimy white walls crushed in upon her fragile self and soon all was black. She could remember nothing of the next few hours but was aware only of a pain in her womb. This was when her soul had gone wandering at the lake, unable to face the trauma of events around her, and when Paralysis had first entered her womb.

For Dianna, this meant so much. Suddenly, she understood the sense of 'stuckness' in her life these last twenty-seven years, the feeling of confusion about what to do with her life, her inability to move forward, which had come to a head once more in feelings of guilt and despondency at the time of a similar event twenty years later, the birth of her son, which had coincided with her physical paralysis.

She realized that she had always had Paralysis within her, but she – the spirit of Paralysis – had only shown herself with the arrival of Dianna's son and she understood how Paralysis, cramped in the womb with her growing child, had needed to find a new home in her body, so had travelled from the womb to her back and then into her face and head, the furthest place she could find from the developing embryo. She had made her new home there and with this event had come all of Dianna's problems of facial paralysis.

Dianna was overjoyed to be able to piece together so much of her missing life. Our next healing adventure together would be to revisit those traumatic moments in the hospital to see what spiritual impact they had had and how to deal with this. Eventually, we conducted a healing ritual together in the woods where I drummed as she laid out an altar on the stump of a dead tree and prayed for the soul of her first child, and for herself. All the time, I drummed for her. With the first beat, the trees bent towards us, forming a natural cathedral as the wind heard the drum and picked up. Then a robin appeared before us in the trees and gorse at the very front of Dianna's altar. Later, she told me that whenever robins had appeared in her life it had always signalled a momentous event of real life-changing importance. Dianna was elated that everything, for once, had started to make sense.

And this is the nature of shamanic extraction healing work. The body remembers, the mind remembers, and when our soul parts are returned to us, or the spirits within us are freed, the soul remembers too and our power begins to flow again. Often, these memories come in dreams or other images, just as they initially did with Dianna, and all of these have messages for us and meanings to impart. After all, what are images but reality before it is made solid in the world? If a thing can be imagined, say the people of Africa, then at the very least it has the potential to be.

THE HEALING POWER OF EGGS

There is one, almost universal, method of extraction medicine which I cannot ignore here, simply because of its widespread practice – and that is the use of eggs in shamanic healing, illustrating how something so seemingly unimportant as a humble egg can become powerful medicine when used with the right healing intention.

In the Mayan tradition of extraction, the ritual of *limpia* is performed, where a fertilized egg is rolled down the patient's body in order to extract the illness or energy disturbance as it is passed over the afflicted areas. In Siberia, Mongolia and Andean Peru a similar practice is followed and the egg is then broken, the shape and state of the yolk being used to determine the exact nature of the spiritual illness, which may then require further shamanic work. In the Mayan application the egg is used in a less divinatory or diagnostic way and absorbs the illness, while in the latter, the idea is to remove illness *and* to better understand the cause.

Eggs are also used in the Vodou healing tradition. In Santeria, the Vodou religion of Cuba (and increasingly, of mainland America), eggs are used in a particular ritual context and are offered in the service of the spirit, Obatala. Eight eggs, coconut butter, powdered eggshell, white cotton and white cloth are used. A bowl of milk, fresh basil and a white candle are also needed.

The cloth is arranged on a plate, then nests are made from the cotton which the eggs will sit in, and each one is covered in coconut butter. One egg is dipped in the milk and basil mixture and rolled in the powdered eggshell. It is then rolled down the whole body several times. The second egg is treated in the same way and used specifically on the neck and shoulders; the third on the left arm and body; the fourth on the right side; the fifth on the chest and stomach; the sixth on the genitals and backside; the seventh on the left leg; and the last one on the right leg and both feet. All of these are areas of magical attack. The illness or bad magic is absorbed into the yolk as the eggs are rubbed down the body in this way.

All of the eggs are then placed on their nests on the plate and dusted with the powdered egg. A seven-day candle, coated with coconut butter, is lit at the centre, and the whole package is placed at the highest point in the house, with the candle left to burn overnight. The next day, the bundle is taken to a place in nature and spun around the head eight times using the left hand. On the eighth spin, the package is thrown away. Immediately, the person doing so must walk away and not look back. The illness goes with the package and, since the action is a complete severance of association, with no looking back, the illness will stay away.

As well as being a priest of Santeria (a *santero*), the person who taught me this ritual is a priest of Palo (a *palero*) and of Vodou. He tells me that eggs are used in the same way in Palo, but here they are used only when the spirit, Mama Chola Guengue is invoked to assist the cleansing.

The ritual is not without precedent, including in Catholicism, where the egg may be used to symbolize the soul, so this practice is, in a sense, 'soul cleansing'. In Palo, eggs also have a specific physical meaning and can be used to represent the head, the eyes, the ovaries, the breasts, the testicles or just about any part of the body with a similar shape. This is like the Law of Similarity we looked at earlier, which is used in many magical traditions.

In both Palo and Santeria, eggs also represent a container which can be filled with 'spiritual grime' and then disposed of. They represent possibility and fertility, and can be given to the spirits Oshun or Yemaya, as 'seeds' for the petitioner's requests – especially for a requested pregnancy. In addition, they represent obstacles which can be broken through, the cracking of the eggshells signifying the action of breaking through these barriers.

The priest that I spoke of writes that he has also 'heard of this egg cleaning being a Mexican and a Gypsy tradition. I know of a Celtic-Wicca-Goddess worshipper who also uses eggs to clean problems away, and I know of a folk-medicine healer who does the same – I believe that this is one of those universal ingredients . . .'

Personally, I respect all of these traditions, but I also like to involve my clients in their own healing whenever I can, since this involvement is, in itself, empowering for them (it means they are not relying solely on *me* to heal *them* but are caring for *themselves*). To involve them and to engage their belief system, I have to make the healing as meaningful as possible for our own Western perspective and to respect some of the constraints of our Western worldview and way of life, so I have adapted the procedure slightly. Many people in the West do not like to be touched, for example – it is unnerving for them and feels intrusive – so instead of rolling the egg down their bodies, I often hold it in my left hand, as a receptacle for the negativity within their energy bodies, and use a feather to cut through and to waft the intrusion away from them and into the egg, using the egg as a container.

I begin with a smudging ritual, working *up* the energy body and from *right to left*. This disturbs the flow of natural energy (which naturally works down and around the body and in a spiral from left to right) and reveals whatever it is that needs to be extracted and shows its location. Then I use the egg and feathers to remove it, before working down the body again to replace and smooth out the energy body. It is important always to hold the egg in the left hand since this is the hand that pushes energy out, while the right hand receives energy, and you do not want to absorb any negativity yourself.

The client then leads the way out to the garden, carrying a white candle. I have empowered various areas of my garden in different ways to work with different common problems. There are certain sacred or power objects buried in these areas and each area has its own small shrine. I think in a couple of hundred years, if anthropologists ever bother to dig up my garden, they will be very puzzled by the curiously archaic religious practices of 20th century urban man!

Sometimes I prepare a burial site for the egg in advance; at others, the client and I dig a hole together. This is especially powerful since the client has full choice of where the egg is buried, and so a deeper realization of the problem which has been removed, and it also involves her in her own healing empowerment.

I then make an offering of thanks to the Earth and the client may say a few words or we may pray together or simply stand in silence.

Usually I follow this with further healing, often a shamanic journey of one kind or another, perhaps back to when the problem first arose so we can understand and deal with it, and I find that the small ritual previously performed is very helpful to relax the client and to set the scene for this. It makes the experience very sacred for her.

As a modern Western man raised from birth in our scientific worldview and, for my sins, also trained in psychology, I have to admit that I am still not sure of the exact mechanism that leads to the healing in all of this. Do we really extract spirits or negative energy from the client's body (I certainly *see* it being removed quite visibly, so perhaps . . .) or is it that the client *believes* she is being helped, and so she is, much like the way in which placebos – tablets with no known pharmacological value – can create real, clinical, curative events? Or is it the power of suggestion which works by opening the gates to the mind and allowing our natural healing powers to flow?

I still wouldn't like to come down in favour of any one explanation – maybe it is a combination of them all. But one thing I am increasingly sure of is that the connection with the 'sacred moment' – the moment, the split second, when another choice is offered to the client, and she is able to embrace that – is what ultimately produces a cure, and all of these rituals, if nothing else, are very powerful ways of creating the sacred space which brings that healing result.

In shamanic traditions there is no distinction between the maintenance of personal power and the maintenance of good health. The two are the same. When the body is powerful and its energy strong, there are no 'gaps' in the energy field where intrusions may enter and take root. The first step to guarding against spiritual intrusions of this kind (besides awareness of the possibility, and daily magical protection using the shields we looked at earlier) is to *be* powerful and *act* powerfully.

It is also possible to remove spiritual intrusions for

ourselves if we feel we have been affected in this way (though I would still always urge you to see a specialist first, or as well). The following exercise will show you how.

EXERCISE: REMOVING SPIRIT INTRUSIONS THROUGH JOURNEYING

Many shamanic traditions believe that we have more than one soul or spirit. Among the Sora of India, the soul is in the blood and so touches all parts of the body. For the Wana of Celebes, the body's souls inhere in the fontanelle, the liver and other internal organs. In Mongolian tradition, each body part has its own *ezhin* or spiritual ruler, while for the Shipibo-Conibo of South America and the Cuna of Panama, every single body part has a soul of its own and these may all be attacked. Thus, a physical ache or pain, especially if arising in suspicious or portentous circumstances, may be the bodily manifestation of a more deep-seated spiritual problem.

Journey now to a part of your body where you are currently experiencing discomfort, with the intention of 'seeing' the energy of that part and any spiritual intrusion associated with it.

If there is no intrusion, all well and good: simply ask that body part what you can do to ease its physical pain and speed its recovery. Act upon what it tells you, no matter how strange or 'rationally' ineffective it may seem. I have seen inspired shamans use orange juice and water alone to cure sprains and ease the pain of cuts. Despite all the very sound medical reasons why this *shouldn't* work, their clients report that it *does*.

If you do find an intrusion, ask that body part how best you should go about removing it. A ritual or ceremony may be suggested, or you may simply be told to pull it out using your hands. See yourself doing so as clearly and powerfully as possible. Actually move your hands to the affected part and pull upon it to remove the intrusive energy. Gather it in your hands and then return to ordinary reality and dispose of it. You do not need to make an elaborate gesture to do so: simply blowing it from your hands will suffice.

Remember, energy which is unhelpful to *you* is, *in itself*, completely neutral. By blowing it from your hands you simply release it back into the universe where someone else may use it for positive purposes.

When our Western dentists and doctors talk of 'extraction', they mean the tangible and physical removal of something we can see. With energy medicine we are working with the invisible, so what proof do we have that such healing is a real phenomenon and not all in the mind?

Dolores Krieger, a teacher at New York University, offers some. She has conducted interesting research into the power of spiritual healing which seems to suggest that real physical events do take place in the body of the patient through the manipulation of the energy system alone.[13]

In Dolores's experiments, a 'laying on of hands' was conducted on bona fide patients, by real nurses, in a genuine hospital setting. There was no physical contact between healer and patient; the healer worked only with the energy body of the patient, somewhat as in reiki or faith healing.

Dolores used sophisticated medical equipment to assess changes in the patients' bodies after these sessions, and found that their haemoglobin values were significantly increased. There was no effect whatsoever when nurses simply sat with their patients, even when they spent extra time with them, and no increase when they talked to them, even in highly positive words. What *was* important was the nurses' *intention* to heal. As long as they held this thought and focus in their minds, the haemoglobin values of their patients would be improved merely by the nurses holding their hands over them.

The interesting thing is that the patients themselves did not have to believe in anything for this effect to take place. During the experiments, they were not even told what the nurse was doing or that any effect of any kind was expected. Even if they had somehow guessed what was happening, they had no way of knowing how to respond; yet the haemoglobin was raised in every case, a delicate physiological change which is difficult for anyone to accomplish 'on a whim'.

Stanley Keleman, Director of the Center for Bioenergetic Studies in Berkeley, California, and the author of *Emotional Anatomy*, also reports a number of cases which show that people are capable of healing themselves of many different disorders when they are shown a new way of being which engages their belief in a way that moves them forward and gives them permission to change.

People who come to see me, or people whose problems I address, will say, 'I'm dissatisfied with life. I feel depressed', or 'I feel lost', or 'I don't understand why I can't love . . .' [Then I] look at [them], how they use themselves, and how they stand – are they stiff-necked, or rigid in the shoulders, or sunken in; is their tissue dense; do they guard themselves by contractions?

When they begin to explore how that tension rigidifies their aliveness, and soften it by a series of exercises which I help them learn, or which they find for themselves, then they are flooded not only with associations of the past, but also with the feelings of being alive. And you get phrases like, 'I realize that I'm connected to everything that's living', 'I feel part of the world again', 'I feel like when I was a young boy or a young girl, in contact empathetically, not cognitively, with that which is living. I feel sympathetic again' . . . people [report] that they are in touch with that which supports all life.[14]

What Keleman's studies suggest is that the body carries and manifests a living memory of limiting events which is reflected in physical symptoms and postural problems. When people realize this and work with the symptoms, they are able to heal not only the physical problem but the event which gave rise to it through a change in their energy bodies. In this research, the key is that they are supported by Keleman in changing their beliefs about themselves in order to create a more empowered future. 'I'm not told I'm silly any more,' as one of Keleman's patients said.

Dolores Krieger's results show that 'faith healing' *is* effective as a technique in its own right, while Stanley Keleman's work demonstrates that the patient can also heal herself through an act of *self*-belief. The evidence from both is pretty conclusive that energy medicine *does* work and, in this sense, it actually doesn't matter how – whether it is personal belief or the healing act itself which changes the dynamic of the illness – it works; that's all that counts.

On the other hand, if the client does *not* believe in the power of the healing (which is as much as to say, in some respects, that they do not believe in their own power to recover), there is little that can be done with any approach (including medical science), as evidenced by a somewhat amusing email I came across from a shaman on a web site discussion list:

> *One day a middle aged lady came into my store and said she was plagued with a spirit who would visit and take – how should I put it – take liberties with her body. I told her what books to read, sold her some white sage, cedar and sea salt, and she took the items and went home.*
>
> *The next month she came back still complaining about the spirit and I asked her if she did any of the things that I explained to her and she said, 'No'. I asked why, and she said, 'I just didn't think that would work'.*
>
> *It was evidence to me that she liked the attention the spirit was giving her, plus the sympathy that she got from it. You can lead a horse to water, but can you teach it to drink if it's not thirsty? We all learn at different rates.*[15]

One of the most dramatic and visible manifestations of the action of faith on the body is the mystery of stigmata. This is when, as a result of intense identification with Christ, the marks of the crucifixion actually become visible on a devotee's own body.

Shamans might call this mystical-physical experience an example of shapeshifting, the ability of the body to take on a new form as a result of a deep and powerfully pervading belief in its capacity to do so. It is an example of faith in action and evidence of our facility to change ourselves which, with direction and focus, can become a force for healing and positive growth.

'History tells us that many ecstatics bear on hands, feet, side, or brow, the marks of the Passion of Christ, with corresponding and intense sufferings. These are called visible stigmata,' says the *Catholic Encyclopaedia* which clearly, even from this description, defines stigmata as linked to ecstacy.[16] This is also the passion of the shaman, of course, as well as the Vodou priest in the throes of possession. The experience of those affected sounds very much like the possession trance of the vodouissant – such as that of St Catherine de Ricci, who is said to have 'conversed aloud, as if enacting a drama'.

'On coming out of the ecstacy,' the description continues, 'the saint's limbs were covered with wounds produced by whips, cords, etc.'

Research by the Catholic Church finds 321 stigmatics in its history, only 41 of them men, of whom the best known and the first recorded case is St Francis of Assisi, who lived between 1186 and 1226.

This research discounts any suggestion of natural causes for these wounds, or the notion that they might in any way be self-inflicted. 'Sometimes the patient has been watched night and day, sometimes the limbs have been enveloped in sealed bandages,' the Church notes. One researcher even 'placed on one foot of a stigmatic, a copper shoe with a window in it through which the development of the wound might be watched, while it was impossible for anyone to touch it'. The stigmata continued unimpeded and obviously without any possibility that it was self-caused.

The Catholic view also discounts the power of imagination alone to produce the effects of stigmata. The Church does concede that 'joined to an emotion, it [imagination] can produce sweat; and as the mere idea of having an acid bon-bon in the mouth produces abundant saliva, so, too, the nerves acted upon by the imagination might produce the emission of a liquid and this liquid might be blood', but notes that 'there is not a single experimental proof that imagination could produce them [stigmatic wounds], especially in violent forms'.

Furthermore, no 'scientific' explanation has ever been offered for three particular qualities of such wounds:

- Medical remedies have no effect on them.
- The wounds usually have no fetid odour, as would be expected from a typical flesh wound over a period of time.
- Sometimes the wounds emit a perfumed scent, as was the case with Juana of the Cross.

In short, according to the Catholic view, stigmata are the result of miraculous intervention.

But what exactly is miraculous intervention? It is simply the unity with sacred power produced through the channel of faith. In other words, if we have faith in ourselves as a part of a divine and living universe, we can produce miracles within our bodies, and this includes a capacity for miraculous self-healing through recovery of our 'soul', as well as the physical signs of stigmata.

SOUL RETRIEVAL AND THE NATURE OF HEALING

Sometimes we need to recover our soul, as in cases of soul loss. In the city, it would be surprising if we did not.

Soul loss is in many ways the exact opposite of spiritual

intrusion. In the latter, some alien force is injected into your spirit-self; in the former, it is a loss of spirit, a depletion of energy, which is the cause of illness.

In the West, we talk of psychological dissociation and 'syndromes', which have a litany of problematic and distressing physical, mental and emotional symptoms associated with them. These arise as a result of traumatic, abusive and hurtful experiences. In shamanic cultures, the same symptoms will be diagnosed as a 'fracturing of the soul' as a result of such events. The soul, say the shamans, is unable to cope with the pain when it is faced with experiences such as these, and so it splits into many parts, some of which take refuge in the lands of the spirits, far away from the harshness of the material world, where their pain is located.

Any event which is associated with emotional distress of any kind will have a spiritual component too. Yet, while our medical doctors are adept at mending the body, and our psychologists and counsellors can deal with our mental and emotional demons, no-one in the modern world is taking care of the soul.

Some of the more obvious causes of soul loss are well known to us all, even though the term may be unfamiliar.

A beloved spouse, child or friend dies and the survivor also 'deadens' for a while. We feel as if the light has gone from our existence, as if we are sleepwalking. Or we return from having major surgery and do not feel as if we have come fully out of the anaesthesia. A client who had been involved in a serious automobile accident reported being 'spaced out'.

A person involved in an abusive intimate relationship may be aware of being locked into destructive patterns but feel too weak and powerless to move away. Or in leaving the relationship, he or she might feel as though something was left behind with the partner. After a workshop, a student of mine said that since breaking up with her boyfriend she felt as though 'a part of me is still with him'.

The soul may leave a child who does not feel loved, or who feels abandoned, by his or her parents. In one of my clients, soul loss was caused by a parent's continual yelling. In another, by the physical pain of falling off a bicycle. A soul might leave the body to survive physical or sexual abuse. In each of these cases, the traumatised person literally escapes to survive the ordeal . . . Literature is full of out-of-body experiences in the wake of illness or accident.[17]

As a recent example of this, I watched as a small child, aged just three, was finally pulled from the rubble which she had been trapped beneath for days in the wake of the earthquake in Turkey.

Physically, she was lucky. She had only a few scratches and bruises and did not seem to be suffering any major effects from dehydration or lack of food. Yet, when she was asked how she was feeling by one rescue worker, she replied simply: 'I've been ill'. The spirit recognizes its own pain, even when the body appears healthy.

But these are just the obvious experiences of trauma that we can all identify with, the 'big events' of our lives which we can imagine as having a shocking and debilitating effect. In fact, every time we go into our workplace to sacrifice eight hours of our lives to an unfulfilling job, or return home to a partner or relationship which has long lost its sparkle, or deal with rude and unhappy officials as part of the normal 'daily grind', there is a cumulative loss of our personal power to the extent that subtly, insidiously, and over time, our souls suffer wounds that perhaps we do not even register until one of these 'big events' forces us to take notice as a wake-up call for our spiritual self-preservation.

Such was the case with Simon K. I never met Simon. He was a client of a friend of mine, a shamanic healer, who asked for my opinion on the best course of treatment, but I got to hear the circumstances of his case in some detail in my role as her informal 'consultant'.

At the age of 47, Simon was 'Mr Reliable'. He had worked for the same company for twenty years, been married for twenty-five, and had two teenage children. He caught the 8.15 into town, the 5.15 home, always did his best, never quibbled about working late or on weekends when required to do so by his boss, helped his wife (who didn't work) with the housework, the children with their homework, and his elderly neighbour with her gardening and shopping on the modern and nondescript suburban estate where he had lived since getting married. He always seemed pleasant, if not cheerful, and was a quiet and undemanding member of the workforce in the executive offices of the food company where he worked in the finance department.

Some people are marked for attention within a company, others strive to be noticed, to make their mark. Not Simon K. He had risen steadily through the ranks and been promoted when his seniors left, filling their place quietly and efficiently. Even when he spoke to his colleagues (which was rare) to check an invoice or on some other company errand, he was hardly even noticed. He was the last person anyone ever expected trouble from. If he had an opinion on company policy (or any other matter), he kept it to himself and never rocked the boat.

Until one day when he came into the office at his usual time and then, crossing the floor, suddenly stopped and began to sob uncontrollably. His colleagues, stunned, were unable even to rise from their seats before the screaming began. As the first of them reached him, the second computer monitor hit the floor as he swiped it from the desk in front of him. He was dismissed later that day.

He had no idea what had overcome him, or why that day in particular but, as he spoke of his life to the therapist he later went to see, the picture emerged of a deeply unfulfilled and unhappy man who had sacrificed his life to a job which was in no way involving for him, let alone enriching, and a lifestyle without adventure. His therapist worked with him for some months then, having some knowledge of soul retrieval, recommended him to visit my friend, which he did.

Normally, soul loss is associated with more dramatic causal events (or perhaps they are a more obvious and compelling reason for people to visit shamanic healers) and so my friend had no experience of a case like this and did not at first recognize it as an example of soul loss. She decided to attempt a shamanic journey on Simon's behalf, however, and that proved the turning point in the therapy.

What she saw during this first journey was a small boy, the child of old-fashioned, almost Victorian, parents with a strong line in discipline, who was restricted in almost every normal boyish pursuit and punished severely for any transgressions. By the age of 10 he was a dour, plain and frightened child who had lost touch with every spirit of adventure within him – literally, for they had taken leave of him so that he could survive the stifling deep brown suffocation of his early years.

My friend began to recover these soul parts for him, in partnership with his therapist, who helped him to explore and reintegrate these forgotten aspects of himself. Some months later, Simon was ready to return to a public life. He has now set up in business for himself and relishes the thrill of the risks he takes every day. He has been reunited with his true spirit of adventure and is a fuller man and more at peace with himself as a consequence.

Howard Charing remarks in an article written for the shamanic magazine, *Spirit Talk*, that 'The separation in Western society from the natural world, with its accompanying myth of man having "dominion over all living things", has led to spiritual disconnection from the universal energy field. At some level we are aware of this and we are experiencing a heart-led desire to reconnect to the universal field of energy.'[18]

This was certainly the case for Simon, who had been forcibly separated from the sense of his own natural flow within this energy by his overbearing parents and, powerless to resist, had allowed this disconnection to continue through his quiet and uneventful suburban life and a job which he never even realized was stultifying and crippling to him.

In a sense, then, the flight of the soul was a positive action of protection and self-healing. Eventually, however, the loss of essential energy has to be felt. Then, if the sufferer does not implode into depression, dislocation or self-harm, he may explode instead, like a pressure cooker which is so tightly clamped that it can no longer let off steam. If Simon had not 'blown his top' that day, his entire system might have blown instead. He was saved by the drama of his emotional crisis, which alerted him to do something fast.

Eileen Nauman has prepared a comprehensive list of warning signs which signal a need for shamanic intervention as a result of such soul loss.[19] They include:

- **Chronic or unusual fatigue** – which is not like normal tiredness after exertion, or due to the body's natural rhythms, but more a sense of apathy or ennui, where you simply cannot be bothered to do anything.
- **Headaches** – which develop after you have been in a stressful situation, or with a particular person.
- **A feeling of physical coldness** – even when it is warm around you. This may be widespread throughout your body or localized in a particular place.
- **A feeling of emptiness or tightening in the area of the solar plexus** – the solar plexus is the seat of the will, the place where we align the world to our intentions. A loss of soul (or power) may, therefore, be physically felt in this area.
- **Anxiety and panic in relation to particular circumstances or events** – even when there seems no obvious cause or reason;
- **Feelings of depression** – this may also manifest as general pessimism, hopelessness, nameless malaise or mental un-ease. Mood swings into unfocused anger; irritation and impatience may also be experienced.
- **Health problems, particularly accompanied by unexplainable pain** – and especially if your medical doctor can find no obvious physical problem.

- **Inability to ground oneself** – constant daydreaming, lack of interest in daily life, escape into unreality through TV, alcohol or drugs – or intense feelings of detachment, as if you are standing outside yourself and seeing the world pass by, accompanied by emotional and/or physical numbness and a sense of helplessness, of giving up.
- **Memory loss** – the soul parts which retain that memory are simply no longer there to be recalled.
- **Addictions and repetitive behaviour** – such as choosing the same kind of abusive partner time and again, or repetitive weight gain or loss (Nauman's experience is that the latter is a pattern typical of women who have been molested or raped as a child, and unconsciously either eat more food to build a protective 'barrier' around themselves, or eat so little that they begin to 'disappear'. Fat becomes a physical symbol of armour or protection, while anorexia may be an attempt by our unconscious selves to make our body invisible to our abusers).
- **Inability to let go** – of a loved one following their death, a divorce, or other emotional trauma, so that life continues to revolve around the past.
- **A vague feeling of impending doom** – where the person concerned feels extremely vulnerable but has no idea why.
- **A history of abuse or violence** – Abusers often steal soul parts from their victims by eroding their power and taking control of their lives, thoughts, actions and emotions, although paradoxically, this can sometimes be an expression of their deep, but obviously misguided, love rather than a deliberate intention to harm. Many have been victims of abuse as children themselves, and so identify abusive behaviour as an aspect of love, so that abuse continues as learned behaviour across many generations. Even if the abuser is dead, stolen soul parts can be buried with her.

Nauman also offers a number of expressions she has heard her clients use over the years to symbolize their feelings of loss. Most of them are recognizable from our own daily lives, suggesting that some deep, intuitive part of us is aware that soul loss has taken place.

- I *gave him* the best years of my life
- She *stole* my heart
- I feel *devastated*
- She was my other *half*
- I just *don't feel whole* any more
- I feel as if there's *a gaping hole* in my life
- *I feel lost*; as if I have no direction, no goals
- He still has a *hold on me*
- I feel as if she is *a part of me*
- I'm tired all the time; I just *don't seem to have any energy*
- *I can't live* without him
- I can't do anything *by halves*; I always have to go to extremes
- She was *my life*
- I dream about him all the time; *I feel haunted* by him
- I feel like I'm *a slave* to her
- I feel like *an emotional cripple*
- *I feel numb*. There's no joy in my life
- I haven't been able to cry for years; it's like *I can't feel* any more
- I feel as if he's controlling me; I just *don't have the strength* to say 'no'
- I feel as if I'm being *torn apart*
- *I feel like a puppet*; I'm always being jerked around by them
- *I'm nothing* without her

Besides these reasons for soul loss, which are all too common in the West and in city living, there are specific factors implicated in the condition of spiritual illness which have been identified by particular cultures. As well as expanding the list of circumstances and things to be wary of, the fact that all societies have given detailed attention to such things in itself suggests a universal knowledge of the problems of the soul. There is no smoke without fire.

318

The Tuvan shaman, Christiana Harle-Silvennoinen, speaks of at least seven types of identified cause of spiritual illness in her culture, all of which can be dealt with by the shaman.[20]

The first two – power loss and its more extreme form, soul loss – are similar to the situations we have looked at, but there are five others which also need specifically to be addressed. These are: *aza, buk, albys*, an illness which arises from not properly honouring our own sacred places, and the transmission of curses through the 'evil eye'.

- *Aza* is a malicious spirit which lives in the lower world and will create illness amongst humans out of what we may perceive as mischief or malice. Presumably, *Aza* has his own agenda, and in his definition of his actions, evil intent is not a primary motivation. From our limited human perspective on events, it may seem so, however. As far as we are concerned, then, *Aza* is a chaos principle of the universe.

- *Buk* describes a condition ('to be *buk*'), a situation, and a result. It is an illness which arises from the malicious actions of one person to another or to another life-form. In a sense, it is like the Western notion of 'instant karma'.

  Christiana gives the example of a case she witnessed where two young boys, in an extreme and uncaring act, castrated a live animal one day during their 'play'. They then returned home and immediately became ill, one symptom of which was inflammation and swelling of their testicles.

  Medical intervention failed and the shaman was called immediately. Recognizing the illness as *buk*, the shaman demanded that the children tell him exactly what they had done to cause its onset. The children, however, overcome with guilt and shame at their actions, refused to confess. Had they done so, this would have relieved some of the traumatic pressure within their bodies and given the shaman vital information and a direction for healing, but they simply could not. Both children died soon afterwards.

- *Albys* is a form of deep love-sickness which causes the sufferer to become withdrawn, distant and melancholy; it is almost like a pining love which takes over the whole of one's life. In Tuva, the object of this love is the *albys* spirit, a beautiful siren, male or female, which causes its victim to desire only it and to forsake all else.

    The only way for the shaman to cure this form of spirit illness is to find out the name of the particular *albys* which has control over the person – which they will typically resist giving him for fear of losing their love. But the shaman must be rigid, inflexible, and demand the name. Once he has it, he can enter the otherworld and capture the spirit, which will then manifest in the form of flat felt-like material, typically to be found beneath the fire in the sufferer's house. The shaman takes this physical representation of the spirit and crushes it. The spell is then broken and the person recovers.

- Dishonouring the spirit of a place can also have dire consequences. We saw earlier that particular places have specific energies or power associated with them and, where these resonate with our own energy fields, they can be deeply soothing and beneficial to us. Some places and things have so much power that they become sacred in themselves. Trees, especially, are important. In Tuva, the sacred tree of the shaman is the larch; in Britain, it is the oak; in Haiti, all trees may be sacred when they are occupied by particular types of spirits known as *djabs*. In all cases, these sacred places must be approached and honoured in a certain way and with offerings to the spirits that live there. When this is done, spirit protection is assured, but if it is overlooked, the spirit will withdraw its protective services and illness will result. This form of dis-ease is therefore one associated with ignorance of the sacred and a lack of connection with spirit.

- Cursing – which, like our European equivalent (a remnant of our spiritual past) is administered through the pointing of a finger and the intention, vocal or otherwise, to do harm to a person – is another cause of illness. In many cultures there is a proscription on pointing at people. In the UK we tell children it is rude to point and stare; in Turkey and in Greece there are particular ways of pointing which deliver the 'evil eye' to a victim; the Hopi Indians of North America talk of 'two hand-edness', where you may speak kindly to a person but your negative thoughts about them (intended or otherwise) can still have a detrimental effect on them.

In Asian communities, the power of the curse and of the evil eye is taken very seriously. Hair removed from combs and brushes is never simply thrown away because, if found by an enemy, it can easily be used to deliver harm to the victim. Instead, the hair is blown upon three times and a prayer said over it. It is then secreted in hollows and crannies in the walls of the house so that it cannot be used in occult rituals. Babies and young children are particularly susceptible to the evil eye, especially from barren and jealous women who are envious of the newborn. Children attacked in this way often cry for no apparent reason or become withdrawn and sullen. To protect against such attacks, young children are often made to wear a black thread around their necks and wrists, and black eyeliner to deflect the evil magic. A child who still falls prey to a psychic attacker can be cured by taking a bunch of cloves (which must consist of an odd, rather than an even, number since odd numbers cannot be divided to leave nothing; something must always remain) and circling the child's head with them three times. The cloves absorb the negative influence and are then burned to destroy the power of the curse. If the cloves burn without a scent, it is certain that the child has been attacked with the evil eye. After this ritual, however, the child will soon return to normal, fully cured of their magical dis-ease.

In Tuva, too, cursing is taken very seriously. To deal with it, the shaman must purify and then bless the person affected. He may also use salt to cleanse them, making a protective circle of it around them and across the thresholds of their house. Interestingly, we in Europe also know of the purifying power of salt but, like many things in our culture, its significance has long been forgotten. Now, we may throw salt over our left shoulder in order to ward off evil, but we do not ascribe real meaning to the event. By not doing so, we are, of course, at spiritual risk.

'Returning a curse to the originator is considered to be well within shamanic ethics,' writes the Mongolian shaman, Sarangerel, in her book, *Riding Windhorses*. 'It is important, however, not to augment the curse by returning it with malicious intent, which does step over the line of good Shamanic behaviour.'[21] One of the ways of deflecting curses and providing spiritual protection is through the use of a mirror, which is 'absorbent of energies in all frequencies, visible and invisible, and it absorbs energy from the universe at all times. A mirror also acts as armour and can protect the person wearing it from attack. For this reason mirrors are given to the sick and to small children. During healing rituals the mirror will be used to absorb intrusions from the patient's body or it can be pointed at hostile spirits to blind them with its energy and scare them away.'

In Peru and Mexico there are quite different reasons for disease than those found in Tuva and Mongolia, and ways for the shaman to deal with them and with the problem of soul loss. This is not surprising since culture, geography, social norms, ways of interacting, and a million other nuances of life and rules of behaviour vary. Once again, the shaman needs to be sensitive to the client and her environment, even though he will well understand the reasons for soul loss and spiritual illness in his own culture.

Elena Avila has produced a comphrehensive list of the physical, mental, emotional and spiritual expressions of these dis-eases of the soul which may affect people in her own Aztec tradition and cause them to visit a *curandera* for healing.[22]

Physical dis-eases

- *Bilis* (rage) – caused by stress, work pressures, and simply the effects of modern life. It is 'an illness that many people in modern society suffer from'. It will usually be dealt with by massage and through prescriptions of herbal teas and baths.

- *Empacho* – blocks to the emotions and the energy body, leading to stomach cramps and digestive problems. It is usually dealt with in the same manner as *bilis*.
- *Mal aire* (bad air) – caused by attacks, usually on children, from invisible spiritual entities (which Elena interprets as an ancient, intuitive, recognition of the existence of microbes and bacteria). It is defended against by swaddling the child affected; this is also a metaphor for spiritual protection through surrounding the child with love and care.

Mental dis-eases

These may be caused by deep trauma, chemical imbalances or genetic factors, but can be eased by the generation of energy by the patient to help her keep her mind and body healthy. 'If we retain a strong spirit and soul, we can learn to live in greater harmony and balance with our afflictions,' says Elena. 'I have learned much from the schizophrenics, manic and depressed individuals with whom I work . . . They respond well to the spiritual cleansings and soul retrievals I do with them, and to the education I give them. But most of all, they respond to compassion.'

This is a point echoed by Robert Holden, a Western writer and workshop leader trained originally in psychology, whom Nick Williams quotes in his book[23]: 'I was trained to be a problem solver,' he says, 'and initially I prided myself on how quickly I could spot people's weaknesses and neuroses . . . I wanted to be able to spot more problems than the other psychologists . . . I began to realize [however] that the greatest therapy is about pointing people towards their own goodness, the love, creativity and health within, not fault-finding.'

Indeed, love and compassion alone can have profound effects on our sense of health and well-being. Nick quotes one study of 159 people undergoing coronary angiograms, which found that those who felt most loved (emotional) actually had fewer (physical) blockages in the arteries of their hearts. The key factor was not diet, or exercise or lifestyle, but love pure and simple, which was able to touch their souls.

Emotional dis-eases

- *Envidia* (envy) – which causes problems for both the envious person, 'who is sick in her soul', and the person envied, 'who is receiving energy that is not hers. When someone is the object of envy, she gets sick in her *tonal* (spirit) . . . even people we love, friends and family members, can harm us without meaning to.' Elena deals with *envidia* by educating her client to use the energy of envy in a more positive, constructive and focused way as the energy of intention to help them achieve their own goals rather than coveting what someone else has. 'When we use envy as a mirror, we can achieve our goals at work, school, and in our personal life faster.'

- *Mal puesto* (hexing or cursing) – as a result of 'black magic'. Elena is sceptical that cursing actually exists but the belief in curses is widespread in her culture and this belief can be enough for the effect of the curse to be felt in the life of the person so 'cursed'. Elena's solution is to educate her clients and empower them to take responsibility for their own decisions and accept their own power. 'I always tell my clients, "Take responsibility for your health . . . You are the architect of your life. Don't give your power away . . . Put your energy into the development of your soul and your spirit. If your spirit is healthy, no harm can penetrate to your soul.'

- *Mal de ojo* ('evil eye') – Specifically, in Hispanic cultures, this refers to an illness which results when excessive attention is paid to a young child, who will then become distressed, restless, unable to sleep and may even get sick and run a temperature. One solution is the use of protective charms and talismans, similar to the cross that was given to me during my own healing session with don Eduardo in Cusco. This has a central circle within it – an 'eye' – which deflects negative energy so that no harm can pass into the body.

- *Mala suerte* (bad luck) – Seen as an emotional illness, since the energies and expectations we put into life have a direct effect on what happens to us, says Elena, and 'once we become entangled in low self-esteem, worry, and feelings of helplessness, we can become enmeshed in a vicious cycle of bad luck.' The classic cures for bad luck are the *placitas*, a sort of in-depth heart-to-heart chat between shaman and client to identify the root cause of the problem, and the *limpia*, a spiritual cleansing to remove the problem and restore the balance of the soul.

In this, 'there is no split between the spiritual and the empirical,' says Peter Cloudsley[24]. 'The concept of health is one of maintaining balance between the individual, his community and the environment. In the urban and popular versions, it is more to do with love, health and money! *Amor, salud y dinero*: in other words, modern problems such as keeping a business profitable.'

Spiritual dis-eases

- *Susto* is classical soul loss caused by trauma or fright. In Elena's healing tradition, the recovery of missing soul parts is carried out in a somewhat different way to the one we have so far looked at. I once drummed for Elena in London as she conducted a soul retrieval for a young woman who was troubled by a complicated and unhappy love affair which had led to the loss of her unborn child. Elena built a trail of flowers and corn from her *mesa* (altar) which she walked with her client, both calling the name of the child and searching for a representation of the lost baby in the form of a child's doll which Elena had hidden in the room. Finally, the client found it, buried beneath a mound of flower petals at the side of the altar. Immediately she was able to release a whole flood of emotions which she had held repressed for years, while Elena comforted her. As she hugged the doll to her chest, she spoke passionately to it of her previously unvoiced feelings for her lost child.

- *Espanto* is another, quite specific, form of soul loss which is traditionally caused by fright as a result of seeing a ghost. There is a belief, for example, that if deceased family members are not honoured during the ritual festivities of *Dia de los Muertos* (the Day of the Dead), when the cemeteries come alive with singing, dancing and family feasting, they may return to haunt the guilty family member. *Espanto* can also be caused by a sudden shock, such as when a person has been sleeping and is suddenly woken up with a start so that their spirit, which has been wandering the otherworld in dreams, has not had time to return to the body. The traditional cure is a *limpia* for the client, along with an energetic clearing of the house and a blessing for the family if the ghost is haunting their home.

From this discussion, we can see that soul loss and spiritual disorders are treated very seriously in a number of different cultures, even though their causes and cures may vary in each. In the West we tend to remain very sceptical about such matters. There are no experts to call upon in matters of soul loss; there is no-one to turn to for help and support. Our spiritual leaders and religious authorities may even deny the existence of a soul, and certainly they have little advice for us in such matters – sometimes with quite dire consequences for those people who feel themselves afflicted with such problems.

WESTERN SCEPTICISM

On matters of the soul, Western religions take a more simplistic – and extreme – view than traditional cultures, which have evolved a detailed understanding of these matters and a wide range of treatment methods.

If the Western Church has an explanation for soul loss, it tends to place it firmly within the context of religious dogma rather than seeing it as a spiritual dynamic, and its 'treatment' methods are largely unrefined and ineffective. It might say, for example, that a person who is morose, depressed, listless, is suffering from 'loss of faith', while dramatic changes of character and 'acting out of sorts' (typical signs of soul loss) are classified as possession. 'The devil goes round like a roaring lion looking for souls to devour,' warns the *Exorcismis* of the Catholic Church.

Such extremes do not give sufferers anywhere to turn with their problems. 'Loss of faith' can only be combated by a return to that belief system which no longer attracts and involves the person, an almost impossible thing to ask; while the Church itself has almost abandoned the notion of genuine spirit possession (the *Exorcismis*, which was updated in 1999, now warns that demonic signs are more likely to be indicators of mental or physical illness rather than possession, and better dealt with by a physician than a priest).

Such an approach, as much as anything, is an indication of a faith which is itself in crisis: when the Church gives up the notion of the soul, defines possession only in terms of 'evil' spirits, and then lets psychiatrists and surgeons handle the problem, it is suggestive of a crisis of belief in an overly-rational culture. In many other traditions, such as those of Haiti and Cuba, by contrast, spirit possession is a daily event, open to all, and seen as a good thing; the spirits are there to help us and are benign, not threatening.

The fact that the Church has given up on the spirits in this way, however, does not mean that its followers have and, with nowhere else to turn for advice, people may take matters into their own hands.

In America just before Christmas 1999, I read and heard about a number of cases where parents, convinced that their child was possessed by the devil, had conducted their own exorcisms on them, sadly using the practice defined by the Church itself many centuries ago – a violent one which aims to make it too painful for the spirit to stay. At least three deaths had resulted as a consequence, and those were just the ones I heard about. In one of these, which had also been reported in the *American Globe and Mail*, a 43-year-old woman was found guilty of manslaughter after forcing water down her two-year-old grandchild's throat in order to 'drive out the devil'. The autopsy showed that 'the otherwise healthy child had choked on her own vomit'.[25]

In shamanic cultures, the diagnosis of spiritual illnesses is far more embracing and comprehensive; there is a solution for the sufferer; and the outcome is typically a happy one.

THE MODERN APPROACH TO SOUL RECOVERY

Modern Western shamans deal with soul loss by journeying to the missing part to recover it and then blowing it back into the energy body of the person affected. This is a practice based on the teachings of Michael Harner and Sandra Ingerman, the Western authorities on soul recovery.

In recent years, however, there has been a modification of the practice, which may better deal with the non-spiritually inclined mindset of the Western world and the urban landscape. Developed by Howard Charing, it is known as Shamanic Core Process, a name deliberately chosen to suggest an alliance with the 'psychological processing' approach of modern psychoanalysis, which is less threatening to most people than talk of 'spirits' and 'lost souls'.

'I considered Western methods which, on the surface, look similar to shamanic journeying, such as hypnotherapy, guided visualization and various models of transpersonal psychology, all of which work with the active imagination, yet view non-ordinary realities as extensions of our inner psyche, deeper levels of mind, inner and collective archetypes,' says Howard.

This approach mainly disregards the spirit worlds, and the universal field of energy is regarded as a projection by our own psyche of what is called the 'unconscious'.

My experience has shown me that rather than we individuals projecting a field of collective archetypes, it is we that are the projection of the universal field or energy matrix. The actuality that we experience as the physical world is but the description of our physical senses rather than being an absolute inherent fact. In some respects, quantum physics is now pointing in the same direction as have the ancient shamans for 50,000 years.

It is within this context of shamanism, outside of linear time, with incorporation of the non-ordinary realities, that the Shamanic Core Process method was created.[26]

In traditional communities, soul retrieval may take only one 'session', the shaman journeying for the client and returning the missing soul part. The client is then able to get on with her life and to recover from her illness. This is fine within those indigenous cultures since the belief system of the client is aligned to this method, the acceptance of the spirit world, and faith in the curative powers of the spirits and the shaman. The patient effectively heals herself once her energy is restored in this way.

Our own culture, however, is one of dependence upon 'specialists', such as medical doctors and therapists, to whom we give the power to heal us, an ability which we do not see as inherent in ourselves; the spirits do not exist since there is nothing beyond the material world we have created; and therapy is an ongoing process with no pre-defined end point when the person will be seen as entirely 'cured'. (I met one therapist in Greece who had been seeing the same client for thirty years – and was proud of it!)

To allow for these differences in perspective on healing, Howard's innovation was to change the structure of soul retrieval in order to make it a process in itself, and one which the Western mentality could more easily grasp.

Soul retrieval takes place over three sessions. The first is a journey taken by the client with guidance from the practitioner, using drum and voice to gently direct the client through the stages of entry to the shamanic lower world to meet with the soul parts that are lost there. 'It is important for the practitioner to remember when working with the general public that there can still be a fear of the "lower world" as being a scary or even demonized place,' says Howard, a reflection again of our lack of understanding of the spirit world, a place which most people have never before visited, but which our religious systems have defined for us. It is therefore important to put the lower world in context, as a place where specific types of information can be found, and with none of the negative value judgements that have been imposed upon it.

People who undergo this journey will usually experience an expanded sense of perceptual awareness, including visionary, auditory and kinaesthetic events. Eventually they will be guided to meet with their personal spiritual teacher, in whatever form is most acceptable to them, who will typically pass on insights and information about that person, which only they could know, and which are deeply helpful in understanding the bigger picture and the patterns of their life. This teacher will then take the role of guardian and protector, leading the visitor through their world to recover their own soul-essences and return these to them.

By the next session, the client has learned the method of journeying and so less guidance is needed. Instead, the shaman takes the role of facilitator and supportive ally as the client journeys for himself to consult with the soul parts of others which he, in turn, may be holding on to.

Once these are identified, they can be released, which will free up more energetic space for the client since this is now no longer occupied by the energies of others which he is unable to use effectively in his own life.

One way of returning these soul parts is through a fire ritual where, in normal consciousness, the client will write down on paper the names of the people whose soul parts he has been holding, then gently tear each one from the sheet, visualizing the person concerned and the nature of the original encounter where the soul part was taken. This strip is then burned, while healing blessings are offered to the person concerned, with the heartfelt intention that these soul parts return home to their true owner.

During the final session, the client journeys to meet with his own returned soul parts, which have now had some weeks to reintegrate themselves back into his energy body. He may then ask questions of them to find out why they left, for example, if this is not known; to understand any deeper pattern in his life symbolized by the type of encounters which have caused these parts to leave; or for guidance on how best to care for these soul parts so that they do not take flight again. This journey is a celebration, a welcoming home of essential parts of oneself and a recognition of the enhanced energy and power that one now has.

'I find the most memorable part of this is the spontaneous fusion of the returned soul parts with the person,' says Howard. 'People describe it as "a magnetic force" drawing the soul part into their hearts. This is a very significant and beautiful experience for many, where they really and tangibly feel their hearts opening and expressing love.

'This is a very special and illuminatory encounter for the person who may not have had this experience during the initial soul retrieval work or in the following weeks. In fact, this kind of experience generally involves feelings of discomfort, confusion and emotional "rawness" that can occur after soul retrieval work which is part of the healing re-union of the life force energy, and can lead to the person reconnecting to forgotten memories and feelings.'

Sometimes, in cases of extreme soul loss or profound physical illness (which the shaman would also see as indicative of a deep loss of soul), the client will be unable to journey on his own behalf, and so the shaman must journey for him to carry out the recovery work.

Gary Gent relates a particularly beautiful journey of this kind which demonstrates also that soul retrieval is a healing approach of value not just to the living, but also to the individual who is preparing to end his time here on Earth.[27]

The journey taken by Gary was for a patient he calls John, who was hospitalized for liver cancer and being given pain medication by his doctors to reduce his suffering until he died.

'The medical establishment could do no more for him. His family background is one of abandonment by his mother and other family members. His mother had disowned him.

'On entering the altered state . . . I was taken to a hospital room that was empty except for a single bed. John's physical body was lying on the bed unmoving. His spirit self was sitting on the edge of the bed, holding his head in his hands. I could feel intense pain, grief and sadness in him.

'His spirit self became aware of our presence (myself and my Spirit Guide) and looked up with fear in his eyes. I talked to John, explaining who we were and what we were doing in his room . . . I asked if he was holding any [soul] pieces from other people that we could return for him. John stood and reached behind him, bringing forth 10 soul pieces that he was holding from others. Two of these soul pieces were returned to his mother, one to a sister, one to his father and the other six to other men and women. With those soul pieces returned, I asked my guides to assist in returning soul pieces that John was missing.

'I was immediately taken to a situation from John's age of 13 to 14. We found John on his knees with his head to the floor in front of his mother. His mother was holding a foot on his neck, maintaining a forceful control on his masculine self. John's 13 to 14 year old soul piece was degraded, angry, trapped and experienced very deep self-image damage due to the forced submission. Our appearance surprised his mother, causing her to jump back. This released John's soul piece and my Guides encircled him so his mother could not reassert her control. We then explained why we were there and asked if he would return to his older self. The soul piece's response was an immediate yes.

'We brought his 13 to 14 year old self back to John, and then travelled to other situations, recovering an additional 24 soul pieces, which were also returned to him. On the return of the soul pieces, John's spirit self took them immediately into his heart. As they were taken in, a sense of peace came over him . . .

'I contacted Jane [John's friend] and related the journey information to her. She said she was going to visit John in a few days and would let me know how he was doing. She related later that John was much more peaceful and even had a few lucid moments during her visit. This was a dramatic change from previous visits, where she found him in an agonized condition.

'Her next visit was in three weeks. On this visit she reported that around John was a peacefulness that had not been there before. Three days later I received a call from Jane. John had died during the night, with no trauma. Like stepping through a door.'

I think Gary's work with 'John' was an act of beauty and I really hope that Gary, or someone very like him, is there for me when it is my time to die.

EXERCISE: RETURNING YOUR MISSING SOUL PARTS

Over the years, and especially as a city-dweller, with all the frustrations, subtle, and not-so-subtle hurts, irritations, and the scrabble for power, promotions and socially-defined meaning you will be part of, it is inevitable, sadly, that your soul will suffer damage in this world. Here is a technique, taught originally by Howard Charing, which you can use to recover the parts of yourself which may leave you over time as a consequence of this hurt.

Begin in the journeying position you now know, with drumming if you have it; otherwise in a still, quiet space and frame of mind.

See yourself as standing before the entrance to a cave or some other doorway which provides an entrance into the Earth, such as a well or a foxhole, and then step into this new world. You will find yourself in a tunnel or passageway. How it looks, sounds and feels in this place will be unique to you. Take all the time you need to look around and get familiar with your surroundings. When you are ready to move on, look for a source of light, which is the natural daylight of the lower world, and walk towards this.

Go through the doorway you find there and look around at this new world.

Begin to focus your explorations and look for a river or a stream or other fresh, running water. Follow this back to its source and there you will find your spirit teacher waiting for you, who will appear in the form most appropriate and recognizable to you. Spend some time with this teacher, as you both get to know each other, and then ask that they guide you to the place where your soul parts, lost over the years through the impact of life on the spirit, are waiting to return to you.

Throughout our life we may lose many soul parts and not all can be recovered in one journey, as we would not be able to cope with this massive influx of new-found energy (the example given by Gary Gent, above, where 24 soul parts were returned, is extreme and unusual and, I imagine, was done only because of the close proximity of his client to physical death). On your own journey, do not ask to be shown more than two – or, at the most, three – soul parts to return with. Make sure, though, that these are the soul parts which are most valuable to you currently in the light of any problems and concerns you are dealing with now.

When you meet these soul parts, speak softly and gently to them, remembering that fear has brought them to this place and they will need to be reassured that you mean them no harm and can be trusted. They may appear to you as symbols or sensations, or in the form of children or younger aspects of yourself, and you may see clearly the circumstances leading up to their loss. Ask them about themselves and what has led them here, and then, when you are both ready, hug them to you and return, via the route you have just taken, back to ordinary awareness.

Remain lying down in this reality and, with your arms folded over your chest, still hugging the returned soul parts to you, feel their energy seeping into your body.

You may feel a little strange over the next few days as this energy finds its place within you and connects again with the other parts of your energy body. Some people report feelings of elation, others that they feel weepy or slightly sorrowful for a short while. The song of the universe is one of deep, melancholy keening, and your soul parts have been there, in the vast cosmic dance of our energy-world. The sorrow that you feel is merely a by-product of your reconnection with the energy flow of the universe. It will pass as your soul-energy becomes reacclimatized to physical reality.

Stay alert to any unusual experiences over the next few days, including reveries or dreams which seem to have meaning for you. The energy you have returned has its own memories and consciousness and it is not unusual for this to be communicated from your unconscious as your soul parts become one with you and you become more whole once again.

SOUL THEFT

There is another side of soul loss, which is just as prevalent in our modern cities – that of soul theft.

Traditional cultures guard their soul-energy carefully. The Aborigines of Australia are wary of having photographs taken of themselves because they believe that their soul can be captured in the image which results. I encountered a similar belief among the Santeria community of Little Havana, when I was warned against photographing even the front of a *botanica* (a magical supplies store) lest I take its energy along with the picture. Among the Lakota Sioux, even looking another person directly in the eyes can be seen as an attempt to steal that persons's soul – an interesting one for us in the West who are often challenged with the words: 'Look me in the eyes and say that', as a direct assault on our own personal power, or who may be required to 'stare someone out' in a business meeting in order to exert our power over them.

In the Western world, at a conscious level at least, we may not readily subscribe to such 'naïve' views. Nonetheless, we all know someone who has tried to take power from us in one way or another. The office politics of most companies is an attempt at self-promotion which is typically, sadly, and usually deliberately, at the expense of another – our 'rival' – whom we will do our utmost to show up in a bad light so that we are the only natural candidates for advancement.

The unbalanced marriage where one partner dominates the other is another example. Often there is a jostling for power, in the modern, patriarchal marriage, where, despite the efforts of the equality movement, the husband makes most of the decisions which affect the family, while the wife will seek to redress the balance by nagging, criticism and sanctions – or, at least, this is the stereotype presented in most of our soap operas and sitcoms, which is, of course, a tutelary message of the social dream.

Just about every relationship we are involved in can, in fact, be described in terms of its power play and every time we play this social game in order to win out over another and take power from them to increase our own, we are involved in soul theft. Sometimes, this is an entirely unconscious act, which stems from our own insecurities, or it is motivated by our desire for self-preservation and self-development rather than being a deliberate attempt to undermine or wound another. The effects, however, are the same at a personal and a social level since our actions uphold the consensus. Perhaps we are acting from insecurity – but what, after all, are we insecure about? At a deep level, all insecurities stem from our fear that we are not good enough for the system, that we don't measure up to its dream reality. The trick to overcoming any insecurity is to forget the consensus and find a new scale by which to gauge our own worth.

Soul theft is often a learned behaviour which reflects the culture and the systems which support it, rather than an act of individual free will. The children of abusive parents often go on to abuse others, for example: while most of our social systems are based on the notion of having a 'winner' and a 'loser'.

The education system is a case in point. From the earliest age our children are rewarded for thinking and behaving in a particular, socially acceptable or socially desirable way, and are punished for 'misbehaving'. Our school examinations are competitive and graded. Some of us win and some of us lose, and those who win go on to become members of the elite and then have control over the mechanics of the system (or are lost within it, becoming functionaries for it) and so the process becomes self-perpetuating. The result is that we are taught the method for soul theft and seizing power from the moment we are born. It is all around us, in our TV heroes, our politicians, the family interactions that we see, the social hierarchy which pervades our lives. And it takes a lot to get out, once we are in.

As Howard Charing says, soul theft may be 'a learned generational behaviour . . . It is an unconscious act and, in fact, if the person knew what they were doing, they might very well be upset.'[28]

According to Howard, we steal or take people's life force for many reasons. These include:

- Jealousy of another person's power or status.
- As a means of supporting ourselves, when we do not have sufficient energy of our own, and so we become dependent on another for everything we do and every decision made, while they in turn become responsible for our happiness.
- When we are so lacking in our own self-esteem or sense of self that we actually *want* another person's identity. We hero-worship or idolize them so much that we want to be just like them.

- When we 'over care' for someone, causing them to become too dependent on us, which results in them losing their own strength or identity and the will to support themselves.

Judgement of another, particularly in our modern world, is a very common way of taking their power, and this is especially so if punishments or sanctions of any kind are imposed because of their deviance from our accepted views.

Judgement, with the punitive actions arising from it, is an important precondition for 'soul loss' and 'soul theft'. In Haiti, for example, where social and spiritual power is considered vital, a person will often deliberately evoke a loa, or use other magical means in order to secure power over someone who has offended them, or to do harm to the soul of another for short-term personal gain.

Mambo Racine explains the Vodou approach to healing such attacks:

'Spiritually-induced illness is treated by direct intervention with the loa, which are called to the head of either the sick person or the houngan or mambo conducting the treatment. Then, after the spiritual problem is resolved and the malevolent entities paid off or sent away, the person is treated with remedies for weakness and debilitation.

'The [Western, psychoanalytical] theory that mental illnesses are caused by parental bad behaviour isn't too much in vogue in Haiti, where parents have god-like power over children, and can beat them or fail to educate them at will. Mental illness is more apt to be attributed to frustration with life's circumstances; to *madisyon*, meaning really awful things done by the ill person's parent, to reproductive health related issues, or a partner's infidelity.' In such cases, all of which are situations of soul theft nonetheless, the loa are called to offer blessings and healing, to take away the negative energies and life issues which have eroded or impacted the person's soul, and to help make them whole again.

The notion of 'judgement' is the central concept behind perhaps the most extreme form of soul theft – zombification, a condition well known in Haiti, and one which is intimately associated in the public mind with the practices of Haitian Vodou.

THE ZOMBI AS AN EXAMPLE OF SOUL THEFT

Because of the beginnings of Haiti, cast as it was in the cauldron of slavery and moulded by years of political oppression and murder, the communities which evolved there became extremely close-knit and defensive. While they would support their neighbours wholeheartedly and in every way, the people were not inclined to welcome newcomers and, even among their own, would not condone any activity which drew unwelcome attention to their community from the authorities who had power of life and death over them.

Even today, unemployment levels of 65 per cent or more exist in Haiti and most people are poor enough to wonder where their next meal – which is typically only beans and rice – is coming from. Theft from a neighbour could not be tolerated where communal loyalty was a matter of survival, while, of course, the conditions of abject poverty encouraged stealing whenever possible as a developed survival skill.

The system of punishments developed by the community to safeguard itself against such transgressions, and the intervention of the state as a consequence of them, was somewhat formalized. A first offence might only receive a warning, but for a second, the powers of the houngan would be summoned. As regulator and pastoral leader of the community, his job was to dissuade the violator from further acts and, if talking failed, he would use his magical skills to cause a sickness to befall that person in order to keep him home for a few days so he could reflect on his crimes and come to think better of them.

In some cases, however, even that failed and the final recourse of the community, in order to control the criminal and keep him out of trouble, was to zombify him in order to make him docile, placid, and unable to create further distress and attract more unwanted attention.

The houngan did not act alone in this. The decision was usually made by a powerful and secret society of mambos and houngans known as the *Sanpwel*, which would discuss each case in detail and on its unique merits. The zombification of one of their own village sons was not a decision taken lightly, even though the community may have requested it.

If it was decided to proceed, however, action was swift. A powerful herbal mixture was prepared which would produce the desired effect and this was administered through stealth to the person whose actions had drawn this punishment to him.

Harvard ethnobotanist, Wade Davis, has written eloquently and convincingly of the origin of the zombi in Haiti, in *The Serpent and the Rainbow*. After painstaking research, he was able to identify and reproduce the herbal poisons used by the houngan in order to create the zombi. The mixture produces a state of narcolepsy which slows down all of the vital signs and, while consciousness apparently remains, the victim gives the appearance, to all intents and purposes, of being dead. In this state of living death, she might even be buried and left underground for a day or so, perfectly able to breathe since her respiration was slowed and the need for oxygen lessened, but aware of every moment of her incarceration in a living tomb.

After a period of time, she would be dug up. Her brain affected over days by terror and by lack of oxygen, and with the residue of the drug still in her system, she would be as a woman with no soul, no power over herself, and easily controlled by others. The community would have its daughter back, but a different, more malleable and acceptable daughter.

Zombification was, and still is, one of the most feared of destinies in Haiti: a living soul loss, with all control over oneself stolen by another. Myths of the zombies still circulate on the island and, over time, the *threat* of zombification has developed its own power.

For a culture born in slavery, where control of the personal inner world was possibly the only existential freedom left, the loss of power in this way is a horrifying prospect, but also an accepted fact. People in Haiti *know* that the houngan has this ability to create a zombi of them if they step out of line. Consequently, it may even be possible to say now that a person who *believes* they have been zombified will come to act in that way, losing their soul completely, which takes flight at the terror of the punishment, even when no poison has been administered.

As Davis remarks:

> *All that can be ascertained is that voodoo death occurs, and that as a process it involves a number of complementary factors. Fear probably does initiate physiological changes. Certainly it makes the victim psychologically vulnerable and this, in turn, affects the physical health. Neurophysiologists still do not fully understand the process, though the response of the victim's family and society would seem inevitably to influence both his psychological and his physical well-being. So, while a universal mechanism to account for voodoo death has not been identified, the basic assumption is clear. As one researcher has put it, the brain has the power to kill or maim the body that bears it.*[29]

I am sure that dead men walk the streets of our cities too, though rarely to the extent of zombification. Nonetheless, there are many ways that we can, unwittingly or otherwise, steal the life force from another: by our conscious decision to accept a promotion at work that we know someone else needs and possibly deserves more than we do; by clinging to old relationships long after they have ended so that they remain, in a sense, incomplete for both parties; by fighting with our neighbours over a few square inches of disputed land; by exercising such control over our children that they are never allowed true independence and the freedom to think for themselves; by encouraging our employees to work so hard that they end up 'selling their souls' to the company. The list is as long as human experience.

The theft of another person's power in this way is ironic and doubly painful since we can never use this energy ourselves because it is simply out of phase with our own life force. Instead, it hangs around within us, cluttering up our own energy system, a burden which drags us down too. Sometimes, too, the energy we take from another may actually come from their shadow self, that dark repository of emotions and feelings which we regard as unwholesome to us. We then find ourselves 'working with another's [darker] feelings, which may be an uncomfortable experience', as Howard Charing points out.[30]

Howard has worked with many people to help them release the soul parts that they are holding on to, and from their comments it is possible to see just how liberating it can be to finally let go of this energy – 'the taken soul parts . . . were holding me back, weighing me down', said one; 'it felt like I was covered in clinging seeds and leaves', are the words of another. It makes sense always to release those energies which we feel we may be hanging on to, not only for the other people affected, but for ourselves – and also, of course, to try to be more conscious of the reality and repercussions of soul theft so that we can do our best to ensure that we are not involved in it again.

It may be that these soul parts will, themselves, return over time (and, of course, not every situation of abuse will necessarily produce soul loss), but it is, perhaps, more wholesome to return these parts to others as a deliberate act of intention, to clear the energetic 'debris' and 'clean the slate' as it were, perhaps after the end of a love affair when we need, fully, to say goodbye to our loved one.

If you would like to do so, the following exercise may help.

EXERCISE: RELEASING THE SOUL
PARTS OF ANOTHER

Journey in the same way as in the soul recovery exercise you have already completed, in order to meet with your guide in the shamanic lower world and ask to be taken to the soul parts of *others* which you are holding on to. Sometimes you will be surprised at the soul parts that are revealed to you as you meet again the people who, consciously, you thought you had long let go of.

Do not pass up the opportunity of speaking with the enlightened spirit who is your teacher and guide in this place. Ask to see the circumstances in which you feel drawn to take the energy from another person, the need in you that stimulates this action, and how best you can control this and draw beneficial energy for yourself from other sources – or any other questions which come to mind.

When you are ready to return, gather to you the soul parts of the other person you are still holding on to, in the same way as before, and return to ordinary reality.

It is a lovely gesture of healing and restoration to have some tangible item ready as a gift, which you have specially selected or made, and which is intended for the person whose soul part you have returned. Blow their soul energy into this gift now, seeing it clearly as it enters this item and comes to rest there. You can then send this gift – anonymously if you wish – to the person concerned.

When I came out of a long-term relationship a few years ago, I made sure I did exactly this, returning my ex-lover's soul parts to her which she had naturally given away to me during the course of our relationship, as our soul essences blended into the mutual future we had planned. I followed the guidelines I have given you here and, when I returned her soul parts, I blew them into a

CD I had bought for her that day. I simply sent it to her with a short note telling her she might like the CD and to give it a listen. I knew that her soul parts would find their own way home when she did so. And I also made sure to take my own soul parts back from her.

If you don't want to use this method, you can use the fire ceremony we looked at in the last exercise instead, or even simply will that the energy is returned to the person to whom it belongs.

Energy is immaterial and does not need to be contained in a gift or any solid object; I just think it is an act of healing on two levels – physical and energetic – to send a gift in this way. It also makes it tangible and more meaningful for you and for them.

A LOVERS' PACT

After all we have said about spirit intrusions and soul loss in this chapter, I was stunned to read an article in the London *Times* in November 1999 about a couple, Kevin and Irena Warwick, who intend to share their emotions with each other by wiring their nervous systems together through the insertion into their bodies of a silicon chip which, via a computer, will 'read' and decode the electrical stimulation associated with various emotional states in each person and then share them with the other partner. 'Kevin hopes his nervous system will become temporarily "possessed" by his wife's, forcing him to perform the physical actions that she performs, and to feel the same emotions she feels,' says writer, Anjana Ahuja.[31]

'It will be the ultimate test of whether human beings are anything more than machines – albeit sophisticated ones – whose physical and emotional behaviour is regulated purely by electrical inputs,' the article goes on. How sad that we even need to ask the question, and how much a reflection of our preoccupation with analysis and rationality rather than any desire to know what it truly *means* to be human.

'If the experiment works . . . it may one day be possible to use implanted chips to communicate emotions and even concrete thoughts – such as "Will you marry me?" – from one person to another through the internet' – as if we do not have enough problems with face-to-face communication right now in a world torn apart by war and exploitation!

'The chip would also prevent marital infidelity by providing "physical" proof of adultery,' according to Ahuja – and so none of our secrets will be sacrosanct any more. We will be reduced to the status of an emotional book, open to all, where questions of ethics and morality become not a matter of personal reflection and soul-searching but a soap opera with voting rights for all. The *Big Brother* of the soul. The mystery of life will be gone, the sacred eroded further, and our conscience up for grabs. And this is what we call progress in our linear-scientific world.

I cannot deny that the modern city-dwelling Western man in me is fascinated by this experiment and intrigued to know the results. At its best, it may even go some way to telling us about the nature of our emotions and the place of the soul in all of us.

But as someone trained and initiated in traditional healing methods, and concerned for the moral evolution of this world we share, I am deeply concerned at the outcome of an experiment which, on the face of it, seems little more than an exercise in deliberate, wilful and consensual soul loss and which does nothing to really connect us as individuals, and everything to turn us further into automata within a private universe and a city sometimes already too full of heartache.

6

GETTING TO KNOW THE SPIRITS
OF THE CITY

The world of our present consciousness is only one
out of many worlds of consciousness that exist, and
those other worlds must contain experiences which
have a meaning for our life also.
– William James, *The Varieties of Religious Experience*[1]

We call it 'energy', the conscious, aware 'beingness' of the universe, which we first experience as raw information, before attaching meaning to it and so creating reality. The energy of the universe is not just 'data', since this would imply a one-sided relationship where we are the only beings of power in the universe, everything streaming towards us nicely packaged and ready for us to assemble according to our whims. The evidence is quite the opposite: this energy is alive, aware, and just as important as we who are a part of it.

What we are talking about, of course, when we describe an aware, invisible 'energy' which has an impact on our lives, is what the shamans call 'spirit'.

Spirit is a word we are not too comfortable with in the West. Nor are we happy to believe that this spirit-energy can be used in matters of healing – or, indeed, that it has any purpose apart from its use in trickery and charlatanism.

Our cynicism was summarized in an article in one of the UK's national newspapers on 20 February 2000. Under the heading, 'Only Fools and Curses', the piece talked of African healers as 'black magic crooks . . . suburban voodoo tricksters

. . . who rake in a fortune with what they call powerful juju and the rest of us call a total con'.[2]

The article goes on to describe an undercover 'investigation' by a reporter, of three London-based healers, one of whom he calls a 'greedy guru', another 'a very strange lady . . . raking cash from the desperate and gullible', and the last, a 'witch doctor . . . dressed in robes that looked like they'd started life as a sheet'.

Naturally, the writer would never dream of calling a hospital consultant 'a greedy guru' or describing a surgeon's gown or a priest's robes as looking like a 'sheet'. His article is a reflection only of his own limited belief system – that 'West is best' and that only *our* own healers have power – rather than any fundamental truth. His worldview is implied in every word. Indeed, the very fact that the article began life as an 'investigation' at all, an 'exposé' rather than an objective feature, is testament to the writer's intentions and already gives the game away. Sadly, however, our media have power over people's beliefs, so anyone reading this might easily mistake such prejudice for 'objective fact'. The consequence is that a person who might really have benefited from seeing one of these healers may now be inclined not do so, all because of one writer's narrow-mindedness.

Of course not everything in the West is as limited, narrow-minded and ignorant as this. Obviously unknown to, or deliberately ignored by this reporter, our National Health Service is currently sponsoring detailed research into the healing efficacy of such 'greedy gurus' in the hope and belief that Vodou healing practices can vastly cut the amount of disease among UK Africans and also help to prevent illness in the wider population.

Writer, Gonzalez-Wippler, notes a similar trend in American healthcare, with psychologists from New York hospitals including Bellevue, Lincoln, and the Columbia Presbyterian Medical Center referring a number of their clients to well-known santeros (priests of the Santeria Vodou tradition). The patients are referred because they believe in the magical powers of Santeria much more than the 'magic' of the psychologist and physician and, according to the clinical evidence, respond much better to the santero's treatment methods. In fact, says Gonzalez-Wippler, 'miracle cures' of a medical as well as a mental nature, 'are very common in Santeria'.[3]

She tells the story of one man who visited a santero because of a problem with a paralysed arm. 'The man had been seen by several doctors who had said the paralysis was permanent because the arm's nerves had been severely damaged. The Santero prepared an *obra* [a healing potion designed to infuse the patient with power], and within minutes the man could feel sensation in the arm. A few days later, the arm was completely healed. The man's doctors could not understand the cure and asked him to explain the treatment he had undergone, but he would not tell them that he had been cured by a Santero.'

One can understand his reluctance, too, given the prejudice, lack of sophistication, arrogance and ignorance of our media and some of our medical professionals.

At the root of this lack of understanding is the sheer reluctance to use the word 'spirit' and to take magical powers seriously. We have moved so far away from a sense of the sacred in our lives that we prefer the risk of damaging our own health so long as we don't have to entertain the notion, or even the possibility, of an unseen world where the spirits walk beside us. Yet the spirits are all around us and will help and teach us if we wish. The starting point is simply to listen, because no healing at all can take place unless we are prepared to hear what they have to say.

THE SOUL AND THE SPIRITS

In the West, our understanding of the 'soul' is as shaky as our view of the spirits. In *The Journey To You*, I told the story of a Western religious authority who was asked by a journalist from the UK papers for the Church's definition of the soul. In thirty years, he said, nobody had ever asked him that before. The best he could do, besides reading from an ecclesiastical dictionary, was to offer his own comment that the soul is 'sacred' – before requesting that the journalist not quote him on that as it might run counter to the official 'line' of the Church.

We are alone in the universe in the urban world. Our religious leaders have no answers for us, and even question the nature and possibility of the soul. What, one wonders, are they trying to save, then? And how can they possibly do their jobs as priests if they cannot, will not, or do not know how to define the soul and what is sacred for us?

The ancients had no such problem, but could define in exquisite detail the nature, cycle and components of the soul, as well as its journey beyond death and its eventual reincarnation. The Bardo Thodol, or *Tibetan Book of the Dead*, dating from as long ago as the eighth century, is exactly such a guidebook and contains descriptions of all stages and challenges in the passage of the soul through the phases of its reincarnation.

According to Buddhist tradition, which grew as a religion from the Bon tradition of shamanism, human beings have three essential components: a physical self, a mental self and a conscious self which exists beyond death and which we would refer to as 'the soul'. At the moment of death a process of disintegration begins – or is begun for the dying person by the priest or lama – where these three elements separate and the soul draws inward to the heart before departing the body. In this it is not so very different from the funeral rites of Vodou which we looked at earlier.

Death, in the Buddhist tradition, arises from one of three causes:

- Having reached the end of one's natural lifespan – a 'natural death'.
- Through the dissolution or exhaustion of personal energy – a form of soul loss, in fact, which depletes personal power so that illness or dis-ease may enter.

- Through sudden events such as accidents or murder which prematurely – and sometimes unnaturally – cut short a person's life, in a way which is, perhaps, somewhat like the Tuvan notion of *aza or buk*.

Death can be avoided in the last two cases if it is known when and how the death will occur. This requires an expert knowledge of the 'omens of death', which will reveal the cause behind the crisis. Omens are of three types:

- *External* – referring to bodily conditions. These will almost always have a spiritual element to them, reflecting a loss of power which is attractive to Death and makes accidents and 'bad luck' more likely since the person affected is less able to defend against them.
- *Internal* – revealed by the patient's symbolic dreams and visions, which may provide advance warnings of the nature or circumstances of death.
- *Spiritual* – signs which are understandable by an examination of bodily conditions. The lama will say, for instance, that if the patient can put pressure on his eyes and not see sparks of light as a result; or can cup his ears and not hear the sound of the sea, these are signs that he will be dead within four weeks unless an intervention takes place.

Death itself is marked for the patient by the sudden appearance of a radiant light – very much like the brilliant white light described by those who recover from near-death experiences. The dead person then awakens in the otherworld, surrounded by strange entities which eventually reveal themselves as enlightened spiritual beings. This is, again, similar to the near-death experience, where survivors report that they are met by beautiful and luminous beings who welcome them to this otherworld.

The precise mental state at the moment of death determines the quality of the experience in the otherworld of this now-disembodied consciousness, as well as its future destiny, so it is crucial that the dying person is helped to maintain a positive attitude throughout life, right up to the point of physical death. Those who have met with sudden, violent, deaths (such as murder victims) do not have time to make preparations for death and may suffer particular problems of disorientation and distress in this new world beyond life, which the shaman-priest may be able to ease. (The Buddhist notion of 'karma' also suggests, however, that those who become murder victims may have drawn this event towards themselves by their own actions, and it is certainly true that 'those who live by the sword' are more likely to die by it. The shaman-priest must therefore be cautious not to interfere with the wider karmic pattern which the dead person may have chosen for herself, including her own eventual murder.)

'Buddhism is based on the idea of the origins and cessation of suffering,' says Ekun, a friend of mine who is both a santero and a student of Buddhism. 'Buddha asked why there is death, sickness and old age and, through his long search, managed to discover the origin of suffering, which he called *samsara* – the endless cycle of birth, death and rebirth. The way to end human suffering, he said, is to escape this cycle of reincarnation, known as *karma*. Then you will reach the "bliss state" of *nirvana* (which means, literally, "snuffing out"), where the ego, or individual self is annihilated and the consciousness returns to the cosmic pool of universal connection. The individual is no longer reborn, and no longer suffers.'

The word *nirvana* was mistranslated to mean 'Heaven' or 'bliss' by Westerners when they first encountered the term, since *nirvana* was understood to be a goal of Buddhism, and must therefore be like our own fantasies of achievement; in this case, 'peace everlasting'. But the true goal is, in fact, the annihilation of the differentiated self, since whenever the self is believed to be separate, it will strive to reincarnate in its quest for divine reconnection.

'We remain in the state of *samsara* as a result of our *karma*, which is what attaches us to experience,' says Ekun. 'Whenever we treat another living being cruelly, exercise control over it, or use our power to abuse it, we create more *karma*; whenever we act kindly and compassionately towards another, that, too, creates *karma*, since by loving another living thing, we become attached to it and attached to this world, so that we are, again, at risk of being reborn. *Karma*, therefore, is entirely neutral in itself – there is no "good" or "bad" *karma*, only *karma*, per se.'

Enlightenment, the achievement of *arhanthood*, is a result of conscious living and mindful preparation for death through awareness and non-attachment.

Theravadan Buddhism, which predates Tibetan Buddhism and is even more shamanic in nature, speaks also of *boddhisatvas*, 'good spirits', who had a chance to achieve *nirvana* and escape the cycle of life and death, but have decided to become reborn in order to return and help others. This a matter of their personal, spiritual, choice. It is the intention to become free which must remain the ultimate goal of life.

Assuming we have lived our lives well by being true to ourselves and practising non-attachment to people or things (in a way very different from the urban, commercial, lifestyle!), we all have a final shot at freedom at the point of our death.

To help his patient make the most of his last opportunity, the lama (the Tibetan equivalent of the shaman-priest) will guide him with instructions from ritual texts which ease his transition to death and then assist his consciousness on its 49-day journey through the realm between lives.

Forty-nine seems to be a magical number which occurs in many separate and otherwise unconnected traditions. There is a similar time frame connected with Vodou rites of death, where the houngan will work with the dead to ensure their own smooth passage and to protect the community by ensuring that they are settled and at peace. A similar ritual occurs among the Darkhat Mongols, where the body of a dead shaman must not be touched or visited for 49 days. Instead, his body, his tools and equipment are left in peace at his own power place in the landscape for the prescribed time so that his soul may become one with the energy of the universe and his powerful ancestral spirit become a protector for the community.

At the end of the 49th day, in Tibetan lore, the deceased is reborn to the world, in a new incarnation which is influenced by his *karma*.

During its journey between lives, the soul will experience moments of spiritual potential which provide an opportunity for it to recognize the true nature of 'reality' as illusion, a facet of one's own perceptions and projected experiences. In so doing, the soul-consciousness is able to shatter the cycle of birth and death to achieve ultimate peace. If it cannot do this, however, it will reincarnate once again into another physical existence.

In traditions such as these, where knowledge of the spirit is practised almost as a science, the existence of the soul is self-evident and the 'psychology' (literally, the 'science of the soul') practised by their spiritual leaders, evolved and detailed. In every tradition, the soul is regarded as a component of man, along with a physical, mental and emotional 'self'. Of all of them, however, the spiritual self is the most important and has the power to transcend life and death, and to retain consciousness, evolutionary potential and free will.

In Vodou, humans have three spiritual components – the *ti-bonanj* ('little angel'), *gwo-bonanj* ('big angel') and *mét-tét* ('master of the head').

The *ti-bonanj* is individual consciousness, the personal experiences of those who have lived, the ethical dilemmas they have faced and their moral response to these challenges. It is this part which is subject to divine 'appraisal', in a way similar to Buddhist *karma*. That is, there is no 'good/bad, reward/punishment' duality as in Christian thought; instead one's actions on Earth have an impact for one's own spiritual self in helping to determine the sort of life one is reborn to in order to learn from the events of the past. No retribution is acted out or moral penance required in the new life, merely ongoing evolution through spiritual development and new life experiences to learn from. It is cause and effect, not 'right and wrong' which is key.

The *gwo-bonanj* is an aspect of 'the one god' and, according to Richard Hodges in his article, 'The Quick and the Dead', 'is entrusted to a man as his life force, his invisible core; it is his vital spirit, his blood, his breath, his disposition, his intelligence . . . Finally, it is what a man's life amounts to, what he as an individual represents in eternity. For those who are his direct descendants, it represents their ancestry, and through them undergoes a kind of reincarnation.'[4]

If the person has lived well or was an individual of exceptional power, such as a houngan or mambo, their soul may even become one of the loa itself, making itself a still-visible part of the community through ritual appearances and spontaneous possession.

The *mét-tét* is an individual's personal protective spirit, whose identity can be established through divination and will reflect the individual's personality and predilections. Prior to my own initiation, for example, my *mét-tét* was determined to be Ogoun, a loa who very much reflects my own character. This patronage was ascertained by my initiatory mambo, who was 2,000 miles away from me at the time, and whom I had never met. She was, however, through divination alone, able to summarize the essentials of my own personality by establishing which loa had 'claimed' me as their 'god'-child at my birth.

The *mét-tét* is actually better seen as a *potential* for one's life guardian rather than an absolute, as the individual still has free will and can choose instead to work with another primary loa (though this is sometimes not without risk since she is choosing to reject a god), and nothing is regarded as fixed in any case until the individual accepts the 'offer' of the loa by undergoing certain rituals of initiation which cement the relationship between the two.

A further force in Vodou, as in most traditions, is that of the ancestors, the benevolent spirits who play a crucial role in the daily affairs of humankind.

'The sacred dead are of paramount importance,' says Hodges.

They represent the ancestral wisdom accumulated from past human experience, and also the channel through which the spiritual emanation of the original creation makes contact with each generation, and finally that which ought to concern every living human being above all else: his most fitting fate and end.

Concerning the importance of a proper burial, there is this saying, uniquely African in flavour: 'a man buries himself while he is alive'. In other words the quality of a person's burial, which is everyone's highest aim, is a mirror of the quality of his life.

This is a statement echoed in most spiritually inclined societies. The Toltec shamans also counsel us to 'keep Death as our advisor' at all stages of life so that we can die well whenever our time may come, while the Sioux have an expression which evokes the central importance in any life of spiritual preparation for death. 'Today is a good day to die,' they say, reflecting their 'karmic' readiness to face death with a good soul and with all duties and responsibilities honoured, all debts paid, all affairs in order, all arrangements – physical and otherwise – well made.

DYING TO LIVE – RECOGNIZING THE SPIRITUAL IMPORTANCE OF DEATH IN OUR LIVES

The Western world has become what psychiatrist, Dr Elisabeth Kübler-Ross, calls a 'death-denying society, a people who even deny the aging process itself'. Informed by the worldview we are born to, we have come to believe that death will arrive in one grand event which stands in dramatic juxtaposition to the rest of our life. Ancient civilizations and tribal peoples know better. They appreciate that life and death are parts of the same continuum: we are all of us dying all of the time. Only by recognizing this and keeping death with us as an adviser on our lives can we ever hope to live authentically and fully while we have the opportunity to do so.

Dr Kübler-Ross has spent decades working with the dying, and as a counsellor on death. In her book, *Death: The Final Stage of Growth*, she has wise words for all of us based on her years of experience with terminal patients and their own recollections on the meaning of their lives and their selfless advice for the still-living.

'There is no need to be afraid of death,' she says.

It is not the end of the physical body that should worry us. Rather, our concern must be to live while we're alive – to release our inner selves from the spiritual death that comes with living behind a façade designed to conform to external definitions of who and what we are. Every individual human being born on this Earth has the capacity to become a unique and special person unlike any who has ever existed before or will ever exist again. But to the extent that we have become captives of culturally defined role expectations and behaviours – stereotypes, not ourselves – we block our capacity for self-actualization. We interfere with our becoming all that we can be.

Death is the key to the door of life. It is through accepting the finiteness of our individual existences that we are enabled to find the strength and courage to reject those extrinsic roles and expectations . . . rather than trying to fit ourselves into some ill-fitting stereotyped role.

It is the denial of death that is partially responsible for people living empty, purposeless lives; for when you live as if you'll live forever, it becomes too easy to postpone the things you know you must do. You live your life in preparation for tomorrow or in remembrance of yesterday, and meanwhile, each today is lost.[5]

There are plenty of other societies that agree. In his remarkable essay, 'Dying Among Alaskan Indians: A Matter of

Choice', in Dr Kübler-Ross's book, Murray Trelease, who spent eight years serving Indian villages in Alaska as a parish priest, reveals how the Indians would often *choose* precisely, consciously and deliberately, the moment and circumstances of their own death, when they had reviewed their lives and decided that their life purpose had been completed.

'Often it was the one dying who called everyone together. And I was told on several occasions that the dying person had spent the past few days making plans, telling the story of his life, and praying for all the members of the family . . . Death would occur soon after they received the sacrament.' These people were so in tune with their lives, and with death as an essential part of it, that they could actually determine in advance the exact moment of their death and make the appropriate arrangements to leave the Earth with their life purpose fulfilled.

Notwithstanding the logic of other cultures and their approach to death, which allows them to honour their mortality and embrace their life more fully, sometimes it is only through *personal* realization, when faced with death itself, that we can come to a true understanding of the power and preciousness of life, which is our real and natural birthright as human beings, in place of an 'empty life' following the rules of the system.

A friend recently forwarded a message to me which had been posted to an Internet newsgroup by Hawk, a Native American flute maker who had been ill with cancer for some time. Despite his devastating illness, his response has not been one of resentment towards his condition, or of self-pity, but of deeper love and compassion for all of us mortal human beings, and a deep respect for life based on the growing realization of its true significance. He offers these words as a healing gift for us all:

> *My Dear Friends, this disease has brought me some of the most horrible days of my life. At the same time, it has brought me some of the greatest blessings of my life.*
>
> *There is something in us that can't be satisfied by the*

materialistic world, that can only be satisfied by things
that can't be seen or measured. Things like being touched
by somebody else's spirit who has been motivated by
love, concern and affection.

Having my mortality hovering around me has given
me a whole new perspective. I used to say 'most things
don't matter', I thought it was a truth of my heart. But
I quickly learned that it was still only a head truth. Now I
know that most things don't matter. I used to say to my
family and friends 'I love you'. I didn't know what the
word 'love' meant until now.

There is much sickness of the spirit in this world today,
and I would like to dedicate the remainder of my life,
however long that might be, to helping and serving
others. I do not have adequate words to express the
blessings you all have already given me.

As Richard Hodges remarks, 'There is an important suggestion in all of this about what the soul really is . . . It seems to
subsist not just in something inside a person, but also in the
network of forces and relationships of a spiritual as well as a
material nature which a person establishes with other people
during his life.'[6]

We in the West, sadly, remain largely divorced from this
potentially life-enriching continuum of life-and-death and out
of touch with the fullness of our experience of life. But that is,
perhaps, not so surprising, as the 'spiritual network' Hodges
talks about is also missing in the faceless system of the city
which is our modern home.

'Some of these relationships [in more traditional societies]
are such that they are not destroyed when the body dies,
and may continue to act for a long time,' Hodges goes on.
'As other people are affected beneficially by these relationships, they spontaneously send good wishes to the person
who is the source of these benefits and, in that way, begin to
feed his remembrance among people. A point can be reached,
these teachings seem to be telling us, where this aspect of a

man's inner and outer structure becomes permanent, able to exist and to act independent of his physical vehicle.'

Hodges seems to be implying a psychological framework here for understanding the spirits, where it is our energetic force which survives death in the form, perhaps, of a collective, communal, archetype which has its own momentum and power, to be drawn upon either as an actual memory of how this person might morally have acted in similar circumstances or, over time, as an ethereal, almost fable-like projection of her core essence.

There is an element of truth in this, though spiritists would say that they are not interacting with 'archetypes' at all, but with real and individual spirits, the ancestors and the loa.

Personally, I do not think it matters greatly how we choose to define these spirits – as archetypes, energy or spirit beings – but we *do* need to honour their place in our lives in some way in order to work *with* them at all.

This is not the case in our modern world. Once the dead are buried, they are gone. If we are religious, we may see them as now in the audience of the divine; if we are not, they are simply a memory which will fade with time. In either case, they are beyond us and do not touch our lives. And when we forget our ancestors, we lose their wisdom; when we forget the gods, we have no moral scale by which to measure our lives.

The sociologist, Emile Durkheim, believed that religion was merely society worshipping itself, projecting its own sense of structure onto the random play of the cosmos in the form of a heavenly father and mother who gave us life. If that is the case, then we children of the city have killed our parents and made ourselves the orphans of the universe.

EXERCISE: THE JOURNEY TO LIFE BEYOND DEATH

In this journey you will reconnect with the spirits of those you have loved and who have passed over to the other-world and experience the continuing love and wisdom they have to offer you.

Take this journey from the exact moment *after* your physical death, not before. Experience yourself drifting upwards, as the soul-essence of yourself, walking down the tunnel between the worlds and into the light of the souls that will meet you there.

Who are these people who welcome you to this new world? What do they have to say about you and the way you have lived your life? Looking back over your own Earthly life from this new perspective, infused with spirit, what do *you* have to say about the way you have lived?

Once you are 'settled in' to the new world of the spirits, you find that you are able to move about, to journey to other places, and to interact with life-forms different to yourself.

Journey back to the physical relatives you have temporarily left behind on Earth. What advice do you have for them – for all of us – about the way we are living our lives here on Earth?

LIFE AMONG THE SPIRITS

There is plenty of evidence in Western literature and research of the existence of consciousness after death. Still reluctant to use the word 'spirit' or 'soul', however, Western writers tend to talk of 'ghosts' or (even better since it sounds more scientific) 'apparitions'. Both words imply a sense of objectivity and distance from the human condition – something 'out there', not quite connected with us.

The effect, however, is the same, and the evidence impressive that spirits do exist and that we are quite capable of sensing and communicating with them.

The archaeologist, Tom Lethbridge, author of *Ghost and Diving Rod*,[7] describes a walk one day with his mother, through a wood near Wokingham. Both became very depressed as they passed a particular spot, for no reason they could fathom, and did not want to continue their walk. A few days later, the body of a suicide was discovered at just this place.

Lethbridge was affected by this experience, and by many similar ones which took place throughout his life. 'From living a normal life in a three-dimensional world,' he wrote, 'I seem to have fallen through into one where there are more dimensions. The three-dimensional life goes on as usual, but one has to adjust one's thinking to the other.'

To make sense of these experiences, he went on to develop a theory that woodlands, mountains and rivers have a special kind of energy attached to them which attracts 'emotions' [read 'spirits'], like tape recordings of past emotional events which may go back millions of years into human history as a form of energetic record of that experience. The 'three-dimensional' physical world, then, was just one expression of reality, one level of being, beyond which was an energy universe, which recorded its events on the magnetic tape of the physical.

All of this is, of course, very similar to the ancient beliefs of the shamans who maintain that rivers, trees, mountains and landscapes are the homes of the spirits, which become the sacred places of their community.

Lethbridge believed that we all have the ability to attune ourselves to this energy, since the human mind has evolved to make this possible, almost as a survival mechanism, so we are more aware of our surroundings and the threats from them to our well-being, which must have been very pronounced in the distant days of our hunter-gatherer ancestors. An awareness of spirit energies and an ability to tap into them is therefore a strategy and a mechanism for health and safety. We can all tune in to these energy recordings when we allow ourselves to become still, to stop the 'inner dialogue', and to listen to what the world has to tell us.

Colin Wilson, who has written extensively on the occult, mentions two cases of just such events.[8] In one, a woman watching her husband repair a second-hand motorcycle (in that meditative state we can all get into while watching

361

another work, perhaps) suddenly became aware of a man who had walked into their yard and was standing watching too. Assuming it to be a friend of her husband, the woman asked to be introduced, only to witness the man vanish before her. From her description, the husband – who had not seen this man at all – was able to tell her that the person she had seen was the previous owner of the motorcycle who had been killed two years before.

In another case, the spirit of a chimney sweep who had died of cancer was witnessed by the whole family repeatedly visiting his bedridden wife to offer comfort to her, on one occasion standing by her bed before the entire family for more than an hour. Again, in the solemn atmosphere surrounding a sick, bedridden woman, we can easily imagine a sense of tranquillity and quiet similar to the air of contemplation which enables us to stop the inner dialogue and allow the spirits to enter.

Even our religious authorities, who (ironically) are non-believers in the spirits, are not immune to their visitations and interventions. In the 1890s, Pastor J. L. Bertrand, overcome by cold while climbing in Switzerland, himself became a 'ghost' for a while, as he succumbed to temporary death and watched his spirit float above his own body as it lay in the snow.

From this new vantage point, Bertrand watched peacefully as the others in his party, who had gone on ahead of him, continued their climb. He watched the guide sip secretly from a bottle of Madeira and steal food from the group; saw the party advance by a somewhat different route than the one previously agreed; felt himself being revived as his colleagues returned and – to their astonishment – was able to tell them all he had seen while 'dead', which turned out to be entirely accurate.

'It is a pity that the notion of "survival" has been made unacceptable to many by the naïve enthusiasm of "spiritualists" who seem to turn the Christian doctrine of heaven and hell into something cosy and comfortable, with dead relatives advising their survivors not to forget to feed the canary,' says Wilson, 'yet much of the evidence is impressive'.[9]

But it is not just the 'cosy-comfortable' pro-spirit lobby which is to blame for the prevailing ideology of suspicion towards all things spiritual. In 1936, the Archbishop of Canterbury himself appointed a special church commission to determine whether the Church of England could seriously accept the possibility of 'communication with the dead'. After much research, the commission reported back three years later that, in all likelihood, the spirits do exist and that there is nothing in this which in any way contradicts Christian doctrine. Their report was suppressed for fifty years. One wonders why.

LIFE AFTER NEAR-DEATH

The findings of extensive scientific research into near-death experiences (NDEs) also offer evidence for a way of life beyond the body. Again, researchers typically veer away from using the emotive word 'spirit' to describe the prevailing consciousness that they invariably discover beyond the physical world. They prefer to talk of a 'survival of consciousness' – although the consciousness which survives is, of course, the spirit.

The pioneer of research in this field is Dr Raymond Moody, who pretty much introduced the subject in his book *Life After Life*, where he recorded and compared the experiences of 150 people who had died temporarily before being revived.[10]

There are, he concludes, a number of consistent elements which occur in every near-death experience:

- Hearing a strange sound, variously described as buzzing or ringing, along with the clear understanding that you are no longer living.
- This is typically accompanied by a feeling of deep peace and contentment, even if the experience leading up to this was one

of intense panic, fear, or physical pain while still 'in the body'.

- A sensation of being out-of-body, of rising up and floating above the physical body and looking down dispassionately at this 'shell', while the self now occupied is experienced as a lighter, less constrained, spiritual body, a living field of energy.

- A sensation of rushing quickly through a dark tunnel towards a source of radiant golden-white light. Sometimes, instead of going 'down' into this tunnel, the person may float or be lifted 'up', looking back to see the Earth as a celestial sphere like that witnessed by the astronauts who first sent pictures back from space.

- Usually a meeting with wise and loving spiritual beings on the other side of the tunnel, entities which glow with an inner light and then become – or are perceived as – the souls of relatives or friends who have already died and are there to greet the person who has 'died'.

- This period of orientation is followed by a meeting with a spiritually powerful being, who is understood to be the 'ruler' of this realm and is sometimes described as 'God' or 'Jesus'. This meeting often inspires feelings of reverence or awe, sometimes even fear, although there is never any sense of threat from this presence.

- This powerful being will present the dead person with a minutely detailed yet cosmically large review of all they have done in their lives so that they relive every act and interaction with others and see how their own life has been part of an entire, intricately woven pattern. There may be a feeling of 'karmic learning' associated with this – not a punishment or making of amends, but an opportunity for deep wisdom and tuition to be received. Those who undergo this experience normally return with the knowledge that love is the most important thing in the world.

- The emotions experienced in this otherworld are so intense and beautiful that there is often a reluctance to come back. The 'Supreme Being' will advise the dead person that she must return, that it is not her time; or, sometimes, will offer her a choice to go or stay. In all cases, there is such a sense of peace and oneness that most people do not want to return to the harshness of life on Earth. When they choose to do so, it is normally only because they sense a need from their loved ones who are still living, and finally do return out of a sense of duty or compassion towards them.

There is something extremely shamanic about Moody's description of the NDE archetype, as well as much in common with the Buddhist description of death and the journey into the otherworld, which we looked at earlier. The shaman's journey also begins with a voyage deep into the Earth (the lower world), through a dark tunnel, or into the realms of the sky beings (the upper world) to emerge into a spiritual landscape which is often described as bathed in light. The journey is one of the spirit outside of the body to meet with guides who may take the form of light-beings, and with tutelary spirits who also have an air of supreme wisdom.

In one journey, which I described in *The Journey To You*, I was spontaneously subject to a life review spanning several incarnations, and so deep was the sense of peace in the midst of this mystery that it was a struggle to return to ordinary consciousness. In fact, the shaman who guided this journey wisely had us write out two things that we would *definitely* return to ordinary reality for, in case he needed to enter the otherworld to bring us back. His experience was that many people do not want to come back from this world. I would personally have stayed there happily if not for my daughters.

The tunnel, the light, the understanding received from spirit and, sometimes, the reluctance to return, are all borne out in the NDE experience.

CHILDREN'S EXPERIENCE OF THE OTHERWORLD

Dr Melvin Morse, MD, paediatrician, neuroscientist and Associate Professor of Paediatrics at the University of Washington, has spent twenty years studying near-death experiences in children.

His interest began when he was called to a young girl who had drowned in a swimming pool and who had had no heartbeat for 19 minutes. Miraculously, he was able to revive her and she went on to recover fully. Strangely, although she had been 'dead' for 19 minutes, she could recount many details of her resuscitation. She said that while she was 'away', she had been led through a tunnel to a place called 'Heaven'.

Dr Morse was sceptical and so began a study of near-death experiences, along with colleagues at Seattle Children's Hospital. Using age- and sex-matched controls, he compared the experiences of 26 children who had been resuscitated after death, with those of 131 other children who were all severely ill and had also experienced lack of oxygen to the brain – but who were *not* near-death.

His results showed that 23 of the 26 children in the 'near-death' group (88 per cent) had undergone experiences consistent with those originally identified by Raymond Moody as the 'near-death archetype', which is so similar to the shamanic experience, while none of the other children had. If near-death experiences were caused by lack of oxygen to the brain, drug side-effects, hallucinations, stress, or by fear of dying – all explanations which have been offered for near-death experiences – then the other 131 children should also have had these experiences. But they did not. Not one.[11]

Dr Morse followed his initial research with a long-term study of NDE children, observing their progress as they grew up. His results show that the survivors of near-death experiences have a much enhanced and richer experience of living, as well as an appreciation of the sacred, and of the importance of compassion in daily life. Adult survivors are more likely to donate money to charity, to volunteer to help in the community, to work in the caring professions, to treat their own bodies better, and are less likely to suffer from drug abuse or other problems.

Another organization, the International Association for Near-Death Studies, has broadly supported Morse's findings in this respect. Their research shows that:

almost every near-death experiencer reports a changed
understanding of what life is all about . . . Besides losing
the fear of death, a person may also lose interest in finan-
cial or career success. 'Getting ahead' may seem like an
odd game that the person chooses not to play any more
. . . Becoming more loving is important to most . . .
Religious observance may increase or lessen, but deep-
ened belief in God or a 'higher power' is almost certain.
People say, 'Before, I believed; now I know' . . . Some
people find they have an increase in intuitive or psychic
abilities.[12]

Dr Morse is also convinced from his research that everyone
has the biological ability to communicate with those who
have died; indeed, that our brains are wired with this capability and there are specific areas of the neural tissue whose
function is to facilitate such spiritual interaction. The fact that
few people do so is the reflection of two simple facts: first,
that we do not believe such communications are real since we
are taught all our lives that the spirits do not exist; and
second, that we are unpractised in using the area of the brain
which enables such communication, although we can learn to
do so.

HOW THE DEAD COMMUNICATE

Bill and Judy Guggenheim are the authors of *Hello from
Heaven!*,[13] which is based on more than eight years of research
and interviews with 2,000 people, young and old, throughout
America and Canada, and across all social, educational,
economic, occupational and religious backgrounds.

Their studies include more than 3,300 firsthand accounts of
people who have been contacted spontaneously by deceased
family members and friends. Extrapolating these figures to
cover the entire population, the Guggenheims have estimated
'conservatively' that 'at least 50 million Americans – or 20%

of the population – have had one or more ADC [After Death Communication] experiences – and the actual numbers may be closer to double these figures.'

The Guggenheims have recorded the twelve types of communication with the dead that people report most frequently, as well as offering advice on how to increase your own chances of such communication.

- **Sensing their presence.** This is the most common form of contact, and is often experienced immediately after the death. It involves a distinct feeling that the dead are near, although they cannot be seen or heard. It is similar to the sensation I felt when first walking into my parents' home following my father's death.

- **Hearing their voice.** This may be external or experienced inwardly, as a voice 'in the mind', but with a real and separate personality capable of taking an active part in a two-way dialogue with you. My eldest daughter experiences this a lot. Her sister and I have watched her sit up in bed, still asleep, and carry on a conversation with another, to us invisible, entity. Even more remarkably, they seem to be communicating in German – a language she doesn't even know (consciously, at least).

Joel Rothschild, in his book, *Signals*, also mentions this sensation when he first walked into his friend, Albert's, apartment to find him dead: 'I felt his presence, as if he were speaking. I did not hear words with my ears, but I sensed a faint cry that no sensory organ could register. I *felt* his voice.'[14]

Joel and Albert had agreed that whoever died first would leave a note for the other. Having searched the apartment, however, Joel could find no such note and initially became upset. At that point, Albert's voice, which he was able to 'sense' rather than hear, told him to go outside to the back of the building, where he would find a trashcan: 'You will find the note that you need.'

Joel ran outside and found the trashcan exactly where he

had been told he would, and began to scrabble through the rubbish in the bin. 'Everyone thought I had gone mad [but] there, at the very bottom, I found Albert's last written words. He had buried the note in the neighbour's garbage so it would never be found . . . The crumpled letter began, "To my most dear love, Joel", and ended, "You are my dearest friend. I shall always love you". That was exactly what I needed to know. I needed to know that I was in his final thoughts.'

- **Feeling their touch.** People often report the sensation of an arm being placed around them, of a kiss or a hug being given, even though they cannot see the entity responsible.
- **Smelling their special fragrance,** often a familiar perfume or some other aroma obviously associated with the deceased.
- **Seeing 'something'.** This may be a fully solid and whole being who is known to you, or perhaps only part of a body. Sometimes it is just a mist or a pattern of lights, but intuitively you understand its significance and its connection to the deceased. 'Loved ones virtually always appear healed and whole regardless of their cause of death,' say the Guggenheims. 'Verbal communication may take place, but not always.'
- **Visions.** Of a different quality to the last category. In visions, you watch something unfold before you and are both part of it and separate from it at the same time, somehow involved but outside of the experience itself. It may be a replaying, actual or symbolic, of an important moment from your lives together, which thereby connects you once again with the deceased; a sort of 'action replay' of a significant event, for example, in a place which holds special memories for you both.
- **'Twilight experiences',** which occur during the altered state of consciousness between waking and sleeping, and which are especially vivid. Information received at this time is usually retained on waking.
- **Experiences while sleeping,** in the form of lucid and intense dreams which have a qualitatively different feel to them from others, and which you 'just know' to have a deeper significance.

- **Out-of-body experiences.** Of a similar nature to other out-of-body experiences but combined with a sense of destination and purpose, where you visit – or are taken to visit – the dead person and are able to interact with him.

- **Telephone calls.** These forms of communication are interesting as there is something very curious about spirits employing modern – yet very indirect – technology! Nonetheless, people report answering the phone in the normal way and hearing the voice of the deceased who passes on a message to them, and sometimes engages in conversation or answers questions. The voice is usually quite clear but will sound distant and 'otherworldly'. Once the message has been delivered, the line will disconnect as if the receiver has been put down at the other end. The fact that the phone is used does, of course, make the experience more 'solid'. A disembodied voice or words heard 'in the mind' can always be dismissed as fantasy or imagination, but it is harder to deny a tangible action such as answering the phone. And, of course, very recently, the researchers at Scole have been told by the spirits that a new form of spirit communication is now evolving which relies on the use and manipulation of energy in order to offer more tangible proof of survival.[15] A phone call from the beyond would certainly fit that category.

- **Physical phenomena.** A wide variety of unusual physical signs are mentioned, which are often associated very directly with the dead. A photograph of the dead person may be lifted or a personal item moved, for example. At other times the phenomena may be more general, such as lights going on and off by themselves, televisions being turned on, and noises from otherwise empty rooms. In my own case it was a robin, which flew into my father's house and made directly for one of his favourite possessions.

- **Symbolic actions.** When people ask for a sign from someone who has died, they often receive it as a symbol of some kind, such as an odd coincidence or moment of synchronicity. My friend, Simon, told me recently that he was driving into the town of Hastings a while ago, which is the place where the great English magician, Aleister Crowley, died, and was thinking of

Crowley as he did so. Crowley often referred to himself in life as '666, The Beast'. At the exact moment that Simon thought that, the milometer in his car clicked over to 666.

'According to our research,' say the Guggenheims, 'the purpose of these visits and signs is to offer comfort, reassurance, and hope . . . They want you to know they're still alive and that you'll be reunited with them when it's your time to leave this physical life on Earth – and they'll be there to greet you when you make your transition. Their most frequent messages, expressed verbally or non-verbally, include "I'm fine . . . everything is OK . . . don't worry about me . . . I love you . . .". You may be asked to give a message from your loved one to somebody else. We urge you to write down the message verbatim and to deliver it, if possible, because it may help the recipient far more than you realize.'

The Guggenheims' research also suggests, however, that not everyone will be contacted by their ancestral dead. This may be a reflection of the fact that few people know how to open their minds so that their natural psychic abilities can be used, but according to many writers in this area, fear, anger, guilt and prolonged grief may also inhibit such communication. The key is to remain open, relaxed, and to welcome the dead with love.

The following technique may help if you would like to try to contact someone in the spirit world whom you have been close to. (Also see the Guggenheims' advice in *Hello from Heaven!*)

EXERCISE: OPENING TO THE ANCESTORS

Express very clearly the intention that you are open to, and wish to communicate with, the spirit of a *specific* ancestor and to receive help with a *particular* problem.

The most effective time for such communication is

when you are feeling relaxed and calm, with the expectation that contact *will* take place. The shamanic journey is ideal for this, enabling you to enter a deeper, non-ordinary state of consciousness in anticipation of a meeting with your spirit guide. Meditation has been reported to work just as effectively, however, if it enables you to relax into a light trance. Alternatively, you may use visualization techniques, as the Guggenheims advise, to clearly imagine your deceased family member, well and whole, standing before you. Then ask that they visit you in your sleep or meditation.

Follow whatever happens next, whether this is a powerful dream, an 'imaginary' conversation, a journey to the realm of spirit, a feeling of being 'possessed' by the sensations of this person, or a physical manifestation of some kind. As soon as you receive such a sign, begin to dialogue with the spirit just as you would a friend.

As evidence for you of the validity of this experience, ask them also for a sign of some kind that you will recognize in your everyday life after this particular encounter has ended. Try to be as clear and unambiguous as possible in this request so you will know the sign unequivocally when you see it.

According to Guggenheim, signs often offered by the dead as proof of survival are 'butterflies and rainbows . . . birds, animals, flowers, and a large variety of inanimate objects – such as finding a series of coins or whatever item you associate with your deceased relative or friend'. This may be what the dead want to offer but I know for a fact that in a country as wet as the UK, I would not be convinced by a rainbow. Or, indeed, for that matter, by any other object or thing that I might well encounter by chance alone – such as a butterfly or a flower – unless the circumstances surrounding their appearance were extremely dramatic and unusual. Call me unsubtle, but I would want something much more obvious and less open to interpretation.

Immediately after my father died I attended a meeting of the Spiritualist church in our town, where the medium was able to tune in to the spirit of my father. He was laughing, she said, because the previous day he had watched my sister and me hiding the family silver, and described exactly where we had hidden certain valuables in the house pending a visit from the probate inspector! Evidence like this is much more convincing to me than the appearance of a butterfly.

Stories of reincarnation add weight to the arguments from near-death research. While they do not suggest the existence of spirits, *per se*, since by definition the person reincarnated now occupies a new physical body, they do provide strong evidence that some form of conscious awareness continues after death as, in many cases, the person concerned not only remembers their previous life but, when the circumstances of this life are investigated, the facts often check out too.

LIFE BEFORE LIFE

Peter and Mary Harrison have assembled a number of re-incarnation stories in *The Children That Time Forgot*, and from their research they conclude that there is 'little doubt that in some instances life does indeed exist before Earthly birth, either in some non-physical realm or on the physical material Earth plane'.[16]

In every one of their cases, the reincarnation concerns a child of pre-school age, normally two to three years old when their memories of a previous life first surfaced. A child of this age has probably never even encountered the notion of re-incarnation and, even if they had, they would be able to make little sense of the rather sophisticated concepts involved. Yet their stories are intricate, their memories alive and vibrant, and the facts of their previous incarnations verifiable by others. Such are the cases of Mandy Hartley and Nicola Wheater.

One day, when she was two and a half years old, Mandy Hartley created a bit of a mess in the kitchen while she was playing. Her mother, Susan, first amused, soon became cross with her daughter for the disruption she had caused and was about to tell her off when her daughter interjected.

'I'm going to tell my mummy of you,' she said.

Susan was a little stunned by this and replied, 'But I am your mummy.'

'I mean my other mummy,' said Mandy, 'from when I was a little girl before.'

'Susan could see that Mandy was absolutely serious,' said the Harrisons, 'so she asked her, "Well, why did you leave your other mummy then?" A rather dejected expression crept over the child's face. Then she answered "Because she hit me with knives." Susan was horrified and asked her daughter "Are you sure? Are you just making all this up, Mandy?" Mandy said, "She did hit me with knives and then I died."'

A few weeks later, more of the story unfolded as Mandy spoke about her death. 'I was very poorly,' she said, 'then I fell asleep and went very small. I woke up and I was with you and daddy and then I grew big again, into a big girl.'

She also told her mother that she remembered being in her womb and some of the sights and sounds she experienced there from the outside world, some of which her mother could remember too. She revealed, for example, that Susan's newborn child [Susan had recently given birth to another child] had once died in her mother's tummy but had come back again. Susan had had a miscarriage in the tenth week of her pregnancy, when Mandy would have been about a year old and quite unable to fully understand what had happened. Susan had conceived again shortly afterwards.

Even more dramatic is the case of Nicola Wheater who, when she was five years old, had an unusual question for her mother, Kathleen: 'Why am I a little girl this time, mummy? Why am I not a boy like I was before? . . . When Mrs Benson was my mummy.'

Intrigued, Kathleen asked her daughter for more information, and Nicola described in some detail life as a young boy in the West Yorkshire village of Haworth, a place that Nicola had never been to before, of having two sisters, both much younger than him, one of them a baby, and a father who worked on the railways. She described her family home as one of the middle houses in a row of four, made of grey stone and backing onto fields near a railway line.

She then went on to describe her death: 'I was playing on the railway lines with Muff [her dog] and my friend and I saw a man walking along swinging a lamp. After that a train came up fast and knocked me over . . . I went to sleep and died and I saw God in heaven before I was born – but I didn't really die. I came to you instead and you got to be my other mummy.'

Kathleen decided to check out Nicola's story and drove them both to Haworth to look for clues. Since neither of them had ever been there before, she managed to get completely lost among the winding country lanes. Nicola, though, was completely unfazed by this and intervened to direct her mother through the isolated, unmarked roads, straight into Haworth village. 'I know the way,' she said, 'because Muff and I used to walk around here.'

Following Nicola's further instructions, Kathleen drove on to the outskirts of the village where they finally stopped – directly in front of a row of four grey stone houses, with open fields at the back and a railway line nearby, exactly as Nicola had described.

Kathleen took a note of the address and then drove on to the parish church to look through the register for the area. She found an entry for the house they had just been to which, in 1875, listed the occupants of the cottage as Mr and Mrs Benson and their son, John, born on 20 June. The father's occupation was given as 'railway plate-layer'.

Totally unknown to Kathleen, another, related, line of enquiry was at that moment taking place in the Archives Department at City of Bradford Metropolitan Council where the census for 1881 was being checked.

The census is a legal document requiring absolute accuracy from respondents in recording the details of their family, so in 1881 the Bensons would have had to record details of every family member living in their home at this time. The census records listed the Bensons as having only two daughters, aged three years and six months, at this time. There is no longer any mention of their son, John Benson, even though his name is recorded in the parish register of 1875.

Since every family member must be included, the only possible explanation for the discrepancy between this and the parish record is that John must have died before the census was taken and his parents then had two more children, both girls. Nicola had remembered having two sisters, one just a baby, in her statements to her mother. As the youngest member of the Benson household at this time is just six months old, this places the death of John Benson fairly precisely between 1880 and 1881. He would have been, as Nicola said, a 'little boy', just five or six years old at his death.

LIFE EVERYWHERE

If only a fraction of all of these reported cases of reincarnations, 'hauntings' and near-death encounters with spirit beings are correct, we still occupy a universe teeming with spiritual life and our cities are alive with the ancestors.

Some modern writers are clear that this is exactly the case, but that these entities are resident in other dimensions to which we have only part-access, and only on occasion. In *The Romeo Error*, Lyall Watson proposed that there is no ending with death; rather it is a form of evolution into a different stage of life.[17] He points to the natural cycle of plants which are dormant for long periods of their lives – particularly some desert species which can remain apparently lifeless for years until touched by rain – and to the regenerative powers of some animals who can lose entire limbs or parts of their bodies and then re-grow them at will. It is a mistake, says

Watson, to write someone off as 'gone' when they 'die'; we need a more sophisticated model than that in order to understand their evolutionary development beyond death.

The idea that the dead may be all around us, but in a different dimension from our own, would not disturb some modern scientists, who have hypothesized that we would require a model of the universe incorporating ten or more dimensions in order even to begin to make sense of the reality we *currently* occupy. We poor humans are limited to just three dimensions, but just because *we* can't see beyond these does not mean that nothing else in the universe can exist in, or experience, other realms.

Many animals have access to a much greater range of sound and a much deeper awareness of the light spectrum than we are capable of, and seem able to sense things far beyond our range of understanding. The Chinese, in rural areas, still use chickens as 'early warning systems' for impending earthquakes and atmospheric disturbances, for example, their increased sensitivity and resultant behaviour proving a reliable indicator of the need to 'batten down the hatches'. And we are all familiar with the stories of dogs who sense their master's arrival well before he reaches the door or are aware, before it happens, that the phone is about to ring.

We can explain such anomalies in one of two ways. We either admit the sensitivity of certain creatures to information which relies on an awareness among their species of dimensions we are not directly party to, or we put it down to 'supernatural causes' – neither of which is an entirely satisfactory solution for the overly-rational among us.

Shamanic belief systems do not have a problem with either explanation, however. My friend, Ekun, who is a santero in Miami, explained it well to me.

'Because I work in a rational, scientific field and have been brought up in 20th-century America, I struggled for a long time with accepting the existence of spirits, even though I was seeing them and interacting with them every day as part of my religion.

'Then I found myself watching a dog one day which was sitting across the street from a pizza house. That dog was practically drooling! And it dawned on me that what the dog was seeing was a *physical* vapour trail of smell from the pizza house – not an invisible thing we might pick up but a real, solid thing like we might see in 3D; like those cartoons where the smell wafts towards the dog's nose as a trail of grey smoke. That's what the dog was seeing.

'Now, dogs see in black and white while we see in colour – that's one ability they don't have – but they make up for it with greater sensitivity in other areas. Seeing the spirits is exactly like that – we just have to develop our skills in those other areas (and to accept in the first place that we do actually have those skills), just as an aromatherapist, for example, can tell you the difference between benzoin and neroli, which you probably couldn't, because he's spent some time developing his sense of smell. So maybe he "sees" smells too now.

'The first step is to *believe* in the spirits so you're concerned enough to look for them, and then to develop the right skills so you can find them. It's just like map reading, really.'

SEARCHING FOR THE SPIRITS OF THE CITY

There is a Native American saying: 'We do not inherit the land from our ancestors; we hold it in trust for our children.' There is, however, much that we do inherit from the people who have gone before us.

On a personal level, this is true of all the physical, mental and spiritual gifts that we have been given by those who preceded us. Genetically, we have inherited many of their abilities and dispositions, which have set us up with the skill repertoire for the life we decide to lead. Behaviourally, we have adopted much of the worldview, the prejudices and the predilections of our parents and grandparents through the simple act of our upbringing and socialization. Mythologically, too, we have absorbed the history of our forebears and our role within the mythological network and the history surrounding them. It really does make a difference to our bearing in the world that we are either the sons of bank robbers or barons. Our ancestors, one way or another, have contributed much to who we are.

On a cultural level, this is even more so. The way our society operates, what we see and believe, the way we live, are all a direct consequence of the actions of those who have gone before us and established the systems we live in today. Had Germany won the second world war, people of our generation, born after 1945, would now be living quite happily under a Fascist regime, in complete ignorance of the alternative unfolding of history which has taken place. Had we been annexed by Russia, we would have been raised in communism. But we 'won' the war and so we were born into capitalism. To the universe, such ideological differences are of no importance at all and, indeed, we might even struggle sometimes to tell them apart ourselves. But at a personal and social level of life experience, our world is very different as a result of the victories and losses of our ancestors.

We have looked at some of the implications of this in earlier sections. For one thing, a capitalist society is forward-looking, concerned with the future and disparaging of the past and this has tangible implications for the way we are allowed by the system to live our lives.

Karen Kelly, editor of the shamanic magazine, *Spirit Talk*, made the point in her article, 'The Search for Spirit in the City'.[18]

Many of us, I think, believe that something in the way our Western society interacts with the world is sick. With our machines and technology we have far more power to destroy our environment and can do so at a speed that no other society in our race's history has matched. And in our cities we are distanced from the damage we are causing; we have become cut off from nature, lost to the cycles of the land and its spirits . . .

If man's relationship with nature needed healing in primitive societies, how much more so is that healing needed now? However, in a society which hardly acknowledges the need for healing for other people, let alone our relationship with nature, how can that healing begin? Well, perhaps by cultivating that intimate and sacred relationship, by listening, and hearing what nature has to tell us . . .

Nature is all around us, the city, too, is part of it, so, even here, we can begin to reconnect with the spirits that surround us. Every city contains the spiritual residue, the essence, of those who lived there before us, some of them pioneers, wise men, and great leaders from whom we have much to learn: the Florence Nightingales, the Jane Austens, the Gandhis, the George Washingtons, the Einsteins, the Martin Luther Kings, the Marie Curies, the Shakespeares and the Mozarts. These spiritual beings are in no way different from any of the others we have looked at and seen evidence of in this book, and they are available to us at all times for consultation and inspiration, if we only decide to acknowledge them.

EXERCISE: MEETING WITH AN ENLIGHTENED CITY SPIRIT

Have in mind one of the great ancestors of the past who is connected with your city and whose advice you would like to seek on a particular issue. In London, this might be Christopher Wren or Charles Dickens or Florence Nightingale; in Washington, DC, it might be JFK or Lincoln; in Paris, it might be one of the great Impressionist painters of the past, or Hemingway and the other expatriate writers who made a temporary home there.

In the shamanic tradition of the ancient Greeks, such spirits, who brought the gifts of music, rhyme and inspiration to mortal seekers, were known as the Muses. You can, if you wish, make a journey to your own, modern muse, such as a great poet, philosopher or musician, who is associated with a particular city or landscape, or someone who simply inspires you in a personal way. An acquaintance of mine, who is a psychotherapist, very often journeys to the spirit of Carl Gustav Jung, who is one of his advisers, and sometimes to the spirit of Sigmund Freud, too, for advice on specific clinical issues.

Keep in mind your intention – for example: '*To meet with the spirit of the poet, W. H. Auden to learn from him how I can develop my own poetic style*' (or whoever you wish to meet with, and for whatever reason) – and then journey to this spirit to consult with him or her.

Allow your spirit to expand within you, seeing yourself so filled with light and power that this conscious energy can now drift beyond your body in the direction you will. You are an energy being which has the same shape as your physical body, but are lighter, translucent, and able to move effortlessly through the world. Guide this energy body with your thoughts and intentions, directing it towards a landmark in the city associated with the spirit you wish to consult. See this landmark in its spirit-form rather than the three-dimensional concrete representation it has in ordinary reality, so you can understand the essence of its meaning for its creator.

As you arrive at this place, notice how the energy changes with your presence since you have an impact on the energy web as well. The change you make will tell this spirit you are there, and they will be drawn to you. You may then ask the questions you are seeking answers to.

Begin to integrate their suggestions into your life and see what impact they have.

The spirits will not dictate to you exactly what is right for *you* in *your* life – that responsibility remains yours –

but their privileged position does afford them a much wider perspective and deeper understanding of what is truly important in life. It is therefore sensible to listen and to try out the information you receive to see if it works for you, exactly as you would with the advice of a good friend whose opinion you respect.

There are city places, too, which have their own spirits. It is not just the ancestral spirits who can help us. Sometimes we can pass by these places unconsciously aware of their spiritual dimension but feel uplifted as a result of the brief time we spend in the presence of their energy field. Sometimes it is the opposite.

Karen Kelly, for example, writes of a group journey taken by a shamanic drumming circle she was part of, which explored the spiritual essence of St Paul's Cathedral in London, a major religious landmark which has an imposing presence among all that surrounds it. In contrast to its assumed spiritual significance, however, 'many of us saw a great pit of fire surrounded by blackened trees and circling ravens', writes Karen.[19]

It is as well to understand these spiritual energies of the city and its landmarks. St Paul's, for example, is held to be a great spiritual centre and attracts many visitors every year, but the reality of its energetic emanations is somewhat different, according to this description. There will be many places you encounter every day, some recognized landmarks, others unassuming, which have an uplifting or depleting energy for you, all the same. Getting to know these places will have a positive effect for you since those personal power spots which resonate with your own energy will fill you with a sense of re-vitalization; those which sap your energies can, at least, be avoided.

There is some interesting research on the power of particular places – negative as well as positive – from recent studies into geopathic stress, which is a distortion of the Earth's electromagnetic field at certain locations. This distortion enables energies to be concentrated and then to rise up through buildings and other structures, often causing people to suffer tiredness, lack of energy and emotional problems. There is some indication that the siting of the buildings themselves causes a disturbance in the natural flow of Earth energies (quite a problem for us in our modern cities), resulting in such problems, a notion reminiscent of the teachings of the ancient Chinese tradition of feng shui.

Christopher McNamey of the People's Research Center in Alston, in a study of 175 nomadic families, found that people who are constantly on the move and whose lives are not centred, like most of us, around occupancy of two particular buildings – home and work – were likely to suffer from cancer in less than 1 per cent of cases. This is against a national average of 25 per cent.

NcNamey believes that his research provides strong support for the theory that 'cancer is primarily a disease of location. Not only do gypsies have a feeling for places which are free from geopathic stress, but should they pick a bad spot, they don't stay there long enough for it to harm them.'[20]

The research organization, Earth Transitions, states categorically that

> geopathic stress has been found to be the common factor in most serious and minor illnesses and psychological conditions including cancer, MS, AIDS, tuberculosis, meningitis, ME, kidney and gallstones, rheumatism, heart and circulation problems, as well as depression, insomnia, suicide, the promotion of stress and high blood pressure, together with resistance to treatment. Geopathic stress is also the common factor in cases of infertility and miscarriages and in most children with learning difficulties and behavioural problems.[21]

The organization produces some strong evidence to support its claims, including research from Dr H. Nieper, MD, a world-renowned specialist, who claims that 92 per cent of his MS patients are geopathically stressed; Dr E. Hartmann, MD, who is convinced, after treating thousands of cancer patients over thirty years, that cancer is a disease of location, caused by geopathic influences; and Dr Von Pohl, whose presentation to the Central Committee for Cancer Research in Berlin proved that a person was unlikely to get cancer unless she spent time in a geopathically stressed area. Dr Hager, MD, has also found geopathic influences present in every one of 5,348 cancer cases he has looked at; while in 90 per cent of cot deaths, it is claimed, a geopathically stressed location is also involved.

There is some support for this last statistic in work by two American doctors who studied 5,000 cancer patients to compare their sleeping positions with the intersection of energy lines as they crossed the area of their homes where their beds were situated. In 98 per cent of cases, the point of origination of the cancer in their bodies was at the exact position of the energy intersection. Research in Australia similarly found that with 3,000 children diagnosed with Attention Deficit Disorder, simply moving their beds produced an improvement in the condition in 100 per cent of cases.

A study from the 1930s by Dr S. Jenny, experimented in Aarau, Switzerland, with the effects of geological faults and underground streams on the well-being of 25,000 mice over a period of twelve years. Results showed that mice placed in cages over disturbances in the Earth's geomagnetic field became agitated, often gnawing their own tails off, and were inclined to eat their offspring. This behaviour stopped when the cage was moved to a geomagnetically neutral area. If the cage was placed part-on and part-off such an area, the mice naturally preferred to stay in the 'healthy' zone.

It is interesting to bear these results in mind as we reflect on the rising levels of rage and violence in our cities, especially if we remember that the very act of building, and therefore of urban development, is also implicated in the incidence of geopathic disturbances. But we should not be too surprised by these findings. Since the dawn of history, mystics and shamans have been consulted over the suitability for occupancy of particular sites and would take into account the spiritual and energetic composition of the land in doing so, as well as its visible physical features.

In China, the practice of feng shui defined an area according to the shape, size, disposition and interrelationship of natural features such as mountains, lakes, forests and rivers, all of which had spiritual energies (*chi*) which lived there and which, between them, directed power to certain locations. It was considered a good omen to have mountains to the rear of the property, for example, since this offered protection; but a corner property, at the confluence of two roads, was believed to be ill-appointed since the roads would direct excess energy towards the building, like an arrowhead, overwhelming its occupants, who would become irritable, ill-at-ease and suffer bad luck as a consequence.

Chinese sages believed that spirits travel along straight paths and so would install winding routes up to the doors of temples and other important places to prevent the entrance of demons and negative energies. Similar methods of protection, in the form of spirit gates called *torii*, are installed before Japanese Shinto shrines.

The Romans were also aware of the natural power of some places, and would leave a herd of cattle on a site for a year before moving there themselves. They would watch closely to see what befell the herd, and a year later would slaughter the cattle and use their entrails in divinations to determine if the site was healthy for human occupation.

Our ancient architects also understood the need for people to build and live in harmony with their surroundings and the spirit of the land. In Cairo, the exact moment that the first city stone was laid was precisely determined to match the ascension of the planet Mars ('*El Kaher*' – the Victor – in Arabic). Work on the site of the Escorial Palace, the seat of Spanish government, meanwhile, began with the entrance of the sun and moon into Aries, symbolizing the height of political and military achievement.

In *Geobiology – the Holistic House*, J. M. Gobet reflects on the care taken by the architects of old to ensure that the *spirit* as well as the *structure* of a building was taken into consideration in all construction work. 'In the Alps of Switzerland a few older carpenters are still inspired by respect for the forest and the wood,' he writes. Trees to be used in construction are felled only between December and February, and always under an ascending moon. The timber may then be seasoned for up to eleven years depending on its future use.

During the construction process, each beam, rafter and stud is carefully positioned according to the original direction of growth of the wood. A tree grows from the Earth . . . thus rafters and studs will always be fixed so as to have their positive pole towards the sky. The beams would have their positive pole towards North or East to ensure a natural flow of energies.

When completed, the structure is always blessed in a small ceremony during which a decorated sapling is nailed on the pitch of the roof. Many chalets, some of them up to 400 years old, are still standing in perfect condition, having never received a coat of paint or wood treatment.

These traditional practices, and the great body of knowledge from which they came, have been slowly discarded with the arrival of the industrial age to give way to 'cost-efficient', less time-consuming building practices and the use of toxic products. The times seem long gone when any stone mason knew it was unwise to build on the 'veins of the dragon', as the Chinese and the Celts called the streams of tellurian forces.[22]

The problems caused by the proliferation of artificial building materials and cost- rather than spiritually-conscious practices of construction is quite real and widely recognized these days. There is even a condition, well known to architects and planners as 'sick building syndrome', where buildings themselves become 'sick' and spread their illness to the human inhabitants as a result of their design and the materials used. The simple act of walking across a normal office carpet made from artificial fibres can release the same energy charge as a lightning bolt, for example. The fact that it doesn't do so more frequently is because the energy is absorbed by soft materials in the environment – including the human body – leading to headaches, nausea and fatigue.

The increase in the use of radio signals and electricity has also become a matter of verifiable concern in recent years. German specialist, Wolfgang Volrodt, believes that electromagnetic pollution has increased 100-fold in the last thirty years, while the New York Power Lines Project, the commission responsible for the New York power grid, *according to its own research* states that up to 15 per cent of cancers in American children may be caused by low-frequency electromagnetic fields from high-voltage power lines.

We have thrown away much by abandoning the old knowledge and rituals of site selection and building. Nowadays, we are more inclined to locate a 'prime site' for construction based only on the economic implications of its postcode and its likely resale value, without any concern for a healthy association with the spirits of the land while we live there.

These subtle energies, in the air around us, are not undetectable to us, however, and do have a real impact on our lives.

Gayle was a successful manager in a Chicago advertising agency. She loved her job but had noticed lately that she often developed headaches and felt drowsy and ill when in the office. The feelings left her when she got home again, but returned with equal force when she got into work the next morning.

I suggested to her that she might like to try an exercise in her office one night, after her colleagues had left: to lie down and to journey to the spirit of the building and ask it to help her understand the nature and the cause of her illness. She decided to give it a try, reasoning that she had nothing to lose by it.

'I began to get very cold,' she told me, 'and, in my mind, I saw the image of an old man walking towards me. He was dressed in a long brown coat, like a school janitor.

'He took me to the corner of the room where our heating and air conditioning unit is situated and pointed towards it. He was quite laconic, but in an amusing kind of way. "You need to get that looked at," he said. Then he pretty much walked back into the mist he came out of.

'The next day I called our maintenance man up and asked him to look at the unit. I wasn't aware of any problems with it, but I told him I wanted to get it checked anyway.

'So he looked at it – and it seemed that there *was* a problem, some kind of blockage so that instead of blowing clean air into the room, it was blowing back exhaust gases of some kind. He got it fixed and ever since then I have felt much better in the office and I don't get headaches at all now.

'I don't know if it was all my imagination, whether I subconsciously suspected all along that there might be a problem like this, or whether I actually met a spirit in the building. Whatever it was, it worked.'

Journeying to the spirit of a building is something you can also do in your own home or office, in order to understand its unique identity and to create a healthier and more energetic space.

EXERCISE: CHOOSING A HEALTHY HOME

According to the Earth Transitions research into geopathic stress, there are a number of things you can do to ensure that the place you live in is healthy and remains that way. If you are thinking of moving, you might want to consult this checklist before you do so. If you are already settled, see how many of these correspond with your own home environment and, if necessary, consult the following section, which offers some remedial actions you can take.

1. Your principal concern should be that your surroundings encourage a sense of harmony between yourself and nature, and that there are plenty of healthy trees and plants in your environment, which will absorb pollution as well as generating new energy for you. The best type of atmosphere is rich in healthy negative ions found near oceans and forests.

2. The ground should not be too clayey, which will encourage energy to seep away, or too sandy, which makes it difficult for energy to stabilize and settle.

3. Your property should ideally face north or west, and be as far as possible from power lines and other unnatural energy fields.

4. Natural features such as hills and woodland behind the house are good signs, but in front of the house, they are blockages for energy flows. Streams, rivers and roads can have quite the opposite effect, and should not flow directly towards you or you may be overwhelmed with energy and end up feeling 'on edge'.

5. Natural construction materials such as wood and stone are preferable to man-made substitutes. Cork floors, wood and woollen carpets are much healthier than nylon fibres and plastics, and much less likely to cause the sort of static build-ups associated with 'sick buildings'.

6. Dimensions should make you feel comfortable, with a good relationship between height, length and width.

7. Ensure that areas where you will spend long periods of inactive time, such as the bedroom, are not cluttered with electrical equipment such as clock-radios, TVs and stereos, which will continue to release electromagnetic energy, soaking your body even while you sleep. Sleep with your head pointing north if you can, so you are aligned with the natural geomagnetic field.

8. Rooms containing too much metal, or built over a garage, for example, become a battery for electromagnetic forces, and should be avoided.

9. Ensure that your house is a perfect square in shape and, preferably that all rooms are also squared as this helps energy to circulate freely, instead of gathering in the pooling areas created by irregular shapes. Feng shui is adamant that any areas 'missing' from the square, particularly if these create an L or 'hatchet-shaped' room, must be fitted with appropriate items to replace the

missing energy and redirect it, such as crystals and mirrors.

10. Do not place furniture in an irregular way so as to block the flow of energy, or *chi*. It is better to arrange chairs and tables in a circular formation, for example. Also avoid sitting directly below ceiling beams if your house has these features, as this will create a feeling of oppression.

Remedial actions

It is quite easy these days to get hold of good introductory guides to feng shui (such as Man-Ho Kwok and Joanne O'Brien's *Elements of Feng Shui*[23], which will give you fuller information on this ancient art of energy manipulation. Always ensure, however, that you never follow rules and regulations that do not sound appropriate to you just for the sake of it. In every case it is better to journey to the spirit of your house in order to find out what is best for the house itself, since what is good for the building will always be good for those who live there.

One of my shamanic teachers also advises walking the entire plan of your house, using incense or herbal smudge mix to clear out old energies and to make your house your own. Clapping or ringing bells in the corners is also important in order to stir up accumulated and stagnant energy. Another of my teachers is insistent that you should stand for a second or two in every space of your house. Not just every *room* but every *space* you can physically stand in, in every room of the house, in order to energetically claim the property for yourself.

My feng shui instructor, however, is less rigid than most. Whereas many will rely on the *lo'pan*, the directional compass of feng shui, which determines with the exactitude of a science the various degrees of direction and impact of energy flow, Charles uses a much simpler method. When you enter any room, he says, keep the door at your back; the areas of the room (or the house) which now face you from left to right, in a circular pattern back to where you stand, represent, energetically, your:

- Career
- Lifestyle
- The Elders and ancestors, and the wisdom of age
- Wealth
- 'Fame' or spiritual illumination (essentially, what you choose to make of yourself in life)
- Children and the wisdom of innocence
- Love, and
- The support of good friends

The centre of the room or building is the point of *tai chi*, or balance, for the whole.

Despite arguments made by purists, Charles's method seems to work just fine. I was once without a job for a short period of time and called in Charles to help. My house was 'hatchet-shaped', the missing area at the back being a patio leading to the garden which, effectively, removed the 'wealth' section of the building completely. I had already carried out some remedial work there, such as planting a tree at the bottom of this section to symbolically end the square of the house, but Charles recommended that I should also paint the garden fence red along this section since this fire colour would create a further energetic charge and attract new wealth into my life. I did more than that; I first painted the flagstones red and then set to work on the fence.

Literally, as I was working on the very last fencing panel, the phone rang. 'I heard that your company made a few people redundant last week,' said the voice, 'and wondered whether you might like a job with us.' It was a friend I hadn't spoken to for about a year and a half.

Some of the remedial actions suggested by feng shui are as follows. The idea is that you use these items within one or more of the nine areas of the room specified above so you can draw more energy into particular areas of your life.

1. If your stairs lead directly down to a front door, place a mirror on the back of the door to deflect and recirculate escaping energy which will otherwise flow right out of the house. This is 'step one' – claim your energy as your own.

2. Place a wind chime or a crystal in your 'career' section in order to stimulate good fortune at work.

3. Ensure that whatever is placed in your 'lifestyle' section accurately reflects your ambitions and aspirations for your *whole self*. A trophy from the office, for example, will create an energetic focus on work alone instead of a more rounded existence. You may need to journey first to discover exactly what it is that you *do* want from life, and the nature of your purpose in being here. In any case, this is likely to change over time as you continue to grow, so whatever is in this section should also be changed periodically.

4. Place pictures of your relatives, or family heirlooms, in the section corresponding to the 'Elders' to ensure that you have ready contact with their spiritual guidance.

5. *Gold*fish, plants, and especially '*money* plants', are recommended in the 'wealth' section to encourage the free flow of good things towards you. A few coins left here or images of money of all denominations is also helpful. This is the Law of Similarity at play.

6. In the 'illumination' section, place candles or a mirror, anything reflective of you, or scrapbooks and other records of your achievements. This section is about you and the impact you will make in the world, so it should always reflect your current ambitions, which may change over time.

7. In the 'children' section of my room I have a photograph of my children, as well as various letters they have written me and pictures they have drawn. By lighting a candle in

this area and allowing myself to relax, I can tune in very easily to their childlike wisdom and know what they would do in any situation, without all the hang-ups and game-playing that adults have to go through.

8. In the 'love' section of my room I have a print of 'The Lovers' from the tarot deck. Just as suitable would be a photograph of a loved one, a lock of their hair, or a personal item given to you by them.

9. In the 'friends' section, you may care to place photographs or mementos of your friends or symbolic representations of their particular skills, which may also be helpful to you.

10. The absolute key point in feng shui is not to live amongst clutter but to clean up your rooms and keep them that way, no matter how painful that may be to you, or you will find your life similarly 'cluttered' and going in no clear direction.

In all of these teachings, the fundamental discipline is to produce areas of focus and intention so that you can direct your will in these spaces in order to achieve results in your life. In a sense, we create 'mini-shrines' of intention in our rooms and when we light a candle there or see and hear a wind chime turning, we are reminded and refocused on our intention. Clutter, by contrast, is a pool of unguided energy which is draining and pulls us away from the direction of our focus. The best thing to do is get rid of it.

Practitioners of Vodou also recognize the importance of purifying the home and workplace to create a healthier living environment. Their practice typically uses the power of the *wanga* (or *ebo* in Santeria), a magical formula based on ingredients and action which also has the effect of focusing the intention towards the outcome desired.

One 'old-fashioned' way of purification was to make up an equal quantity of basil and eucalyptus leaves, add myrrh to the mix, and then set fire to the leaves and walk the length of the house, distributing the smoke in all rooms. Nowadays, aromatherapy oils, mixed together in a burner, probably do the job just as well. It is your *purifying intention* which counts. Close all the doors and windows to ensure that the scent of the oils cannot dissipate, and leave the house for a day. It will be purified on your return.

To remove unwanted spiritual influences from your home, it is said that a coconut should be rubbed with powdered eggshell and placed in the room farthest away from the front door. It should then be kicked through every room until you get to the front door. Opening the door, kick it out into the street, and the 'negative influence' (or 'bad energy') you are experiencing will also leave.

The American Navajo Indians have a different way of protecting their homes. To the Navajo, the home is a living entity in its own right, which must be respected as a sentient being with its own will.

According to Charlotte Frisbie, who has written extensively on the spiritual practices of the Navajos, '*Hogans* [homes] are personified . . . they are alive; they need to be fed, cared for, spoken to, and shielded from loneliness.'[24]

There is a special ritual ceremony for doing so, known as *hooghan da ashdlisigil*, which is a blessing offered to every home upon its original construction, and by those who subsequently live there. The objective of this ceremony is to 'feed the house, show proper treatment and respect to it, prevent timber breakage, and [most importantly], remove the *Hogan*'s loneliness, since its loneliness and sense of separation, its lack of connection with the occupants who will be its partners in life, is a dangerous thing. Without the community of belonging, loneliness can attract evil spirits to the *Hogan*, just as people may also succumb to dark influences, to depression, or to madness, as a result of their own isolation.'

The House Blessing Ceremony will prevent this misfortune, as well as protecting those who live there against hardship, illness, bad dreams and spirit visitations, while at the same time promoting health, longevity, peace, harmony and good luck.

The ceremony is performed by the head of the household, who will begin by thoroughly cleaning the *Hogan* (in a way similar to our own 'spring clean'), to remove any old or inappropriate energy, and to cleanse and purify the living space. He will then light the central fire as a further act of purification and, symbolically, to 'take ownership' of the environment his family is to occupy.

Moving in an anticlockwise direction, the *Four Directions of the medicine wheel* are then marked with corn meal, the 'food of the gods', which is symbolic of power and plenty, and will attract good spirits and good fortune to the home. The marks are made inside the *Hogan*, at the highest points in each direction, and in an upwards direction to represent strong energy, which also rises.

The penultimate act is the offering of prayers and songs to the *Hogan* itself, which usually take the form of blessings for good fortune, and include the wishes and desires of the people who will live there for a peaceful existence, a long and healthy life, and whatever else they most desire for that home. Frisbie records one such blessing prayer which, as the words imply, is delivered as a strong *intention* for the future, not as limp 'wishful thinking':

> . . . *This fire shall be for the good of the family,*
> *and the children that may be born in this Hogan will*
> *all be in good health.*
> *Any plans we make in this Hogan will be for*
> *the good of the family.*
> *May this be a good place for us to live again;*
> *may it be happy in this home.*
> *May our lives be long and happy in this home.*
> *May I live in this home happily and peacefully*
> *and with respect . . .*
> *My wife, my children, my relatives, whoever*
> *may come to this Hogan,*
> *may they relax peacefully and rest up.*

May all of us have no sickness, no misfortunes.
May my house be in harmony . . . may it be happy . . .

The final stage of the ceremony is the sharing of a communal meal, similar in a way to our own 'housewarming', where further blessings are offered for the happiness and future well-being of the new occupants and of the *Hogan* itself.

It would, of course, be very easy to adapt this ceremony for your own home in order to create blessings and protection for yourself.

THE VISION QUEST – MEETING THE SPIRITS

The same energy that we are using for remedial work, self-protection, and for blessings in these examples, can also be used for more pro-active and positive work. The vision quest is an ancient spiritual practice which enables us to develop our relationship to these energies and use them in our personal development in just such a way.

Many people think of the vision quest as a wholly Native American phenomenon, but there are precedents in all religions and spiritual traditions of the world, including Christianity, Buddhism, Hinduism, Vodou, the Aborigine 'walkabout', and shamanism in all its forms. It is a way of 'getting back to basics' so we can work more effectively and pro-actively with the energetic world around us, just as men and women have done for centuries.

The fundamental principle behind the vision quest is that we all need to spend time alone in the company of the spirits – time focused on defining our specific relationship to the world and how we will live within it. It is a time for looking deep within yourself, for making commitments to a particular spiritual and philosophical approach to the world, and also for challenging that view by testing yourself so that when this period of aloneness ends you can truly affirm, stand up for, and defend your personal beliefs.

Our society is noticeably lacking in rites such as these which celebrate the great transition periods of our lives; instead, the system 'grants' us certain 'rights' at a particular age, such as the 'right' to vote, to enter a pub, or to have sex with another person without being prosecuted for it.

Among the Dagara of Africa, a young man is expected to go out into the wilderness alone, and then to be instructed by his Elders in the ways of the spirit; it is a challenge which not all of them will survive. Malidoma Some tells us of his own initiation in *Of Water and the Spirit*,[25] where he came close to death himself, and watched another member of his tribe die in front of him as a result of his own contact with primal forces beyond our Western comprehension.

In Haitian Vodou, initiation takes a prescribed course of isolation and visible trials are undertaken before the whole community. Initiates may be required to plunge their hand into boiling oil to demonstrate mastery over fire, for example. Miraculously, they sustain no injury during this, since they are under the protection of the spirits.

In our culture, by contrast, our children are simply 'absorbed' into the system through the power of the law, at exactly the same age as their counterparts in traditional societies are undergoing these trials of becoming. When we reach those 'milestone' ages in our life and are ready to celebrate our next step into man- or womanhood, consequently, we feel empty, as if something is missing and no real celebration has taken place. There is nothing in being simply 'absorbed' into society which really presents a test to our young people, or offers them an adventure, a sense of purpose. None of it affirms their absolute right, through their own efforts, to be respected; and none of this, perhaps crucially, is about a *personal* vision; rather it is a power-play where we 'accept' young people into 'our way of life', a way which we, by definition, see as more powerful than their own. It is as if we are granting them access to an exclusive club rather than enabling them to become powerful in their own right.

By denying our children the right to self-affirmation, we

deny them the right to self-direction, to think and act for themselves, to follow their own dream – and then we expect them to run the country for us. And they do – as clones of ourselves, social robots following an empty dream.

There is a Lakota prayer for the vision quest, a personal prayer for every seeker:

> *Great Spirit, whose voice I hear in the winds,*
> *and whose breath gives life to all the world . . .*
> *Make me wise so I may understand the things*
> *you have taught my people,*
> *Let me learn the lessons you have hidden*
> *in every leaf and rock;*
> *I seek strength, not to be greater than my brother*
> *But to fight my greatest enemy – myself . . .*
> *So when life fades as the fading sunset,*
> *My spirit may come to you without shame.*

We are all seekers, and we all deeply need to feel that we have found our own answers and connected with something truly important in life, so that we can avoid this sense of 'shame', of an inauthentic life never really lived.

Enacting a personal vision quest is entirely feasible, even within our cities. It does not demand days in the wilderness alone, merely alone-time within the still, empty centre of ourselves. We all feel differently when we are in a foreign country, or on holiday, where the old rules and patterns are removed from us. In a sense, the vision quest is a holiday from the world, but with the added focus of concentration on the spirit.

The anthropologist Arnold van Gennep described the characteristics of all rites of passage as a *severance* from normal, habitual practices; a time of aloneness, at the *threshold* of personal change, where we journey deep into ourselves, see what we have created, and take steps to renew ourselves.

Finally, we *emerge* back into the community with a clearer way of seeing our lives and, typically, with tasks to be performed so that we may change, and change the world around us for the better.

In traditional societies, this three-stage process is normally represented by a period of fasting and prayer in preparation for the quest, during which time the candidate readies himself for separation from the normal, expected and habitual life of his people. In certain communities, most prominently, those in North America, this may be followed by a sweatlodge, where the boy will purify and cleanse himself to remove all traces of the old self.

The sweatlodge experience is one of symbolic death. The person you were 'dies' as you enter the heat and darkness of this Earth womb, a hollow carved into the soil and covered with tarp to create a pregnant belly from the Earth. In the darkness there may be visions and mystical experiences as the shaman-leader calls for the spirits to enter this sacred place and prays, in rounds, for the initiates, for their families, for the community as a whole, and for the Earth and all her people. *Mitakuye O'yasin*; 'for all our relations'.

Some who take part in the sweatlodge ritual report strange sounds, voices and singing in the drums, visions of lights and faces in the darkness, or the presence of the ancestors, as the spirits move among them in answer to their prayers.

In one sweatlodge I was part of, the pulsing glow of the hot rocks in the pit at the centre of this Earth womb was the only light. As we prayed for the burdens of the past to be lifted from us, I heard gentle sobbing from across the fire, not of pain but of release. Later, I asked who had been crying and Gwendolyn told me it was her. 'It was so beautiful,' she said. 'I asked for my hurts of the past to be taken away from me and, as I stared into the fire, a group of angels appeared and came towards me. They were smiling and laughing, and so loving that I didn't feel any fear at all. Each one came up to me and took a particular burden from me. I saw it in their arms, like a dark bundle. Then they walked back into the fire with it and took it away. I felt lighter and lighter as each weight was removed until, at the end of the sweat, I felt completely purified.'

After the sweat, the candidate will enter the 'threshold' stage fully, walking by himself into the natural landscape where he will remain in isolation from all others for a period of several days. He will draw on his intuition and inspiration to find the place most conducive to a deep spiritual experience. Sometimes this will be an active search for a particular power place, but often it is a sensation of being 'drawn' to the right area and a feeling of peace when he finds it.

He will then create a sacred circle on the ground, of rocks and other natural materials, and this circle will become his home for the period of his quest. He must not move now from this place. The air is charged with energy and the spirits are aware of him. He is vulnerable, deliberately so, before the great mystery of the Earth, and the circle is his only protection.

Usually, the vision quest will take place for four days and five nights. The candidate does not eat and does not move, but remains in stillness, journeying within himself for answers and watching his environment for clues. There must be no distractions, no making notes or keeping diaries or marking off the days – all the typical rationalistic distractions of our overly-analytical minds. Instead the candidate must remain focused and intent.

For modern vision questers, this requirement to sit still, to remain quiet and to not distract oneself with trivia is one of the most demanding, and most powerful, aspects of the experience. It will typically produce an initial feeling of boredom, irritation, sometimes frustration and despondency, it is so very alien to our way of life.

After a while, however, you notice that you are slowing down to the natural pace of the Earth, that *its* rhythms have become *your* rhythms and that a dialogue can now begin between you. The features of the landscape and the natural world become, in themselves, the answers to your deepest questions of existential meaning.

Experiences like these put the candidate on the 'threshold' between ordinary and non-ordinary consciousness of himself, the world around him, and the spiritual connections between the two. Sometimes this threshold awareness can be liberating and enlightening, producing a very much deeper understanding of oneself and one's path in life; and sometimes this new view of the world can be a little unnerving or disorientating at first. It is like waking up from a deep sleep and realizing that the world you were just a part of and so deeply believed in was, in fact, a dream, an illusion, and this new world you have woken to is the real one.

Such realizations can be shattering, in the sense that the whole of the intricate structure and meaning system we have built around ourselves for the last several years of our lives is suddenly falling apart; all that the system has taught us and the city acclimatized us to seems no longer valid. The candidate's quest then is to reconcile his experiences and emotions so he is able to integrate them, to build a new structure in place of the old, and to come away from his experience remade, so he is whole and together again, re-membered by spirit.

This is the greatest challenge of the vision quest. As one of the first steps on the shaman's path, it is no less than a search for true meaning in one's life, which requires a stripping away of all that we have been taught is real, including our own illusions, fears and socially conditioned sense of ourselves. We must stand naked before the universe. Only then can we finally meet the gods and find the secret of ourselves.

'A shaman has walked up to the gates of his or her personal hell and then walked in,' says the American shaman, Jamie Sams. 'The self-created demons of fear, insanity, loneliness, self-importance and addiction have been confronted and conquered by the shaman, who has gone through the gamut of shaman's deaths.

'The quality that always shines in a true shaman is compassion for the paths that others must walk. This comes from the fact that the shaman has also walked through the underworld of the shadow and knows first-hand the pain involved in breaking the stranglehold of inner darkness.'[26]

When the boy returns to his tribe he has become a man. He has died in the sweatlodge, been reborn small and vulnerable in the wilderness, and fought for his life, his authentic, personal vision of life, during the vision quest itself. He returns with the victory of adulthood and has earned respect – not been 'given rights' by his society – for the challenges he has faced and battles fought. His return to the group and to feasting and celebration is his time of re-emergence into a new world.

Despite the traditional focus on the wilderness experience as part of the vision quest, there is nothing in van Gennep's description of the stages involved which implies that a journey *must* be taken deep into the desert, or the jungle, or in some remote hilltop cave in order to produce these profound personal changes. I have taken vision quests in the middle of San Francisco, London, Paris, and at my home, with equal success, and I am convinced that the location is much less important than the intention behind the quest itself. Perfectly wonderful visionary experiences can be achieved on rooftops, in gardens, or in bed-sits, as long as you can create a time of aloneness for yourself, so you are able to remain undisturbed, and powerfully *intend* that you will have a vision for your life.

One of the most enlightening vision quests I have undertaken in recent years was on the rooftop of a hotel in San Francisco. More rightly, I suppose, this would be described as a 'night vigil' since I had decided that I would only quest for 12 hours and my intention was quite specific – to understand the energy of the city amid the bigger web of the world, to see how they interacted, and to discover where I fitted into all this. I was staying in a modern American business hotel in the Bay Area at the time. Having spent a week in meetings and presentations, I was feeling as if I needed to reconnect with a less artificial life.

I planned the vigil earlier that week so I knew I would be free of meetings and dinners and able to fast for 24 hours before it. Then I took the lift to the roof of the hotel and made a circle for myself, high above the city. The sun was still in the sky when I settled down, clear in my intention for this quest.

I watched the city change, from a creature of the day, to a darker, more mysterious animal, as the sun descended and the neon took over. With it came new passions and freedoms, screams of excitement and pain from the revellers and victims of the night, those the city comforted and those it condemned. The energy became palpable, rising in clouds from the street to hang over the city like a mist which began to descend again in the early hours of the morning. Its rise and fall, I realized, was the breath of the city, charged with the emotional respiration of its occupants.

Then the dawn began to rise, a wildly powerful rush of energy from the ocean which washed the streets as it crept across the city structures, cleaning away the traces of the night until the day woke fresh and stretched itself.

I understood then that the city is a living thing with its own heart and lungs and life force. But it is only one part of a much vaster energetic flow which is the pulse of the universe, and I am just one passing thought in its colossal mind, a mind which may be finite but, to me, is beyond all measure. And I have a choice – as we all do: to be a thought which gathers impetus and force, or a passing notion, soon forgotten in the mind of the city and the consciousness of the Earth.

As surprising as it may seem, a night in the open in the city is wonderful for reconnecting with the energy flows of nature. There is something about the architecture and the scale, the height, of the city which is especially conducive to sensing the opening into another world, as well as a beauty in the intricate details of its buildings, its ebbs and flows of people, the lights on the freeway at night, which we so often miss as we hurry past with downcast eyes.

As part of one of the training courses I run in shamanism and energy awareness, I ask participants to spend a few weeks just looking at the tops of buildings as they walk through the city. I have never offered an explanation for this, allowing them instead just to see what happens.

One day I got an email from Chris in America, who said she had been doing this exercise and was experiencing some strange sensations. 'It is like I get light-headed and the world around me seems to get fuzzy and out-of-register. I have looked up at buildings and down at them from a higher floor and at mountains and hills as well, and always the effect is the same.' She was curious to know what was happening and why.

This was the first time that a student had asked me for an explanation of this phenomenon, so I was pleased to hear from her.

I originally got the technique from John Grinder, one of the founders of Neuro-Linguistic Programming (NLP). A patient had been referred to him suffering from chronic depression, unable to snap out of her feelings of gloom and despondency. John had asked her to gaze up at the tops of buildings for a few weeks, taking particular note of their alignment with the sky and the specific area where the building met the blue around it. In a few weeks his patient returned – completely cured of her problem.

NLP is a very powerful psychology and one of its tenets is that the mind holds memories which have an impact on the body – so a memory of an unhappy event may make us flinch quite involuntarily, for example, a body language which offers a valuable way of understanding people and the impact of their history upon them. But the reverse is also true: the alignment of the body causes old and unsatisfactory memories to come to the surface too.

Depressives, like John's patient, spend a lot of time looking down. By asking her to look up instead, John was realigning the neural pathways of her body and creating new and more uplifting sensations in her mind. By retraining the body, the mind was also eased and the impact of the past negated.

Since reading this I had also come across literature from the European Saami tradition of shamanism and from Mexico, which both pointed to the same effect, though their explanation was quite different to that of the psychologists. 'There is a crack between the worlds and it is more than a metaphor,' said don Juan, referring to the Toltec tradition in Castaneda's *The Second Ring of Power*.[27] 'It is rather the capacity to change levels of attention. Don't try to reason it out.' The point was the same for the Saamis – the crack between the worlds is that thin membrane at the top of mountains which is neither the mountain itself nor the sky, but the layer of 'in-betweenness' that separates the two. It is at this point that the worlds of physical and spiritual reality meet. The body senses the existence of something vaster than itself and is uplifted as this energy begins to flood it. Our skyscrapers are the mountains of the city, whose architecture can be an unwitting ally for the soul.

A night vigil can be taken anywhere by anyone. My suggestion is that you do so at least once to understand the spiritual nature of our reality, and your own place within it. The following exercise offers some guidelines.

Exercise: the night vigil

Spend a few days refining your thoughts so you are clear on the purpose for your vigil: to find a guiding vision for your life and to know the direction of your destiny, perhaps; or, like my own vigil, to see the energy of the city, to understand its character and personality, the vital role you play in this, and to reach some decisions for yourself on how you want your life to be here.

Set yourself a time limit for the vigil and make arrangements to be undisturbed. Tell your friends not to call, unplug the phone, and choose a location which best serves your purpose for this. Begin the process by fasting for 24 hours before the vigil, drinking only mineral water during this time. Immediately before you begin, take a bath, then dress in comfortable loose-fitting clothes which you are happy to remain in for the duration of your quest.

Purify and 'seal' your space with incense or with a sprinkling of water to make a circle around you or, if you are undertaking this quest outside, build a circle of stones around yourself.

Be aware of your thoughts and feelings during the vigil, but do not give in to distractions and do not take notes;

instead, allow yourself to flow with your sensations. It may take a little time before you can fully achieve this state of flow but go with it and don't give up.

When the vigil ends – which is at the time you earlier agreed with yourself and not at some new and arbitrary time which occurs to you during the process itself – take another bath and change into your ordinary clothes.

Begin to review the events of the last few hours and write down your thoughts, feelings and experiences. Look at them again in a few days' time when they have had a chance to 'settle' so you do not reach any hasty conclusions based on this information.

THE RECAPITULATION: INTEGRATING THE SPIRIT

Recapitulation, originating again from the Toltecs of Mexico, is a term popularized by don Juan in Castaneda's *The Eagle's Gift*.[28] It describes the process of 'recollecting one's life down to the most insignificant detail'.

Recapitulation works well as an extension to the vision quest since, in questing, we are redefining our lives and making a conscious decision, based on spiritual information, to reinvent ourselves and change the future. The recapitulation is a method of casting off the energetic chains of the past to free our unconscious and empower ourselves to make the changes we intend. In simple terms, we revisit every meaningful memory from our past and examine the detail of the event which gave rise to it in order to release the energy that we have invested in it. This energy can then be used for other purposes in our lives.

In a sense, there is nothing esoteric or mysterious about the process of recapitulation – it is a simple reliving of a past event in order to discharge the emotions surrounding it and, in doing so, in effect, to rewrite the past. When this is done effectively, the energetic and emotional links to the present are also released since, very often, our interpretation of the past is what defines for us the present and this, in turn, is what dictates our future.

There is a parallel here with the methods of cognitive and some behavioural schools of psychotherapy, where the event that is causing trauma or pain is relived and retold time and time again, in as much detail as possible, until it becomes just a story, with no emotional attachment for the teller. At this point, the patient is free of the trauma connected to that experience, even though the memory itself remains, and he can therefore move forward from 'ground zero', a 'neutral zone' of understanding the past without being dependent on it or threatened by it.

The shamanic method of recapitulation is a little different from its psychotherapeutic cousin in that it is rather more involving than the simple relating of an event, more direct and powerful as a consequence of this and, crucially, it is open to anyone as a device for freedom, not just those who must seek therapy as a means of coping with a traumatic past.

According to Castaneda's scheme for recapitulation, the first stage is to produce a list of all the incidents in our lives that stand out as obvious candidates for examination. These will tend to be 'defining moments' which we still feel an emotional attachment to as we recall them. Whether the emotion is melancholy, distress or delight is irrelevant; it is the *emotion itself* which holds us to this event and which must be released if we are to move on as independently powerful beings (without an attachment to karma, as the Buddhists would say).

The second stage is a detailed recollection and re-examination of every single aspect of each emotional event in its entirety, so that the whole of one's life is retraced, from the point of sitting down to look at the list you are working from (i.e. from this instant *now*) to a moment which could extend back to the very second of one's birth. 'Theoretically' says Castaneda, '*stalkers* [those in search of themselves through the use of recapitulation and other methods] have to remember every feeling that they have had in their lives.'

As an example, if you were recapitulating an event from

your childhood, a confrontation with your older brother, say, you would relive the image of the event itself, in its entirety, and then go through it again, focusing on particular elements. Your brother was wearing a red shirt. What associations does the colour red now have for you? You would need to revisit all of these. A particular record was playing at the time. What does this now mean for you? What are your feelings about music in general? And so on.

Such a detailed reliving tends, in my opinion, to produce quickly diminishing returns since once the major emotions connected with an event have been released, it can become an exercise in navel-gazing to continue going over old ground. For example, once you have dealt with the big issues of humiliation and abuse connected with an unpleasant event from the past, I do not see the point in going over it once again because, at the time, you also felt queasy as a result of something you ate at lunchtime.

There is also a degree of irony involved in the continuous recapitulation of a single event since, in the Toltec path, the aim of this exercise is to release the habits and actions caused by dwelling on the past – while prolonged recapitulation is itself a form of dwelling on the past, of course, and may end up equally damaging or debilitating; certainly, it seems pointless. Taken to real extremes (which some people do), we would even have to start recapitulating our recapitulation and get trapped in another negative feedback loop, when the whole point of the exercise is to become free.

Nonetheless, the method is extremely effective when used correctly, in appropriate moderation and with proper intention. Perhaps we can make a distinction, then, between recapitulation which is taken to extremes, and the beneficial action of reviewing and releasing the unhelpful past. There are, after all, some memories which are useful and empowering for us in themselves; attempting to rid ourselves of these too is a little like throwing the baby out with the bathwater.

As well as reviewing our life events, there are two special techniques used as part of recapitulation. One of these is a breathing and movement technique, the other a form of sensory deprivation.

The breathwork of recapitulation is very important since, according to Castaneda, every event begins with a breath; it is how we absorbed the information of the life event in the first place, and took it into our energy bodies, and it is the key to its release.

'The procedure starts with an initial breath,' says Castaneda.

As stalkers remember the feelings they invested in whatever it is that they are remembering, they inhale slowly, moving their heads from the right shoulder to the left. The function of this breathing is to restore energy . . .

Every situation of interaction, or every situation where feelings are involved, is potentially draining to the luminous [energy] body. By breathing from right to left while remembering a feeling, stalkers, through the magic of breathing, pick up the filaments [projections of energy from their energy bodies] they left behind. The next immediate breath is from left to right and it is an exhalation. With it stalkers eject filaments left in them by other luminous bodies involved in the event being recollected.[29]

According to Castaneda, this sweeping motion with the head, and the controlled breathwork which goes with it, is very important to the success of recapitulation. But just as important is the use of a device he calls 'the box'.

Originally, this was an actual box, somewhat like a coffin, just larger than the human body, which the person recapitulating would enter in order to constrain the energy body and force it to focus on the events to be replayed. Experiments with flotation tanks show how useful non-threatening sensory deprivation can be, not only as an aid to concentration, but in shifting awareness into a non-ordinary form of consciousness, where deep insights and greater capacity for recollection and philosophical understanding are enhanced (see *The Journey To You* for a discussion of this).

Modern shamans do not always go to the extremes of using a box of the kind described by Castaneda, though they do, of course, recommend a time of quiet solitude in order to carry out the work effectively.

Taisha Abelar, a contemporary of Castaneda and fellow student of don Juan, at a public talk in California in January 1994, stated her somewhat looser view of the recapitulation method: 'There *is* a method but it is not important whether you move your head from right to left or from left to right or set aside a regular time or a lot of time. What is important is the *unbending intent to recapitulate*. Then, spirit will guide you into the right form and time and amount of practice . . . Therefore: (1). Intend it. (2). Have an integrity about it – don't brag or compete. (3). Most people make a list [of significant life events] and work backwards. (4). Breathe. Direction is not important. What is important is using the breath to pull the energy back.'

This is a much better approach to recapitulation, in my view. As much as anything, the technique exists to help people reclaim their own power by taking back the energy they have invested in a particular event. Reclaiming power means a personal action of individual choice rather than a rote following of instructions. Abelar's interpretation of the approach seems more inclined to enable this by allowing individual freedom of expression.

There is one key point to make in using recapitulation – *do not feel guilty or remorseful or attach yourself to any other self-blame as you carry out the life review*. As Castaneda himself put it in *Journey to Ixtlan*: 'You should not have remorse for anything you have done, because to isolate one's acts as being mean, or ugly, or evil, is to place an unwarranted importance on the self. Well-being is a condition one has to groom, a condition one has to become acquainted with in order to seek it . . . The trick is in what one emphasises. We either make ourselves miserable, or we make ourselves strong. The amount of work is the same.'[30]

Don't make the mistake of beating yourself up for past life choices or actions. They were the best you could do in that moment. To dwell on them is to enter a cycle of guilt which is more likely to increase the chances of them happening again, since you are not yet free of their attractive power. Remember, during recapitulation, that you were as perfect as you could be at that time, just as you are right now.

EXERCISE: RECAPITULATION – CONDUCTING A LIFE REVIEW

Set aside at least a morning for a first attempt at this exercise. First, write down on paper the episodes from your life which immediately present themselves to you and then place them in order of their appearance, beginning with the most recent. Refine your list by itemizing, in as much detail as you can, the specific experience of each event. This then becomes your 'checklist' for reliving these events.

Find a quiet dark place for the next stage and enter as fully as you can each event you have listed. Don't just remember what happened, *be there*, experience it again, feel all the same emotions, see everything around you, relive it completely.

As you do so, breathe out as you work through each reliving, clearly visualizing all of the energy of that event and all emotional connections leaving your body. Then breathe in clean, fresh energy, as a new sense of power and freedom enters you. Theoretically, you should keep this up for as long as it takes to completely work through the event you are recapitulating, until you feel its hold over you start to diminish; in practice, it may be better to attempt the exercise in stages, working through each episode from your past for 30 minutes or an hour, depending on the time you have available.

When you are ready to do so, move on to the next experience.

Recapitulation is an incremental exercise and you may need to repeat each reliving a few times before you feel fully cleansed of it. That is fine. At each pass you are making significant progress in reclaiming your power from the event itself.

When you feel that you have truly let go of that memory and recovered your energy from it, tear off the item from your list and burn it, visualizing the event as truly gone as the paper turns to ash.

Without the weight of this experience in your energy body, you now have greater capacity to create the life you wish, which your vision quest will have revealed to you.

THE POWER OF 'SO WHAT?'

In this chapter we have considered a new way of looking at the world and the city around us – as a place of life in infinite forms, spiritual and energetic as well as physical – and some of the ways of working with its energies so that we experience more of the reality around us.

I suppose the question remaining is, 'Why bother?'

The ancient shamans considered this too. Just like you, they were busy people with no time to waste on trivia. Their conclusion was that we have a responsibility to embrace as much of life as we can, to be the best we can – for ourselves, but also for the planet – since it is only by changing our consciousness and *seeing* a better world that this new reality can begin to manifest. We are all Beautiful Mutants, evolving into a new and *conscious* future, and with consciousness comes choice. We can't easily go back to non-awareness but now that we have consciousness, we *can* choose the future we want to live.

'Responsibility' is a heavy word, though. We all have enough 'responsibility' already in our daily lives, without adding a duty to the world at large. And so the shamans had a test for the validity and importance of any statement or action we intend to take, so that we can check the depth of its personal meaning for us, instead of blindly accepting it as another instruction from 'on high'. I call it the 'So What?' test.

413

The test itself is very simple to use; it is really just the ability to be inwardly contrary!

Society can tell us till it is blue in the face that the world operates in a particular way – according to some mysterious laws of production, some alchemy of economics, some divine right of kings and rule of social justice – as if the *definition* it is using, and the implications behind this definition, are the *truth* of the matter itself. But if we refuse to accept the definition, then so what? The definitions and their implications for us cease to have meaning or power over us.

What happens then is that we can move beyond determinism based on social 'facts' like these and begin to question those things in the world that we have been habituated into and now take for granted. In doing so, we get closer to ourselves and our own truth of the world, beyond the imposed meaning of others.

Here are a few examples:

Statement: 'But I had a tragic childhood.' [Limiting belief]
[**Implication:** . . . and I have given up on having a future as a consequence of this.]
Counter: *So what?*
[**Counter-implication:** *You can change it right now, if you choose.*]

Statement: 'My doctor says it's incurable.'
[**Implication:** . . . so I guess it must be. [Limiting belief]]
Counter: *So what?*
[**Counter-implication:** *What does your doctor know of the human spirit and the power of the individual that he didn't get from a science book? So why are you giving away your power to him?*]

By questioning the things that are often presented to us as a 'certainty' in this way, including the limiting beliefs which often hide behind them, we are able to discover what is *really* being said and asked of us.

We can use this very simple 'So what?' argument to question everything in the world, and to do so is incredibly liberating. It gives us back our own power.

If the vision quest reveals a truth to you, if the act of recapitulation returns energy to you, then you better believe it is real. The only person who can tell you it is not is you.

And why is that important? 'So what?'

It is important because whenever we allow anyone to dictate our reality to us, we lay ourselves open not only to the curtailment of our right to freedom, to experience and to play in this beautiful world, but to the threat of global suicide through the actions of others. As the evidence of recent years has shown, the consensus worldview we live in, which legitimizes our abuse of the Earth and dominion over nature, is leading to dire consequences for us all. We can only live the dream of the system for so long before we crush ourselves as a species.

Both the shaman and the modern scientist are now telling us that we must clean up our act and see ourselves as just one strand in the whole complex web of life if we are to survive at all. The following quotation, actually from don Juan in Castaneda's *Fire from Within*, could just as well be taken from the latest thinking in current biology or physics.

> *The Earth itself is a living being. The old seers saw that the Earth has a cocoon. They saw that there is a ball encasing the Earth, a luminous cocoon . . . The Earth is a gigantic sentient being subjected to the same forces we are.*[31]

That, for me, answers the 'So what?' question. It is why it is vital to fight for our personal beliefs, to overcome the social inertia generated by a system that hands us our 'beliefs' on a plate, to start thinking for ourselves, and to accept responsibility for our own actions – because it is important for the survival of the planet and for all of us. The more we take from the Earth, the less there is. A simple equation, really. And the Earth is aware of our actions.

In the next chapter we look at the evidence.

7

EARTH HEALING, SELF HEALING:
TOWARDS A *CONSCIOUS* EVOLUTION

We now stand at a crossroads.
Do we lead ourselves into everlasting life or
into total destruction?
We believe that the spiritual power of human beings
in prayer is so strong that it decides life on Earth . . .

Be well, my children, and think good thoughts of
peace and togetherness. Peace for all life on
Earth and peace with one another in our
homes, families and countries.
We are not so different in the Creator's eyes.
We are one after all

Dan Evehema, Hopi Indian Chief, in his farewell 'Message to Mankind',
immediately prior to his death, at the age of 108, on 15 January 1999

Perspective is everything. If you place a magnifying glass against this page you will see that the words in this sentence are made up of dots of ink, each one separate and alone on the page, surrounded by white space. It is only when you take the glass away and see the bigger picture that the dots become words, the words become sentences, then paragraphs, then pages, and, finally, make sense as a book.

In the same way, you – as a single 'dot' – are part of a family, a community, a country, a world, a solar system, a galaxy, a universe, and you can only truly make sense of yourself and your life in this context, as part of the whole – essential and unique, but really very little on your own.

416

You and I are related, just as we are sons and daughters of the Earth and of the sky above us. One of my shaman friends uses a beautiful expression to describe the unique place we all have in the world, a uniqueness which connects us all: 'We stand beneath the Earth and the sky. The rest is just details.' We are all of us working out the details together.

In the 1970s, this 'working out' of the world took a new turn – and the planet changed as a consequence. Perspective is everything.

It changed from dry, dead rock with a few interesting specimens of animal and plant life, quite a lot of not very useful salty water, a creeping evolution based on large-scale acceptable murder called 'survival of the fittest', and a few freak weather conditions which gave us something to talk about in the pub. Suddenly, the Earth was no longer just another big rock in space, on a dull, predictable, rotation round its axis, like a giant machine, and we were no longer just machine operators who doubled up occasionally as librarians and cataloguers of the more interesting specimens in our charge.

It became instead a world that was, literally, *alive*. Its rocks, animals, plants, oceans and atmosphere were all individually sentient and at the same time part of one single, giant, living and consciously evolving organism, with humanity just one interesting specimen in a vibrant and complex, interconnected web of change.

We were Beautiful Mutants, but so was the planet itself. Perhaps even god was evolving too.

The person responsible for changing the world was James Lovelock – not a shaman, a priest or a prophet, but a NASA scientist, President of the Marine Biology Association, a Fellow of the Royal Society, and Visiting Professor of Reading University.

Lovelock takes himself very lightly for a man whose theories have had such a major impact on contemporary scientific, environmental and social thought. He notes, for example, that the word 'theory' has the same Greek root as 'theatre'. 'Both are concerned with putting on a show.'[1]

Nonetheless, Lovelock's own theory – which he calls the Gaia hypothesis, after the Greek Earth goddess – has given birth to a whole new field of understanding of people's relationship to the planet they are a part of; a way of thinking, and of living, which accepts that we are all just tiny cells in one vast life-form which is self-regulating and, like the gods themselves, concerned with the grand cosmic picture of which we are but a part.

In a sense, Lovelock was proving what the shamans have always maintained: that the Earth is alive – not just poetically, but *actually* – and she has a spirit and a soul as real as our own.

Gaia theory discounts the Darwinian notion of human evolution based on the 'natural selection' of the species best fitted for the job of dominion over the Earth; instead, it suggests that the Earth itself is an entity which maintains a state of equilibrium conducive to *all* life – however 'life' is defined.

This need not be a state which supports *human* existence; in fact, the planet has no conception of 'human' existence, only of whether our job as a part of the whole is being performed effectively or not. If not, then the planet itself will take action to redress the balance and safeguard the existence of all species in its care – whatever the consequences for human life.

The situation of Gaia is very similar in this respect to that of our own bodies. We are composed of millions of micro-organisms, bacteria, cells and subatomic particles, all of them alive since they are connected to (and intimately a part of) our entire living being, just like the many different species which make up the whole of life on Earth. But we are no more conscious of them than the planet is of us. Our approach to our bodies is, if anything, quiet acceptance of its parts or, often, sublime ignorance until something goes wrong, at which point the offending part may be removed and the rest of the body will continue, quite happily, to exist without it.

This, says Lovelock, is very much like the Earth, which tolerates human life in ignorance; it is the *total system*, and its own survival, which counts. It is a humbling perspective for humanity, the self-appointed head of the animal kingdom, to learn that we are in fact no more important than penicillin mould or a cold virus, despite our self-aggrandizement. But it is a perspective which seems to be true.

Lovelock makes the point, for example, that our present concerns about global warming, acid rain, deforestation, overpopulation, and so on, are really just human problems and, in truth, First World issues at that, which have only been of interest at all for the last fifty years or so. To Gaia, they mean little, if anything; the entire First World was buried beneath glaciers only 10,000 years ago, and less than two centuries ago people were able to skate the frozen Thames as a mini Ice Age swept through Europe.

Gaia, the *planetary* system, does not care to hear about our *human* problems, or to listen to our excuses for having created them. She does not even understand our language or, perhaps, perceive them as problems herself. She will merely become aware, over time, of a 'dis-ease' within the system and remove it, just as we might have a faulty organ removed by surgery. There is nothing personal in it.

In other words, if we have a future as part of this total system, we need to recognize our place as just one aspect of the whole and get with the programme rather than maintaining our state of separation from it as a result of arrogance or ignorance.

DAISYWORLD

Lovelock's hypothesis is not simple conjecture. To test his theory, he developed a sophisticated computer model to demonstrate the way in which the planet maintains equilibrium of life. On this planet, which he called Daisyworld, only daisies grow (more advanced models were developed later, with other inhabitants and a more complex relationship between them; the results were the same).

Two kinds of daisies live here – the Dark and the Pale. Both grow best at a temperature of 20 degrees C and cannot survive outside of the range 5–40 degrees C. But that is OK, since Daisyworld is pleasantly warm.

If Daisyworld should grow too cold, however – a fate similar to that which befell the dinosaurs when clouds of dust, thrown up by an asteroid that crashed into the Earth with the force of an atomic explosion, blocked out the warmth of the sun for centuries – then the situation would change drastically. The Dark population, which absorbs the most heat, will grow and proliferate, while the Pales will die of cold before they can seed themselves, until only a few remain in more tropical areas of the planet.

The proliferation of Dark daisies which now takes place, however, means that more light and heat are absorbed by the planet (since dark colours are more absorbent of heat), and the Earth itself starts to warm up. And the ironic consequence of this is that the Dark population – the one 'best fitted' for survival, in Darwinian terms – will then start to die off as the planet heats up beyond the limits within which they can survive.

The Pale daisies, meanwhile, reflect more warmth, and so their temperature remains comfortable. This tiny population starts to grow as it reacclimatizes itself and begins to seed, until eventually they are the dominant life-form on the planet once again.

But there is also a sting in the tail for the Pales. Since they are lighter in colour and now so dense on the surface, they begin to reflect much of the heat reaching the planet until, once again, it becomes too cold to sustain them. The Darks begin to dominate and the whole cycle begins once again.

The point of this modelling is to demonstrate that all of our planning, analysis and manipulation of the environment is entirely irrelevant to the development of the planet. We may think, in our blindness, that we are kings of creation but the intelligence of the planetary system is more powerful than that, and we are merely a part of it. This ebb and flow of life, based on the temperature of the planet, is worth pondering in this age of global warming and pollution-ridden cities.

Here on Earth, we are like the Pale daisies, the bright stars who shine temporarily in the cosmic night until our closeness to the sun destroys us and another race takes over. The result is the same for Gaia; the universe survives, whatever species occupies the surface of its planets and considers itself god.

So what, then, is our real purpose here, within the context of Gaia?

THE PURPOSE OF HUMAN LIFE

Lovelock's evidence for the Earth as an entire holistic, living system made up of the planet *and all it contains* demonstrates the unity which keeps our world in balance. Everything is connected in this homeostatic system and we all have a job to do for the common good.

The job of humankind is not to turn its back on its technological heritage but to use this power for good. Going back to nature or running for the hills will not help us right now. We are creatures of the city, 'techno-sapiens', and we can use our consciousness, our evolved intelligence and sophisticated technologies to work *with* Gaia – if we choose. We can monitor the environment and provide early warnings and corrective action when things begin to fall *out of balance*, instead of when things fall *out of our control*, for example. All it takes is a change of perspective.

The urban, techno-shaman already operates within this framework, as part of a global worldview where the whole of humanity is one 'tribe'. The Internet, the TV and the satellite, are the channels for his intent and he can be connected in seconds to someone on the other side of the planet with a vastly different culture and experience of the world. The dream of the 'global village' is becoming a reality.

We are all a part of this new world tribe. By embracing it, we will become less introspective, less fearful, less focused on

the day-to-day and the claustrophobia of our own city structures, and more open to the spiritual invitation of the infinite.
As Lovelock himself said, in *Gaia: A New Look at Life on
Earth*: 'City wisdom [is] entirely centred on the problems of
human relationships, in contrast to the wisdom of any natural
tribal group, where relationships with the rest of the animate
and inanimate world are still given due place.'[2] Words which
emphasize the division we have created between ourselves and
spirit with a cityscape which divorces the 'real world' from
the sacred and ourselves from each other.

The legacy of Lovelock has been an even more dramatic
reconsideration of our role on the planet, with input from
some of our most innovative thinkers.

IS THE CITY 'MAD'?

One of Lovelock's contemporaries is Theodore Roszak,
Professor of History at California State University and author
of *The Making of a Counterculture*. His work has been highly
influential in the development of eco-psychology, which states
that people are ultimately indivisible from the environment
they are a part of since they both create their world, which is
a reflection of the human psyche and our personal and collective worldview, and, of course, we are also participants in,
and at the receiving end of all that we have dreamed up.

This may seem to make obvious sense to us now, but the
very origins of modern psychotherapy have been founded on
quite the opposite view, and this is not without its political
dimension, of course, since the 'science of the mind' is what
has, for centuries, defined what is 'normal', 'abnormal', 'right'
and 'wrong' in our relationships with each other and with the
world around us, as well as what is healthy or otherwise in
terms of our adjustment to it. Putting it bluntly, people have
been locked up (or worse) according to their degree of adaptation to a society which may even, according to current
thinking, actually be mad itself. If that is true, we have been

locking up our saviours and our sane, while the lunatics have taken over the asylum.

Roszak observes, for example, that Sigmund Freud, the father of modern psychoanalysis,

> *thought of himself as a scientist examining a scientific material he called the human psyche . . . [a definition which] haunts the practice of psychiatry and psychotherapy down to the present day . . . it has led to the assumption that you can treat the psyche in isolation from the natural environment because there's no signifi-cant, meaningful, human connection . . . [and there is certainly no] outreach to the world beyond – the non-human world – that surrounds us and out of which we evolved.*[3]

Yet ironically, and in contradiction almost to all Freud said, his own theories cannot, with hindsight, be separated from the culture and the times he himself occupied. Freud was writing at the turn of the century, at the height of the indus-trial revolution, and his theories were themselves a product of his age, a proud new age which revered materialism, physical science and the factory.

His approach to the mind reflected this reverence, his career based on dividing and compartmentalizing the psyche, ascribing functions to developmental aspects of the human condition and 'taking apart' the mind, as a mechanic will take apart a car. His definitions of 'madness' were based on his patients' lack of adjustment to this mechanical and 'non-human' system, a system which he was himself a child of, and one we are increasingly coming to view as crazy merely as a result of our own experiences of it.

'In traditional societies, among primary people, it is under-stood that sanity and madness have to be defined always in relationship to the natural habitat; and that, indeed, to a very large extent, madness is understood to be an imbalance between the individual and the natural environment, or between an entire tribe or a people and its natural environment,' says Roszak.

This is a perspective very different from our own (which is based on a separation from, and dominion over, nature). Our cities, the visible face of the system, even cut us off from the countryside and the natural world, as little havens of materialism. But there is nothing in the rulebook which says that our Western definitions are right and the rest of the world is wrong – so how exactly can we now define madness?

Paulo Coehlo puts the contradiction brilliantly in the fable he relates of a powerful magician who once set out to destroy a kingdom by polluting its water supply with a potion that made all who drank from it become mad.[4]

Only the king and queen did not drink the poisoned water, so when the king tried to control the people and rescue them from madness, all those who had drunk the water thought his orders were crazy and ignored them, believing that it was the king, and not they, who was mad.

The only choice left to the king and queen, as the only remaining 'sane' people in the world, was to drink of the water if they were to survive as rulers, issuing orders which would be listened to:

And that was what they did: the king and the queen drank the water of madness and immediately began talking nonsense. Their subjects repented at once; now that the king was displaying such wisdom, why not allow him to continue ruling the country?

The country continued to live in peace, although its inhabitants behaved very differently from those of its neighbours. And the king was able to govern until the end of his days.

When Freud spoke of 'collusive' or 'communal' neurosis, where an entire society may be mad, he was referring to 'primitive' societies, whose Earth-honouring practices he viewed as examples of group hysteria. But his theory is equally applicable to any social system, including our own, as Coehlo's story shows, and we may well be colluding in the maintenance of our own social insanity. This raises a number of interesting challenges for modern psychoanalysis:

- If the entire society is mad, how would you recognize it since you, yourself, would be part of it and, therefore, presumably, also insane?
- What would give any therapist the right to try to cure a single individual of this madness?
- How, in fact, is it possible to 'cure' them? You would, by definition, have to move them away from the prevailing worldview into one not even yet developed or conceived of if society itself is mad. You would have to be 'outside the box'.
- And if you did so, you would be no better than a cult leader, and probably labelled 'insane' yourself. Where would your authority come from? How would it be recognized?

Once you begin even to look at these questions, by definition you enter the shamanic world, which sees every viewpoint as equally valid and every one of us as born with exactly the same power. We are alone in the universe, all of us the kings and queens of our own reality. It is this very separateness which, paradoxically, links us all.

William Bloom put this well when he commented that 'old psychology reflects the old scientific paradigm. Put at its worst, it wants to understand people as if they are biological machines responding to fixed stimuli, rewards and punishments . . . From a holistic perspective, the approach of the old psychology is less than human. Where is the complexity, the genius, the eccentricity, the soul? . . . To say that the brain produces all the manifestations of consciousness is as untrue as suggesting that the inner wiring of your television set produces all the material you can see on its screen . . . What is beginning to emerge in the holistic field, therefore, is an understanding of the human psyche as a dynamic system in which various energies are working independently together.

Each aspect only makes sense when understood in reference to the others.'[5]

We are all the children of Gaia and all linked in the same cosmic consciousness which gave birth to all life, and we are all members of the same world society. It has been estimated that there are only six degrees of separation between any and all of us – we are all related – and we need a way of relating to each other and to being together. What is the answer for us to this eternal paradox?

'The way I take up this issue,' says Roszak, 'is to suggest that there is a madness involved in urban industrial society that has to do with our lack of balance and integration with the natural environment and this might be an interesting baseline to use for the definition of sanity . . . That is, we need to recapture the sense of being embedded in nature, being in the condition of reciprocity with nature that you find in traditional forms of healing.'[6]

Roszak's definition of madness certainly seems appropriate to me. After all, it does not take an expert psychoanalyst to hear the thunder of insanity in a culture hell-bent on global self-destruction. Lovelock may indeed be right when he observes that 'the fact that the Earth is more raped than loved may come from our unnatural separation from her in the cities', but the opposite may also be true. As the system continues to destroy the planet, to burn up our resources, to scorch the skies and poison our air, without a care for our survival beyond today and the profit that accrues from it, perhaps our only escape *is* a willing flight into madness, a sort of moral shell shock that means we don't have to look at the repercussions of our actions. In this sense, the mental illness of our culture will only be cured through our spiritual reconnection with the Earth, and the taking of our rightful place within the Gaia system.

Recently I found myself, bizarrely, standing in the middle of a rainforest with the American vice-president of an oil company. We didn't have much in common but, in a lyrical moment which came out of nowhere and passed quickly

426

between us, we managed to spark up a short conversation. Looking around at us at the beauty of the natural landscape we stood in, I asked him why his company wanted to destroy all of this and whether, at some deep, personal level, he was aware of the global implications of such destruction.

'Son,' he said, 'if I didn't burn her somebody would.'

'But whoever "burns her",' I persevered, 'the outcome is the same – NASA is already warning us that global warming is now off the scale. That's NASA, not a tribe of hippies and eco-warriors. Doesn't that tell you something?'

'I'm 55 years old,' he sighed. 'I reckon I've got about ten more years. There's money in oil and I wanna play golf. You know how much it costs to be a member of my club?'

Somebody tell me that's a sane response.

EXERCISE: JOURNEY TO THE CENTRE OF THE EARTH

In this journey we will voyage beyond the physical boundaries of the Earth and look back at our world with the intention of 'seeing' and sensing the holistic system, the energy connections, which make up Gaia.

Begin in the journeying position you are now used to from the other exercises in this book, and, closing your eyes, allow the energy of your body to flow out from you so that you become a being of light, able to travel anywhere in the cosmos. Drift peacefully up into the night sky, full of stars, away from the Earth and into the heart of what we call 'space'.

Of course, it is not really 'space', it is sentient, alive, awareness, just as you are. Reflect on this and get a sense of your own energy body within the whole of this energetic flow. How do you feel yourself connected to the entire system? What sense do you get of your place within Gaia and within the natural order of our world?

How do you differ on the energy level from your life in

the physical realm? What is your purpose, and what part do you play in the bigger cosmic picture? What is your reason for being on Earth?

And which is really 'you' – your job in the city or this energetic purpose you are here to fulfil? Are they both you? How can you better align the two?

When you have explored enough, allow yourself to drift back to your physical body and come back to consciousness. Remember what you have learned, though. Are there any lessons for you which you can now put into practice in your daily life?

THE PARALYSIS OF ANALYSIS

'The human mind is very deeply linked to every aspect of nature, from the furthest galaxies to the tiniest cell organisms at the bottom of the sea,' says Roszak. 'Western analysis leads to inaction because the world can't be analysed, it's too uncertain.'[7]

We have built a culture based on packaging of facts and figures, data analysis, and justification for our actions based chiefly on economics and political considerations, on the needs of the system instead of human concerns. All of this suggests to us that the world can be analysed, planned for and controlled. Yet modern science is now telling us just how erroneous and overly comfortable this view is.

At the deepest level of reality, we occupy a world where the beating of a butterfly's wings in Tokyo may indeed cause an earthquake in Rome, just as the ancient mystics predicted and atmospheric factors like El Niño are proving in the 'real world'; where our memories and perceptions of events *are* the reality of that event, there is nothing else. This world defies such analysis and the tidy packaging of information. Our response cannot be analytical, it must be moral and personal.

Again, it is perspective which counts if we want to change

the world for, as the shamans tell us, *everything* in life begins with an idea.

This may even be true of genetic evolution, and so, of what we are becoming – or choose to become. Castaneda was once told by don Juan that the dinosaurs evolved into flying lizards, and then into birds, because they *chose* to do so; they didn't just 'evolve' and then figure out what to do with their new abilities and body shape. There was no 'survival of the fittest' based on an accident of birth, a freak of nature, or adaptation to a landscape they stumbled blindly into. *Choice*, based on the idea of change, was the central point, not Darwinian evolution which gave them new qualities over generations. They chose to fly and so evolved wings; they did not 'get wings' and then learn what to do with them.

Castaneda struggled with this concept and we, too, might initially find it baffling. Is it really possible that choice and ideas create evolutionary change and not vice versa? Well, although by no means clear-cut, the evidence is impressive that something else *is* going on beyond the remit of purely Darwinian theories of development and evolutionary growth – something beyond the body and more connected with the concept of free will, personal choice, and the ability of all of us to *create* our futures with conscious intent.

In America now, for example, there is a new genus of 'killer bees' which have adapted so that they are larger and more aggressive than other species. They can attack and oust the current occupiers of rival hives, who are smaller and more placid, by biting off their heads and then taking over their hive. They move through the hive like a Chieftain tank driving over daisies – and they have developed in this way *so* that they can do this.

Meanwhile, the smaller bees, unable to defend themselves with brute force against their larger attackers, have come up with a rather ingenious defence. Instead of tackling their enemies head on, where they know they will lose, they have evolved a defensive strategy. As soon as an enemy bee is seen, a number of them swarm it, so it cannot return to its own hive and alert the others who would return in force. Then, with the larger enemy bee now contained within their midst, they begin *en masse* to flap their wings at high speed, which has the effect of raising the predator's body temperature and, effectively, roasting it.

They have learned to do this, not over generations, as Darwinism might predict, but in months. But how did the bees know that they could survive four degrees of body heat more than their larger adversaries? Who taught them this? And how did they know what to do with this information when they had it – that swarming an attacker and raising its temperature would kill it?

By the same token, there is a story from Japan of the Samurai crab. The legend is that many years ago, the Samurai, sworn to protect the emperor, failed in their duty. Attacked by an invading army, the Samurai launched their fleet of ships and rushed the emperor out to sea in order to get him away from the advancing army. They were pursued, however, and, with their fleet in tatters, the emperor was killed by a well-targeted enemy arrow.

The Samurai, in shame, threw themselves fully armoured into the sea and drowned.

Stories began circulating among the fishing village where this event took place, of ghostly Samurai who wandered the seas at night, unable to rest with their duty to their master unpaid.

Then the fishermen began to notice that the crabs they were catching locally had a strange design on their backs, which resembled the face of a weeping Samurai warrior, in full armoured headgear. Believing these crabs to be sacred, fishermen threw them back into the sea.

The crabs, meanwhile, recognizing their own encounter with death and the fact that they had survived, began to refine the pattern on their backs so that the design on their shells looked more and more like that of a warrior's mask. The event became self-fulfilling and the crabs, indeed, became sacred and are now revered and never eaten in Japan. They had *learned* how to survive through interaction with a myth and had done so in just a few generations.

At the very least, we can suggest that this evolution is due to some form of conscious interaction between the crab and the world around it, rather than a chromosomal or developmental 'accident' over time; an interaction not just with its environment, but with a mythological event and the beliefs of mankind based on a phantom reality.

More recently, Darwinism has also been challenged by the scientific work of a team of investigators on the Galapagos Islands, where Darwin worked out his own theories of the 'origin of species'.

These researchers released a number of lizards into the environment and recorded their evolutionary progress. What they found is that, over just five generations – not the thousands of years predicted by Darwinists – significant physical changes have already taken place across the species according to the precise nature of the new environment each lizard, or group of lizards, occupies. In particular, those who live in steeper areas have developed longer claws than those on more level terrain, so they are able to cling to the surface of their landscape more effectively.

Lyall Watson called such developmental incidents '100th monkey events'. He noticed one day that a single monkey, a member of a group which lived by the sea, had started to wash its bananas in the ocean to get rid of the dirt before eating them. Within days, others had copied this behaviour and began to follow suit. Then something remarkable began to happen – the monkey colony on the next island began to do exactly the same thing, *without once having any form of contact with the first group*. He called it a '100th monkey' event because as soon as this behaviour was adopted by the 99th monkey in the original colony, it seemed to reach a critical mass of adopted behaviour and jumped islands, so that the 100th monkey to carry out this washing behaviour was effectively in a different country from the first.

What is going on here?

Scientists will ponder away until they reach a 'conclusion' and make a 'scientific pronouncement' about the nature of reality and evolution, which is supposed to clear the matter up for us (just as Darwin was supposed to have cleared up the mystery of evolution a couple of hundred years ago, and our religious advisers to have solved the mystery of creation with references to the first couple, Adam and Eve – before Stephen Hawking came along and ruined it for them). But at another level, of course, we don't even have to ask the question 'What is going on?' because we already know the answer: ideas give shape to reality and everything stems from the will, the focus of these transcendent ideas into workable form.

Imagine how powerful we could be if we merely accepted the power that is already ours – for self-healing, for planetary change, for transformation of energy and matter, for *conscious* evolution where we direct our will towards a future intent, to bring ourselves the future we truly want to live.

In fact, perhaps we don't even have to 'imagine' what our potential might be; we can see it in the world today in the form of the so-called 'Indigo Children'. Heralded as a completely new race of 'super-beings', these children (called 'Indigo Children' because their aura seems to glow with this highly spiritual colour) even have power over life and death.

The new phenomena first came to the attention of scientists in the early 1990s, with the birth of an AIDS baby in America. The child was tested at birth, at six months and at one year and confirmed on every occasion to be positive for the AIDS virus. When he was tested again at the age of six, however, doctors were amazed to discover that he was completely free of AIDS, without even a trace that the disease had ever been in his body.

Further tests were conducted by doctors and UCLA scientists, who were dumfounded to find that this child did not have normal DNA, like you or I. Human DNA contains four nucleic acids which combine to produce 64 different patterns called codons. Every human being in the world has 20 of these codons 'turned on' and the rest inactive – apart from this child, who had 24 codons turned on: four more than anyone else alive on this planet.

Another remarkable thing about this child is that he had extraordinary powers of self-healing. When his cells were placed in a petri dish and bombarded with the AIDS virus – even at a dose 3,000 times stronger than that needed to infect a normal human being – his cells remained disease-free. When the cells were bombarded with an equally lethal dosage of cancer cells the result was the same. There was no disease in the world strong enough to hurt this child.

That would be remarkable in itself, but UCLA scientists then began a search for other exceptional children and, within a relatively short space of time, were able to locate more than one million 'new children' worldwide with similar healing powers. They now estimate that one per cent of the world's population – or 60 million people – have this new DNA, all of them Beautiful Mutants who are no longer human beings according to the definitions we have been using up until now.

Furthermore, some researchers have apparently discovered that people without this new DNA structure have only to stay in the presence of an Indigo Child for a short period of time for the extra four codons in their own DNA to mysteriously 'turn on', giving them these abilities too.

The characteristics and personality traits of Indigo Children are also interesting since they seem to exhibit very lofty, spiritual aspects to themselves, not like 'normal' children at all. They *know* they have a right to be here and an important mission in life; they reject any authority which seems unjust or nonsensical and which is imposed rather than requested and are bored and frustrated by rigid systems and bureaucratic structures; they have esoteric, philosophical and spiritual interests and show compassion towards all things; they live in the Now, are anti-materialistic and often resent and defy adults who have given away their power to the system or try to impose the rules of the system upon them; many of them remember past lives and are openly talking about their previous life experiences by the age of about two.

Indeed, so strong is this spiritual impetus, that some researchers even believe that it is the heightened spirituality itself which is creating the physical changes in the DNA of these children. Drunvalo Melchizedek, who has studied this phenomenon for some time, puts it like this:

We believe there are three parts to this phenomenon. The first part is a mind which sees unity . . . it sees everything interconnected in all ways. It doesn't see anything as separate.

The second part is being centred in the heart – to be loving.

And the third thing is to step out of polarity – to no longer judge the world. As long as we are judging the world as good or bad, then we are inside polarity and remain in the fallen state. I believe these people (with the new DNA) have somehow stepped out of judging and are in a state where they see everything as one and are feeling love . . .

Researchers think that by the very expression of their lives these people . . . are changing these four codons and, in so doing, becoming immune to disease. What they don't know – and this is where a lot of research starts to happen – is, so maybe they're immune, but is there anything else? They might be immortal, who knows. Maybe there are other characteristics that we haven't even dreamed of? I often wonder if they are all linked together. Is there some form of telepathic connection that goes on?

I see it as a phenomenon like the E.T.s, except they aren't coming here in spaceship form, they are coming here in spirit form and making it personal by coming into the Earth's evolutionary cycle and joining with us.

And you know, there is another thing that happened last year [2000] – AIDS dropped something like 47 per cent, the largest drop of a single disease in the history of the world. I believe that it had a lot to do with this very thing we are talking about.

These may seem like strong claims, but they are really no different from the perspective that shamans have held for thousands of years. If Melchizedek is right, these children are conscious evolutionaries whose advanced spirituality is leading quite naturally to a new adaptation to the the world (a development far removed from Darwinian law) and changing the world as a direct consequence of that.

The first step for us in consciously creating our own evolutionary future as part of this new world, then, is to strip away the old definitions, to refuse to have our realities dictated to us by scientists and politicians, town planners and bureaucrats, economists and priests, and to start to live comfortably with the acceptance of our own divine power and connection to all things.

This is what don Juan meant when he instructed Castaneda on the conscious evolution of the dinosaurs. We all have choices, and our choices and the ideas that flow from them can literally change the shape of the world.

MOVING TO NEW CONSCIOUSNESS

Fritjof Capra, in *The Turning Point*, predicts the rise of a new, holistic, integrated culture, which will come to pass through such individual action at a local level. With it will come the decline of the old Western model and its mechanistic structure and exploitative nature.[8]

The development of consciousness and of society, he says, is a cyclical process where cultures and civilizations rise, reach a critical mass beyond which they can simply go no further as they become unsustaining, and then a new culture arises to deal creatively and ingeniously with the problems of the old. The change comes not with new technology to address old problems, but with a new worldview which makes the old problems redundant.

'This is what happened at the turn of the [20th] century . . . the old culture, which was basically the scientific culture of the seventeenth century, of the Enlightenment, Newtonian physics and the Copernican revolution – this way of seeing the world in mechanistic terms, in reductionist terms – has come to a close and is now declining. And what is rising is a more holistic or more ecological way of seeing things.'[9]

Capra makes the point that all cultures develop essentially around new ideas and consciousness which gather force, become accepted as popular worldviews and are then absorbed into mainstream culture as a force for change, so that every society is basically formed from *concepts* which are made concrete through human action to direct our collective imagination. In other words, as the shamans say, we dream our own reality.

The last few centuries were a 'blip' in history where the prevailing ideas were materialistic, in counterpoint to the thousands of years in our evolution when we were far more deeply connected to the world, as spiritual and natural beings as dependent on the Earth as she is on us.

These ideas, which gave rise to our present, drew their validation from the sciences, which have described a physical, rather than a spiritual or transcendent universe, which worked like the mechanism of a clock, a machine and, finally, a 'supercomputer', and we, by implication, were all 'cogs' or 'robots' or 'software'. But now we have reached a turning point in our history as science itself moves away from material qualities to paint a picture of a universe of change, created daily from the interplay of individual ideas and beliefs so that all physical reality is, at best, merely a 'probability' which relies more on the method of measurement than the existence of solid objects and unequivocal facts. Science has become a spiritual discipline, as it was in the days of alchemy, and it is now leading our culture away from a hard-edged black and white world to a kaleidoscope of new possibilities.

Referring to the findings of this new science and the holistic conception of reality it reveals to us, Capra has remarked that 'the properties of the parts can only be defined in terms of the dynamics of the whole. So it's a complete reversal . . . in fact, if you go further and ask, "What are those parts?" then you will find that there are no parts – that whatever we call a "part" is a pattern in an ongoing process.'[10]

He offers the analogy of cloud-gazing. If you look up into the sky, you will see clouds in the image of animals, people, mountains, cars, aeroplanes, events. Indeed, some traditional cultures divine the future in just this way, relying on the synchronicity of *exact moments* – the exact moment of looking up with a question in mind and the exact moment of the cloud formation which suggests an answer. (In fact, given that modern science, with all of its state-of-the-art instrumentation, can offer us only the *probability* of an outcome, it seems as good a system as any – and a lot cheaper than our multi-million-pound solutions to the same life puzzles.) And yet, if you look up at the sky again a few minutes later, what you saw with certainty as a tree or a human face will have changed into some other form.

This, he says, is very much like the approach of modern science. 'With particles, the patterns change much faster, but whatever you call an object or a particle or an atom or a molecule are patterns in an ongoing process . . . people in other traditions, like the Buddhist tradition, have been saying that for a long time. There's emptiness out of which comes form. But the forms are not *things*, not isolated objects. The forms are forms of the whole.'[11]

Capra wrote *The Turning Point* when he recognized that all things are connected in this way – just as atoms or clouds are *parts* of the whole which also *contain* the whole – and that includes the current social problems which face us, like war, economic crisis, and rising levels of crime. They are problems of worldview, 'systematic problems. They are all interlinked and they are, in fact, reflections of the limitations of an outdated worldview . . . most of our social institutions, the large corporations, the academic institutions, the political institutions, all subscribe to this outdated worldview and are therefore not able to solve the major problems that we have.'[12]

According to Capra, who has spent many years researching the interaction – or lack of it – between these major institutions and the world around them, the situation is now reaching crisis point.

The old system shows us such a spectacular failure that the 'experts' in various fields don't understand their fields of expertise any longer. Researchers, for instance investigating cancer, don't have a clue, in spite of spending millions of dollars, of the origins of cancer. The police are powerless in the face of a rising wave of crime. The politicians and economists don't know how to manage the economic problems. The doctors and hospitals don't know how to manage the health problems and health costs. So everywhere it's the very people who are supposed to be the experts in their fields who don't have answers any longer – and they don't have answers because they have a narrow view; they don't see the whole problem.[13]

Again, we come back to the problem of separation. We have taken ourselves out of the natural flow of the evolutionary cycle and tried to control the process, losing our foothold and our perspective as a consequence.

Some of this was quite deliberate. We have fought for and institutionalized the divisions of labour we see in our cities, revelling in the idea of experts and authorities who are specialists, essentially, in the control of production and output in one form or another – the factory owner/manager/shop steward/worker; the bishop/priest/minister/faithful; the consultant/doctor/nurse/patient – and made it difficult for ourselves to scramble back to a position where we can see ourselves within the full interplay of our own humanity connected to a world at large.

Those cultures which have remained untouched by the Western world's drive to dominate our specialist corner, or fought to retain independence from our narrow worldview, universally see themselves as connected to the whole – it never occurs to them that it even could be otherwise – and their problems are not ours.

Dr Claudine Michel of the University of California and author of *Aspects éducatif et moraux du vodou haïtian*, in her article on 'Morality in Haitian Vodou' writes, for example, that Vodou belief

> *presupposes a fundamental holism grounded in the ideas of oneness and unity of all forces of nature, in the idea of interdependence and interconnectedness of these forces . . . the universe is a seamless cosmos where every force of nature has a meaning and a connection with other entities.*
>
> *Creating dissonance in nature's polyrhythms, disturbing the harmonious flow of things, bringing about division in the community, are all acts which represent moral transgressions in the Vodou world.*[14]

How different this is from our own moral system which fundamentally asserts the rights of the *individual*; and how different the problems of the Haitian, which are essentially ones of Third World neglect stemming from slavery and European exploitation, rather than deliberate separation from the natural flow of things.

We have lost this sense of community and connection in the Western world, to a great extent. Many of us do not feel able, even, to speak with our neighbours, to exchange problems and secrets, to feel their support, to ask for something as simple as a cup of sugar without feeling guilt, let alone connect more widely with a community in the city. There is a 'north–south divide', a division between the sexes, a growing sense of xenophobia in our country which we read about each day in the attacks on foreign students and the labelling of refugees as 'spongers'.

The consequence of this isolation is some of the problems we experience in today's city living.

EXERCISE: WHEN DID YOU LAST FEEL TRULY CONNECTED?

Journey back to a time in your life when you felt truly at one with everything around you, intimately and un-questionably a part of the whole, the entire universe. Note how old you are. Look around you at your circum-stances. Where are you? What are you doing? Who else is there with you? Really get a feel for this situation. Be there. Live it again.

What would you need to do right now in your life to have that feeling again?

Move further back in time now. See yourself aged 10, 5, 1, then beyond that to the womb, and beyond that to the moment when you decided to be born into this world. What was your reason for choosing this life? What is the essence of you? What are you here to do?

Note any similarities between the sense of true connec-tion you once felt in life and the purpose that drove you to be born to this world. What can you do to ensure that you fulfil this purpose and feel this sense of oneness once again? What risks do you need to take? Will you take them? What are the benefits of doing so?

For Capra, such reconnection will provide the answer to the fundamental problems of social – and personal – evolution. But it can only come from a movement in our system of belief: 'Not only a shift *in* consciousness, but a shift *towards* consciousness, or toward mind – a mindful universe, a spiri-tual, conscious universe.'[15]

DEVELOPING INTUITION

As a cartographer of these changes, Capra is optimistic. The much-needed shift in our worldview is taking place, he says:

440

'a shift from physics to life sciences as the centre of our view of reality – that the universe is a living universe . . . For simple people it's much easier because they experience life as a wholeness and they're much more intuitive rather than analytical and rational. The intuitive mind is a non-linear mode of functioning, a way of experiencing everything at once and not splitting it up into chains of cause and effect.

The more intuitive people are, the easier they will find it. So one way of making the shift would be to cultivate one's intuition.'[16]

How do we do that? Think back to our discussion of the First Attention of the energy body and, in particular, to the concept of our two minds. In the second chamber of the mind is all that society finds it hardest to mould and limit about us: our spiritual and emotional dimensions.

1st mind	2nd mind
Physical	Emotional
Mental	Spiritual

All intuition is 'in-spiration' – 'the breathing in of spirit' – and so the development of intuition begins with quiet stillness and inner silence which facilitates spiritual connection by strengthening the second mind and creating an energetic barrier to social concerns and socially imposed limitations. Don't look for enlightenment in your stillness, look for quietness, a centred mind, and enlightenment will follow along with it. Meditation, prayer, chanting, journeying, visualization and focused physical activities such as yoga and martial arts are all helpful in achieving this sense of calm centredness, then the inspired and intuitive ideas can start to flow. 'God does not proclaim himself,' says the Katha Upanishad. 'He is everybody's secret.'

Once this spiritual connection is re-established and your intuition is more alive within you, it is the emotional self – your will and your desire – which energizes these new ideas and perceptions and begins to give them form. Your mental self, the thinking mind, will then provide focus and intent to your desires, shaping them into aims and objectives, until you have a strategy for living, a 'right way to be' in the world. It is your physical self which then enables this strategy to emerge through your words and actions, your behaviour in life, which is the mirror to your soul.

This progression of the Spiritual → Emotional → Mental → Physical is the way in which we manifest all things in the world and it is the route to some of our greatest human achievements. Our most celebrated and accomplished writers, artists, philosophers and scientists down through the ages all acknowledge that their best ideas emerged from the pool of quiet stillness when their minds were otherwise engaged in meditation and relaxation. They talk of 'the muse', of meaningful 'reveries', of the 'Eureka!' sensation. They mean by this that they were available to spiritual inspiration, insight and intuition when these great ideas emerged.

Intuition, then, is developed through still reflection and meditation. But to *live* intuitively, we must also use our emotional, mental and physical powers in a fully integrated way, so that spirit may be made visible through action. As Lao Tzu wrote: 'These two things, the spiritual and the material, though we call them by different names, in their origin are one and the same. This sameness is a mystery – the mystery of mysteries. It is the gate of all wonders.'[17]

More recently, and less prosaically, Herman Hesse wrote in *Damian* that 'only ideas we really *live* have any value'.[18] This, then, is the point of spiritual intuition – to live in the world as better people.

EXERCISE: WHAT DOES THE EARTH WANT?

Journey to Gaia, our planetary system. In the otherworld, she will have a spiritual identity and may be represented to you in human form – as a beautiful goddess, for example, or a wise old crone who is at one with the secrets of the universe.

Spend some time in her company. Walk with her through her kingdom and see what this world has to offer you. Ask her what *she* would like us to do as a species in order to fulfil our obligations to the cosmos we are a part of, and what we can do to repair some of the damage of the past.

What can *you* do on a personal level to play your part in this healing and to create a more positive world in the future?

When we discover our true purpose and decide to live in the world with integrity and in accordance with our vision, all sorts of extraordinary and miraculous things can start to happen. For one thing, according to radical biologist Rupert Sheldrake, nature herself can begin to resonate with our vision and adapt her evolutionary plan so that the future of mankind, and of the world, is transformed.

Sheldrake is a highly respected academic who has degrees from Cambridge and Harvard, and a PhD in biochemistry from Cambridge University. In books such as *The Rebirth of Nature, Seven Experiments That Could Change the World*, and *The Evolutionary Mind*, he advances a theory of evolution which is quite different from that of the old school Darwinists. Sheldrake's hypothesis is one of 'formative causation', where 'each member of a species draws on the collective memory of the species, tunes in to past members of the species, and, in turn, contributes to the further development of the species'.[19] Usually these things are ascribed to the genes, with most people assuming that evolutionary development depends on biochemicals and DNA. 'What I'm saying is that that view of biological development is inadequate,' writes Sheldrake.

Instead, he believes that all entities emanate 'morphogenetic fields' of group evolutionary memory which all others in their species can learn from, so that development takes place 'in leaps and bounds' rather than the slow, straight path of genetic inheritance across generations. Think back to Lyall Watson's '100th monkey', where knowledge of how to respond in a better way to a particular situation simply jumped islands when the species had absorbed the information needed for healthier progress. The individual 'morphic field' of the single creative monkey, Sheldrake would say, had emanated outwards and so spread to the entire species, which also has its own field.

'The form of societies, ideas, crystals and molecules depends on the way that previous ones of that kind have been organized. There's a kind of inbuilt memory in the morphic fields of each kind of thing . . . one field influences another field through time and space.'

One of the testable implications of Sheldrake's theory is that crystals should be easier to grow in the laboratory once the first batch has matured, since every batch should contain 'a memory of that social group in the past, a group memory – and also, through morphic resonance, a memory of other similar social groups that have existed before', as if each new generation is not just *developing from* but *learning from* the one that preceded it. And, of course, this is exactly what we *do* find. Crystals do grow more quickly in the laboratory when they are able to 'learn' from others. As Sheldrake says, 'It is well known that the addition of "seeds" or "nuclei" of the appropriate type of crystal greatly accelerates the crystallization of supercooled liquids . . . chemical and biological forms are repeated . . . because of a *causal influence from previous similar forms*. This influence would require an action across space and time unlike any known type of physical action.'[20]

But Sheldrake's ideas are not confined to the world of crystals. 'In the human realm, for example, it leads to the idea of a collective human memory on which we can all draw, which is very much like Jung's idea of the collective unconscious. In terms of social groups, it gives rise to the idea that the whole social group is organised by a field.'[21] As conditions change, so adaptation begins and new habits form and we, in turn, inform the coming generation of how best to deal with the changing circumstances they will face. All of life begins with a history, but it is a history we change in the moment according to our responses to environmental stimuli now. In so doing, we change the future not just for ourselves, but for everyone.

Our creative ideas and responses not only impact the moment, but have repercussions for the whole of evolutionary development – which is what don Juan meant when he spoke of evolution coming *after* the decision to change, and not before it, and what I mean when I say that now, for the first time in human history, we are capable of *conscious* evolution, of *creating* a future with heart.

To put this in the terms that a priest of Vodou would identify with better: we are informed by the spirit of our ancestors (the genetic memory and 'morphic field' of our forebears and our past) and by their living memory which is an ever-present, spiritual, part of our immediate daily lives – but it is *we* who must decide on our actions and so shape the future.

Our own ideas are what make a living history for ourselves and for our species. Once we – every single one of us – accept that we *are* powerful, intuitive and creative at levels we perhaps never expected before – then we become a part of conscious evolution as Beautiful Mutants shaping the world.

BEST LAID PLANS

The development of intuition is important at a personal, grassroots level, since society will only change through the individual, and then the collective, dreams of its members.

In the meantime, however, we live in a system which is not intuitive, but which operates from the analytical side of its institutional brain. Its solution to the global problems which now face us is not to step outside of its worldview and habitual self-destructive patterns, but to step further into the quagmire of analysis, and so precipitate further the oncoming crisis it must face. We try, for example, to employ industrial techniques for environmental control and protection – when it is the dream of industrialization that created the problem in the first place, and now we must feed the machines. For every few trees we save with these methods, we chop down another to power our 'saviour' machines. It is always two steps forward and one step back when analysis and not true inspiration is used.

There is an inherent problem with trying to plan our way out of crisis, says Donald Michael, Professor of Planning and Public Policy at the University of Michigan, and former policy analyst for the Joint Chiefs of Staff and the National Science Foundation. *The problem is that planning doesn't work.* Too much is unknown, our human view too narrow, and the future too uncertain; just a fleeting pattern in a cosmic picture. And because we refuse to accept uncertainty as one of the inevitable parameters in our plans, 'the threat is greater and makes it harder and harder for governments or organisations to do anything constructive because they keep getting caught in this swamp of backlogged problems'.[22]

It is, as the psychiatrist, R. D. Laing, wrote in *The Politics of Experience*,[23] difficult to make sense of a world, and predictions for a future when 'change is so speeded up that we begin to see the present only when it is already disappearing'.

The paradox and the irony of this 'uncertainty principle' is that people, as social beings, may engage in one activity only to find that the result is the opposite of their original intentions. Thus, for example, the Christian Church, motivated (probably very genuinely in some cases), by a sense of love and compassion, has been responsible for some of the worst violations of human rights in history. This included thousands of deaths, along with slavery, oppression and enduring poverty in many countries of the world, as it sought to eradicate the 'heathen practices' of tribal religious worldviews from the native lands it annexed, demanding that its own religion be adopted wholesale instead. In his book, *Voyage aux Isles de l'Amérique*, the missionary priest, Father Labat, describes his own part in this on the island of Haiti where, without any sense of remorse or shame, he engaged in thrashing slaves to death for their dedication to their own African religion – all in the name of Christian love.[24]

Just like Father Labat, genuine missionaries, motivated by love of God, were too frenzied and caught up in their own Christian passions to see the bigger picture of their actions. This is uncertainty at work, where actions from a sense of love beget systems based on violence and hatred.

We can see the same situation in the 'Holy Land' today, with all of its wars and violence, just as it has been for generations. When I 'buried' my father there twenty years ago, I made a trip to Bethlehem to visit the site of the stable which was the supposed birthplace of Christ and is now a shrine to peace. I cannot even remember how many armed guards I saw around this place, or how many checkpoints I had to pass through in order to get there, or how many explosions of violence I witnessed while there, as people of different religious and political beliefs tried to claim the site as their own. Each side had very good arguments why only they should have access to god! And this is the problem and the paradox of such 'rational' analysis: that peace leads to violence and god becomes a branded commodity, the exclusive province of humanity and under the control of bureaucrats and religious scholars – which is surely a reversal of the facts!

We see uncertainty at work, too, in our business dealings. Despite 'five year plans' and 'corporate vision statements', most of our companies don't have a clue what they are doing. In March 2000 in the UK, one of our major banks managed to launch a very self-satisfied advertising campaign where it declared itself powerfully 'BIG' – at exactly the same time as it closed 171 of its local branches, leaving many villages without access to any banking facilities because, it said, it could not afford to keep them open. These paradoxical events were entirely accidental and ostensibly unrelated, two quite different business decisions taken as a result of the impossibility of even a little foresight, let alone detailed planning. The overall effect was a public relations disaster for the bank in question, reflecting an organization which was not powerful, but distant, cold, insensitive and uncaring.

To add insult to injury, and to give the final lie to the myth of business planning, the bank's Board picked exactly the same week to announce multimillion-pound pay hikes for its members – at the same time trying to argue that the local branches had to close because they cost too much to run. It was a 'BIG' mistake. The bank threw away millions of pounds of investors' money on an advertising campaign which blew up in its face.

But it is not just the banks which are subject to the fallacies and foibles of trying to plan ahead even by a few weeks or months. Our modern laws and institutions are in the same boat right along with them. In April 2000, for example, the UK Police Commission recommended the decriminalization of certain 'soft' drugs, noting that societies which take the most repressive stance against drugs (such as Britain) often also have the worst drug problems, while those with more liberal attitudes (such as Holland) are relatively problem-free. In other words, once again, where we have planned for one effect, we have actually ended up with its opposite.

Despite the evidence and the logic of this report, politicians began their predictable moral outcry. No matter that British children may be dying at the hands of black market suppliers who cut their drugs with rat poison and scouring powder, and that the legalization of drugs might help to prevent this through tighter quality control, such legalization is not a vote-winner. It does not fit in with their plans. And so, through the power of the uncertainty principle, we continue to 'come down hard on drug traffickers and abusers', and thereby prolong and exacerbate Britain's problem as one of the most repressive *and* drug-fuelled societies in Europe.

Still, uncertainty or not, says Michael, 'you still have to act. And given the choice of acting for peace or against peace, you act for peace'.[25] What we need is *conscious* awareness of the repercussions of our actions and an all-pervading, intelligent and informed foundation of *compassion* as a means to manage the present and to plan *intuitively*, instead of rigidly, for the future.

RANDOM ACTS OF KINDNESS AND SENSELESS ACTS OF BEAUTY

Compassion – the philosophy of connection with the whole of Gaia and with spirit – is essential if we want a human future for our planet, instead of more systems and rules. When we realize how much is unknown, uncertain in the world, we need a way of relating to this world, and to each other, which remains simple, flexible and universally appropriate in order to take our species forward, not ever more complex analytical frameworks, outmoded laws which do not resemble reality, and intricate planning regimes which confuse and constrain our potential. And sometimes, of course, acting from a sense of compassion means that no physical action is taken at all – we leave the 'heathens' to themselves – in recognition that, no matter how offensive to our Western worldview, other cultures have a right to their own quiet enjoyment of life as *they* dream it. Action from compassion in Michael's sense would instantly mean no more war, no more famine, no more destruction of world resources, no more exploitation, no more suffering. And all it takes on our part is a conscious decision to act in a compassionate manner – to ourselves and to others – during our interactions with them.

Michael offers inspirational advice when he asks us to consider our own lives from the perspective of uncertainty.

To my mind there are three aspects we have to recognize, that every person and every organization faces, whether they know it or not . . .

One is that you really don't know the outcome of your actions. Even if you think you've got them pinned down, you really can't know in any way for sure.

Second, that we live a storytelling life; we create our reality. Everybody does and all cultures do, and they're alternative realities . . .

And thirdly, everybody is struggling with the meaning of life, with living, and with dying.

If you accept that that's the condition in this turbulent and uncertain world that everybody's in, whether they know it or not – including oneself – it means you really have to support one another – using all the knowledge one can bring to bear, recognizing all the ignorance one lives in, in the face of that knowledge. The only choice under those circumstances is a compassionate state of being toward oneself and toward others.[26]

Surprising as it seems, it doesn't take much to change the world.

In the 1990s I became aware of a revolutionary (perhaps, even evolutionary) new trend which had begun to sweep the world: an act of guerrilla 'lovefare' (as opposed to warfare), which had started in the States but caught the imagination of the global community. It began after an American journalist, tired of hearing the same expression – 'a random act of violence' – used on the news every night to describe another senseless murder, or rape, or drive-by shooting, decided to reclaim the streets by means of a peaceful protest in order to create new and Earth-changing direct action.

He invented the term 'random act of kindness' as a direct counter to the acts of violence he was hearing about, little imagining that he would create a worldwide epidemic as more and more people became infected by the revolutionary bug.

It started small, with reports of a motorist stopping at a toll gate and paying for his own car to pass through, along with the next two cars behind him in the queue – and then driving off anonymously without waiting for thanks. It seemed the action of a madman, behaving 'randomly' and 'senselessly' with compassion and kindness towards people he did not even know. But it spread like wildfire because fundamentally, when we decide to escape the rules of the system and the need to play the game, the natural state of human beings is one of compassionate caring.

And so others began copycat acts of senseless kindness, growing more and more creative until a whole insurgent movement grew up of people acting kindly, with complete anonymity, towards perfect strangers. If reality is political, this was the equivalent of a coup, an attempt to overthrow society! People acting kindly towards one another in a social system predicated on competition, the survival of the fittest, dog eat dog.

It is also an example of conscious evolution at play: by focusing on positive examples of caring and compassion, instead of acts of violence, the news media were creating a new assemblage of reality, a new channel for people's energies. The result was a newly created option for people to act with kindness and, given the choice, many people opted to do so.

One of the most wonderful and moving 'acts of kindness' I heard of at that time came from a child, as is so often the case. Our children are naturally giving; they have not yet been educated by us to be otherwise, to look out for number one, to watch their own backs, to do as they would be done to.

It concerned a young boy (let's call him 'Robert', as his real name escapes me and he probably would not care to be named anyway) whose brother ('Jack') was seriously ill and needed a kidney transplant in order to live. His parents, having looked for a compatible donor for many months, were resigned to never finding one, while Jack's condition continued to deteriorate until he was severely ill. Then the doctors discovered that Robert's tissue type was an exact match, that he was the perfect donor they had been looking for. A kidney transplant, while it should not be life-threatening, is not without its risks and Robert's parents, obviously concerned about the possibility of harm befalling both of their children but unable to sit by and watch one of them just die, took an incredibly enlightened approach. They decided to calmly explain the situation to Robert, including all the pros and cons, the risks and rewards of his donating a kidney to his brother, and then to leave the decision entirely up to him.

Robert listened to what they had to say and then grew quiet. 'I'd like to think about it for a few days,' he said.

A few days later he told his parents that he had decided he would like to help his brother and would give him his kidney.

The operation proceeded smoothly and proved a complete success. Recuperating in the hospital afterwards, however, Robert seemed unusually quiet and concerned, and, realizing this was not just the normal after-effects of a fairly routine hospital operation, his parents eventually asked him what was wrong.

'Oh,' he said. 'It's nothing really, I was just wondering when I will start to die.'

This beautiful child had gone through with the transplant operation believing that he would die at the end of it but was prepared to do so anyway in order for his brother to live. I am still very moved by this story of true compassion and kindness.

Not every act of kindness needs to be on this sort of level to make a difference. I remember spending a wonderful summer one year conducting guerrilla raids of kindness on unsuspecting strangers. My girlfriend and I would 'accidentally' drop coins in people's driveways for them to find later, just to brighten their day, stick notes onto the windscreens of cars parked in the 'parent and child' spaces at supermarkets so that when their fraught owners returned to them they would find a message that told them how much we respected the work they were doing for the planet in bringing up their child in a loving way. Once or twice, on a whim, I decided to pay someone else's lunch bill as we were leaving a restaurant. My girlfriend, who was a teacher, got her children involved, with 'random act of kindness' projects – the kids loved it! I told a few friends what we were doing and they decided to join in too. The 'project' became infectious, exactly as Sheldrake's morphogenetic model might predict, as each person learned from the actions of others and then, consciously and creatively, chose the kindness option, too.

Now there are whole web sites devoted to the Random Act of Kindness movement, with stories of actions, big and small, taken by ordinary people determined to change the world through compassion at an individual level, to do something for themselves, to make a difference and not just moan about the state of modern living or expect 'someone else' to sort it out for them. Instead, they are seizing back power for themselves and exercising their own right to change the world they are a part of.

It is remarkable, too, how often these people express how liberated and happy they felt when they were able to help out someone else – and how often they report that the recipient of their kindness has gone on independently to help another, as if these compassionate actions simply *have* to be spread as part of our natural humanity and predisposition to life before we are curtailed by systems and modern expectations. These are human beings at play; Beautiful Mutants creating a new future. The fact is that the energy we experience around us and between ourselves *is* changed very easily through the power of intention. If we approach the world from a perspective of distrust, blame, unhappiness, that is what we see there, but if we change our minds and see a better world, that is what we create.

As the psychotherapist, Gwen Randall-Young, remarks on the Random Act of Kindness web site at *www.intouchmag.com*: 'Allowing a spirit of kindness to permeate our collective lives would be a quantum leap, from an evolutionary standpoint.

'Eliminating meanness, pettiness, gossip, criticism, judgement, polarity, and blame would be a superb act of kindness. It is also a fundamental step along any spiritual path.

'Negative qualities reflect a very dense, heavy energy, vested solidly in ego, and they block the light of the spirit. Random acts of kindness amidst the darker energies are certainly a positive start. We can do more. Much more. We can resolve to be kinder, gentler beings. All day, every day. We can treat those closest to us with the same respect and politeness that we reserve for friends and colleagues. We can refuse to litter the lives of others with negative energy. If we do this, we will be doing our part to create a world in which kindness is never a random act, but rather a way of life.'

It is the little things, as she remarks, which often make the biggest difference – the parents who decide *consciously* to treat their children with love and warmth, even if they themselves come from a violent or uncaring family, since in that action they heal the past, set themselves free, and create a better world right now with a more positive future for their children.

As Randall-Young writes:

Teachers can strive to remain patient and forgiving, no matter how frustrated they might feel with a particular student . . .

Employees can choose to cooperate and remain positive about employers, rather than going into polarity . . . Employers can honour the individuality and dignity of each staff member, placing the significance on the human over the material . . .

Men and women can choose to focus on what is beautiful and special about the opposite sex, rather than battling for superiority . . . Children can learn to let everyone play, rather than setting up exclusive games . . . We can all begin to celebrate adolescence and help teens to feel proud of themselves, rather than raising our eyebrows in disgust . . . Teenagers can learn to be patient with, and accepting of, adults in spite of our limitations . . . Drivers can realize that there is enough road to share, and time to get there.

Here are some of the stories I have come across which illustrate how we can all make a contribution immediately in the kindness war, some of which can be found, along with others, at the Random Acts of Kindness Home Page at *www.noogenesis.com/malama/kindness.*

Healing the wounds of love

Many of us will start out in new relationships brimming with love for our partners, thrilled and optimistic at the prospect of a wonderful future together, only to find that feeling fading over time until divorce or separation is inevitable, and then the emotional vacuum can be filled with quite the opposite feeling for our once-true love.

Such feelings – both love and loathing – are projections of ourselves onto the other, leading to demands and expectations, self-hurt and blame. Only by owning our own emotions and healing the wounds can we ever heal ourselves and become whole once again.

One man found himself better able to deal with the pain of divorce once kindness entered the equation. After being inspired by a spiritual book, he decided to take a good look at his life and realized that he had sometimes been less than kind and loving to those he most loved.

One of the people he wished to make amends to was his ex-wife. 'We went through a very painful (emotionally) break up and separated as less than good friends,' he wrote. 'Here was someone I loved dearly at one time and now, due to circumstances, I could hardly tolerate her . . . I knew that she was in financial need, so I called her and made arrangements to pay off her bills.'

For him, this act of kindness was a healing on a soul level, like returning the soul parts of others once a relationship ends.

A Christmas gift

There are opportunities to act kindly towards others in many situations and circumstances every day. Often, we may choose to ignore these opportunities – which come to us themselves as gifts, a shot at liberation from expected and conditioned patterns – but it can often be rewarding for all concerned if we do choose to seize these moments. One New York postal worker wrote about the benefits of doing so: 'Some years ago I found out that there were thousands of letters addressed to Santa Claus, North Pole, at the Main Post Office in Manhattan. I was curious so I went and looked at some. Most of them were lists of toys that children wanted. But among the letters, I came upon a number that were so sad they made me cry. So I sent each child a telegram "Will be at your house. Wait for me. Santa." My wife made me a costume and I showed up. It was so wonderful that I did it for the next 12 years.'

Compassion in action

The simplest of actions can have a disproportionate and quite profound effect on the people who benefit from them. Here is one woman describing the lasting impact on her life of a small kindness by another:

'It was 1991, a few weeks before Christmas. My husband had left me for another woman eleven months earlier. This was the first Christmas alone with the children and financially things were tough. On December 12th eve, there was a knock at the door and when I opened it, I saw a small box of cookies with a note "On the first day of Christmas . . ." I was touched and more than a little curious. I had, but a few minutes before, been crying – feeling very alone and sad. This gift brightened my day.'

The same thing happened the next night, and the next, throughout all twelve nights of Christmas. They were small gifts – some bubble bath, a few colouring books for the children, 'but they meant so much . . . I didn't feel so alone. I never did find out who sent these gifts [but] that random act of kindness helped me through a very difficult time.'

Ticket to kindness

Once again, it is often the small things that make the most difference. When we reach out to another and share, for a moment, their humanity – the thing that unites us all – it doesn't matter whether we express that connection between us with a gift of a million dollars or a few coins. It is the *act* of connection which matters.

'Many of us living in towns where we must pay for streetside parking meters find the allotted time at the meters too short to run all the errands we have in a given day,' writes one person who was the subject of a small act of kindness.

'The other day I parked at a meter and ran off to do my errands. I was gone over 30 minutes. Fearing a ticket on my window, I ran back to my car. Someone had paid the meter, and put a very nice note on my windshield asking me to do the same for someone else sometime. I was very moved by this simple act. Now I will often look for other cars with an expired meter and put the coins in to give that shopper a little relief from the meter patrols . . . the small ways we affect one another really do make a difference.'

Working together, creating community

In the city we live lives of quiet isolation where 'community' can be a forgotten word. But it doesn't have to be that way. We can *create* community. A simple kindness may be all it takes, as this writer found out.

'I have lived in this community of mostly professionals and retirees for over three years, but I had met only a few of my neighbours. After the snow had stopped falling from the blizzard of '96, we were left to fend for ourselves because the city and state services were overwhelmed. I went out to the parking lot to dig out my and my girlfriend's cars . . . After about 30 minutes of digging, some of the neighbours came out with snow shovels and told me if I helped them, they would help me. I agreed and we dug out each others' cars [then] we all put our heads together and figured out who was too old or too ill to dig themselves out and went about, as a team, digging out people most of us had never met. As the day went on, more and more people joined us . . . We became an army of snow diggers, our only motivation being concern for the people who were stuck and our growing friendship. I made a lot of friends that day.'

Appreciating what others really go through

We get caught up in our lives, our sorrows and frustrations, and find it hard to appreciate that others are in the same boat too. A very simple act of kindness is sometimes just to treat another person with respect, when our habitual response would be to act very differently, as this writer remarks:

'Telemarketers. I dislike them as much as anyone [but] I have always told myself that most of these people are simply trying to make a living with a tough and thankless job. I try to tell them quickly but kindly, in a cheerful, friendly way, that I am not in the market, that I want to save their time because I know they're trying to make a living and I wish them good luck. This, I find, is better than pretending to be interested, raising their hopes unnecessarily and wasting their and your time and patience. If you know someone so hard up they have to make ends meet by telemarketing, give them some flowers. Anyone who has to wallow through that much rejection every day needs some random kindness!'

And finally, a story I find remarkable in a person so young and which, once again, illustrates the natural kindness of children which we, as parents, could do more to appreciate, honour and support. This would be an act of kindness in itself, for our child and, in the longer term, for the world as a whole.

At the age of seven, Taylor Marie Crabtree started a business called TayBear, making and selling hand-painted hair clips at local stores. But there was no selfish motivation in this; it wasn't that Taylor wanted extra spending money. Instead, she wanted the money so she could buy teddy bears for children with cancer. 'She said the kids probably have a lot of sadness in their lives and and she wanted them to have something special to hug and to hug them back. Taylor wanted them to know that even strangers care about them,' said her mother.

The media became interested in Taylor's project and she began to receive donations from strangers living thousands of miles away, from word of mouth alone. 'With her scribbly second grade handwriting, she wrote each person with her appreciation.' She then expanded the project to involve more than 100 other children, so they, too, could feel they were helping others.

'Taylor has been touched by so many people on her journey,' says her mother. 'One woman began questioning her about the project [and] was very suspicious about just where the collected money was going. Taylor gladly talked on and on about all the little steps she had taken to that point and about children and cancer. Looking on, I noticed that the woman's suspicions had turned to sadness. She became teary-eyed and stopped Taylor in mid-sentence. She then leaned down and hugged Taylor from a place deep in her heart. She told Taylor that her eight-year-old son had died just five months before from cancer and that he would have been very proud to have had one of her teddy bears.'

There have been some remarkable acts of healing as a result of Taylor's work, as her mother explains. 'Maybe it was the homeless man that had donated 11 cents and was surprised when he was told that was plenty of money to buy a hair clip. He and Taylor stood together choosing just the right hair clip for his lady friend. Or maybe it was the young woman who was flying back home the next day to say goodbye for the last time to her father, who was dying from cancer. Perhaps it was the man that drove all the way to his bank and back in order to buy a hair clip for his mom. He said that his dad had recently died from cancer [and] he wanted a child to have a teddy bear in his dad's memory. With each hair clip or donation have come so many memories and a realization that when working toward a goal from your heart, the journey too is part of the experience. Taylor once told me "how could people not see angels, they're everywhere".'

As soon as I read Taylor's story, I sent her an email of appreciation and encouragement. Despite her heavy workload and her young age, she replied the next day, asking me about myself and telling me *I* was kind for thinking of her. If you would like to send her your thoughts, you can reach her via email at *TayBear@bigfoot.com*. I can't think of anybody more deserving of your kindness.

There is a wider, deeper, aspect to random acts of kindness, one of personal liberation as well as cultural change. We have been socialized since birth to see the world as a foregone conclusion, that this is the way things are, unchangeable, immutable, forlorn. The reality is different. By acting from our intuition and innate spiritual wisdom, we set off a whole chain reaction of world-changing events. The person's life we affect is energized, revitalized, and who knows what positive 'chance' event might flow from this? And we, in turn, are empowered by the recognition of our own ability to make a real difference in the world and, as a consequence, our relationship with, and to, others is changed for the better.

The effect of random acts of kindness is deeply shamanic – and you don't have to be a shaman to practise it!

EXERCISE: RANDOM ACTS OF KINDNESS, SENSELESS ACTS OF BEAUTY – SOME SUGGESTIONS

- Make coffee for the whole office, especially if you don't do it normally, and particularly if you are the boss.
- Send your partner a note of appreciation, telling them all the things you really like about them. Don't stop writing until you find at least ten – and make them things you wouldn't

normally have the courage to say to their face. Slip it into their coat pocket or their lunchbox so they find it at random some time later.

- Write to your local newspaper to tell them about someone you know and admire, who is doing a really great job in the face of personal difficulties – why she's a wonderful mother, all the things he does for charity, whatever. Send the person themselves a copy of your letter too – anonymously.

- Tell your child today all the reasons why you love them and why they are truly special. Tell them you're sorry for any of the things you now regret, that you were learning to be a good parent and you know you got it wrong sometimes, but from now on you will try your hardest to do better. And mean it.

- Forgive your own parents for their mistakes as well. Tell them you forgive them if you wish but, more importantly, forgive them in your heart.

- And forgive yourself for the things you have done to others which still bother you. Make amends and let the feeling go.

- Next time you are asked for money by a homeless person, give it graciously and ask what else you can do to help. Nobody asks to be homeless.

- Spend some time thinking about the worst case of bureaucratic meddling in your life that you can remember – when some faceless bureaucrat who was 'just doing his job' really ruined your day through some mindless action of the system – then send them flowers. Believe it or not, they're human too – and you might just start a kindness revolution which will bring back some humanity to the system!

The remit of the 'neo-shaman' is to use all of his skills, all of the tools at his disposal, in the most creative way possible, to heal, to balance and to support the Earth and all its children. There is nothing more natural than using our innate love and generosity in the battle for world and self-empowerment.

How do we save the Earth? Simple. We start by saving ourselves.

In this chapter we have seen that the Earth is a living system, that the way we live as part of it, and the type of society we create, is an expression of our own ideas and consciousness, and that kindness and compassion are the keys to change.

In his wonderful book on Hawaiian shamanism, Dr Serge Kahili King offers us seven powerful principles for freeing ourselves from old habits so we can start to live compassionately towards all things – including ourselves – and so begin this process of global transformation.[27]

1. *ike* – the world is as we think it is

The glass in front of you is either half full or half empty – depending entirely on your perspective. In other words, how we choose to see reality *creates* our reality. This is often the hardest spiritual insight since we are conditioned to approach the world in a socially approved way and to accept the social model without thinking. Indeed, it can often be disturbing, to us and to society, when we find ourselves at odds with the majority view. Nonetheless, it is true that our complicity in the worldview of the system is required to uphold it and also true that no-one has dominion over our minds. We can choose a different reality – one that makes sense to *us* – if we wish to: all that is required for our mental and physical health is that it is consistent and congruent for us and better answers our needs.

There is nothing mystical or metaphysical about this; it is merely common sense – we simply choose to see what we *want* to see so we can build a life based on these more empowering perceptions.

The way to change, therefore, is simply by changing – which is why, perhaps, this is the hardest lesson of all to learn.

2. *kala* – we are beings without limits

The only limitations to our abilities are those that we agree to impose upon ourselves. The system would like very much to control and direct our thinking so that we will go along with it without challenge. The system may try, but it is *we* who either accept or reject its limiting beliefs and dictates.

Sometimes accepting limits can be a positive thing, enabling us to enjoy specific experiences in a universe which is itself infinite, by giving ourselves useful boundaries. So, for example, we might choose to ignore the rest of the world in order to capture in a photograph one particular moment – the smile of a child or the face of a lover – which, for us, *is* the entirety of the world in that moment.

There are other limitations, however, which are the outcome of ideas and beliefs imposed upon us by the culture we live in, and which we have come to accept without thinking. A few hundred years ago, the world was flat and the Earth the centre of the universe, so nobody thought to explore our environment in order to expand our horizons. It was an act of supreme deviance and creativity when someone dared to make the journey one day and discovered that the Earth was round; and an act of heresy when it was first suggested that our planet was not the centre of all things. These deviants changed the world. Thanks to them, the Earth does, indeed, now have the potential to become a true 'global village', while Gaia herself is part of a much wider system – the cosmos – making us all children, not just of one world, but of one entire universe, ideas we could not even have conceived of if not for our 'deviant' forebears.

I remember gazing at the stars as a child and wondering if they weren't just atoms, along with the Earth itself, spinning together, as part of some colossal entity we were too small to see in its entirety. I journeyed to the stars many years later and saw them as dots of ink on a blank white page, spilling from the imagination of some cosmic author and making up a single word – 'Why?'

We are aspects of the same question asked on infinite worlds across endless time, all of us searching for meaning, and the meaning we find will always be the meaning we provide. Out there, there are no limits, but within us are all the limitations we may care to apply.

EXERCISE: EXPLORING COSMIC ENERGY

Journey in the normal way, this time with the stars as your destination. What is the energy which holds them together? Why do the stars not just fly away? Why are we conscious beings amidst this tear-like diamond sprinkling? Are we alone in this universe?

We project images into the sky to make sense of the random configuration of the planets and the stars – the Big Dipper, the Pole Star, Orion's Belt. These are human projections, like our creation of reality, not true qualities of the stars and planets themselves. We see a 'man' in the moon; the North American Indians see a 'rabbit'.

Look beyond these projections and ask yourself what is the real purpose, the shape, the reality of the stars, and what holds them there for us? My own experience of the stars is that they are the final destination, the next phase of life, for conscious human beings; they are what we become when we are sufficiently, spiritually, evolved. It would be interesting to hear that you had seen this too.

Now journey beyond the stars. They are tiny fragments of a cosmic whole. What is that whole and what is it spelling out for you?

3. *makia* – energy flows where directed

One very valuable application of this principle is offered by Gay Gaer Luce, author of *Your Second Life*, and founder of the Nine Gates Mystery School. 'There are other cultures that are far more civilised than we are in the sense that they don't spray their emotions over each other,' says Gay. 'They understand that emotions have to be released and that this is a compressed energy, a labelled energy [which] has to be given some outlet . . . but instead of saying "You did such and such" and "You're doing this to me", they say, "I am going to feel this energy, see these images, and allow this to transform by changing it. It has nothing whatsoever to do with you".'[28]

In other words, releasing energy such as anger is a very healthy thing to do, but rather than venting our frustrations on the person closest to us (who may not even be the cause of our anger), as is so common in our society, we can use this energy as a tool in our own development. Instead of just blowing the energy by blowing our top, we can begin to process it, asking 'What's behind this feeling?' and then, 'What is the essence of the feeling which now begins to arise?' until we come face to face with ourselves, like adventurers of the soul, uncovering new insights into our own nature and the wider nature of the world we live in. 'And then there's a magical moment when all of a sudden the anger turns to sheer energy or excitement and you *know* – Aha! – and you begin to understand that you held that anger in place with a belief, and that you can change that belief voluntarily.'(ibid.)

EXERCISE: FORGIVENESS AND FREEDOM FOR SELF

The simple act of writing can be a powerful way for us to get in touch with our feelings and our creativity, allowing a story to unfold of our place in the world. Through writing we can 'get it all out', 'get it down on paper', instead of bottling our hurts up inside ourselves.

Recall the worst episode of hurt and betrayal you have ever had to live through. Write down on paper all that happened to you at that time and truly feel all the pain you experienced then.

Now identify and name the person you hold responsible for that pain and write a letter of forgiveness to them. You do not have to post it to them; you can, if you wish, choose simply to burn it, but it is important that you let these feelings go.

There is a story of two Buddhist monks who arrive at a river and find a woman waiting on the shore who needs desperately to cross but cannot negotiate the current. One of the monks picks her up and carries her across safely, leaving her at the other side.

A few miles later, his companion, who has been silent, turns to him and asks 'Why did you carry that woman across the river back there? You know it is forbidden for us monks to touch a woman in any way.'

The 'guilty' monk simply laughs and turns to his friend. 'Are you still carrying that woman?' he asks. 'I put her down some miles ago.'

Blame and recrimination is like that. It does not matter what another has done; it is how we react to it, whether we let it become a central and unpleasant part of our life, that counts, and whether we can finally put it down and let it go.

There is freedom in forgiveness; a freedom which enables us to wipe the slate clean and start living once again.

Using our energy in a positive way like this is, in a sense, a 'hygiene factor' which helps to keep us and the world around us clean of negative forces. But the act of focusing can also be used pro-actively as a force for good. By deciding to invest our energy single-mindedly in a particular direction, towards a specific goal, we develop a strategy for our lives and begin to attract the necessary changes to us.

Many of us drift through life using daydreams and fantasies to escape from boring jobs and dead-end relationships, as a crutch to get us through the stress of city life. Then suddenly we find we are 60 years old and all we have to show for our lives is a few photo albums of holidays in Tenerife and a two-up, two-down house in the suburbs with the same relationship we dreamt of changing for the better forty years ago.

Maggie had a dream of 'doing something' for the environment, leading a more exciting life, travelling. But it seemed just a fantasy, albeit a sustaining one which continued to give her hope in an otherwise mundane life. At 45 she was locked into a twenty-year marriage which had long ago become stale and predictable, and a 'pointless' job that drained her energy. The conditions were right for her to change; she had 'done her duty, brought up two great kids': now it was time for her to begin living. The problem was, how.

What was missing from her life was focus. Once she decided to sit down and itemize all the things she *really* wanted to achieve, to recapitulate on her life, and to list her aspirations for the future (along with the degree of risk she was prepared to take in order to achieve her dreams), her options became instantly clearer. In fact, thinking it through and getting it down on paper was the hardest part; after that, everything else fell into place 'as if by magic'.

She began by researching and then writing to a number of charities involved in environmental action, volunteering her services after work and on weekends, and was met with enthusiastic responses. She began to work for a few of these agencies and enjoyed it so much that she negotiated new hours with her employer, enabling her to work part-time and to develop her campaigning interests. Her commitment was soon noticed and, when a job became available, she was offered a full-time salaried position with one of the charities she had donated her time to. Then, in due course, a more senior role presented itself until, a few years later, she is now helping to run field trips overseas for other volunteers – she is exactly where she had said she wanted to be.

The key for Maggie was *focus* – and the development of a singular course of action which enabled her to invest her energies most effectively in order to liberate herself from drudgery and create a more fulfilling life. Her happiness, in turn, created benefits for her marriage, for the recipients of her charitable energies and, through her work, for humanity as a whole.

4. *manawa* – NOW is the moment of power

'What lies behind us and what lies before us are tiny matters compared to what lies within us,' said Ralph Waldo Emerson,[29] and this is the essence of this fourth principle.

The past does not exist. It is not the past which limits us or makes us what we are today; it is our *beliefs* about the past and the actions we take as a consequence of these. Nor does the future exist. What we do *right now* determines how the future will unfold for us as we ourselves create it in the moment.

If we allow ourselves to carry old and unhelpful beliefs and emotions from the past into the future, we create a continuum of crisis in our lives, which becomes self-fulfilling as we inevitably recreate the patterns we know and are attached to. We use our past to justify our present unhappiness and the inevitability of our future fate. But the real choice is always ours and it is always Now.

The fact is that the past is arbitrary and the future unwritten; the present moment is all that matters. This second, as you read these words, is, as don Juan expressed it, 'your one square centimetre of opportunity'.[30] You can change the world in an instant. It may not be easy, but it can be done: look at Maggie. The choice, once again, is entirely yours.

5. *aloha* – what love is

In Hawaii, the traditional greeting of 'aloha' means 'love'. The root of the word also means, in a sense, 'to share an experience'. To Be Here Now, in other words, happy or satisfied with what you have. Love exists only to the degree that you are content with all that exists in your life, right now.

We each have a right to love and a right to *be loved*. What else is truly worthwhile in our lives – working for 'a living'? Committing to a political ideology? Is that really how you want to sum up your life to yourself and your children? It does not matter who you are, it does not matter what you do – it is *what you do with who you are* that counts. Rich or poor, over-indulged or under-privileged, what are *you* going to do with *your* life – and if the life you are living does not make you happy, what are you going to do *about that*?

Only when we are connected, feel part of the whole and have a life with meaning, do we sense ourselves to be truly happy. The time to act is *now* if that does not sound like you.

Assume – rightly or wrongly – that we get one shot at the world and this is yours. Is this all you wanted from it? No? Then recognize the signs. True love should not make you nervous or concerned, dependent on another, or lacking in power; it should be energizing, supportive and liberating. True passion does not mean sleepless nights and daybreaks filled with dread at the journey to the office and the day ahead.

6. *mana* – *Your* power comes from *You*

All the power you have comes from you. Your own experiences and interpretations of events assemble the world each day. There is nothing more. The way you choose to interpret events therefore has a profound effect on your life and – since we are all you, and you are us – on the entire matrix which connects us.

No-one else has the power to make you happy or unhappy, to hold you back or set you free – only you. People may interact with you, they may be the cause of certain events in your life, but it is your reaction to them, not what 'they have done' which determines the impact of the event. Your partners leaves you – So what? Does she break your heart? No, she leaves you but *you* break your own heart. You are fired from your job – does this make you destitute? No, *you* make you destitute.

You always have a choice in the interpretation of the events of your life. Taking true responsibility for your own feelings, actions and way of life is both healthy and liberating – for as soon as you give your freedom up to another, allowing them to decide on the meaning of any event for you, you are sacrificing and reneging on your own power. Understand that this is *your world* and that you are the only person who really lives here and you maintain control of your own sacred destiny.

7. *pono* – 'truth' is what works for you

I began this book with a question: 'What is Truth?' The answer is that, ultimately, *there is no Truth*. Others will tell you to 'abide by the rules', 'play the game', 'obey the law', 'do the "right" thing', as if 'the rules', 'the game', 'the law', the 'right thing' had some objective meaning outside of ourselves. They all have the same meaning – 'do what I do or what has been institutionally approved'. They are no more *the* Truth than your own view of reality is any reflection of an Ultimate Reality, merely your own unique perspective. I didn't sign any 'social contract'. Did you?

The truth is what works for you. All any of us can ever do is to follow what don Juan called 'the path with heart', the truth that is ours and holds our own meaning, but which is compassionate towards others too, and recognizes *their* right to do for themselves what works for them.

This demands a great deal of self-discipline since, in every situation, you must get beyond the system and its social conditioning to find your own truth. You must also ruthlessly explore your own motivations so you do not get bogged down in petty concerns. Then, you will arrive at the heart of what is meaningful and important to you. In the final analysis, what works for anyone is what makes them most happy – whether this is money, success, security, love, whatever. And whatever makes *you* happy adds to the positivity quotient of the energy of the universe – providing it does no harm to others along the way.

THE FUTURE IS WHERE WE ARE

If you asked me to summarize these seven principles which King offers us, I would say simply that the world you see around you is the world of your own imagination. 'As I am, so I see', to quote Emerson once again.

If what you dream around you works for you, that is great, you are in the midst of the experience of love, the divine love of the universe; but if it doesn't, you have the power to change it in an instant by making the decision to do so and then acting upon it with spiritual insight, emotional clarity, mental focus and, finally, directed physical action as your guides.

When you change, the energy of the world changes and, in all likelihood, you will act differently, think differently, move differently in the world too, so that solid, practical and beneficial changes will also result, creating a better and more compassionate world for us all.

I think it is really important to state clearly that *you are not to blame for the problems of the world*. No-one is to blame. There is not a person alive who deliberately set out to create suffering on Earth, a dying planet, a world of despair. I believe this is true even if you are a despot or a dictator. You may be hell-bent on your own happiness and so intent on power that you are willing to take it by any means, even hurting others, but this abuse of others is still an *outcome* of your behaviour, not the purpose of it.

Too often, guilt is used as a spur for action by our politicians, the environmental movement, our religious leaders – anyone who desires from us a personal change in a particular direction which aids *their* cause. To my mind, this is ineffective and a negative energy in itself. None of us need feel guilt for our world; we are all just as perfect as we can be.

We know more now about our planet and we can benefit from the educational work of people like Lovelock and Roszak and choose to act as ambassadors for a better world because *we want to*, because *we believe it is right to do so*, and because we are motivated by a sense of connection, compassion and love, not because we are told to, or shamed into action.

We are all 'urban shamans', caretakers and healers of the Earth – if we choose to be. As Lovelock says:

> *It all depends on you and me. If we see the world as a living organism of which we are a part – not the owner, nor the tenant; not even a passenger – we could have a long time ahead of us and our species might survive for its 'allotted span'. It is up to us to act personally in a way that is constructive.*
>
> *If living with Gaia is a personal responsibility, how should we do it? Each of us will have a personal solution to the problem . . .* [31]

As creative individuals, your own solutions are the most important because they will carry your heart with them.

EXERCISE: HEALING THE EARTH

This works best as a group journey taken with like-minded friends, but there is no reason why you should not do it alone.

Adopt your preferred journeying posture and enter the shamanic state of consciousness together, via the energy of the drum, having agreed with your friends on a task in hand, typically your arrival together at a particular place on the planet – a geographical landmark, a social situation, an area of political oppression, of war, or of poverty – where you would like to carry out healing work.

When you arrive at this place and meet with your

companions, seek out the spirit of the place you have chosen and ask how you should proceed in the best way to provide healing.

You may be shown a particular spot which is the focal point, the power place, for that area, or given other specific instructions. I was once instructed to 'spring clean' an entire road system, for example, lifting the road itself as it cut through the landscape and tending to its wounds, then cleansing the whole area to purify and rebalance it. Both the environment and I knew that this was only a remedial action of recovery and not a permanent healing for the future – there could be no healing for the future since the roadway itself still existed – and that this 'spring cleaning' must be a periodic event in order to safeguard the status quo or until we stop 'developing' the land with roadways which create further congestion and pollution.

If you are not given specific instructions, then come together as a group, join hands and focus your energies on the landscape in general, with the intention of healing and sending positivity to the environment as a whole.

Notice how the energy of a place is much different, much bigger, and more powerful than when you are healing an individual or journeying for yourself. You are a part of a much vaster living system now – which is why, to be truly effective, this journey is better taken as part of a group where you can combine your energies.

When you return to ordinary consciousness, share your personal experiences with the others and see where they coincide. We have conducted journeys like this many times in the shamanic community I facilitate at *AJourneyToYou-Shaman@egroups.com* and always there are points of similarity and coincidence shared by group members, which is powerful validation of the reality and effectiveness of your healing actions.

Of all the actions, practical or energetic, we may choose to take in order to heal our world and thereby heal ourselves, the most crucial is a change in our mindset. We must move from a position of *ego*-centricity to one of *eco*-centricity, where we are no longer separate from, but at one with, all that is. Whatever we do to get there will be worthwhile.

As the Vodou priest, Oswan Chamani, once said, for all of us, 'Behind living and dreaming lies the most important thing – waking up.'

8

BECOMING A BEAUTIFUL MUTANT: IDEAS TO CHANGE THE WORLD

To begin to be what you are, you must first come out of what you are not.

His Holiness, Shantannand Saraswati Maharaj

We all have the power to change things and there is nothing really stopping us from doing so, once we get beyond the notion that we have to be the pawns in someone else's game.

The biggest illusion of all is that we are who we are, we all have our place, and the system which governs us is an immutable fact of life. The truth is that the system we have created is there to serve us, not the other way around, and is there to be changed if that is what we wish.

The houngan and the shaman have their belief systems, too, of course, which are quite different from those of mainstream, accepted reality. The ultimate aim of the shamanic worldview is to create a sense of greater community and connection between people and all living things, while for the houngan, and for Vodou in general, the community is *the* most central aspect of reality.

Yet, both views are also fiercely individualistic, recognizing and respecting deeply the rights and responsibilities of every single one of us to live a life of *personal* vision, fulfilment and compassion which stems from our own appreciation of essential spiritual values. The 'politics of shamanism' are probably closest to anarchy in this sense – in the true sense of the word – since it expounds the fundamental right to personal, individual, freedom, which is the exact opposite of our automatic subscription to a political and social system – unless, of course, *you choose* to belong.

'Anarchy', like 'Vodou' and, to some extent, like 'shamanism' itself, is one of those frequently misunderstood words which is most often used by the establishment from a position of fear or wilful misinterpretation rather than knowledge. Yet the path of shamanism must lead us first to the place of anarchy since both are concerned with the sovereignty of the individual, the right to free choice and the absolute power of us all to make our own decisions, despite the dictates of others.

Only by exercising our freedom and owning our own power can we ever say that we are truly free. And only if we do so will we ever, as a species, be able to overcome the inertia of governmental systems and big business structures which can detrimentally impact the life of the individual and the world at large. We will then be able to create the destiny that our dreams may lead us to.

This destiny may be the recreation of a new culture, another society which we agree to be a part of. But that is a next step. Because that, then, is our individual choice. First, we must decide on the type of society that we want for ourselves, and this necessitates a break-out from the dictates of the existing system. In this sense, it is similar to the 'initiation crisis' of the shaman and the houngan, where he frees himself – deliberately or otherwise – from the constraints of all he 'knows' so he can finally discover who he truly is.

'SHAMAN-ARCHY'

Most people seem to have a view of what anarchy is, though few actually know. Often it is equated somehow with communist regimes and totalitarianism – though that is the exact opposite of its meaning. Webster's dictionary defines anarchy as 'from the Greek, *anarchos*, having no ruler . . . a utopian society of individuals who enjoy complete freedom' – which is, in fact, the antithesis of totalitarianism – while the philosopher, Alex Comfort, defined it as a 'philosophy which advocates the maximisation of individual responsibility and the reduction of concentrated power – regal, dictatorial, parliamentary: the institutions which go loosely by the name of "government" – to a vanishing minimum. It has no connection with bomb-throwing radicals: it has, in fact, been a point of view which has attracted biologists, such as Kropotkin, the founder of ecology, and anthropologists.'[1]

Misunderstandings and fears about anarchy are not at all surprising, however, since a philosophy which puts the *individual* first runs so counter to the needs of the social *system* that successive rulers have allowed the negative connotations of the word to go uncorrected as the fear of disorder and chaos it engenders is entirely conducive to their purposes. Yet anarchy is one of the most gentle and humanistic of philosophies. It is about the right to freedom and free-thinking for all, in place of habitual reliance on the consensus view. It cannot be about violence or revolution since 'freedom for all' means exactly that – the right to free choice, not the imposition of one system and one worldview in place of another, including an anarchistic or a shamanic one.

Henry David Thoreau, in his *Essay on Civil Disobedience*, wrote that such intelligent questioning of the state and its systems is important if we are to be whole once again, the perfect, sentient human beings we were born to become.[2]

In his view, there are three types of people in modern life. The first two are the representatives of (and so, respected within) the state system. Actually they are slaves to it, who manage to go through life without any exercise of thought or free will in their own affairs. They are the 'one-dimensional men' referred to by Marcuse, the 'hollow men' of T. S. Eliot. The third group, while a challenge to the system, like those who discovered that the world is round, and the true place of the Earth in the solar system, are actually its saviours since it is from them that all true innovation will come.

'The mass of men serve the state . . . not as men mainly, but as machines,' wrote Thoreau. 'In most cases there is no free

477

exercise whatever of the judgement or of the moral sense; but they put themselves on a level with wood and earth and stones ... Yet such as these even are commonly esteemed good citizens. 'A very few – as heroes, patriots, martyrs, reformers in the great sense ... serve the state with their consciences also, and so necessarily resist it for the most part; and they are commonly treated as enemies by it. [But] a wise man will only be useful *as a man*, and will not submit to be clay.'

The shaman must, perforce, agree, since, no matter what his culture or the system that he lives within, shamanic consciousness means that he understands its limitations and will seek to improve it for all its children, even while he is its member, perhaps even its leader. Before there is anything else in the universe, there is energy, pure and simple. Not systems, not structures, not rulers or slaves, but pure, nameless energy.

When we take this energy and add our interpretation to it, as we all do, we apply judgements and values, and so create a world in our image. The problems arise when this worldview becomes self-sustaining as a result of the systems we put in place to reflect our beliefs, and to make the job of interpretation an easier, routine task. Then our systems can come to govern us, rather than the other way around, and the spirit of the system is a tyrant. The essence of shamanism is to break through these limitations and re-empower ourselves so that we are in control of our own lives and morally responsible for our actions in the world as they touch us and those around us.

The evidence we have looked at from writers such as Lovelock, Roszak, and Michael suggests that our civilization today is facing three principal areas of crisis. All of these stem ultimately from our worldview; there is nothing in the energy of the universe which makes it so. Looked at another way, these crisis areas are all opportunities for transformation.

They are:

1. Community breakdown, which is typically centred on our cities and reflected in the rising rates of crime, poverty, homelessness,

alienation, drug and alcohol abuse, social isolation, and the erosion of community, compassion, and support for ourselves and others. The *opportunity* is to reach out with kindness towards others and to *offer* help and support where we see that it is needed, instead of waiting for state intervention and governmental dictates which further erode our power and damage the spirit of community.

2. Eco-destruction, as we continue to take a blunt view of the complexity of our environment, assuming we can go on taking from it with impunity; that Gaia will support us, despite our own best efforts to make our species an intolerable part of its fragile ecosystem. The *opportunity* is to respect the environment and our part in it at a *personal level*, knowing that we *do* have the power to create change with our actions.

3. Violence towards ourselves and others, at a personal and local level. We have seen an increase in depressive and suicidal tendencies in recent years, as well as a rise in the incidence of more and more extreme forms of homicide, serial killings, and the migration of violence to classroom murders by six-year-olds. At a global level, we continue to stockpile weapons of mass destruction, and to develop new ones based on biotechnology and chemical and germ warfare. Despite international arms limitation agreements, there are still enough nuclear weapons in the world to destroy the planet many, many times over. The *opportunity* is to fight fire, not with fire, but with water; with guerrilla lovefare instead of warfare; to create a community based on respect and tolerance.

These are not separate problems which can be tackled in isolation from one another; they stem from a common cause, which is a particular way of looking at the world and the systems we have put in place to manage this. And the solution in every case comes down to direct action based on an entirely different worldview – one built on *compassion*, through acceptance of the sacred.

How do we want to live?

Knowing that we *can* rebuild the world if we choose, what kind of society will we choose to create where we are all free to realize our own full potential, without doing so at the expense of others? What would such a society look like and how would it be managed?

The models are right there in traditional communities. Clearly, we cannot go back to a pre-industrial society and abolish our technology, forget we ever knew about nuclear fusion and our visits to the stars. Still, there is much we can learn from the philosophy, approach and organization of such communities.

In his superb article, 'The Americas That Might Have Been', Julian Granberry of the Bahamas Archaeological Team looks at indigenous cultures within pre-Columbus America, before the Western worldview arrived at those shores, and identifies three different types of social system which were all well established before we ever got there.[3]

The importance of this article is to show that there may be many other worldviews and social structures that can work effectively for their people, and certainly as well as the one – our own – which we have come to see as the only possible solution for our future.

One of these societies, which Granberry calls a 'Unitary' society, offers a very beautiful model for a future we may wish to create. Exemplified by the Aztec and Inca empires of South America, and by many Far Eastern cultures (though practically non-existent in Europe), these are communal systems where all members of society are equal partners in the creation and welfare of the whole.

There is only one social class – 'the people'. Although certain individuals may be elected to positions of social responsibility in order to serve the whole community in specific ways, they will never become a permanent political fixture or enjoy the privileges we give our own governments and ministers.

In Unitary systems, there is little sense of the polar opposition we find in the West. Boundaries of time and space do not exist as such, and all humanity is one, governed by the same rules, which are accepted by all. This creates a quite sophisticated worldview which is based, in itself, on a more intricate, complex and spiritual relationship to the universe.

As Granberry remarks: 'Good and bad, right and wrong, even yes and no do not exist as polar quantities . . . Everything is equal and everything is relative. The yin-yang symbolism, which we erroneously view as a dualism, an 'either/or', is a national expression of this concept of oneness. There is never any need for compromise, since good and bad, right and wrong, correct and incorrect are all inherently present in everything at all times. It is interesting to note, in this context, that some of the best practitioners of modern physics and its relativistic world have been ethnic Chinese.'

In the Inca system, which exemplifies this society, the elected leadership would be replaced *by the people* if it did not govern at all times *for the people*, and training for leadership emphasized responsibility to the community rather than political self-preservation.

In return for benign and responsible government, the people provided labour and agricultural produce, in lieu of taxes, which were then redistributed equally to all. As a consequence, poverty was unknown, except among those who did not make their contribution to the state, and so received nothing back in kind. This was not a punishment for non-compliance but a form of natural justice based on the right to individualism; but with the obvious downside that there was no personal accumulation of benefit through a natural economy of scale.

The system worked and the society flourished. The capital city, Cusco, the political and organizational centre, achieved miracles in development, including a 10,000 mile highway system which surpassed anything produced by the Romans, and an education system open to all who wished to learn. More than eighty languages were spoken there. In short, says

Granberry, 'It is hard to find anything to criticise adversely in the Inca system . . . The overall democratic concern of the system, as administered by the chosen rulers, for the welfare of all without distinction – conquered as well as native son – has an undeniable appeal in this age of dog-eat-dog.'

The Inca lifestyle still survives in Peru, where community welfare comes first and they still await the spiritual return of the last Inca ruler, quartered by the Spanish invaders, who will be remembered and made whole again in the beautiful town of Cusco, and where 'they still call themselves Runa, *The People*, and look forward to a time when their time-honoured values will once again govern their land'.

This simple, almost innocent, yet philosophically and politically advanced system offers a wonderful model for our own aspirations – and one which clearly worked.

Every social or political *system* begins with *personal* aspiration: how we as individuals decide to operate collectively and compassionately in the world. Social change must always stem from personal change. Through our efforts now, such a world of tolerance, sharing and respect for the individual may come to pass, if we are prepared to act with compassion towards those who may seek to abuse us during the change-over of power, when their own worlds are threatened, without once giving up our own power or reneging on our own decisions. A better world is not beyond us, given sufficient time for our society to adapt to the world we each create as an individual.

Could we really give up what we have now and create something new on such a social scale? I believe it is possible.

Just outside the temple known as 'the hitching post of the sun' at the ancient community of Machu Picchu in Peru, there is a stone shaped somewhat like a bed or a doctor's couch, which other writers have described as a 'death stone'. But it is not a death stone, it is a launching pad, a stone of flight.

Lying down on this stone, just a few months ago, and closing my eyes, I found myself transformed into a bird, soaring through the surrounding valleys and circling the mountains which encompass the sacred city of Machu Picchu.

Nobody quite knows how this fabulous citadel ever came to be, what this complex network of temples, palaces and observatories, perched at the impenetrable height of 2,300 metres at the peak of a jungle mountain, was ever meant to accomplish, or what happened to its several thousand citizens once they decided one day, and for unknown reasons, simply to leave.

But in my soaring vision, I saw it clearly. The people there had simply tired of the old ways, of the systems they lived by, and decided to create something harmonious, to evolve something beautiful and new – an ancient Findhorn, if you like, where everyone was equal and connected through energetic exchange to a much bigger philosophical and energetic purpose. Then, when the time was right, they had simply 'turned out the lights' and left, to find other places to be in the world and to spread their message of unity. It was simply a 'hippie' community which served its purpose at the time – but nothing to get attached to. Similar centres of energy can be found, or created, anywhere. It just takes the coming together of like-minded people sharing a common intent.

I awoke from my vision at Machu Picchu, got up and walked off to explore the temple and the other sacred surroundings. When I returned there were others on the stone I had recently vacated. Just listening to their words made me smile: 'I was an eagle,' said one. 'This whole area is about flight,' said another, 'about escaping the world where we must always be looking down and the desire to be up among the gods.' So the vision I had seen was in no way unusual. Everybody who touched that stone got the same message and saw the same things.

There is a human desire to explore, to transcend, to get beyond the mundane and to work co-operatively with like-minded souls, and to (re-)connect with the gods, which was the point and the purpose to Machu Picchu. And that desire is no different for any of us today. We are all tired of looking down. Now we want to soar with the gods and fly with the eagles.

The philosopher, Mikhail Bakunin, wrote that '[A] person is strong only when he stands upon his own truth, when he speaks and acts from his deepest convictions. Then, whatever the situation he may be in, he always knows what he must say and do. He may fall, but he cannot bring shame upon himself or his causes.'[4] Such a view is, I am sure, one of the motivating factors for the architects and citizens of Machu Picchu. But it is far from merely a Peruvian or Andean phenomenon; it is at the heart of all shamanic belief. In her beautiful collection of Aboriginal stories, *Wise Women of the Dreamtime*, Johanna Lambert remarks that

> *traditional Aboriginal society is founded on the pre-eminence of the characteristics of the Universal Feminine, epitomised by its unwavering respect for the Earth, which Aborigines refer to as 'the mother'. Their social order encourages, from infancy, empathetic concern and compassion towards all creatures of nature, as well as deep loyalties and responsibilities to their kin and the group as a whole. While these feminine characteristics are paramount, they do not translate into power-based hierarchical social structures as have the excessive masculine qualities within our patriarchal society. Within the Universal Feminine qualities such as receptivity, mutability, interrelatedness, and diffusion that are predominant in Aboriginal society, the creative Universal Masculine characteristics such as limitation, order, structure, and definition also find balanced expression . . . [Only] after men have obtained the highest degrees of male initiation . . . do they become eligible for initiation into women's law.[5]*

The search for balance between universal polarities such as 'maleness' and 'femaleness' is one that has occupied writers and philosophers for centuries, and some anthropologists have even charted our human evolution from prehistoric to contemporary times in terms of the historical swings between masculine creative energy and feminine receptivity and integration.

I have been fortunate enough to live through two 'revolutions' – the very 'yin' revolution of the hippie 1960s, based on peace and love, and the 'yang' explosion of energy during the punk 1970s – and there are those in shamanic circles who see that the speed of the world and the vibration of change is growing ever faster, so it is possible to predict further, faster, changes, with less time elapsing between such evolutions in consciousness, as we learn from the 'morphic resonances' of each preceding evolution. Right now, we are emerging from another highly masculine era, the 'Me Generation', into a more compassionate and loving one as our time of recovery from the spiritual bankruptcy of the 1980s and 1990s.

One of the most interesting episodes in British history arose when these two streams of energy – the masculine energy for action and the feminine energy of compassion – came together to create a brief period of peaceful revolutionary progress. It is an episode which also demonstrates the approach of the 'ShamAnarchist' – at once individual *and* collective, creative *and* logical, passionate *and* compassionate. This short episode – which sowed the seeds of much wider social change to come – is a model we might aspire to in our quest for world change.

It took place in the 1640s, against a background of starvation. Food prices had risen to record levels, exacerbated by the impact of war, disease, and the severity of the winter. In the face of this living death, in April 1649, twenty men, led by Gerrard Winstanley, assembled on the waste land at St George's Hill, in Surrey, and began to dig. This innocent action for survival led to a revolution in political thinking which, though short-lived in itself, continues to have an impact across the centuries.

Calling themselves the Diggers, the group maintained that common land belonged to everyone, as its very name suggests, and that common land which was otherwise unused should morally be made available for cultivation by the poor and the hungry. Their colony more than doubled during

1649 as more and more people were swayed by the simplicity of this seemingly obvious and ethical truth. But then the government, once prepared to turn a blind eye, caved in to mounting opposition from the big landowners who were threatened by this 'insurrection' and demanded ownership of the common lands, even though they already controlled vast estates.

The Diggers, who refused to use force to protect themselves, were crushed in less than a year and their group disbanded. But they managed to raise a number of important questions during the time of their occupation – like whose land is this anyway, and who has most moral right to its common usage: the poor and the starving or the big landowners and the government system?

Gerrard Winstanley, a great mystic and a prolific writer, produced a document to explain the actions of The Diggers, in which he answered some of these questions. 'We are all born equal, born free and born of spirit,' he wrote. 'It is only when man's baser instincts take over that he falls into the trap of "covetousness", that "the Earth is bought and sold, and kept in the hands of a few".'

This division between the 'haves' and 'have-nots', the in-group and the out-group, means ultimately that 'the spirit is killed in both'.[6]

The community that Winstanley envisaged and created was an honourable and Earth-honouring one, built from compassion, where people could live and work together as equals: not so very different from the Unitary system described by Granberry.

Winstanley's community was forced to disband in 1650. But spirit moves in some very strange ways – and so the Diggers re-emerged, more than 300 years later, as part of the counter-culture movement centred in San Francisco's Haight-Ashbury, in 1960s America.

Taking their name and their philosophy directly from Winstanley's group, the San Francisco Diggers believed in a society where all could be free to act from compassion, without having to be dictated to about morality – and they were prepared to 'walk it as they talked it'. Much of their activity centred on the distribution of free food each day and the donation of 'surplus energy' to a number of stores they created where nothing was for sale and everything was free. These were random acts of kindness on a grand, organized scale.

EXERCISE: ENERGY FLOWS

The San Francisco Diggers claimed they were able to fund their give-aways through a spiritual belief in the natural flow of energy, summed up in their expression: 'What goes around comes around'. 'Somehow', money and provisions were always available for those who needed them.

Reflect on this principle in your own life. Can you remember any instances where your belief in a particular outcome actually created that outcome for you? What, *specifically*, did you do to produce this effect? How can you learn from this in order to apply these principles pro-actively and at will to create the outcome that you most desire in your own life?

The San Francisco Diggers were a highly creative group, offering free theatre and concerts to the people as well as free food. They were also the progenitors of a number of innovative ideas which have now entered mainstream culture, among them the development of the first free medical clinic (the inspiration behind the free clinic movement). Their vision is summed up in two phrases which they also coined and which are now in popular use: 'Do your own thing' and 'Today is the first day of the rest of your life'.

In 1966, in an article in *Berkley Barb*, entitled 'The Ideology of Failure', the group announced its philosophy in more detail. The article is, if you like, a modern reworking of Winstanley's own ideas in words I am sure he would have used himself had he been born 300 years later:

> *From the time we begin to call our childhood our past we seek to regain its simplicity, its sense of presence. We tumble into drugs and cleave reality into so many levels of game. We turn our backs on the mess and walk into the woods, but only for a time. A game is a game is a game is a game and we return to the silent – crowded – uptight sidewalks with our pockets full of absurdity and compromise between cowardice and illusion . . .*
>
> *Well, when some of us get to that . . . we look at ourselves and remember the 'funk' that pushed us into the lime, and we react. We may open peace centres with our money and contribute to the cause of freedom, or we may plough ourselves into the corner of 'who cares' and paddy-cake fortunes, or we may drop out all over again and go back to the woods, and stare at the preposterousness of doing our thing within the frame of a reality that can incorporate and market anyone, anything, anytime. And then we may begin to understand that if some attempt is not made to manage the world with love, it will run mad and overwhelm everything . . .*
>
> *We won't, simply won't, play the game any longer. We return to the consumer society and refuse to consume. And refuse to consume. And we do our thing for nothing. In truth, we live our protest. Everything we do is free because we are failures. We've got nothing to lose, so we've got nothing to lose.*[7]

It is a long time since the 1960s, but the vision of the Diggers is still going strong. If you go to *www.diggers.org* and hit the 'Free Store' button, you will be taken to a 'virtual shop' where Diggers from around the world are offering thousands of items for free. Any of them is yours for the asking. You can also contribute by adding items of your own that you would like to give away.

The San Francisco Diggers lived their beliefs directly, at an individual level in the 'real world', and in this they are not alone. The new shamans of today are also incorporating a spiritual perspective into their work in the 'real world'.

Drums in the Boardroom

A few hundred years ago, in the wilds and deserts and rocky hill places of America, indigenous people would go into the wilderness in search for a vision of their lives and to understand their spiritual selves. Nowadays, you are as likely to meet a senior business executive around the campfire with colleagues on a wilderness quest of their own where they will touch their creativity, build stronger relationships, and seek insights into the vision, philosophy and future direction of the company they work for.

This is the 'new shamanism' of the corporate office and its popularity is growing as a result of the spectacular results which programmes like this can achieve. Sports and leisure giant, Nike, for example, now routinely sponsors trips deep into the Amazon rainforest for their people to work with ancient shamans who will show them how to 'shapeshift' their future and create a new focus for their organization.

Even scientists, who might have laughed at such an idea until very recently, are now using shamanic techniques to aid the creative process behind research and development. Dr Eve Bruce, a respected plastic surgeon and American medical professional, and an initiated shaman herself, uses shamanic techniques with her patients in order to help them find that part of themselves they are unhappy with and to change their vision of it before trying to remove it or cover it up with surgery.

In the UK, shamanic practitioners such as Vera Waters are working with social services departments to facilitate bureaucratic shapeshifts and to support the healing of their clients by taking 'families with difficulties' on week-long therapeutic holidays where shamanic healing techniques are a major part of the programme. Vera's work is so successful that her participants write to her of 'life-changing' experiences and her work is even being quoted in parliament as a new model for the caring professions.

At the other end of the scale, 'personal spiritual trainers' like Nick Williams, author of *The Work We Were Born To Do*, works with individual employees and groups within an organization to help them find the 'vision' of the company they want to work for. His technique is not dissimilar to the *placitas* consultation (defined as a deep, *heart-to-heart* discussion) used by Mayan and Peruvian curandera shamans.

A friend of mine, Julie, is a lawyer working primarily on child protection cases. Using shamanic techniques, she is often able to 'tune in' to the spiritual truth behind each new case, simply by touching the case notes folder. She is then able to identify the soul purpose of the abused child at the centre of the trial and discover the best possible outcome, spiritually and legally, for the child concerned. Using these same techniques she can also often discover vital pieces of missing information (such as the time an incident took place or an undiscovered piece of evidence) which subsequent investigation then confirms – simply through contact with the case notes folder and journeying to the truth behind the case.

Such an approach is far more honourable and appropriate, it seems to me, than the typical legal focus on the punishment of offenders. Julie's approach is to help the child, first and foremost and in the fullest sense, as a spiritual being, to understand and resolve the conflicts in the family and the abusive background – and to encourage a new flow of love and forgiveness. It is not just a question of going for the biggest fine or the longest sentence.

Shamanic techniques work in all these settings as well as any other since we can, of course, dream any possible future – for ourselves, our company, our society, or for the world as a whole. All it takes is the liberation of our creativity to facilitate the vision. Sometimes this liberation is hard to come by as a result of the systems we put in place in modern business, or the need to make profits or appease shareholders, which then locks us into a system which simply does not work, and which we find ourselves powerless to change because of the immensity or inertia surrounding it. Shamanism, however, can often find a route through the mire.

John Perkins has acted as an adviser to corporations for over thirty years, and has taught shamanic business techniques to executives, medical doctors, government agencies, educators' and lawyers' associations. He has also written a highly acclaimed book on the subject: *Shapeshifting – Shamanic Techniques for Global and Personal Transformation*.[8] 'This is a time of incredible change, of cultural and global transition,' says John. 'No longer is the yardstick of profitability sufficient by itself. The corporation must respond to challenges never before faced. Satisfying market demands means empowering the individual employee while building a cohesive, creative, flexible team. It requires extreme sensitivity to environmental and social concerns.'

Shamanism offers this possibility since it opens up the bigger picture and adds a spiritual dimension to the place of work. Without their laptops, business suits, expense account lunches and titles to sustain them, people are allowed to be people once again and to find understanding, community and fulfilment in their lives, which they can then bring into the workplace through their more human interaction with colleagues.

It is a win-win situation for the company too, since the executives given access to shamanic techniques and training normally return with renewed vigour, more resources, as well as greater access to creativity and a shared vision with other team members. As the president of a large Italian corporation, which has been working with shamanic techniques for some time now, remarked: 'It has absolutely transformed our organization and corporate culture!'

John, Vera, Eve, Nick, Julie . . . these visionaries are not alone; there is a whole grassroots movement of people 'walking their talk' and bringing their beliefs into work, refusing to be constrained by the outmoded corporate thinking which has made work and city living such a stressful experience nowadays. There is something very beautiful about that.

THE TOMORROW PEOPLE

The Beautiful Mutants will be the people in this world who are able to best absorb these new ways of being, of seeing the world, and who can accept them, act upon them and stand before the forces of mundanity, oppression and 'normality', unflinching in the face of fearful challenges from the system. They will be the pockets of quiet, centred, peaceful resistance to the frantic efforts of the system to bring us all back into line. And, eventually, we will win and the world will change.

In *A Way of Being*, psychologist, Carl Rogers, asked, 'What is the meaning, the significance, of all these current developments in modern life?' (some of which we have looked at in this book).

'Taken together, these trends profoundly transform our concept of the person and the world that he or she perceives,' he answered. The people of tomorrow – the Beautiful Mutants – will have 'hitherto undreamed-of potential. This person's non-conscious intelligence is vastly capable. It can control many bodily functions, can heal diseases, can create new realities. It can penetrate the future, see things at a distance, communicate thoughts directly. This person has a new awareness of his or her strength, abilities, and power, an awareness of self as a process of change. This person lives in a new universe, where all the familiar concepts have disappeared – time, space, object, matter, cause, effect – nothing remains but vibrating energy. In my judgement, these developments constitute a "critical mass" that will produce drastic social change . . . the process will be in persons and social systems.'[9]

Who will be the people leading this change? From Rogers' research, the people of tomorrow, able to live in an 'utterly revolutionized world', will have certain characteristics in common:

1. A sense of openness – to new ideas, experiences and ways of being

2. A desire for authenticity. 'These persons . . . reject the hypocrisy, deceit, and double-talk of our culture . . . They are open . . . rather than leading a secretive double life'

3. A healthy disregard for the pronouncements of officials and especially of a science and technology that is 'used to conquer the world of nature and to control the world's people'

4. A focus on whole-ism, away from the current fixation on living a compartmentalized life. Instead, they strive for 'a wholeness of life, with thought, feeling, physical energy, psychic energy, healing energy, all being integrated into the experience'

5. A desire for intimacy, with new forms of closeness, community and shared purpose. They want experiences, not second-hand dictates and hand-me-down rules

6. An involvement in the journey, rather than the outcome. 'They are keenly aware that the one certainty of life is change . . . they welcome this risk-taking way of being and are vitally alive . . .'

7. A caring approach. While they are 'suspicious of professional "helpers"' [whose institutionalized care is itself a part of the system], the people of tomorrow are 'eager to be of help to others [as part of] a gentle, subtle, non-moralistic, non-judgemental caring'

8. A closeness to nature. They are 'ecologically-minded' and repelled by concepts (which are foolish and unrealistic anyway) that rely on an attempt to 'tame' or 'conquer' the natural world

9. An anti-institutional approach. They have 'an antipathy for any highly structured, inflexible, bureaucratic institution [believing instead that] institutions should exist for people, not the reverse'

10. A sense of faith in their own moral being, 'they make their own moral judgements' and have a 'profound distrust of external authority'. They are willing to openly disobey laws, norms, rules and bureaucratic regulations which they personally consider unjust

11. An indifference to material possessions. 'Money and material status are not their goal'

12. A desire for the spiritual. They are seekers on a quest to find meaning in their lives. They search for peace, for new principles of being, for new states of consciousness, for personal truth and the experience of 'the ultimate'. These people are the shamans of the city, the Beautiful Mutants who will change the world.

'Persons with these characteristics will be at home in a world that consists only of vibrating energy,' says Rogers, '. . . a world with no solid base, a world of process and change, a world in which the mind, in its largest sense, is both aware of, and creates, the new reality.'

I would be very surprised if Rogers is not describing you.

Discovering that you are not alone, that there are others like you, who share your worldview, your sense of boredom at the futility and emptiness of modern life, your desire for change, and your willingness to live your own life and 'play your own game' – all of that is helpful and supportive in your quest for personal and global transformation. But what are you supposed to *do* with this new approach? How are you supposed to live?

Very recently a friend of mine sent me a document entitled *12 New Rules for Life*, which was composed by Frederic M. Hudson, PhD and Pam McLean, PhD, the President and Vice-President, respectively, of the Hudson Institute of Santa Barbara. This offers some suggestions as to how we might begin anew to see our own place in the new world now emerging. Putting these principles to work in your own life will be a start.

1. *Understand that no-one owes you anything – not the government, your employer, your family, or your spouse . . . To rejoice in living you must invent your own future, entrepreneur your life, and expect surprises.*
2. *Global change is the major force in your life, and in the lives of everyone on Earth. We are all in training for a new era for all humanity. Take advantage of*

the expanding possibilities now available to you in our world of constant flow.

3. *You have no ultimate safety, security or guarantees, so don't expect any. What you have are endless opportunities to rearrange your priorities for work, play, and life. Choose wisely, and expect more choices to follow.*

4. *Your life is an adventure, a journey . . . Everything is flow – just keep moving . . . Learn how to say 'hello' and 'good-bye' with grace and style.*

5. *Know how to recycle yourself. Live each chapter of your life fully, then invest in a transition and begin the next chapter . . . No matter what your age or situation, design your future as your manifest destiny.*

6. *The best way to guide your life through infinite change is to follow your own values and vision.*

7. *Your best future happens when you have the courage to be . . . Embrace the unknown ahead. Live on the outer edge of your possibilities, not on the inner edge of your security. Be active, not passive. Lean into the wind.*

8. *Conduct your journey by having a long-term purpose and short-term goals. Be definite and flexible. Trust the ocean but stay in charge of your boat. Ride the waves.*

9. *Refuse to be defined and consumed by your work . . . Your deepest agenda is your soul's work, your holistic calling to create success and caring in all the parts of your life.*

10. *Everyone on Earth is linked to the same destiny. We share the same air, water, food, and capacities for total destruction. We are in each other's hands . . .*

11. *Learn how to grow older and better . . . Leave a legacy that makes a difference.*

12. *As you find better rules – and you will – replace these rules with them.*

The more times I read these 'rules', the more they seem to make absolute sense as guidelines for modern living. I would only clarify the first of them by saying that, while no-one owes you anything, the reverse is also true; you owe nothing to anyone, except what you are prepared to give through your own free choice, even in the face of 'demands' from the system.

Think seriously about these observations on life, each of which was developed from *real* experience in the world. Do they make sense to *you*? And, if so, can *you* live them?

If we can follow these guidelines ourselves and share them with others, then we will already be living shamanically within our cities, and as part of a new and more compassionate worldview, based on the eternal, living principles of the 'new primitive', the Beautiful Mutants which, like it or not, we are all now becoming in the world.

A SENSE OF WONDER

There is one other thing which is of overriding importance for maintaining health, power, personal fulfilment and the creation of a better world around us, and that is maintaining a sense of wonder at the world and at our lives.

We must look at the world afresh, through the perfect eyes we used as children, so that our life in the city does not weigh us down with boredom, frustration and inertia. It is this sense of wonder and of awe which connects us with the sacred and enables us to define ourselves as members of a beautiful, vast and wonderfully evolving universe, when others would seek to impose their own limited worldviews upon us and define our existence as a tiny and insignificant mechanical fact.

We begin living miraculously, and life becomes a miracle, when we choose to see the miracle in life itself. Perhaps all it really takes is a truly *open* mind.

As Auden said, 'We must love one another – or die.'

Life is a miracle.

Scientifically,
the processes of life,
its formation and evolution,
its aspects,
and even its dissolution can be described,
quantified,
diagnosed,
adjusted,
treated,
affected,
effected,
and ended.

But what is life,
Actually?

Poets,
philosophers,
religious figures,
scientists,
and healers can't answer the question objectively.

What creates the difference between a clumping of
matter,
and a living thing?

What is it that transcends a human body,
for example,
and gives emotions,
intellect,
personality,
spirit,
and 'soul'?

What mechanism provides for us to 'feel' a breeze,
when our bodies perceive motion in the air?

I know,
technically,
it can be described by sense receptors in the skin,
and neurological stimuli,
but what grants us the ability to appreciate it?

An amoeba can perceive changes in its environment,
but I don't know if it 'enjoys' its surroundings.

I don't know why I find the smell after a rain
exhilarating,
but I consider it a miracle to enjoy it.

I consider the process by which rain produces the air we
breathe and the food we eat miraculous.

I consider how food and drink becomes our bodies,
miraculous.

I consider how life comes from life,
miraculous.

– Bon Houngan Izrayel Pale Lape (Israel Speaks Peace)

GLOSSARY

Ayahuasca: The hallucinogenic 'vine of souls' used by Amazonian shamans to enter the otherworld of the spirits.

Ayahuascero/a: Shaman/-ess who uses ayahuasca for otherworld journeys and in healing rituals.

Babalowa/Babalao/Babalawao: A high priest of the Santeria Vodou tradition who typically works with a 'clear eye' (i.e. never becomes personally possessed but is able to work with, and call the spirits, for others). The differences in spelling occur because the languages of Cuba and Haiti are not 'fixed', and have only been formalized for a few years. Spellings, all of which are valid, will therefore differ according to the correspondent. Vodou may, for example, also be spelled Vadau, Vaudau, Vodou, Voudo, – or even Voodoo; ti-bonanj as ti bon anje, gwo-bonanj as gro bon anje and mét-tété as met tet.

Curandera/o: South American shamans who may often be expert herbalists as well as spiritists.

Djevo: The 'heart' of the Vodou temple, where secret teachings take place; usually restricted to the houngan or mambo and selected others.

Double, The: The 'dream body' which is the energetic essence of oneself; the soul, or spirit; sometimes the doppelganger who is also you.

Dreaming: The ability to separate the soul from the body during sleep or shamanic journeying in order to explore the otherworld or enter the 'dream' of another. All people and things have a dreaming, which is also a way of seeing the world, sometimes quite unconsciously, and projecting our views onto the world of physical reality.

Gaia theory: The hypothesis that the Earth itself (and, quite probably, the entire universe) is a sentient organism of which humanity is but a part, like the single cell of a body.

Houngan: The Vodou priest who acts as shaman for his community.

Limpia: In South America, a cleansing ritual to remove an energetic or spirit intrusion which would otherwise cause illness or death (for example, Tokolosh).

Loa: In Vodou, aspects of the god-energy, roughly equivalent to Christian saints or angels.

Mambo: The Vodou priestess, shamaness of the community she serves.

Palero: The priest of Palo who is shaman to those he serves.

Palo: A form of Vodou practised in the West Indies and Caribbean.

Santeria: The shamanic practice of Cuba, now widely adopted by the Hispanic community of Miami and, increasingly, of mainland America.

Santero: Priest of Santeria who acts as shaman for his community.

Tokolosh: A spirit entity directed by a magician to harm another, causing illness or death.

Vegetalista: Shaman expert in the curative powers and the spirits of plants and herbs.

Vodou: The shamanic practice of Haiti.

Vodouissant: Believer in the power of Vodou; the faithful of the Vodou religion.

Voodoo: Strictly, the Vodou practices of New Orleans. More generally, the term by which all Vodou (including Santeria, Palo, etc.) traditions have come to be known in the West.

Wanga: In Vodou, a spell or charm meant to deliver practical effects such as greater income, protection, or harm to an enemy.

NOTES

Introduction

1. Elisabeth Kübler-Ross, *The Wheel of Life*, Bantam, 1998.
2. Maya Deren, *At Land*, 1944 (directed by Maya Deren and Talley Beatty).
3. Nick Williams, *The Work We Were Born To Do*, Element Books, 2000.
4. Carlos Castaneda, *A Separate Reality*, Pocket Books, 1991.
5. Martin Prechtel, *Secrets of the Talking Jaguar*, Jeremy P. Tarcher, 1999.
6. Maya Deren, *The Very Eye of Night*, 1959 (directed by Maya Deren).
7. Emma Restall Orr, in Terry and Natalia O'Sullivan, *Soul Rescuers*, Thorsons, 1999.
8. Ross Heaven, *The Journey To You*, Bantam, 2001.

Chapter 1

1. Paulo Coelho, *Veronika Decides to Die*, HarperCollins, 1999.
2. Milan Kundera, *The Unbearable Lightness of Being*, Harper & Row, 1984.
3. Priscilla Cogan, *Winona's Web*, HarperCollins, 1999.
4. Professor Ian Kennedy, 'Doctors Arrogant Over Organ Stripping', at BBC Health News, *http://news.bbc.co.uk/hi/english/health*, May 10, 2000.
5. Malidoma Patrice Some, *Ritual: Power, Healing and Community*, Gateway Books, 1996.
6. Heaven, *Journey To You*.
7. Jim Haskins, *Voodoo and Hoodoo: The Craft as Revealed By Traditional Practitioners*, Scarborough House, 1990.
8. Maria Rainer Rilke, *Letters to a Young Poet*, Vintage Books, 1986.
9. Carlos Castaneda, *The Wheel of Time*, Penguin, 1998.

Chapter 2

1. Coleman Barks (trans.), *The Essential Rumi*, Penguin 1999.
2. Augustin Rivas Vasquez, in Jaya Bear, *Amazon Magic*, Colibri Publishing, 2000.
3. Polly Ghazi and Judy Jones, *Downshifting: The Guide to Happier, Simpler Living*, Hodder & Stoughton, 1997.
4. Ceridian Performance Partners/MT study of 2,000 readers, August 1999, quoted, ibid.
5. Herbert Marcuse, *An Essay on Liberation*, Beacon Press, 1969.
6. John Zerzan, *The Mass Psychology of Misery*, Future Primitive and Other Essays, Autonomedia and Anarchy: A Journal of Desire Armed (1994). Autonomedia, PO Box 568, Williamsburgh Station, Brooklyn, New York 11211–0568, USA.
7. Carlos Castaneda, *The Active Side of Infinity*, Thorsons, 1999.
8. Zerzan, *Mass Psychology*.
9. Richard Bandler and John Grinder, *Frogs into Princes*, Eden Grove, 1990.
10. Frank Farrelly, *Provocative Therapy*, Meta Publications, 1974.
11. Arnold Mindell, *The Shaman's Body*, HarperSanFrancisco, 1993.
12. Farrelly, *Provocative Therapy*.
13. Bandler and Grinder, *Frogs into Princes*.
14. Elisabeth Kübler-Ross, *The Wheel of Life*.
15. Elena Avila, *Woman Who Glows in the Dark*, Thorsons, 2000.
16. Ghazi and Jones, *Downshifting*.
17. Ibid.
18. Heaven, *Journey To You*.
19. Reuters Health web site is at *www.Reuters.com*.
20. Elmer and Alyce Green, *Beyond Biofeedback*, Delacorte, 1977.
21. Ian Pearce, in Colin Wilson and John Grant, *The Directory of Possibilities*, Corgi, 1982.
22. Iris Owen and Margaret Sparrows, *Conjuring Up Philip: An Adventure in Psychokinesis*, Harper & Row, 1976.
23. Wilson and Grant, *Directory of Possibilities*.
24. Alexandra David-Neel and Lama Yongden, *The Secret Oral Teachings in Tibetan Buddhist Sects*, City Lights Books, 1981.
25. Walter Yeeling Evans-Wentz, *The Tibetan Book of the Great Liberation: Or, the Method of Realizing Nirvana Through Knowing the Mind*, Oxford University Press, 1983.
26. John Perkins, *The World is as You Dream it*, Inner Traditions, 1994.
27. Itzhak Bentov, *Stalking the Wild Pendulum: On the Mechanics of Consciousness*, Destiny Books, 1988.

28. Maya Deren, *Divine Horsemen: The Living Gods of Haiti*, Documentext, 1970.

Chapter 3

1. Tom Cowan, *Fire in the Head: Shamanism and the Celtic Spirit*, HarperSanFrancisco, 1993.
2. Wilson and Grant, *Directory of Possibilities*.
3. Arthur Grimble, *Pattern of Islands*, John Murray, 1952.
4. Felicitas D Goodman, *Where the Spirits Ride the Wind: Trance Journeys and Other Ecstatic Experiences*, Indiana University Press, 1990.
5. Mircea Eliade, *Shamanism: Archaic Techniques of Ecstasy*, Princeton University Press, 1972.
6. Cowan, *Fire in the Head*.
7. John G Neihardt, *Black Elk Speaks*, University of Nebraska Press, 1988.
8. Karen McCarthy Brown, *Mama Lola: A Vodou Priestess in Brooklyn*, University of California Press, 1991.
9. Knud Rasmussen, in Wilson and Grant, *Directory of Possibilities*.
10. James Chaytor, *Plantas En La Cultura Andina*, 2000.
11. Peter Tompkins and Christopher Bird, *The Secret Life of Plants*, Penguin Books, 1974.
12. Haskins, *Voodoo and Hoodoo*.
13. S Jason Black and Christopher S. Hyatt, *Urban Voodoo: A Beginner's Guide to Afro-Caribbean Magic*, New Falcon Publications, 1998.
14. Alfred Metraux, *Voodoo in Haiti*, Schocken Books, 1989.
15. Brown, *Mama Lola*.
16. Mambo Racine Sans Bout, web site: *www.members.aol/com/racine 125/index*.
17. Cowan, *Fire in the Head*.
18. Mambo Racine.
19. Luke Rhinehart, *The Dice Man*, Grafton Books, 1972. Quotation is from Rhinehart, *The Search for The Dice Man*, HarperCollins, 2000.
20. Restall Orr, in *Soul Rescuers*.
21. Mambo Racine.
22. Migene Gonzalez-Wippler, *Santeria: The Religion*, Llewellyn Publications, 1996.
23. Deren, *Divine Horsemen*.
24. Brian Bates, *Sacred Trees*, *Resurgence* magazine, March 1997. Web site: *www.gn.apc.org/resurgence/ADMIN/articles*.

25. Christiana Harle-Silvennoinen, *In the Land of Song and the Drum*, *Sacred Hoop*, Issue 25, 1999.
26. Black and Hyatt, *Urban Voodoo*.
27. Deren, *Divine Horsemen*.
28. Eliade, *Shamanism*.
29. Luis Eduardo Luna and Pablo Amaringo, *Ayahuasca Visions*, North Atlantic Books, 1993.

Chapter 4

1. Fritjof Capra, *The Tao of Physics*, Flamingo, 1992. Michael Talbot, *The Holographic Universe*, HarperCollins, 1996.
2. Carlos Castaneda, *Tales of Power*, Arkana, 1970.
3. Wilson and Grant, *Directory of Possibilities*.
4. Ibid.
5. Edgar Cayce, *Auras*, A.R.E. Press, 1945. Association for Research and Enlightenment web site at *www.edgarcayce.com*.
6. Jonathan Cainer and Carl Rider, *The Psychic Explorer*, Book Club Associates, 1986.
7. Desmond Morris, *Manwatching: A Field Guide to Human Behaviour*, Cape, 1977.
8. Luna and Amaringo, *Ayahuasca Visions*.
9, Both of these beautiful blessings were emailed to me by a friend and
10 the original source is not known. I would be delighted to hear from the author or from anyone who knows the origins of these.
11. *Positive Health* magazine web site is at *www.positivehealth.com*.
12. Prechtel, *Secrets of the Talking Jaguar*.
13. Mark Solms in *How You Can Save Your Life With Dreams*, Mary Salmon, *Sunday Express*, January 21, 2001.
14. Robin Royston in *How You Can Save Your Life With Dreams*, *Sunday Express*.
15. Green, *Beyond Biofeedback*.
16. Wilson and Grant, *Directory of Possibilities*.
17. Tompkins and Bird, *The Secret Life of Plants*.
18. Mitch Krucoff, on Reuters Health web site.
19. Harold Koeing, on Reuters Health web site.
20. Ibid.
21, 22 *Time* magazine, June 24, 1996, Vol. 147, No. 26.
23. Michael Harner, *The Way of the Shaman*, HarperSanFrancisco, 1990.
24. Harle-Silvennoinen, *The Land of Song and the Drum*.
25. Peter Cloudsley, *The Art of the Shaman: Healing in the Peruvian Andes*, *Journal of Museum Ethnography*, No. 11, 1999.

26. See web site discussion group at *ajourneytoyou-shaman@egroups.com*.

27. Wilson and Grant, *Directory of Possibilities*.

28. Ibid.

29. Grant and Jane Solomon, *The Scole Experiment: Scientific Evidence for Life After Death*, Piatkus, 1999.

30. Ken Eagle Feather, *A Toltec Path*, Hampton Roads, 1995.

31. Nicky Arden, *African Spirits Speak: A White Woman's Journey Into the Healing Tradition of the Sangoma*, Inner Traditions, 1999.

32. Eagle Feather, *A Toltec Path*.

33. Ibid.

34. Martin Lee and Bruce Shlain, *NLP in 21 Days*, Grove Press, 1992.

35. Kevin Warwick, *March of the Machines: Why the New Race of Robots Will Rule the World*, Century, 1997.

36. W Y Evans-Wentz (ed.), *The Tibetan Book of the Dead: or, The After-Death Experiences on the Bardo Plane, According to Lama Kazi Dawa-Samdup's English Rendering*, Oxford University Press, 1978.

37. Albert Hoffman, *LSD: My Problem Child*, McGraw Hill, 1980.

38. Deren, *Divine Horsemen*.

39. James Frazer, *The Golden Bough: A Study in Magic and Religion*, NTC/Contemporary Publishing, 1998.

40. Cloudsley, *The Art of the Shaman*.

41. Luna and Amaringo, *Ayahuasca Visions*.

42. Bill Broadway, *Visionary Visitor From the Amazon: Shaman Teaches Love of Nature*, The Washington Post, September 11, 1999.

43. Cloudsley, *The Art of the Shaman*.

44. Ibid.

45. Deren, *Divine Horsemen*.

46. D. H. Lawrence, *Fantasia of the Unconscious and Psychoanalysis of the Unconscious*, Penguin, 1991.

Chapter 5

1. T. S. Eliot, *The Hollow Men*, in *Four Quartets*, Faber, 1979.

2. Williams, *Work We Were Born To Do*.

3. Cloudsley, *The Art of the Shaman*.

4. Harner, *Way of the Shaman*.

5. *East African Standard* on Reuters news at *www.reuters.com*.

6. Sandra Ingerman, *Soul Retrieval: Mending the Fragmented Self*, HarperSanFrancisco, 1991.

7. Eileen Naumann, *Soul Recovery and Extraction* – information on soul recovery and the work of Eileen Naumann is available at *medicinegarden.com/sre*.

8. Stanley Krippner, in conversation with Jeffrey Mishlove on the television programme, *Thinking Allowed*. 2560 Ninth Street, Suite 123, Berkley, CA 94710, USA. Web site: *www.thinkingallowed.com*. Transcripts available at *www.intuition.org*. Also see *Thinking Allowed: A Book of Selected Transcripts*, and Jeffrey Mishlove, *Roots of Consciousness*. Information from *Thinking@ThinkingAllowed.com*.

9. Deren, *Divine Horsemen*.

10. Bandler and Grinder, *Frogs into Princes*.

11. Deren, *Divine Horsemen*.

12. Olga Kharitidi, *Entering the Circle*, HarperSanFrancisco 1996.

13. Dolores Kreiger research quoted by Stanley Krippner, *Thinking Allowed*.

14. Stanley Keleman, on *Thinking Allowed*.

15. Sacred Hoop web site at *sacredhoop@egroups.com*.

16. Michael Quin (ed.), *The Catholic Encyclopaedia*, Virtue, 1965.

17. Ingerman, *Soul Retrieval*.

18. Howard Charing, *Shamanic Core Process*, *Spirit Talk*, Issue 5, Winter 1998.

19. Naumann, *Soul Recovery and Extraction*.

20. Christiana Harle-Silvennoinen, London workshop, 1999.

21. Sarangerel, *Riding Windhorses*, Destiny Books, 2000.

22. Avila, *Woman Who Glows in the Dark*.

23. Williams, *The Work We Were Born To Do*.

24. Cloudsley, *The Art of the Shaman*.

25. *Globe and Mail*, *Woman Admits Guilt in Exorcism Death*, Thursday June 22, 1995.

26. Charing, *Shamanic Core Process*.

27. Gary Gent, *Death and Dying – A Change*, Athena Mailing List: *Athena@Lyghtforce.com*. Web site: *www.medicinegarden.com*.

28. Howard Charing, *Soul Theft: The Other Side of Soul Retrieval*, Spirit Talk, Issue 2, Autumn 1996.

29. Wade Davis, *The Serpent & the Rainbow*, Simon and Schuster, 1985.

30. Charing, *Soul Theft*.

31. *The Times*, *The Chip That Could Stop Adultery*, Friday, November 5, 1999.

Chapter 6

1. William James, *The Varieties of Religious Experience: A Study of Human Nature*, Penguin Books, 1982.
2. *News of the World*, *Only Fools and Curses*, Sunday February 20, 2000.
3. Gonzalez-Wippler, *Santeria*.
4. Richard Hodges, *The Quick and the Dead: The Souls of Man in Vodou Thought*, 1995, at *www.cnmat.berkley.edu/~hodges/QandD*.
5. Elisabeth Kübler-Ross, *Death: The Final Stage of Growth*, Touchstone, 1986.
6. Hodges, *The Quick and the Dead*.
7. T. C. Lethbridge, *Ghost and Divining Rod*, Routledge & Kegan Paul, 1963.
8. Wilson and Grant, *Directory of Possibilities*.
9. Ibid.
10. Raymond A Moody, *Life After Life*, Bantam Books, 1978.
11. Dr Melvin Morse. Web site: *www.death-dying.com*.
12. International Association for Near-Death Studies. Web site: *www.iands.org*.
13. Bill and Judy Guggenheim, *Hello From Heaven!*, Bantam Books, 1997.
14. Joel Rothschild, *Signals*, Bantam, 2001.
15. Solomon, *The Scole Experiment*.
16. Peter and Mary Harrison, *The Children That Time Forgot*, Berkley Books, 1991.
17. Lyall Watson, *The Romeo Error: A Matter of Life and Death*, Anchor Press, 1975.
18. Karen Kelly, *The Search for Spirit in the City*, *Spirit Talk*, Issue 2, Autumn 1996.
19. Ibid.
20. Christopher McNamey, *Can You Live Geopathically Stress-Free as the Gypsies Do?*, at the Earth Transitions web site: *www.earthtransitions.com*.
21. Earth Transitions, 1726 Lemon Heights, Oceanside, CA 92056, USA. Email: *CHBABA@aol.com*. Web site: *www.earthtransitions.com*.
22. J M Gobet, *Geobiology – The Holistic House*, at the Earth Transitions web site, op. cit.
23. Man-Ho Kwok and Joanne O'Brien, *The Elements of Feng Shui*, Element, 1997.

24. Charlotte Frisbee, *Ritual Drama in the Navajo House Blessing Ceremony*, in Southwestern Indian Ritual Drama, 1980.
25. Malidoma Patrice Some, *Of Water and the Spirit*, Arkana, 1995.
26. Jamie Sams, *Dancing the Dream: The Seven Sacred Paths to Human Transformation*, HarperSanFrancisco, 1999.
27. Carlos Castaneda, *The Second Ring of Power*, Pocket Books, 1991.
28. Carlos Castaneda, *The Eagle's Gift*, Pocket Books, 1991.
29. Carlos Castaneda, *The Journey to Ixtlan: The Lessons of Don Juan*, Washington Square Press, 1992.
30. Ibid.
31. Carlos Castaneda, *The Fire From Within*, Pocket Books, 1991.

Chapter 7

1. James Lovelock, *The Ages of Gaia: A Biography of Our Living Earth*, Oxford University Press, 1990.
2. James Lovelock, *Gaia: A New Look at Life on Earth*, Oxford University Press, 1979.
3. Theodore Roszak, on *Thinking Allowed*.
4. Coehlo, *Veronika Decides to Die*.
5. William Bloom, *The Penguin Book of New Age and Holistic Writing*, Penguin Books, 2001.
6. Roszak, *Thinking Allowed*.
7. Ibid.
8. Fritjof Capra, *The Turning Point: Science, Society and the Rising Culture*, Bantam Doubleday Dell, 1988.
9. Fritjof Capra, on *Thinking Allowed*.
10. Capra, *Thinking Allowed*.
11. Ibid.
12. Ibid.
13. Ibid.
14. Claudine Michel, *Morality in Haitan Vodou*, at *www.ahad-kreyol.org/newsletter/number15/morality*.
15. Capra, *Thinking Allowed*.
16. Ibid.
17. Timothy Freke, *Loa Tzu's Toa Te Ching*, Piatkus, 1999.
18. Herman Hesse, *Damian*, Picador, 1995.
19. Rupert Sheldrake – articles and interviews at *www.Sheldrake.org*.
20. Ibid.
21. Rupert Sheldrake, *A New Science of Life*, Paladin Books, 1983.
22. Donald Michael, on *Thinking Allowed*.
23. R. D. Laing, *The Politics of Experience*, Ballantine, 1972.

24. Father Labat, *Voyage Aux Isles de l'Amerique*, in Laennec Hurbon, *Voodoo Truth and Fantasy*, Thames and Hudson, 1995.
25. Michael, *Thinking Allowed*.
26. Ibid.
27. Serge Kahili King, *Urban Shaman*, Simon and Schuster, 1990.
28. Gay Gaer Luce, (author of *Your Second Life*, Merloyd Lawrence, 1980).
29. Ralph Waldo Emerson, *Essays*, Franklin Watts, 1973.
30. Carlos Castaneda, *The Teachings of Don Juan*, Ballantine, 1972.
31. Lovelock, *The Ages of Gaia*.

Chapter 8

1. Alex Comfort, Preface to Harold Barclay, *People Without Government*, Left Bank Books, 1982.
2. Henry David Thoreau, Civil Disobedience, *Walden and Civil Disobedience*, Houghton Mifflin College, 1960.
3. Julian Granberry, *The Americas That Might Have Been*, at *www.millers.edu/~colombus/data/spc/GRANBER1.SPC*.
4. Mikhail Bakunin, *God and the State*, Dover Publications, 1970.
5. Johanna Lambert, *Wise Women of the Dreamtime*, Inner Traditions, 1993.
6. Gerrard Winstanley, *The True Levellers Standard: Or, the State of Community Opened and Presented to the Sons of Men*, 1649.
7. George Metesky, 'The Ideology of Failure', *Berkley Barb*, November 18, 1996. Diggers web site articles at *www.diggers.org*.
8. John Perkins, *Shapeshifting: Shamanic Techniques for Global and Personal Transformation*, Destiny Books, 1997.
9. Carl Rogers, *A Way of Being*, Houghton Mifflin, 1980.

INFINITE JOURNEYS
TRANCE DRUMMING FOR THE SHAMANIC JOURNEY
BY ROSS HEAVEN

Shamans use many methods to achieve the altered state of consciousness necessary for the shamanic journey, but their principal technique remains the use of sacred sound, whether it is the singing bowls of Tibet, the click sticks and didgeridoo of Australia, or the drums of Haiti and Africa.

This high-quality tape has been specially recorded by the author as a companion to the books, *The Journey To You* and *Spirit in the City*, and offers a combination of shorter and longer trance sound accompaniments for the journeys described in these books – and for any others you may wish to take.

The cassette features drums (the shaman's 'horse'), rattles and other traditional instruments played at the specific tempo required to induce the shift in consciousness which facilitates entry into the otherworlds – just as they have been played for thousands of years by shamans and priests to support and guide their own journeys of the soul.

Each track includes an orientation beat to allow you to express your intention and phrase your question for the spirits, a journeying beat, and a call-back signal to assist your return to normal consciousness.

Featured instruments: Growler drum, bodhrán, Vodou gourd asson (priest's sacred rattle), African pod-rattles, hand-crafted English rattles, and African rain stick fetish.

Price: £10. Please send payment (cash by registered post; cheques made payable to 'Ross Heaven') plus a stamped addressed *padded* envelope to:

Cloud 2
48 Eversfield Place
St Leonards on Sea
East Sussex
TN37 6DB
United Kingdom

Please note: This address is different from and supersedes the one given in *The Journey To You.*

WORKSHOPS AND COURSES

For information on workshops by the author, presentations, training material and other activities, please send an A4 sized stamped addressed envelope to the address above.

SHARE THE DREAM
OF
THE VILLAGE COMMUNITY

Ross Heaven is working with The Sacred Trust and Veritas Projects to establish a new form of community living in the UK, based on shamanic and Earth-honouring principles of holism, respect, connection and co-operation.

The Village will be a permanent eco-village based on a sustainable approach, which will operate as a European centre of excellence for healing and education in traditional and indigenous practices. It will offer an on-going curriculum of workshops, courses and trainings in cross-cultural and Earth-based spiritual work which will help people to make positive changes in their lives and contribute to a healthier tomorrow for their children and their children's children.

All approaches taught, shown and experienced will be entirely *practical* so that participants may take these new experiences and techniques back to their own social groups and communities and *apply* them during their daily lives. There will be on-going support for them to do so.

A key intention which underpins the work of The Village is *open access*. Recognizing that access to this type of work and environment is typically restricted to a narrow minority of the population, The Village will commit time and resources to working with 'socially excluded' families and children. We will also establish an on-site school, blending mainstream curriculum activities with traditional and Earth-honouring practices, as well as an open access healing clinic which will combine traditional medicine with mainstream healthcare approaches.

The Village will also develop research, outreach and support programmes in order to protect, preserve, explain and introduce into wider society, the wisdom and practices of traditional cultures, particularly those under threat from Western development. This will include, for example, the introduction of a 'resident Elders' scheme, and European expansion of the POLE (Pollution Offset Lease for Earth) project for environmental preservation.

Our financial target for this project is £5 million. If you share this dream and would like to make a financial contribution to its realization (and receive exclusive information, progress reports and the offer of site visits as this project develops), please send your contribution (however small) to:

The Sacred Trust [Please mark your envelope 'The Village' Project]
PO Box 603
Bath
BA1 2ZU

Or directly to:

Trodos Bank
Account number 02652700
Sort code 16-58-10
Account name: The Sacred Trust

We are truly grateful for your support.